SOUNDIN' CANAAN

SOUNDIN' CANAAN

Black Canadian Poetry, Music, and Citizenship

PAUL db WATKINS

This book has been published with the help of a grant from the Federation for the Humanities and Social Sciences, through the Awards to Scholarly Publications Program, using funds provided by the Social Sciences and Humanities Research Council of Canada. Wilfrid Laurier University Press acknowledges the support of the Canada Council for the Arts for our publishing program. We acknowledge the financial support of the Government of Canada through the Canada Book Fund for our publishing activities. Funding provided by the Government of Ontario and the Ontario Arts Council. This work was supported by the Research Support Fund.

Library and Archives Canada Cataloguing in Publication Data

Title: Soundin' Canaan : Black Canadian poetry, music, and citizenship / Paul db Watkins.
Names: Watkins, Paul db, author.
Description: Includes bibliographical references and index.
Identifiers: Canadiana (print) 2024032014X | Canadiana (ebook) 20240320166 |
　ISBN 9781771126212 (softcover) | ISBN 9781771126229 (EPUB) | ISBN 9781771126236 (PDF)
Subjects: LCSH: Music and literature. | CSH: Canadian poetry—Black Canadian authors—
　History and criticism.
Classification: LCC PS8089.5.B5 W38 2024 | DDC C811.009/896071—dc23

Cover design by Guybrush Taylor. Interior design by Lara Minja.
Front cover image by Juliana Caicedo.

© 2025 Wilfrid Laurier University Press
Waterloo, Ontario, Canada
www.wlupress.wlu.ca

Every reasonable effort has been made to acquire permission for copyrighted material used in this text, and to acknowledge all such indebtedness accurately. Any errors and omissions called to the publisher's attention will be corrected in future printings.

No part of this publication may be reproduced, stored in a retrieval system, or transmitted, in any form or by any means, without the prior written consent of the publisher or a licence from the Canadian Copyright Licensing Agency (Access Copyright). For an Access Copyright licence, visit http://www.accesscopyright.ca or call toll-free to 1-800-893-5777.

Wilfrid Laurier University Press is located on the Haldimand Tract, part of the traditional territories of the Haudenosaunee, Anishnaabe, and Neutral Peoples. This land is part of the Dish with One Spoon Treaty between the Haudenosaunee and Anishnaabe Peoples and symbolizes the agreement to share, to protect our resources, and not to engage in conflict. We are grateful to the Indigenous Peoples who continue to care for and remain interconnected with this land. Through the work we publish in partnership with our authors, we seek to honour our local and larger community relationships, and to engage with the diversity of collective knowledge integral to responsible scholarly and cultural exchange.

to be here. sound

of the stones going, 'Canaan Land'

fulla honey. going, 'steal away.' stage

whispering. breeze blowing. knowing only

one way, one direction. Flowing. crossing.

—WAYDE COMPTON, "The Book,"
49th Parallel Psalm, 108

CONTENTS

Prelude 1

Overture
DJ Methodology: Re-sounding the Past 7

Coda
Dialogue and Dissonance 65

1

Blues Vernacular and "Harmonious Dissonance" in George Elliott Clarke's Colouring Pentateuch: *Blue, Black, Red, Gold,* and *White* 69

2

Listening to a Listening: The Disruptive Jazz Poetics of Dionne Brand's *Ossuaries* and *The Blue Clerk* (A Call Toward Freedom) 143

3

Dub Poetics and Improvised Chant in M. NourbeSe Philip's *Zong!* 187

4

Wavin' the Multicultural Flag: Canadian Hip Hop and "Sonic Citizenship" in K'naan's Music   241

5

Recovery and Remix: Wayde Compton's Turntable Poetics   295

Outro

The New Black Can(aan)Lit and the Community to Come   359

Shout Outs!   375

Notes   377
Selected Discography   419
Bibliography   423
Copyright Acknowledgements   445
Index   447

Prelude

"For only love can conquer hate."

—MARVIN GAYE, "What's Going On"

"Hate cannot drive out hate: only love can do that."

—MARTIN LUTHER KING, JR., *Strength to Love*, 47

"Without justice there can be no love."

—bell hooks, *All About Love*, 30

Marvin Gaye

Music has the power to sound across generations, crossing borders both physical and in the mind.♭ For the people creating and listening to music, it can be an act of resistance. It can also be an act of deep love in the face of hate. While in prison, anti-apartheid revolutionary Nelson Mandela drew strength—momentarily dissolving the prison walls—while listening to Marvin Gaye's "What's Going On": an anti-war, anti-poverty, and anti-injustice post–civil rights anthem.¹ Mandela drew power from the energy of the civil rights movement in the United States and related it to his own struggles in apartheid South Africa. "What's Going On" (the album and the song) calls on the listener to confront hatred, suffering, and injustice within the Black struggle for liberation. The lyrics could have been written yesterday: "Mother, mother / There's far too many of you crying / Brother, brother, brother / There's far too many of you dying … / Picket lines and picket signs / Don't punish me with brutality / Talk to me, so you can see / Oh, what's going on." Sonically, *What's Going On* is an easy album to like, but as composer and trumpeter Terence Blanchard points out, "how many people listen to the groove and the melody of this song, without really hearing the words. And that made me realize that many well-meaning people have heard only the melody of our plight, without knowing what the song means for us." For Blanchard, now is the time to "see the pain that doesn't go away. To understand the smile that hides the immense hurt."² How a song sounds can convey its meaning, and as listeners—particularly non-Black folk who have picked up this book—now is the time to build the capacity to really *hear*, *feel*, and *love* the music.

Liner Notes

♭ Nicely done—you found this footnote / flat note. If I have more than one on a page I move to a sharp (#) and then back to a flat. These "liner notes" (like in albums) provide additional commentary about the music and occasionally larger themes of the book and are different than the more traditional endnotes found at the end of book for each chapter. You will also notice artist names in the margins that correspond to the songs in the playlist for a given chapter. You can find the playlist for the Prelude, Overture, and Coda through the QR code at the start of this chapter, or here: https://open.spotify.com/playlist/7nMj0VvKiEGsXBZrUiklzq.

With similar verve and affect, Nina Simone's "Mississippi Goddam" captures the anger and spirit of the civil rights movement. The song responds to the murder of civil rights activist Medgar Evers in Mississippi and the 16th Street Baptist Church bombing in Birmingham, Alabama, which killed four Black girls. The song was banned in several Southern states, in part because of the use of "Goddam" in the title. Simone juxtaposes the jaunty show-tune structure with lyrics that speak out against the brutality of state-sanctioned violence toward African Americans. Now, as it was for Simone, is not the time "to do it slow" and take a moderate approach to change, but to fight in this moment and across generations for the full rights of citizenship. The song was performed in front of 10,000 people at the end of the Selma Marches when she and other Black activists crossed police lines. Simone's "Mississippi Goddam" is a radical act of love for her people in response to the abject violence of white supremacy. While the song confronts a particular moment of terror in the United States, it speaks across the continuum of time and place (back to "picking the cotton") and sounds Black pain and resistance to a white culture that seeks (but fails) to stifle Black humanity and creativity.

Nina Simone

Drawing on the energy of the Black church, and speaking across borders, Black Montreal-based musician Oscar Peterson conceived of "Hymn to Freedom," which was sung in various places in the United States as an anthem to the civil rights movement. While Peterson didn't initially imagine his song in this context, his blues-soaked hymn speaks to the parallel conditions in Canada. As Peterson said, "I was bothered particularly by the fact that I didn't see many nonwhite performers on television and in commercials."[3] Peterson's "Hymn" sounds citizenship across borders and articulates a pivotal moment of radical change along the road toward freedom and equality for all. Peterson, Simone, and Gaye used music to traverse borders, displaying a global anti-oppressive alliance at work. It is precisely this creative force in Black music, resistance, and culture—exemplified by the collective power of the "long civil rights movement" and its influence—that I find exemplary to how we can challenge state-sanctioned violence (whether in policing or in oppressive immigration laws) and model a more inclusive society in Canada and beyond.[4]

Oscar Peterson

In a Western context, Black skin has been a qualifier for exclusion, representing a supposed lack of dignity and access to citizenship rights. I work with the idea that citizenship, conceptually, serves as a contract where we can unify as a cohesive group to promote good things for our fellow citizens, regardless of one's somatic or ethnic identification. Fighting anti-Black racism requires direct sounding, action, and resistance. At the time of writing, the recent deaths of George Floyd, Ahmaud Arbery, Breonna Taylor, Regis Korchinski-Paquet, Andrew Loku, Jermaine Carby, Tony McDade, Chantel Moore, Rodney Levi, and Sonya Massey, and far too many others to list here, show that the white settler state (in the United States and Canada) continues to harm Black and Indigenous people who should still be alive today. Anti-Black racism is not just a public health risk (made more visible through the lens of the coronavirus pandemic); it is also a systemic injustice that informs nearly every Canadian's sense of who they are. Anti-Blackness includes the erasure of Black presence in history and media. There is a specific dimension of colonial violence that underpins the foundation of Canada and the United States and it is vital that we recognize, name, address, and redress this colonial violence and inherent racism if we are to imagine a better future.

Citizenship is sounded: it is more than a passport, just as multiculturalism is idealistically more than a policy. While a truly egalitarian multicultural Canada is largely myth—reflected in particular through the lived experiences of Black and Indigenous folk—it is a malleable myth with parts worth reworking, especially as countries like the United States, France, Germany, and Britain turn to nationalism and call out that "multiculturalism is dead," labelling it an utter failure while trying to return to "traditional" American, French, German, or English values. Canada is hardly immune from such dangerous rhetoric; Maxime Bernier—a former Member of Parliament and founder and leader of the People's Party of Canada—warned of the dangers of what he called "extreme multiculturalism" on Twitter and during the 2019 federal election debate.

Part of the conceptual confusion around multiculturalism is that it often serves as a catch-all for many minority histories. At its best, as Cecil Foster attests, "multiculturalism is the living out of faith, the belief that the good that humans choose will be a good not only for their time but for the future as well."³ Multicultural policy in Canada is tied very closely to the civil rights movement in the United States: the surge of violence and chaos in America's largest cities following Martin Luther King Jr.'s assassination shared front-page headlines in Canadian newspapers with the convention victory of Pierre Elliott Trudeau, who borrowed (sometimes problematically) the language of King when discussing the Just Society.

A truly multicultural citizenship is more than tolerance, and it is certainly more than integration: it is one in which community rights coexist alongside individual rights. In the Overture I frame this negotiation as an act of "sonic citizenship" (a term I adapt from Vincent Andrisani). This book—*Soundin' Canaan*—whose title refers to the code name often used for Canada in spirituals during the Black migration, looks at Black Canadian poetry and the ways that poets incorporate music and sound across borders as they expand the categories of community and citizenship rights. Ultimately, I am motivated by my love of the music and poetry herein, as well as by a deep admiration for the poets and musicians sounded in this book. The work is made possible thanks to a community of writers, students, educators, supervisors, poets, and musicians who have shared their ideas, words, and sounds with me over the years. I am particularly thankful to the poets who made time for interviews. Any misunderstandings or mistakes are my own.

Overture

DJ METHODOLOGY: RE-SOUNDING THE PAST

Listening: John Coltrane: "Alabama" and "My Favorite Things"

So much of the music of John Coltrane is intricate and dense, at times intensely beautiful and at others primal and unsettling. Coltrane's music was also very spiritual as he envisioned a cosmic understanding of peace. One of his most directly political tracks is "Alabama" (1964) from *Live at Birdland*. Like Nina Simone's "Mississippi Goddam," "Alabama" was a response to the 1963 bombing (orchestrated by the KKK) of 16th Street Baptist Church in Birmingham that left four young girls dead and another twenty-two injured. This act of white American terrorism was a turning point in the civil rights movement as mass support grew for the *Civil Rights Act* of 1964.

> John Coltrane, "Alabama" & "My Favorite Things"

Coltrane's music was transformative in theme and sound, and he had an incredible ability to transform a standard into something wholly new. This is perhaps most evident in his classic, "My Favorite Things" (1961), originally composed by Rodgers and Hammerstein and featured in the musical *The Sound of Music*. Coltrane, on soprano saxophone, and McCoy Tyner, on piano, would improvise over the melody and the two tonic chords, E major and E minor, in waltz time (3/4). While the album version clocked in at a whopping 13:41, live performances could be stretched into an hour-plus-long performance, highlighting Coltrane's skills as a consummate improviser (explored more in chapter 2). Coltrane turned "My Favorite Things" into something fluid and contextual, which he adapted to different audiences and spaces every time he performed it.♭ This speaks to the unique power of Black art and two of its central tenets: remix and signifying. Moreover, it emphasizes a key goal of this book and introductory chapter, which is to show how music, poetry, and by extension citizenship are active processes that are made in the moment and then remade in the next.

This chapter—an overture of ideas, soundings, and openings—maps a critical framework to guide the reader through the poetry explored in the subsequent chapters, in which I read history and early Black literatures through the lens of sonic exchange. I introduce thematic concerns that will be expounded throughout this book: an overview of Canada (Canaan land) as a Promised Land and its frequent failure to fulfill this role; a focus on the history of Black Canadian writing and poetics; a breakdown of how music, improvisation, and genre function in the book as a central aesthetic and rhetorical trope for freedom; and a look at what defines creative "sonic citizenship." On one level, this sounding appeals to our basic intrinsic need to be heard and sounded, as well as to the indeterminacy of sound, which speaks to the malleable framework I have in mind for how we can *citizen* with one another. The other possibility, and greater leap, is that this sounding from the various poets shows us that being a full citizen in multicultural Canada happens at a sonic level—a frequency that defies total appropriation much like Coltrane's music does—that moves beyond ocular and xenophobic categories of race, ability, sexuality, language, and ethnicity, even as those markers remain visible.

Liner Notes

♭ Coltrane's influence can be heard in hip hop, such as in Outkast's cover of "My Favourite Things" or in "Trouble Man" by the Juggaknots, which samples Coltrane's track (https://www.youtube.com/watch?v=12Y-iVzo3H4). Both tracks and the Julie Andrews original that Coltrane reworks have been added to the playlist for this chapter, which you can find here: https://open.spotify.com/playlist/7nMj0VvKiEGsXBZrUiklzq.

I. Sing Canaan Land

> "I learned that to the north, in a land called Canaan, all men were free."
>
> —LAWRENCE HILL, *Any Known Blood*, 82

> Canaan Land
>   I dreamed a dream . . .
>   a fitful dream.
>   The life I lived so long ago,
>   in 'Canaan' land.
>   False 'Freedom' land—
>   strained welcome—
>   subtle hatred—
>   covert discrimination—
>   Slavery . . . Canadian style.
>
> —GEORGE A. BORDEN, "Fashions of Slavery," *Canaan Odyssey*, 7

This book envisions what a just society might look and sound like as conceived by Black Canadian poets who resist the settler state and the legacy of slavery and colonialism in Canada. Many white Canadians remain ignorant of the fact that slavery existed in Canada for more than two centuries before Canada was an "official" country. Dub poet and critic Afua Cooper asserts that slavery is "Canada's best kept secret, locked within the National closet."[1] White Canada suffers from what Yvonne Brown describes, in reference to slavery and the Middle Passage, as "collective amnesia" because "a history that involved those fourteen European nations could be omitted completely, an event that lasted 350 years—omitted completely."[2] In Canada, the official denouncement of slavery did not occur until 1793, and its formal abolition wasn't established until 1834. In contrast, just south of the border in America, during the Constitutional Convention of 1787, delegates made the decision to permit the continuation of slavery within American territory, setting the groundwork for the enactment of the *Fugitive Slave Acts* of 1793 and 1850. The Underground Railroad, a surreptitious network of paths and safe houses that led to the slave-free Northern states and Canada, was a response to these acts. According to a conservative estimate by historian Robin Winks, as many as 30,000 fugitive slaves (between 1830 and 1860) survived the journey from the United States to Canada—to Canaan land, that heaven coded in the African American spirituals.[3] For runaway enslaved people, Canada represented reprieve from a life of dehumanized imprisonment and offered freedom from what abolitionist Frederick Douglass described as "the hell of slavery."[4]

Many "freedom seekers" (Daniel Grafton Hill) fled to Canada knowing that capture along the way meant being placed back on a plantation, or worse, public humiliation and torture, or a gruesome public lynching. Despite the risks, freedom seekers set out to follow their North Star, the drinking gourd, journeying along the Underground Railroad that started in the South and ended in Canada.

At the helm of many of those dangerous trips was Harriet "Moses" Tubman, providing passage and bearing the cross of thousands of freedom seekers who travelled toward Canaan land. This journey paralleled the biblical parable of the Israelites' escape from Egyptian bondage to the promised land of milk and honey: they travelled (as if) across the Red Sea and the Sinai desert and through the rocky wilderness into Canada with nothing more than a hope for a better life. Canada was seen as a place where the freedom seekers might be free from racism, extreme poverty, and "the hell of slavery."

These rebel warriors, fugitives, and survivors of the crossing found to their surprise that upon entering Canada, many of their ambitions were stymied. Instead of biblical vindication, they found a new group of oppressors. They encountered very direct racism from "anti-slavery Negro hater[s]," devastating poverty, and segregation, and faced the vestiges of slavery in Canada.[5] This is what Saidiya Hartman refers to as "the afterlife of slavery": "skewed life chances, limited access to health and education, premature death, incarceration, impoverishment."[6] As BLM-TO co-founder Sandy Hudson has pointed out, "it is important to note that the first type of movement that could be described in a similar way to the Underground Railroad was with people moving from above the 49th parallel to below in order to escape the brutality of racism of what was then Upper Canada."⁷ White Canadian settlers saw these escaped people as a monolith, comprised of visitors unfit for integration into Canadian society.⁸ White Canadians tolerated Black refugees largely to bolster their own perceived self-righteousness over the United States and its ongoing institution of slavery.

Canada proved not to be the place that the astute Frederick Douglass envisioned as where "the wild goose and the swan repaired at the end of winter."⁹ In truth, Canada was and remains a "settler colony founded on colonization and genocide."¹⁰ Despite this bleak reality, the freedom seekers founded their own Canaans—Dawn, Wilberforce, the Refugee Home Society, and Elgin—and continued to plant their hopes and dreams in the soil of Canadian society. We can celebrate their legacy and survival while also critiquing the settler state. Furthermore, we can learn from the interventions Black people have made against the colonial state. It takes collective anti-racist and anti-colonial work to build a more inclusive future as envisioned by the freedom seekers. This book is predicated on the hopes of those freedom seekers, improvising songs along those wild tracks, in the belief that we have not yet achieved that just society but that one day, we might.♭ The poets with whom this book engages—most directly George Elliott Clarke, Dionne Brand, M. NourbeSe Philip, K'naan, and Wayde Compton—provide nuanced critique of the settler state and speak from the lived experience of Black Canadian and Afrosporic people.

My working explicitly with Blackness as an academic praxis, literary framework, and sonic model—defined extemporaneously, improvisationally, and within communal networks—has the intention to work against imperialist approaches to teaching and writing about Black literature. There is no simple way to divorce oneself from one's

---

♭ I borrow the "just society" from the language of Canadian Prime Minister Pierre Elliott Trudeau, civil rights leader Martin Luther King Jr., and philosopher John Stuart Mill before them.

choice of study. As cultural theorist Stuart Hall articulates, "We all write and speak from a particular place and time, from a history and a culture which is specific. What we say is always in 'context,' *positioned*."[11] Because of my background as a non-Black scholar and settler of Anglo-Indian (British and South Asian), French Canadian, and Irish ancestry, I will always remain outside of the experience of being Black. My theoretical identification isn't one of genotype (hereditary/biological), but rather of phenotype (morphology and practice), which means I will apply and foreground Black artistic practices to challenge the hegemony of symbolic whiteness in literary studies as the default position when discussing the human.[12]

CanLit scholars have historically debated whether there even *is* literature in Canada. Black writers have always been excluded from such conversations.[13] Dionne Brand describes how she was forced to read and learn about white writers in the academy, and hardly at all about African American or Black Canadian writers. That observation is echoed by social geographer Joseph Mensah as well as by James W. St.G. Walker, who attests that "the student of Canadian history can go right through our school system, university courses, and even graduate school, without ever being exposed to the history of blacks in Canada."[14] While earning my BA, I discovered poets like George Elliott Clarke and Dionne Brand by chance, and was struck by the beauty, rhetorical force, and musicality of their poetry. Prompted by a love for the poetry and the music (which for me, are closely linked modes of creation), I was inspired to take a closer look. But why is this? Surely Canadians, and particularly historians, must be interested in the rich, complex, and tumultuous history of Black people in Canada. Of course, there is also a danger of outsiders claiming this history.

Leslie Sanders, a self-identified white scholar of Black literature, convincingly argues that "white scholars of Black culture have often represented the academy at its most imperialist." Sanders challenges the belief that the scholar is an absolute "authority" on a subject, labelling scholars who attempt to ascertain absolute truth as "extremely dangerous": "What is at stake is power, who gets to decide what is true."[15] Sanders challenges the claim that the scholar has a privileged right to create and define—essentially cutting off the possibility of fruitful dialogue. This is relevant, as much of early Canadian literature is marked by its relation to whiteness. As George Lipsitz argues in *The Possessive Investment in Whiteness*, "white settlers institutionalized a possessive investment in whiteness by making blackness synonymous with slavery and whiteness synonymous with freedom, but also by pitting people of color against one another." He goes on to argue that "those of us who are 'white' can only become part of the solution if we recognize the degree to which we are already part of the problem—not because of our race, but because of our possessive investment in it."[16] By re-sounding the past, we can productively deconstruct racism as a corporeal machination of hegemonic forces by larger institutions and work to imagine and create a better society.

What W.E.B. Du Bois was telling us when he talked about the problem of the colour line was that race is ultimately about how racism and power are correlated and socially constructed. Despite this construction, Lipsitz argues that "race is a cultural construct, but one with deadly social causes and consequences."[17] As a case in point, Adrienne Shadd reminds us that Black "descendants, particularly in the Maritimes, have been living in quasi-segregated communities for over 200 years."[18] Black Canadian literature constantly reflects the horrifying experience of being read somatically as Other. Dionne Brand and Lois De Shield's *No Burden to Carry* provides personal accounts that examine the narratives of Black working women in Ontario from 1920 to 1950. In much the same vein, we have a detailed historical account of the Brotherhood of Sleeping Car Porters in Canada (BSCP) from Stanley Grizzle, who in *My Name's Not George* speaks about his experience working as a Pullman porter, and later, as Canada's first Black citizen judge, recounted in relation to the birth of modern Canada and the struggle for citizenship rights in Cecil Foster's *They Call Me George*.

Power and gender further complicate issues of belonging and race. While many Black activists fought anti-Black racism, Anne Cools, the first self-identified Black Canadian to be appointed to Canada's senate, and who held that seat from 1984 to 2018, describes how Black men fought for equality while oppressing Black women: "Black women, the slaves of the slaves, can have no peace, no rest until they have evolved new social structures within which men can be Men, women can be Women, and their children, free-thinking total creative human beings."[19] Cools was speaking in 1971, and her sentiment echoes Fern Shadd Shreve, who in 1924 emphasized her desire to simply be read as fully human. Shreve said, "I look at myself as me, not as a woman, or as a Black, and I want people to take me as they find me, and not as a Black, or as a woman, or as a woman who is Black. It's just that I hope that it's just the me that shows through, and you like me for me, not because I'm Black or a woman."[20] One's inclusion in or access to Canadian identity is concomitant with a contingent access of power, gender, and whiteness. Given the volatile nature of modern sovereignty, might one be simultaneously Canadian and Caribbean? This book argues that certainly one can be, but historically racist immigration policies and ignorant public opinion make such polyphonic iterations difficult to achieve. Thus, I work in this chapter to re-sound the past in the present with an eye and ear to the future.

The past, after all, as Frantz Fanon wrote, can be "an invitation to action and a basis for hope," and the poets of *Soundin' Canaan* push us toward social justice and a collective calling to imagine, as Rinaldo Walcott writes in *Queer Returns*, "differently the present and the past as a way of setting in place the conditions for a different kind of future."[21] *Soundin' Canaan* is a theoretical manifesto of hope: the music and poetry herein allow us to resist simple binaries, cross borders, and imagine a truly just society.

Soundin' Canaan

For me, *Soundin' Canaan* signifies the active affixing of a vernacular adjective (*Soundin'*) upon a noun (*Canaan*) so as to emphasize the lively, cacophonous, and sound-filled nature of place. Canada signified as Canaan represents faith and contradiction, embodying the hopes of thousands of freedom seekers and Black folk, among many others who believed in the pursuit of justice, who envisioned Canada—amid the hell of slavery—as heaven. Canaan (Hebrew, *Kĕnā'an*), as defined in the *Oxford English Dictionary*, is "the ancient proper name of Western

Palestine, promised to the Children of Israel; hence *fig.* (esp. in hymns and devotional use) land of promise, land of heavenly rest across the Jordan of death, heaven."[22]

It is also important to acknowledge that while Canaan is a displaced Hebrew trope for the "promised land" taken up by African diasporic cultures, it is also the name of the West Bank/Palestine.[23] Examining the troubling language of Michael Walzer's *Exodus and Revolution*, cultural theorist Edward Said confronts the disturbing "injunction laid on the Jews by God to exterminate their opponents, an injunction that somewhat takes away the aura of progressive national liberation which Walzer is bent upon giving to Exodus."[24] In fact, there are strong parallels between the story of Canada and that of Palestine: both involve settlers committing genocide against the Indigenous population. In Noam Chomsky and Ilan Pappé's *On Palestine,* Chomsky looks at Zionism in Israel as part of a global settler-colonial movement that implicates the larger Anglosphere, which includes Canada. This sentiment is reaffirmed in Jeremy Wildeman and M. Muhannad Ayyash's edited collection, *Canada as a Settler Colony on the Question of Palestine*, which explores Canada–Palestine relations through a settler-colonial lens. Additionally, the term Canaanites often becomes a catch-all term for ethnic otherness (particularly Jewish and Palestinian) and there are many connections to larger global struggles for freedom that could be made beyond the scope of this book. Still, the term's usage remains in the historical context between the United States and Canada and the dream of freedom seekers looking for their own land of promise.

And how appropriate that Canada is nearly a visual cognate to Canaan, holding homophonic connections with rapper/poet K'naan, who is the focus of chapter 4. In addition, I appreciate the sonic similarity of "cannon" and "canon" to "Canaan." I think there is value in forming "new" canons, but I am aware of the pitfalls of canon formation, heeding Cornel West's admonishing of canon creation, since it "reveals the worst of academic pluralist ideology."[25] Nevertheless, Gayatri Spivak reminds us that "canons are the condition of institutions" so we "must make room for the coordinated teaching of new entries into the canon."[26] Canons are tools of socialization that are inherently exclusionary and essentialist, but by reworking old canons and introducing new ones, while acknowledging that canon formation is a discursive act, canons can function as units of understanding (and play) that disturb the idea that there is one theoretical approach to a given body of literature. I would like to see more Black Canadian texts enter and/or challenge the larger Canadian canon—an imaginative bonding of texts—since that very passage into mainstream education would be an affirmation that acknowledges Canada's own literary formation and exclusion.[27] I agree with novelist and scholar Nathaniel Mackey when he argues in *Discrepant Engagement* that "creative kinship and the lines of affinity it effects are much more complex, jagged, and indissociable than the totalizing pretensions of canon formation."[28]

Lastly, canon means, although rarer in usage, a piece of music in which an extended melody in one part is imitated successively in one or more other parts, such as the phrases of a bird singing being *canoned* in similar or new phrases. Sonically this can be heard in South African pianist and composer Abdullah Ibrahim's "Moniebah," from *Good News from Africa*, which is gradually drawn into the pull of the previous melody from "The Pilgrim" (*Good News*).[♭] *Soundin' Canaan* presents a nascent canon of Black Canadian poets who make use of music in their poetry to sound citizenship—*canoning* the performances of various musical styles. Through this lens we can explore citizenship beyond state definition and open spaces of belonging outside white-supremacist and heteropatriarchal racial capitalist culture.

[♭] This song was originally performed by Dollar Brand before Ibrahim converted to Islam in 1968 and changed his name. The version on the Spotify playlist features saxophonist Archie Shepp as the original (featuring the canoning) is not available. You can hear that version on YouTube. See "Dollar Brand Duo "Moniebah (The Pilgrim)" YouTube video, https://www.youtube.com/watch?v=w-11CDGp1Mw.

Abdullah Ibrahim

Approaching Black Canadian History

> "Let me be clear: trying to write total stories of any cultural group is an impossibility and in the case of black Canadian cultures this impossibility presents itself from the first instance."
>
> —RINALDO WALCOTT, *Black Like Who?*, 13

There are many Black writers in Canada who valorize dissonance, divergence, and formal disruption, often through the lens of music. While hardly all Black Canadian and Afrosporic texts employ musical techniques in direct praxis, a prevalent body of this literature concerns notions of mobility and disruption in their resistance to various normative forces. Akin to musical dissonance, there is theoretical discordance among the various writers with whom this book engages, from politics around self-identification, to concepts of citizenship and multiculturalism, to notions of how to approach literary and social history. While I use music as a unifying element, Black writers in Canada—like all writers and scholars—hardly write or perform in a conclusive homogenous fashion.

Some of the tensions between the Black/African Canadian writers I explore are put forth through my own personal interviews.[29] For example, forms of naming based on ethnicity directly attest to the complexity of constitutive Blackness, participating in age-old quarrels over labels, which are particularly complex here because of the way "ethnic" literary products are commodified. Such dynamic debates around labelling and identity are hardly new, as evidenced, for example, during the Harlem Renaissance (often referred to as "the New Negro Movement") with the castigation (some one hundred years ago) that Langston Hughes gave Countee Cullen for his rejection of the label "Negro poet." Similarly, many Black Canadian writers, such as Ayanna Black, Lawrence Hill, and Rinaldo Walcott, express discomfort with the label "African Canadian."[30] Afrosporic writers living in Canada, but not born here, often disavow the "Canadian" label, which is why I often (cumbersomely) shift between Black, Black

Canadian, and sometimes African Canadian to acknowledge the desires of the various writers I engage with. For example, Dionne Brand rejects both the Canadian and Trinidadian poet labels, and embraces the role of the stateless, saying, "places and those who inhabit them are ... fictions."[31] In addition, when I was writing a biography of M. NourbeSe Philip for an online interview, she told me, "I am a Caribbean writer/poet or AfroCaribbean, or Afrosporic Caribbean writer. Not ever Canadian!"[32] Perhaps, ironically, being "Canadian" allows people to self-identify as they choose and to change those identities as they see fit. To illustrate the issue for those who still want Canadian as an identifier, Walcott prefers to use the terms "blackness" and "black Canadian" over "African Canadian," which he sees as a borrowing from the use of "African American," which has connotations, he argues, "related to distancing oneself from the black urban poor and working class."[33] "Black communities are," as Robyn Maynard articulates in *Policing Black Lives*, "after Indigenous communities, among the poorest racial groups in Canada."[34] By contrast, George Elliott Clarke prefers "African-Canadian" (African-Canadianité), which for him constitutes an archipelago of Blackness based upon a Caribbean model of Antillanité: a model that unites the Caribbean islands through a shared history while recognizing their unique diversities, which is akin to a kind of multiculturalism.[35]

In "Treason of the Black Intellectuals?" (1999), George Elliott Clarke takes a number of Black Canadian scholars to task (such as André Alexis, Djanet Sears, Dionne Brand, Cecil Foster, and, most fiercely, Rinaldo Walcott) for what he sees as an "unexamined, facile black nationalism and Pan-Africanism" that largely overlooks the history and the achievements of early African Canadian settlers of Canada (particularly the "Africadians" of Nova Scotia).[36] While Clarke is concerned with a particular Africadian history, he doesn't offer, as Walcott argues, much in terms of "theoretical and conceptual frames for making sense of blackness in Canada."[37] Walcott is correct that while Clarke is a remarkably adept chronicler, his "mapping supposes an authentic older and rural black Canada set against an inauthentic newer and urban black Canada, as if the two have not always and cannot live side by side ... Clarke lacks a diasporic sensibility:

his love is not so much for black people as it is for the nation."[38] There are two stories at play vying for authenticity. Clarke's approach is rooted in the historical specificity of early African Canadian people and loyalty to the Black Canadian nation, while Walcott's thinking is informed by a "diasporic sensibility." Both stories concern the past and how one fits within or outside the confines of the Canadian state. While Clarke's and Walcott's positions have evolved, their debate reminds us that belonging remains markedly complex.

This relationship to place and home is especially varied since many of the writers I explore (Dionne Brand, M. NourbeSe Philip, K'naan) could be read as self-exiled poets. As Philip writes, "It is as well to note that legal citizenship in no way affects the profound and persistent alienation within a society at best indifferent, if not hostile, to the artist's origins, her work, and her being."[39] The ambiguity of identity is the reality of the exiled, or globally defined, jazz poet and citizen; even more complex is the refugee, who takes the issue of belonging—or not belonging, which can be positive at times—toward complex boundaries that challenge any simple understanding of identity and foretell utopian hopes for a "coming community" (taken up in chapter 2).[40] Immigrants and refugees are a big part of Canada's make-up. Canada brings in more than 400,000 refugees and immigrants per year, as well as tens of thousands of students, temporary visitors, and workers. Sadly, Canada seems—at times—to be a country of immigrants and refugees who hate immigrants and refugees. As philosopher Giorgio Agamben argues, refugees "[break] the continuity between man and citizen, *nativity* and *nationality*, they put the originary fiction of modern sovereignty in crisis."[41] That is one of the crises this book will grapple with as I venture toward an understanding of what performed citizenship sounds like. Thus, to approach Black Canadian history, we need the skills of the DJ/archivist and poet.

History is open to social construction, recovery, and remix. Just because historical interpretation is porous, it does not mean we can avoid specificity, nor can we avoid how historical discourses and events shape and inform the present. As Christina Sharpe reminds us, using the metaphor of the wake (the path behind a ship and the legacy of slavery), "the past that is not past reappears, always, to rupture the present."[42] Like a turntable needle touching down on the historical record, the past sounds in the present and echoes into the future. History is, as dub poet Clifton Joseph argues, "to be found/out-about, to learn, and to make."[43] Black Canadian history is "to make," because such histories have often been elided by white settler narratives.

There is a need, as George Elliott Clarke states, for literary scholars "to accept the historical (or 'indigenous') African-Canadian population and its cultural production as a constitutive element."[44] A deeper understanding of Black cultural production in Canada needs to encompass historical figures (people like Mathieu da Costa, the first recorded free Black person in Canada, and Viola Desmond, who challenged racial segregation at a cinema in Nova Scotia in 1946) as well as Black communities put under erasure such as Africville and Hogan's Alley, as well as the nascent canon of Black writers in Canada dealing with contemporary experiences.[45] Creating space for these histories is, as poet Dionne Brand attests, "redemptive and restorative; inasmuch as it binds us in a common pain it binds us in a common quest for a balm for that pain."[46] As Cherokee and Greek writer Thomas King explains, "Most of us think that history is the past. It's not. It's the stories we tell about the past. That's all it is."[47] Engaging with past involves understanding Canada's xenophobic, racist, and settler-colonial past, including historical lacunae around slavery and the ongoing legacy of white supremacy.

Early Black Canadian history could easily fill numerous books. Robin Winks's *The Blacks in Canada* was the beginning of that project, and there have been a number of other books since.[48] A more recent book, Winfried Siemerling's substantial *The Black Atlantic Reconsidered*—which has a useful companion site (http://blackatlantic.ca/) and a timeline in the appendix—demonstrates that Black writing in Canada is multilingual, transatlantic, and more than two centuries old, with Black speech being even older. Responding to culpable omissions that leave Canada out of the Black Atlantic (such as Paul Gilroy's influential book *The Black Atlantic*), Siemerling covers Black immigration and mobility, the abolitionist movement in

Canada, and jazz music and its influence on Montreal's French and English literary scenes; it also devotes considerable case study space to African Canadian literary texts, which he weaves into the warp and weft of the Black Atlantic world. While I hardly have the space to present such a substantive history in this chapter, I want to provide some historical context to riff on before I move to examine Black Canadian writing and citizenship through the lens of music and poetry.

Those who can name someone kept as an enslaved person in Canada might recall Marie-Joseph Angélique, who in 1734, after learning about her impending sale by her mistress, likely burned Montreal to the ground; she was subsequently tortured, burned alive, and hanged in public. Angélique's symbolic act of rebellion and her subsequent public torture have made her an important inspiration for a variety of Black Canadian intellectuals and writers, including Afua Cooper, author of *The Hanging of Angélique: The Untold Story of Canadian Slavery and the Burning of Old Montreal*, and of the poem "Confessions of a Woman Who Burnt Down a Town" (in *Copper Woman and Other Poems*), and Lorena Gale, who wrote the play *Angélique*.[49]

More important than whether she set the fire, is, as Katherine McKittrick puts it, that she "represents a long-standing racial meeting point that discloses geographies of wonder."[50] Thus, one of Canada's early race rebels was a Black woman and an enslaved person. It is an ignominy that many Canadians likely have no idea who Harriet "Moses" Tubman or Mary Ann Shadd were, although the success of Kasi Lemmons's 2019 film *Harriet* has likely changed this in the case of Harriet Tubman, at least to a degree (although this says nothing of the film's missteps).[♭] Harriet "Moses" Tubman, dubbed "Black Moses," led "freedom seekers" on the Underground Railroad to its terminus in Chatham, Ontario. The Underground Railroad remains a persistent signifier of resistance (see Colson Whitehead's *The Underground Railroad*) and an "emancipatory lifeline."[51] Mary Ann Shadd was the full-time editor of the radical paper *The Provincial*

♭ There are several songs about or dedicated to Harriet Tubman, but the jazz group Sons of Kemet's 2018 song, "My Queen Is Harriet Tubman" feels lively and apt for this moment.

Freeman and the first woman publisher of a newspaper in Canada.[52] These Black women achieved the seemingly impossible at a time when white women were not even legally considered persons. The efforts of Mary Ann Shadd and Harriet Tubman are even more commendable when we consider their ability to forge new identities transnationally across borders with the hope of resettling escaped "freedom seekers" in Canada. They did all this while fighting the injustices of slavery back "home" as they came to a violent apex with the Civil War.

Canada, while hardly a land of equal opportunity for Black folk, became for many a space of possibility to construct ideals along an axis of freedom. Exodus to Canada became a "business" of resistance to American policy, as one writer in *The Provincial Freeman* stated:

> Well, notwithstanding these brutal arrests and the ever vigilance of the slaveholder and slave-hunter, the number of fugitives escaping, and of those who are ready and willing to aid them to Canada are daily increasing, and there is not the least room to doubt but that the underground Railroad will do this year, according to what has already been done since the year set in, just double the amount of business that was done last year.

Canada could, idealistically, as Mary Ann Shadd wrote in *A Plea for Emigration*, be Canaan: nirvana. The legend of Canada as being akin to Canaan (heaven) has continued to grow over the years. However, this mythic space exists alongside Indigenous genocide, slavery, segregation, *Chinese Exclusion Acts*, racist immigration policies, Japanese internment camps, and a robust colonial system that perennially excludes many from achieving full citizenship.

Nonetheless, the myth of Canada as a Promised Land remains a powerful trope of possibility. No wonder that, even if it's described as such for dramatic effect, the moment Josiah Henson (a founder of the Canaan Dawn settlement and an inspiration for Stowe's *Uncle Tom's Cabin*) crosses into Canada he falls to the ground in an ecstatic fit and kisses the soil of an earthly heaven. This belief was echoed by Martin Luther King Jr. (often thought of as a contemporary Moses), who praised Canada as more than a neighbour to Black folk: "So standing today in Canada I am linked with the history of my people and its unity with your past."³³ However, for many of the "freedom seekers," and for those who fought on the side of the Loyalists, it became apparent that Canada was something else, and not quite the heaven on earth many thought it to be. This disappointment is reflected in Austin Clarke's 1964 novel, *The Survivors of the Crossing*, which begins in the Caribbean with a letter from a friend describing "*Canada* [as] *a real first-class place!*" and later, "*Life up here in Canada is the same thing as living in Goat-heaven and Kiddy-kingdom* [italics in original]." The letter provides the Barbadian protagonist (Rufus) with the strength to stage a protest in the cane fields in Barbados, which ultimately fails because it is predicated on what Clarke sets up as a fictitious Canadian heaven. Toward the end of the novel, the friend sends a more honest letter that describes the racism and unemployment the Black man faces in Canada, calling it the very same type of racism he had hoped to escape: "I sorry to paint a technicolour picture o' the place but, Jesus Christ, man! I couldn't let you know that here in this country is the same slavery as what I run from back in the island."³⁴ This passage recalls Canada's attempt to construct an empire predicated on the privilege of whiteness. History is cyclical; we work through the past to make sense of the present. History is not determinism; we can, and do, create a history of possibility, one that recognizes, as Paulo Freire did, "that History is time filled with possibility and not inexorably determined—that the future is problematic and not already decided, fatalistically."³⁵ Like the DJ digging into the archives, history is there be resounded and remixed.

My approach in this book involves not so much discovery as engagement, critical assemblage, and careful listening. As Miles Davis states poignantly in his *Autobiography*, "White people used to talk about how John Hammond discovered Bessie Smith. Shit, how did he discover her when she was there already? ... It's like, how did Columbus discover America when the Indians were already here? What kind of shit is that, but white people's shit?"³⁶ In order to avoid another self-effacing undertaking about "white people's shit," this book—an assemblage of remixed ideas—offers a layered contribution to the fields of Black Canadian poetry, performance, and citizenship.

Bessie Smith

While *Soundin' Canaan* works thoroughly through a vast amount of material—literary, musical, philosophical, and historical—it does so to provide a "mix" to aid in understanding the selected poets and their texts. Remix is one way to unify disparate sounds and histories that resist linearity.

M. NourbeSe Philip states that to "'write' about what happened in a logical, linear way is to do a second violence."[57] I accept that history as disunity tells us more than ordered histories that claim a singular truth, often on behalf of other peoples' histories. Furthermore, as Ajay Heble asks, "whose histories count as knowledge and whose get disqualified as unpleasant and inharmonious noise?" Very insightful, since histories that are "out of tune"—ones that do not fit rigid and often biased versions of what is considered harmonious—occasion, as Heble puts it, "a purposeful disturbance to naturalized orders of knowledge production in Canada."[58] Perhaps we need to opt instead for less universal and more particular approaches. To say that there is one story of Black history in Canada would be to reduce the presence of Black people to a monolithic whole. As a fictionalized Nelson Mandela states in Clarke's dramatic long poem, *Trudeau*, "History isn't born, it's made," which echoes Clifton Joseph's notion of a history "to make" and resounds with Hortense J. Spillers's view that "traditions are not born. They are made."[59] Uncovering, making, and even remixing history is never a simple process.

Telling the total stories of any culture is an absolute impossibility. History can be a useful aid and reminder of why music and poetry—and the intersections between the two—work against canonicity and specific guidelines for literary merit. Furthermore, certain histories can be oppressive; hear Wayde Compton riffing on Countee Cullen: "What is Britannia to me?"[60] It is precisely this divergence between the inescapable mark of history and indifference toward a certain strand of enforced history that Compton disavows, and it is within (and between) these ruptures that I engage in my sonic literary mix.

Resistance and Black CanLit

There is a substantive body of early Black Canadian literature. Much of this material was (and is) on the fringes of the mainstream publishing industry, and much of the style and format was in the form of pamphlets, leaflets, poems, religious tracts, public orations, and songs, rather than novels, but nevertheless, Black folk have had literary audiences—albeit not always white ones—since they've been in Canada. One particularly early African Canadian text is Boston King's "Memoirs," written in 1798 and published in *Methodist Magazine*. King's "Memoirs" tell of his experiences as a former enslaved American, and then a Black Loyalist, who gained freedom and resettled in Nova Scotia following the American Revolutionary War. The narrative recounts his journey to Sierra Leone, where he played a significant role in establishing Freetown as the first Methodist missionary there. Due to a lack of interest and marginalization by academia until recently, many Black Canadian writers have had to dually play the role of writer and archivist of Black Canadian material.

For example, George Elliott Clarke began mapping the breadth of African Canadian literature in his anthology *Fire on the Water: An Anthology of Black Nova Scotian Writing* (1991), followed by *Eyeing the North Star: Directions in African-Canadian Literature* (1999), *Odysseys Home* (2002), which Clarke describes as responses to the revelation of "the existence of a canon of texts dating back to 1785," and lastly, *Directions Home* (2011).[61] Clarke argues that these early texts work against the perception "that 'Black Canadian' literature consists of two or maybe three writers, and, if pressed, [one] will struggle to name Austin Clarke and Dionne Brand."[62] Since *Odysseys Home*, a plethora of archived material has appeared, often in the form of anthologies or larger surveys of Black literary cultural production, most of it by Black Canadian writers.[63] These texts and others emphasize the expanding canon and massive literary output by Black Canadian writers, particularly since the 1970s, and the desire of anthologists to record this material for future generations.

However, Black cultural production and writing continues to lack mainstream acceptance and is critically undervalued. That is why the anthologizing of Black writers, such as in Wayde Compton's *Bluesprint: Black British Columbian Literature and Orature* (2001), or in Karina Vernon's *The Black Prairie Archives: An Anthology* (2020), is so important. An archive can draw more people into the mix, and the need to establish counter-canons (informed by counter-narratives) is a reminder, to appropriate from Margaret Atwood's *Survival*, that African/Black Canadian literature exists and is distinct.⁶⁴ This is perhaps all the more important given the elision of Black Canadian writers from many mainstream anthologies.

There remains persistent truth in Margaret Atwood's *Survival: A Thematic Guide to Canadian Literature* (1972), which states that literary maps help us learn about the shared history of Canada: "we need to know about here."⁶⁵ Yet, I wonder who this collective "we" speaks to and for, especially since Black voices are particularly absent in Atwood's manifesto, although she does include the work of Austin Clarke in a section titled "Failed Sacrifices: The Reluctant Immigrant." It would after all, be another four years until the important anthology of Black writers in Canada, *Canada in Us Now*, edited by Harold Head, would appear in print.⁶⁶ It was this concept of the unknown, once again rather Eurocentric in origin, that would be adapted by Northrop Frye as he mused, in his "Conclusion to a *Literary History of Canada*," that Canada "is less perplexed by the question 'Who Am I?' than by some such riddle as 'Where is Here?'"⁶⁷ It was French and English communities that forced Black Canadians, Indigenous peoples, and all other visible minorities out to the perceived margins so that they could maintain a vestige of cultural survival. Yet the myth-making process of the Canadian nation-state as white is but one story among many, for I agree with Dionne Brand: "Canada is not (and cannot ever claim to be) a homogenous culture."⁶⁸

So, while I'm apt to deal with the literature of the now, I also realize that the five main poets in this book (George Elliott Clarke, Dionne Brand, M. NourbeSe Philip, K'naan, and Wayde Compton) are rooted in what the past can tell us about the present, and in the hopeful construction of an unknown future. These writers, among many others, have helped put Black Canadian literature, and Canadian literature more broadly, on the literary map, and not just in Canada. It is my hope that the renewed and continued interest in these poets will also expand our interest in earlier poetic texts by Black Canadian writers, beginning with some of the diversely complex poetic texts I encountered in my own archaeological digging for poetic texts written by or about Black Canadians, such as Liz Cromwell's *Canadian Jungle Tea Poems* and Charles Roach's *Root for the Ravens*, from the 1970s, Clifton Joseph's *Metropolitan Blues*, George Borden's *Canaan Odyssey: A Poetic Account of the Black Experience in North America*, and Dany Laferrière's incredibly musical beat-like novel *How to Make Love to a Negro without Getting Tired*, from the 1980s, and the vast explosion of literary output since the 1990s.[69] Perhaps as Black Canadian texts gain popularity, publishers will reissue them, although given the current state of the publishing industry, it seems unlikely.

Such preservation has become the work of archivists and/or remixers. Nevertheless, the accolades bestowed upon Black Canadian writers are a promising indication that although the publishing industry may not have changed in leaps and bounds, the critical reading public certainly has. One need only do a quick search on recent accolades for Black writers to realize this: the prestigious Canadian Griffin Poetry Prize was won by Dionne Brand in 2011, Kaie Kellough in 2020, and Canisia Lubrin in 2021; the Scotiabank Giller Prize was won twice by Esi Edugyan, in 2011 and 2018, and by Ian Williams in 2019; and David Chariandy's 2017 novel *Brother* won the Rogers Writers' Trust Fiction Prize, the Toronto Book Award, and the Ethel Wilson Fiction Prize. These honours, and there are many more, are hardly indicative of a just society, nor do they constitute a claim for a literary landscape where Black writers are on equal footing with "white" authors. Rather, they are a testament that Black Canadian writers continue to change, respond to, and form an integral part of the vast literary community of Canada. We should celebrate these accomplishments while pushing for material change.

The dearth of Black Canadian writers in larger CanLit anthologies is part of the same point that Aldon Lynn Nielsen makes in *Black Chant* with regard to critics of avant-garde poetry, whom he argues "seldom look at black writers while compiling their genealogies of aesthetic evolution."[70] I would argue that some of the most resistant writers—in lived praxis and poetic form—have been Black Canadian and Indigenous writers and that any anthology of resistive poetics must include a large number of them. Canada may not have produced a poet quite as militant as Amiri Baraka, who calls for "Black scream / and chant," but it does generate radical poets from all backgrounds who resist the practices and racism of mainstream society and who labour against the standardization of education and poetic form.[71] One such collection of Canada's radical poets—that is, poets who challenge dominant world views, values, and aesthetic practices—is Pauline Butling and Susan Rudy's *Writing in Our Time: Canada's Radical Poetries in English (1957–2003)*. This collection shows that Canada has its own tradition of radical poets, focusing on writers such as Nicole Brossard, Daphne Martlatt, bpNichol, George Bowering, Roy Kiyooka, Fred Wah, and Frank Davey; it also nods to Dionne Brand, Claire Harris, and a few other Black writers, although it barely examines the truly innovative works of Black writers working in Canada. For instance, the lack of engagement with the work of M. NourbeSe Philip speaks to the failure of CanLit to fully consider Black work and life as innovative and foundational. Black Canadians, particularly those writing today, have in most cases used poetry as a tool to resist and challenge dominant modes. As Steven Green and Karen Richardson contend in *T-Dot Griots*, an anthology of Black communities in Toronto expressed in fiction, poetry, articles, plays, and songs, we can think of the artist "as a mouthpiece of resistance with tongues as sharp as swords."[72] The radical poet perpetually reshapes the past to resist in the present.

Black writers resist oppression by writing back. Black English, like Black music, is—as James Baldwin has argued—a record of brutal necessity. For poets such as Dionne Brand, the personal, the political, and the historical are not easily separated, and the same could be said for the other poets I examine. The long history of oppression of Black Canadians includes an equally long history of resistance. We are thus challenged, as Robin D.G. Kelley argues, to "not only redefine what is 'political' but question a lot of common ideas about what are 'authentic' movements and strategies of resistance." Politics, as a "history from below," also functions by what Kelley defines as "infrapolitics," a term he uses to describe the circumspect struggle waged daily by subordinate groups who function beyond the visible spectrum.[73] Many Black writers—certainly the ones I engage with in this book—use infrapoetics at the level of how they sound language and enact Black resistance in the face of a white hegemonic static finality. I argue that the radicalism of the poets in this book—primarily George Elliott Clarke, Dionne Brand, M. NourbeSe Philip, K'naan, and Wayde Compton—resists and models new forms of being and citizenship through the incorporation of music.

II. DJ Methodology: Poetry, Music, and Listening

DJ Methodology

> "The languages evolve and learn to speak in new forms, new thoughts. The sound of thought becomes legible again at the edge of the new meanings."
>
> —DJ SPOOKY (Paul D. Miller), *Rhythm Science*, 25

For me, sample-based DJ practices offer an improvisatory path towards blurring the lines between scholarly practice and engaged citizenship. By looking at citizenship through the lens of music as an often-dissonant site (or text) of struggle and identity formation, I seek to show how music in Black Canadian poetry is not solely aesthetic; it is also a form of social, ethical, and political expression. My methodology is closest to the practice of DJing, which provides a guide to my murky topology: DJs mix multiple records using various elements of rhythm, timbre, texture, and overall sonic experience. In essence: what happens when the mixer's crossfader moves among several diverse cultural realities?

DJing facilitates my theoretical linkage between varied musical practices, oral poetics, and "sonic citizenship," all of which are incorporated, negotiated, and mixed in the history, texts, and musical recordings I explore. Such mixing recalls the use of mashup in contemporary culture. As Lisa Coulthard outlines, "mashups rub sources against each other, layering incongruous cultural products and reworking references through new combinations, associations and contexts."[74] I think there is real value in employing mashup, especially for myself as an educator and a DJ. At their best, classrooms are multi-sonic spaces where truth (ideally) is worked out in dialogic engagement. That is, the classroom can be a mashup, a creative and intellectual mix where ideas rub against one another and where different opinions are discussed and reworked to form new combinations of thought. Indeed, a DJ/mashup methodology can push back and challenge what has been received by society as normal and provide new ways of engaging with tradition and modernity.

In several ways, my work operates under what poet Wayde Compton describes as "schizophonophilia," which is the "love of audio interplay, the pleasure of critical disruptions to natural audition, the counter-hegemonic affirmation that can be achieved through acoustic intervention."[75] I like the notion of acoustic intervention, of disrupting the pretence of naturalism, as a reminder that democracy (as embodied in sound) is itself most effective when it is most discordantly free. Sampling becomes a new way of doing something that has been with us for a long time, a means to create new contexts from old ones. Rather than an archive, the material I draw from becomes a "living repertoire" (a concept I've adapted from theorist Diana Taylor), a source of "embodied memory" where various multimodal texts are collaged together to create a sonic mix that draws the reader/listener and myself as the DJ/conduit into direct relation with the work.[76] Music—whether in performance or in listening—is an activity about making sense of the world as much as it is about enjoyment. Music is not a "fixed" product. I agree with Christopher Small's assertion that "there is no such thing as music. Music is not a thing at all but an activity, something that people do."[77] By replacing the noun "music" with the verb "musicking," Small highlights that each musical work is not an autonomous creation of one-way communication between creator and audience, but rather a social undertaking where musical works ultimately exist to give performers something to perform.

In one of the first anthologies of Black writers in Canada, *Canada in Us Now*, Harold Head argues that "it is the rhythm of our music that is the formal basis of our poetry. Music, and especially rhythm, syncopates our entire existence in the here and now as it has throughout our history."[78] However, one must be careful to avoid drab clichés about the Black writer being solely a musician, as it is more productive to examine how poets are able to turn phonemes into poetic phrases that sound music on the page. For example, Nathaniel Mackey argues that "the rush to canonize orality as a radical departure from the values of an 'eye-oriented' civilization runs the risk of obscuring the attention paid by recent poets to the way the poem appears on the page."[79] I would further argue that a poem can simultaneously be read in page-bound and sounded/performed format; in fact, many poets intend for their work to operate in both media.

Few Canadian critics—beyond the poets themselves—have written at length about how music functions in Black Canadian literature. We find no shortage of this approach in African American literature, but in Canadian scholarship we encounter reluctance to take such approaches, with novelist Austin Clarke (the first Black Canadian novelist to have his work published by a mainstream publisher) stating, "I don't know of a single reviewer who has seen the significance of music in my work... If reviewers missed something as fundamental as the role of music in the structure of my work, how many other points did they miss?"[80] For writers like Austin Clarke, narrative—or poetic content—is often related directly to blues, jazz-variation, signification, call and response, and so forth. Of course, not all Black writers in Canada want to be read this way, and such a generic approach would be myopic. That said, African diasporic cultures have deep roots in the Black musical tradition: historical roots that sustain life and connect the individual to larger communities, often across geographical borders.

Recounting the emotive and philosophical power of slave songs, Frederick Douglass attests, "I have sometimes thought the mere hearing of those songs would do more to impress some minds with the horrible character of slavery, than the reading of whole volumes of philosophy on the subject could do."⁸¹ Douglass declares that the slave song is the final province of resistance to slavery. Ralph Ellison expresses a similar understanding of the power of Black music in his description of the blues: "The blues is an impulse to keep the painful details and episodes of a brutal experience alive in one's aching consciousness, to finger its jagged grain, and to transcend it, not by the consolation of philosophy, but by squeezing it from a near-tragic, near-comic lyricism."⁸² This is echoed by the improvising artist and bassist William Parker: "Black improvised music has had to fight for its life since the first slaves were brought here in 1619."⁸³ And again by M. NourbeSe Philip in her potent improvised dub text, *Zong!*: "*Zong!* is Song! And Song is what has kept the soul of the African intact when they 'want(ed) water . . . sustenance . . . preservation.'"⁸⁴ Music functions within these sampled texts as a reminder that song is often a plea to listen, if not merely on an intellectual level, then at least on a human level. Music is a way for Afrosporic people, immigrants, refugees, settlers, and Indigenous people alike to find—and I risk essentialism here—that which binds us in our shared creative existence.

> William Parker

Nevertheless, there is a specificity to Black voice and song, as NourbeSe Philip describes in her engagement with Lindon Barrett's *Blackness and Value: Seeing Double*, which "come[s] out of a particular history of pain, trauma and a determination to make meaning of one's life no matter what; it is sound lodged in commitment to matter to and value one's self and one's community in the face of a culture that continues to assert that Black lives lack meaning and are irrelevant except and in so far as they are useful."⁸⁵ Although the history of Black music in North America is deeply embedded in a Black radical tradition that responds to the abject violence of slavery through unscripted performances, shouts, moans, and cries, that history also concerns traditions of celebration, unity, play, and constant revision. Riffing, signifyin', and revising can function as respectful modes of response by critics and musicians alike. Performance and song offer medicine and healing.

In addition, Black dialect and writing is not perennially folksy—perhaps folk culture never was or is—but is always created, as the texts make use of many complex techniques found most in Black Canadian, African American, and diasporic musics: signifyin(g), heterophony, bent notes, elisions, hums, moans, grunts, vocables, epistrophe, echo (duppy), oral declamations, and melisma, among other techniques. Because the music itself might be unfamiliar to some CanLit scholars and readers, I dedicate space in each chapter to a discussion of Black musical traditions, making judicious links between certain genres/styles and a given poet's work (although all the poets incorporate multiple musical registers). Each chapter opens with a listening that canons (echoes) and provides a sonic and generative entryway into a given author and body of texts. I like this approach since all the writers I explore, at some point or another, talk very explicitly about how music is central to their poetic craft; indeed, many would welcome readings that move away from racial or gender-codified analyses that view Black Canadian writing solely as a kind of sociological service camp. While I dwell on both rhetorical and aesthetic analysis throughout this book, I do not find value in discussing Black Canadian literature solely in terms of its rhetorical functionality—how it teaches us to live—or solely under its aesthetic prowess. The mix (and remix) remains central to my approach.

As engaged critics, we are challenged to be witnesses to any polyvocal poetic text, echoing Houston A. Baker Jr.'s assertion that hip hop critics are "at least as exacting of their knowledge of rap as the rappers they pretend to discuss, defend, categorize, or witness."[86] Essentially, under Baker's assessment, and as this book claims, the act of reading becomes the act of listening: good listening creates good critics. Baker's analysis of the blues as a *matrix* is a good starting point because it beckons towards a "point of ceaseless input and output, a web of intersecting, crisscrossing impulses always in productive transit."[87] Because much of my work involves embodied praxis with material consequences—mashing, mixing, sampling, spinning, signifying—I consider the politicized and embodied reality of lived practice. As with a good DJ mix, there needs to be balance, transition, and occasionally disruption (I have an affinity for what I hope are productive tangents and juxtapositions) to achieve a fruitful blending of constituent elements. My approach mixes metaphoric musical belief systems that scholar and creative musician George E. Lewis has called "Afrological" and "Eurological" perspectives, but ultimately favours the "Afrological." Rather than define these terms as ethnically essential, Lewis contends that the Afrological tends to valorize performance and community whereas the Eurological tends to start with the musical work itself and move away from personal narrative, culture, and convention.[88]

I have always felt, like the West African griots and ancient Greek rhapsodizers before me, that music and poetry are often part and parcel. Jamaican Canadian poet, feminist, and arts advocate Ayanna Black felt a persistent desire to fuse poetry and music, reflected in her desire to write poems in an avant-garde jazz tradition; she told Nigel Thomas in an interview that there was, for her, a strong link "between poetry and avant-garde jazz—the composers such as John and Alice Coltrane, Cecil Taylor, [The] Art Ensemble of Chicago, Sun Ra and John Cage. It's the world presented in sound and images."[89] Furthermore, the traditional connection between poetry and music finds solidarity in dub poet Afua Cooper, who sees poetry as an aural–oral literary form that can include music, as she says in an interview: "I think of ancient poets like Celtic Bards who sang their poetry accompanied by musicians; or the West African poets: the griots, who are accompanied by musicians—ballaphon players, cora players, and sometimes drummers ... It's poetry that relies on music, whose very soul is music."[90] The Greek root of poet, *poiein*, means "to make, create, produce" (OED), which is essentially what musicians do with the raw materials they have at hand. Musicians and poets create using the tools they have available. Poetry is a practice in the pursuit of new forms that are often beautiful, as well as a search for alternatives to normative ways of knowing and being. We find such alternative models in the fluid particularities of Blackness.

Rinaldo Walcott argues that Blackness, like improvisation, is an open-ended approach that exceeds somatic identification, biology, or ethnicity: "Blackness for me, like black Canadian, allows for a certain kind of malleability and open-endedness which means that questions of blackness far exceed the categories of the biological or ethnic." Walcott further clarifies this within the specificity of Black resistance as a sign that signals "particular histories of resistance and domination" and as a discourse "embedded in a history or set of histories which are messy and contested." Thus, the mix is both aesthetic and a rhetorical in function, and here I call attention to it as a non-axiomatic liberatory process that disavows simply locating oneself within national boundaries.⁹¹ Sound takes us outside national boundaries, and a complex (Afrologically informed) DJ mix compels us to consider how creative disruption can function in literatures that deconstruct colonial narratives, enact resistance, challenge our listening approaches, and offer ways to retool the academy and, even, society at large.

While many Black Canadian writers are interested in the hybrid, they still want to maintain a connection to old epistemic traditions. Many poets in *Soundin' Canaan*, particularly M. NourbeSe Philip and Wayde Compton, apply innovative techniques while maintaining cultural (often multiple) epistemes. Thus, their work connects with what Alexander Weheliye terms "sonic Afro-modernity," which "envelops both temporally and conceptually any putative original." Essentially, as Weheliye argues, "no Western modernity without (sonic) blackness and no blackness in the absence of modernity." Weheliye's contention is that modernity involves cultural and sonic confluences between sound, sight, and text, and he operates with the intention to "establish a dialogue between literary texts and current popular culture to conjecture how sonic technologies and production have fruitfully contaminated each other."⁹² While such innovative confluences of sound, sight, and text are commonly explored in African American literature (see Jean Toomer's *Cane* [1923] for an early example of a variety of creative forms exploding generic boundaries without offering an easy resolution),ᵇ I argue that

---

ᵇ Jean Toomer's *Cane* is a radical text that heralds the Harlem Renaissance. *Cane* moves from aesthetically simpler forms to more complex ones (dancing between prose, poetry, and play-like dialogue), as it moves South to North, and North to South, through a series of beautiful and very musical vignettes. The creative novel inspired Gil Scott-Heron's song "Cane," where he sings about two main characters of the novel: Karintha and Becky. Currently the song is not available on Spotify, but it can be found on YouTube, https://www.youtube.com/watch?v=v6uJyUrHE7c.

such confluences are happening in Black Canadian literature.⁹³ We might call Philip's *Zong!* and Compton's *Performance Bond* "Afro-postmodern" texts, which, as scholar and musician Jesse Stewart suggests, involve a "kind of fragmentation, plurality, and intertextuality normally associated with postmodernism, but locates these processes within the cultural matrix of the African diaspora wherein they often function in unique ways."⁹⁴ Afro-postmodern forms of pastiche, intertextuality, and irony function as strategies of identity formation, reconstructing the past while imagining a better future. The in-between—like a crossfader on a DJ's mixer—defines the drift (movement) of my mashup approach towards Black poetics and sound.

Black Poetics and Sound

Bob Marley

Music, poetry, and art contain ideas. The ideas of this book echo Bob Marley's song "War." Marley makes the case that freedom must move beyond class, race, and second-tier citizenship. Amiri Baraka contends that this liberatory potential in art can happen at a purely aesthetic level, since he points out, *"Ideas do not require lyrics! Sound carries ideas, that's why you get sad at one song, happy with another."*⁹⁵ Music allows performers and listeners to co-perform community. The idea that music and literature carry ideas that might be dangerous to those who hold power is hardly anything new. After all, in Plato's *Republic* poets are barred from the Republic because, as Plato argues, they give a "distorted image" (377e) of reality, gods, and heroes. Poetry and music continue to speak truth to power.

My approach in this book is multi-sonic and models what scholarship might look like as a DJ mix. At various points, the reader is challenged to listen to two different mixes, as I move between aesthetic and rhetorical registers (discussed in the coda following this overture/introduction). Hence, we can appreciate a poet's work for its aesthetic qualities and for its ability to reframe the human and the citizen. Reading is an act of cultural improvisation, and music and poetry are ways of organizing sound and words, often across a multitude of borders. As an aesthetic experience, a jazz musician manipulates sound and rhythm to allow the listener to transcend everyday experiences.

The prologue to Ralph Ellison's 1952 novel *Invisible Man* models an experience of sonic transcendence when the invisible man gets into "grooves of history," listening to Louis Armstrong's "What Did I Do to Be So Black and Blue?" on his phonograph.[96] Ellison's unnamed narrator states: "Now I have one radio-phonograph; I plan to have five. There is a certain acoustical deadness in my hole, and when I have music I want to *feel* its vibration, not only with my ear but with my whole body. I'd like to hear five recordings of Louis Armstrong playing and singing 'What Did I Do to Be so Black and Blue'—all at the same time."[97] Ellison's choice to foreground Armstrong's performance of "Black and Blue" (initially composed by Fats Waller) allows him to locate the music's aura, as Alexander Weheliye argues, "not in the original musical utterance but in the mode of mechanical reproduction itself, making [Ellison] one of the foremost intellectual architects of sonic Afro-modernity."[98]

Louis Armstrong

The DJ mix—certainly for Ellison—is an act of identity and citizenship, since both, like a sound recording, are open to remix. It is from the sonic underground, what Ellison calls "the lower frequencies," that I work to make visible that which remains hidden from the mainstream view of Canada as a just country. The music speaks a whole historic sounding, including a chronicle of enslaved people praying for deliverance, and "longing for [that] truer world" that W.E.B. Du Bois articulates in *The Souls of Black Folk*.[99] Ellison's narrator, who desires to play multiple recordings of Armstrong's song in a simultaneous mix, provides an articulation of the kind of sonic blending that interests me, and fits Amiri Baraka's notion that "sound carries ideas" that are both aesthetically pleasing and rhetorically dense. From Bartók, who incorporates Hungarian folk songs in a cosmopolitan mix, to Duke Ellington, who fuses classical and jazz traditions. First and foremost, my analysis is predicated on close listening.

I negotiate a dual role as listener and performer. As Canadian poet Earl Birney wrote in regard to teaching poetry: "Persons employing this text for authoritarian purposes are the enemies of all genuine students."[100] I am a scholar of literature and music, but I am equally a student, so rather than teach readers about what Black Canadian poetry precisely is, as if such a thing could even be done in one book, I hope I can help others enjoy the imaginative craft and pleasure these poets have provided for me as a critical thinker. The poets herein offer profound readings of belonging, race, and citizenship, and they do so by mixing beauty and powerful meanings in the stories they tell.

Nigerian storyteller Ben Okri states that "if we change the stories we live by, quite possibly we change our lives."[101] This is similar to how scholar Paul Barrett in *Blackening Canada: Diaspora, Race, Multiculturalism* describes Canadian multiculturalism: it "is about the stories Canadians tell themselves about their nation, and this language of Canadian multiculturalism sets out the imaginative terrain from which Canadians narrate their nation from both the centre and the margin."[102] There is the story of crossing into Canada and being freed from the shackles of slavery, and there are competing stories for what signifies meaningful citizenship in Canada. Deeply listening to Black Canadian poetry recalls postmodernist Jean-François Lyotard's notion that "the capacity to speak to others is a human right."[103] I would add that the ability to sound is a human right.

My privileging of text/sight, sound, and hearing might also raise questions about why I exclude readings that would include taste, smell, and touch, to which I respond that my area of focus is on sonic and textual confluences. However, my approach can be applied—and should be, by others more fitted to the task—to other physiological capacities of perception. The idealized notion of a multicultural Canada as a site of social justice and full human actualization regardless of race, ethnicity, nationalism, ability, sexuality, and language is one that engages with all the senses. Every person in Canada deserves rights to be a legal person who sounds in relation to others, and the poets explored do just that from coast to coast.

The United Nations continues to recognize Toronto as "the world's most ethnically diverse city," surpassing even New York City.[104] In this book, four out of six core chapters focus on poets and rappers primarily based in Toronto, emphasizing its significance.

However, chapters on Wayde Compton's poetry, focusing on Vancouver's historical Black community in Hogan's Alley, and George Elliott Clarke's Africadian poems, remind us that Blackness in Canada extends beyond Toronto. This cultural tapestry challenges the prevailing notion of Canada as exclusively white, a belief that persists today, as articulated by Desmond Cole, who highlights "a system of power that seeks to benefit white people above all others" and which "designates Black people as less than full human beings."[105] All the poets, with varying degrees of influence (George Elliot Clarke has served as Toronto's Poet Laureate and Canada's Parliamentary Poet Laureate), use poetry to speak truth to power.

Poetry—hardly a "dead" literary medium relegated to the past—articulates textual soundings of engaged citizenship, poeticizing a negotiation of the self in relation to others. An apt comparison of this cooperative sounding can be found in jazz groups. Nathaniel Mackey describes how jazz groups, particularly in the 1960s, provided a view into the future of a "freedom within a collectively improvised context," which "proposed a model social order, an ideal, even utopic balance between personal impulse and group demands."[106] Mackey describes the force of Black music, most focally in free jazz, as an artistic desire for both individual and collective freedom: it is a freedom signified not by homogeneity but rather by disruption, disparate sounds, fragmentation, sonic adventurism, and an imperative sounding for freedom and equality, particularly as voiced from "minority" perspectives.

So, while Black writers, performers, and poets have often been read as marginalized, as operating on the peripheries of Canadian literature and history, a more useful approach would be to read and sound the poets herein as writing back to the centre, and from the centre of cultural multiplicity. As Dionne Brand has argued, "I don't consider myself on any 'margin,' on the margin of Canadian literature. I'm sitting right in the middle of Black literature, because that's who I read, that's who I respond to."[107] Brand's statement suggests multiple centres, and her riffing upon the perceived margin as the centre testifies that literature as community is about textual engagement between writers and their communities. When the various poets and larger historical imperatives are read together, we can envision a varied map that charts an ever-widening gyre of intellectual influence, conversation, exchange, riffing, debate, and reciprocity.

Soundin' Canaan acknowledges the resilience, creativity, and humanity of Black artistic practices. Ideally, the modern citizen can freely improvise through self-determination: an ethical disavowal of the notion that skin colour defines the person, even as it remains an important and forever embedded part of one's identity.[108] This is an exercise in a kind of idealization of Black culture and praxis as being iterative of the kind of society we can imagine, and it is informed by my desire to make sense of how a theoretical apparatus of Black hope and creative praxis can work to dismantle powerful structures of white supremacy. As the renowned scholar Robert Farris Thompson put it in his own studies of Black artistic practices, "until we consider the dreams and loves of Africans and Afro-Americans as well as their politics and social structure, we shall never know black people." Part of this desire to know is informed by the incredible pleasure and benefit I receive in studying and dialoguing with Black poets and musicians as a kind of conduit (DJ). Like Thompson, "I see myself as a medium, under possession—metaphor, perhaps" while acknowledging what Thompson sees as "indestructible lines of happening" that exist outside the critic who works to explain and trumpet such practices.[109] *Soundin Canaan'* draws from these "indestructible lines of happening" as a governing metaphor to render whiteness as unstable and ultimately untenable in the modern multicultural world. I am under the perception that we cannot truly exist as individuals unless we reconcile ourselves with others in shared and intersecting cultural spaces, and acknowledge the specificity of Black cultural production.

I've believed for some time now that what we say as literary critics should contribute to an ongoing conversation that is part of the wide spectrum of literary understanding, and that what we say should take part in creating new conversations that help us understand the value of literature for changing the world. I consider myself a *cosmopolitan humanist* who is deeply interested in understanding how literature creates new epistemologies that change intellectual and public opinion.♭ The epigraphs/quotations that introduce each section of this project provide voices from a variety of literary spheres that, for me, engage with the works in dialogic ways, often illuminating the interconnectedness of diverse opinions while highlighting their inherent ruptures. These quotations—out of context, as such is the definition of a quotation—are also reminders that certain voices stay with us, refusing to be silenced. This reflects my practice as a DJ, sound poet, and general music enthusiast, for music (and its ability to communalize) is the central metaphor of *Soundin' Canaan*.

As gender theorist Judith Butler argues in *Precarious Life*, "I cannot muster the 'we' except by finding the way in which I am tied to 'you,' by trying to translate but finding that my own language must break up and yield if I am to know you."[110] At its best, *sonic multiculturalism* (explored in chapter 4) is this precarious act of yielding to the potentialities of others in order to allow for the maximum agency of every individual, improvising upon new amalgamated spaces—riffing on them, if you will—with our own unique jazz soloings.

Music and Improvisation: The Backbeat of *Soundin' Canaan*

> "I contend that the Negro is the creative voice of America, is creative America, and it was a happy day in America when the first unhappy slave was landed on its shores."
>
> —DUKE ELLINGTON, *The Duke Ellington Reader*, 147

♭ I use (and coin, I believe) "cosmopolitan humanist" as an ideology that views all human groups as belonging to a shared community—although this hardly limits the spectrum of communities within communities—and that emphasizes the agency of human beings, both individually and collectively, preferring individual thought and evidence over established dogmas. The term "cosmopolitan humanist" may seem contradictory at first glance, but it underscores my aspiration to place the individual within a broader framework. In fact, we can extend "cosmopolitan" to "*cosmo*politan," emphasizing our role as stewards within the interconnected universe to which we all belong.

Music and poetry, I argue, provide creative modes to resound the past and understand what it means to be a sonic citizen within multicultural Canada. In the way that poets arrange words on the page in a certain order for effect, so too do musicians arrange sound, particularly in musical media such as jazz, hip hop, and other improvisatory styles that cannot be easily conscripted into orthodoxy. Musicologist Christopher Small asserts that "no human being ever invents anything from nothing but is guided always in his invention by the assumptions, the practices and the customs of the society in which he or she lives—in other words, by its *style.*"[111] To really understand music, and the same goes for poetry, we must let it go.

Nina Simone While no one owns music, as bassist William Parker says, there is inherent value in understanding the beneficial role that African Americans—often at the helm, but always across cultures—played in creating and continue to play in shaping the blues, jazz, soul/funk, hip hop, and countless other musical media. We can think of these genres as freedom music because they articulate what resistance and freedom sound like. They were (and are) the sound of what people were thinking and feeling, and the music helped push political movements forward, notably during the civil rights movement. The music also sustained various activists, such as Charlayne Hunter—one of the first African American students to attend the University of Georgia—who was able to overcome the persistent racism and tolerate the constant banging on the ceiling of her dorm room by the white students living above her because she had Nina Simone to listen to, who affirmed she was, indeed, "young, gifted, and black."[112] Hence, we must acknowledge the close link between Black music and politics; moreover, Black people continue to invent and shape music, which is often appropriated by those with little recognition of the Black progenitors of that music. We must learn to be better listeners and improvisers.

By looking at the ever ubiquitous and elusive practice of improvisation—with an emphasis on improvised musical styling/genre—we can better understand much of what Black Canadian and Afrosporic poets are doing when they blend traditions and sound off against the past to make meaning in the present. Derek Bailey argues that "improvisation enjoys the curious distinction of being both the most widely practiced of all musical activities and the least acknowledged and understood."[113] At its core, being human *is* improvisation: from the first steps we take as a developing child, to the first time we pick up an instrument and try to play it, to every single time we enter a space with others. Living through the COVID-19 pandemic has reminded us that improvisation is key to our ability to adapt and change, potentially for the better. Man Booker Prize–winning Indian novelist Arundhati Roy speaks about the coronavirus pandemic as a portal: "Historically, pandemics have forced humans to break with the past and imagine their world anew. This one is no different. It is a portal, a gateway between one world and the next."[114] With systemic injustices more visible than ever, she asks us to use this opportunity to imagine another world. Scholar Robin D.G. Kelley agrees

> that this pandemic is a portal. And as a portal, it is just an opening . . . it's an opening because it exposed the structure of racial and gendered capitalism and the violence meted out to people who are most vulnerable. So Covid-19, of course, exposes the fact that it's a lot of poor people dying, exposed, not protected. That the healthcare industry and the industry assigned to care for the aging have utterly failed for lack of resources and forms of structural racism . . . What kind of society will we have? And this is an opportunity to change it all.[115]

For Black people, improvisation is about not just change, but survival.

Nikki Giovanni describes how African Americans have turned survival into an improvisational art form: "Style has a profound meaning to Black Americans . . . If we can't have ham, we will boil chitterlings; if we are given rotten peaches, we will make cobblers; if given scraps, we will make quilts; take away our drums, and we will clap our hands. We prove the human spirit will prevail. We will take what we have to make what we need."[116] It is through tactics, improvisation, and appropriation that Black culture is able to spatially reimpose upon the terrain that has been imposed on it.

Improvisation is not only about these "off the cuff" and spontaneous experiences, but also about the experience itself: the process of undergoing change. It is better to think of improvisation under a constellation of possibilities, such as spontaneity and change upon a standard, rather than as any one single thing. Because improvisation is always changing, this enables us to think about what it means to negotiate differences within a community, and ultimately what it means to be living in a multicultural society that is itself frequently changing. It is hard to pinpoint improvisation as any single entity—in fact, improvisation resists any single all-encompassing label—yet in the context of music, it can be reasoned as an act of remembrance and, most productively, as hope and possibility. Ajay Heble and Daniel Fischlin argue "that improvised music archives historical practices and speaks to a community about its past and present," a process that opens the possibility of "solidary relations"—the common interests of a group—held together by the unified desire of musicians.[117]

These "solidary relations" make sense within the spirit of Black musicians, who—dealing with a legacy of erasure produced by the inhumanities that arose out of transatlantic slavery—find creative yet often dissonant ways to articulate a horrific past to a common community. Yet improvisation, given its universal quality, is a reminder of the greater poetic need to sustain life in the moment, which is why we find so many invaluable expressions of the medium—often in music—by Black people across the diaspora, even if these utterances were rendered mute by outside/mainstream listeners. As Frederick Douglass's words suggest, improvisation for the slave is often an artistic act that sustains life in moments of desperation: "This they would sing, as a chorus to words [that] to many would seem unmeaning jargon, but which, nevertheless, were full of meaning to themselves."[118] Thus, to understand how meaning or anti-meaning is made, we must reflect on how meaning is always open to being reworked in the alacrity of the moment. The Douglass example provides a poignant instance of how improvisation can be used to make sense of the world, especially when it is most fragmented. Improvisation helps us connect beauty and meaning and envision a better world despite the disorder and violence of the present.

To improvise involves engaging with the music as a social practice while forming dynamic interrelational communities. Improvisation is about listening (as well as performing, reading, and so on), but it is also about the risk involved in trying something new. These unexpected aspects of musical improvisation allow bridges to form between multiple creative and interdisciplinary practices, often within a single space, and with an unforeseen result. Improvised music invites exciting cross-disciplinary collaborations, such Langston Hughes's (the poetic) and Charles Mingus's (the musical) joint album, *Weary Blues*, and Pharaoh Sanders, Floating Points, and the London Symphony Orchestra's *Promises*.♭ Improvisation defies simple categorization and has ignited furious debates about whether the music belongs to the jazz tradition or not, particularly since Ornette Coleman dropped the album *The Shape of Jazz to Come* (1959), and then the even more harmonically open *Free Jazz* (1961). Improvisation, when at its most provocative, is usually at its most free, innovative, and powerful. Improvisation provides not only a model of social organization but also one of oppositional struggle, as reflected in the work of the best improvisers, who include free jazz luminaries John Zorn, Anthony Braxton, the Association for the Advancement of Creative Musicians (AACM), Sun Ra, Ornette Coleman, William Parker, Cecil Taylor, John Coltrane, and too many more to possibly list.

Charles Mingus and Langston Hughes; Pharaoh Sanders and Floating Points; Ornette Coleman

Improvising helps create new thought patterns, symbols, or ways of being in the world.[119] In many ways, improvisation threads throughout the book, weaving the various writers together in a vast tapestry of spontaneous poetic creation. Few scholars have written at length about the musical qualities in Black Canadian poetry; even fewer have written about improvisation in poetry, and perhaps this is one of the first attempts to write about both in a Canadian context, albeit it is not the main focus of this book. There have been those who have previously written about improvisation in relation to poetry, and I

Charlie Parker

♭ I've included a few songs from these collaborations (as well as a few pieces from some of the other mentioned artists) in the chapter playlist. You can hear Langston Hughes read his poem "The Weary Blues" on YouTube, https://www.youtube.com/watch?v=PPjo4903UpU.

am grateful for the willingness of those writers to trudge through the unknown to make it a little easier for me to do so.[120] Understanding improvisation in Black Canadian literature can help us see how poets subvert standard Western notions of notation in music and poetry, as well as reclaim voice and community. Improvisation cannot be easily concocted into orthodoxy—although people try: think of how many of Charlie Parker's improvised solos have been transcribed exactly for performance and popular consumption (such as "Embraceable You"). This serves as a reminder that improvisation is about possibility, especially where life is difficult.♭ Additionally, improvisation is about experimentation, something the poets in this book venture in earnest. As Steven Green affirms in *T-Dot Griots*, "We are improvisers, and spontaneous creators; off the cuff performers whose traditions are largely oral."[121] Black Canadian poets use improvisation to subvert Western academic devices, and by doing so they call us to listen.

Deep Listening

Pauline Oliveros

The ear functions like a microphone that is constantly inputting sound; by comparison, deep listening, as Pauline Oliveros told neuroscientist Seth Horowitz, is very close to what we call consciousness.[122] Our ability to listen, carefully and deeply, can be trained, and technology is changing the very nature of the way we listen. The DJ is the person who notices sound (digging in the crates/archives) and through remix opens space for previously unheard or dormant voices and sounds. By extension, listening on the part of the critic/teacher/student is itself an improvisational act that ventures toward the unknowable edge—the space that Sun Ra called "the other side of nowhere." This unknowability does not limit our participation, but rather opens alternative spaces where listening to others becomes possible, and even essential. To sound, to echo, to listen, and then to

---

♭ As Charlie Parker is assumed to have said (I can't find a proper source), "Master your instrument. Master the music. And then forget all that bullshit and just play."

remix speaks to the human condition. Sound, the most foundational of our human capacities, encapsulates, as Johnathan Sterne states, "what it means to be human."[123] There is no one way to sound, just as there is no one way to be a human.

In this book, I listen closely to the work of four major poets—George Elliott Clarke, Dionne Brand, M. NourbeSe Philip, and Wayde Compton—and one rapper: K'naan (although others, like Shad and Michie Mee, are brought into the mix). I contend that poetry and musical intertexts in their work provide alternative models for imagining citizenship across time and geographical borders. In this way, the book participates in a politics of deep listening. In *Listening Publics: The Politics and Experience of Listening in the Media Age*, scholar Kate Lacey draws attention to the active nature of listening (whether through a *listening in* or a *listening out*) to contend that listening is fundamentally ethical, arguing that our citizenship is performed in relation to a listening public. Furthermore, my close listenings provide alternative avenues to the printed readings of poems by considering the poet's own performances and voice, and the various musical intertexts. The sonic can change the way we understand a printed work. Through performance we can, as Charles Bernstein writes in *Close Listening*, challenge "the idea of the poem as a fixed, stable, finite linguistic object." Bernstein encourages listeners to move with a poem's multiple meanings and soundings, going on to say that when we sound out language "we ground ourselves as sentient, material beings, obtruding into the world with the same obdurate thingness as rock or soil or flesh."[124] For poetry to be heard, it must be sounded. Similarly, to be heard, a citizen too needs to sound—to materialize in the non-material sense of sound. I am interested in the process of co-creation; for me, DJ practices help me sound in multiple experiential registers, and it is my hope that these various soundings will show that a poem is far from a static object. How else are we to go out and broadcast their meanings if not first through an engaged practice of listening and public imagining?

Reimaginings of citizenship present an opportunity to moderate disorder and fragmentation by embracing difference through fraternity. While this is only a book—a set of words and thoughts on paper—I hope it is a valuable place to create some new conversations, and hopefully some interventions, around the power of poetry and music and how we think through the notion of citizenship. Ultimately, and realistically, since poetry is the primary focus, I also hope this book will provide beneficial readings of an influential group of Black Canadian poets, bestowing "new" tools for how *we* approach any multinational, multimodal, multicultural, and multilinguistic Black text in Canada. That is, it is my hope that close readings of these texts will open more space for Black avant-garde practices to work against the narrow classifications that often come with genre and generic understandings of music, literature, and citizenship.

III. "Sonic Citizenship" in Multicultural Canada

> "We have to start thinking about planetary citizenship. Not just national."
>
> —ANGELA DAVIS, "Black History"

Soundin' Citizenship

Richard Iton asks a useful question around citizenship status: "What happens when the shadows are foregrounded and those not normally seen as citizens with full rights—the disposable—are brought more into the picture?"[125] The plight of refugees continues to grow, particularly for those fleeing totalitarian governments, the most devastating effects of climate change, and Western bombings and occupation. In principle, refugees, the disposed, the exiled, and those often deemed Other (usually BIPOC LGBTQIA2S+) by the white heteropatriarchal majority challenge the doctrines of the nation-state and pose the question: What exactly is a citizen? The Universal Declaration of Human Rights (1948) establishes the right to leave a country, to enjoy asylum under certain circumstances, and to maintain and even change nationality (Articles 13–15). I take the philosophical stance that poetry is an act of citizenship and that for citizenship to have real meaning it needs to be performed, although there are infinite representations of that performance. Likewise, identity, which novelist Lawrence Hill views as "fluid" and "evidently evolving," is hardly a static entity.[126] We must expand our definition and practice of citizenship rights, particularly for the underprivileged and underrepresented. Considering those who are often excluded from those rights, I define citizenship from below—those subsonic bass notes— for those people whose presence is often felt but rarely heard.

In his article "The Sweet Sounds of Havana: Space, Listening, and the Making of Sonic Citizenship," Vincent Andrisani explores the significance of sound in Havana, emphasizing how the city's spaces are interconnected through sound. He particularly focuses on ice cream vendors: despite historical changes and external regimes of power, their sound remains a constant, symbolizing the collective interests of Havana's residents. "Listening to the sound of the ice cream vendor," he argues, "constitutes an act of citizenship—an act of *sonic citizenship*—that momentarily claims Havana's spaces according to the aims, aspirations, and desires of those who live there."[127] His conceptualization of sonic citizenship develops a bottom-up account of the city: he renders audible the enactment of citizenship by listening for sounds that ground citizens in spaces historically destabilized by forces from above. I too, contend, that listening to the poets in this book—that is, listening closely to the poems, sounds, and musical samples they bring into the mix—constitutes "sonic citizenship." In other words, this co-performative reading, listening, and sounding serves as a reminder of how citizens inhabit and negotiate life in Canada from beyond the formal legal framework of the nation-state, even though our understanding remains influenced by it. Such "sonic citizenship" supposedly grants equality in a fraternal state, but often there is a disconnect between the promise of equality and the reality of exclusion under the auspices of citizenship for all.

Rogers Brubaker examines the global perspective on citizenship as "a powerful instrument of social closure, shielding prosperous states from the migrant poor. Citizenship is also an instrument of closure within states. Every state [has] established [a] conceptual, legal, and ideological boundary between citizens and foreigners."[128] Essentially, Brubaker, while presenting citizenship as a universal feature of the modern sociopolitical landscape, shows that citizenry is a public act that acknowledges a set of persons as members while rendering all others residually as non-citizens, or aliens. Because only citizens have a right to enter (and remain in) the territory of a state, he concludes: "Citizenship is thus both an instrument and an object of closure."[129] For example, during the ongoing Syrian refugee crisis, then Saskatchewan Premier Brad Wall asked Justin Trudeau to "suspend" the Syrian Refugee initiative.[130] This act of closure becomes one about who is an ideal citizen and who is not, and these claims for validity are often rooted in whiteness. What happens when we expand this definition and move away from stable citizenship or conceive of it as meaningful and/or sonic enactment? For example, what does it mean for a Canadian citizen to think of themselves as predominantly Québécois, yet still Canadian? Can one maintain "Indian" status and be a Canadian citizen? What about a recently arrived Afghan fleeing the Taliban? Can they be both Afghani and Canadian? What does it mean for a Canadian citizen to think of themself as a Jamaican Canadian? Attempts to define citizenship must consider not just who a citizen can be, but how one can be a citizen with multiple allegiances and identities.

While citizenship accords rights, most notably the right to vote, historically citizenship has also been about exclusion. Until emancipation in 1863, millions of Americans were denied citizenship status; indeed, they were not even considered free. Women in Canada were not granted the right to vote until 1918, and in Quebec, women did not gain full suffrage until 1940.[131] Furthermore, Native Americans were not accorded citizenship until 1924, and in Canada, Indigenous rights were not enshrined until the *Constitution Act, 1982*.

Citizenship sometimes entails a rejection of special status, as illustrated in Canada in the late 1960s by "The White Paper," a document commissioned by the Trudeau government that called for an end to the *Indian Act*. Such a move would essentially have abolished land claims and Status Indians, thus making way for the gradual integration of Indigenous people into Canadian society (arguably filling the initial unspoken goals of the *Indian Act*). Thomas King argues that the "White Paper" had a single goal: "To get the government out of the 'Indian business.'"[132] This circles back to the very notion of Canaan land, and I realize that many of these questions around land also border uncomfortably on "the myth of *terra nullius*—or 'no one's land,' a territory supposedly empty of human habitation and prior claims —dehumanizing the peoples who were there first, and who, in most cases, still remained to contest and offer physical testimony of the falsehood of that myth."[133] Tiffany Lethabo King, in dealing with the dual terrors of slavery and conquest, challenges conquistador-settler knowledge systems that mediate discussions between Black and Indigenous perspectives. In doing so, she highlights the interconnectedness of Black and Indigenous deaths in the Western Hemisphere, deaths that are often overlooked in colonial discourse. Clearly, citizenship is a complex business, and not having the rights that are afforded by citizenship or special status is, as Sharon Morgan Beckford states, "like living in hell; as [Northrop] Frye argues, 'it is like living outside the bush garden, with its culture, cultivation, and civilization.'"[134]

As this chapter has shown, it was never intended for Canada to be a multicultural country, and its policies and immigration laws have long been anti-Black.[135] Citizenship, as it exists, and as Robyn Maynard details, remains a legitimate, widely and formally accepted form of exclusion, allotting rights and protections to some and withholding it from others, who then fall victim to state violence by virtue of their designation as 'outsiders.'"[136] Many of Canada's policies, around policing and law in particular, remain markedly anti-Black; for example, Black Torontonians are much more likely to be carded by a police officer, or shot by one.[137] As Rinaldo Walcott writes in *On Property*, "In a post-slavery world, such practices [like carding] work to devalue Black citizenship, rendering it less-than-citizenship."[138] Yet we would not have an expansive understanding of citizenship without efforts by Black folks to bring greater rights to their communities and others.

Cecil Foster's *They Call Me George* focuses on the Black train porters in Canada who fought for social justice, particularly around citizenship rights. In 1954, the Negro Citizenship Association travelled by train to Ottawa along with porters and former porters "to create a

Canada that would be a just society, where individuals would receive all to which they were entitled simply by virtue of their membership; enjoying, that is, all the rights, obligations, and entitlements that come from being a citizen."[139] It is through acknowledging minority rights, and the rights of those deemed aliens, that we can arrive at freer and more just concepts of the citizen. As Derek Heater usefully asks, "Is it perhaps the very concept of a singular form of citizenship that should be questioned?"[140] If we are to study citizenship meaningfully in today's world, we need to understand the concept as a mosaic of identities, responsibilities, allegiances, nationalities, soundings, and rights, rather than as any single unitary concept. Rather than a *damnosa hereditas*—a ruinous inheritance—we should strive to leave the world a better place, which includes taking care of the planet as well as the people and living creatures that inhabit it.

And while citizenship is often conceived within national boundaries, and even within provincial or state boundaries, as the Dred Scott Case of 1857 exemplifies, there is value in conceiving of a planetary citizenship.[141] As Angela Davis said when she spoke in Guelph, Ontario, in 2012, "We have to start thinking about planetary citizenship. Not just national." This echoes Roman emperor and philosopher Marcus Aurelius, who stressed cosmopolitan citizenship, believing that wherever a man lives he is a citizen of a world-city. Under this model the responsibility of being a citizen is applied on a planetary level, insisting that all people deserve life and liberty, the right of access to clean water, and much more. Further, it implies that animals and the environment have rights as well and that citizenship is performed in the moment because we can no longer sit comfortably if another citizen elsewhere in the world is being poorly treated.[142] It also means we must put pressure on multinational companies to change their neoliberal policies if they adversely affect people or the environment.

I also acknowledge that at times, nationalist movements, such as the Black Arts movement, or George Elliott Clarke's desire for national paradigms, are formed in response to other, more opressive nationalisms (explored in the next chapter). The notion of a diasporic nationalism can be empowering as we consider the political possibilities of diaspora, or what Richard Iton, in his book *In Search of the Black Fantastic*, refers to as diaspora's "geo-heterodoxy," its "capacity to imagine and operate simultaneously within, against, and outside the nation-state."[143] As Winfried Siemerling maintains, the move "to 'transnational' cannot mean abstracting from national paradigms; it rather implies reconstructing the national as relational effect that need perspectives beyond itself to explicate its specifications."[144] Most of the writers in this book—aside from George Elliott Clarke (and even here I'm simplifying)—are more interested in transnational models and are working in favour of more malleable borders.[♭]

I'm not going to delineate what all the rights of citizenship are. That would be far outside the scope of this book. But I will be turning to poetry in subsequent chapters to show how citizenship within the works being studied functions—poetically and sonically—as both a right and a responsibility for change. Citizenship is more than a piece of paper. As the Gate Keeper tells Lacuna in Wayde Compton's fable "The Blue Road: A Fairy Tale," "If you sign papers and become a citizen, you can come and go as you please . . . Citizens like yourself are required to take possession of a special mirror, which they are to carry on their person at all times."[145] The parable sounds comparable to citizen cards in Nazi Germany. Citizenship binds a group of individuals together, typically to the state, or world (however defined), whereas ethnicity binds individuals to their cultural group. I fervently reject all incarnations of second-class citizenship. Rather, citizenship should come with the intended premise that citizens are to work together for the betterment of the society to which they belong—working most diligently for those who hold the least power in society—if the term is to be useful at all. "Sonic Citizenship" as an active individual right provides a model of improvisatory citizenry

---

♭ M.I.A., an acclaimed rapper, singer, and producer, as well as a refugee who escaped civil war in Sri Lanka, released the video "Borders," which shows people traversing deserts, climbing fences, and moving in boats across bodies of water. Poignantly, the video only features male refugees to humanize the people that Western countries most often stereotype as criminals and terrorists. You can find the song on the playlist and/or watch the video, here: https://www.youtube.com/watch?v=r-Nw7HbaeWY.

where we take turns soloing within the larger group—a form of individuated transnational identity.

Despite the challenge that power is multiple, diffuse, and ubiquitous, I believe an improvised and "sonic citizenship" provides a possible template for how we can begin to think about change, and the just society. *Soundin' Canaan* attempts to demonstrate how improvised beings—that is, individuals allowed to exercise their identities as mutable constructs open to constant change—when theoretically read in relation to jazz innovation (and disruption), gesture towards what Cecil Foster describes as "genuine multiculturalism."[146] It might appear anachronistic to point out that Pierre Elliott Trudeau (a white Canadian prime minister), whose robust liberalism (which emphasizes equality of individuals) took shape through multiculturalism, championed the ideals that jazz and the American civil rights movement heralded freedom for most African Americans; yet upon a closer look, multiculturalism in its most idealized form (far beyond Trudeau Sr.) provides a framework for radical social change in the spirit of Black creative praxis and freedom.[147] When I asked Cecil Foster what the connection was between Canadian multiculturalism and jazz and, more specifically, the civil rights movement in the United States, and he assured me, "It is difficult to see a separation between multiculturalism and the Civil Rights Movement":

> But by the 1960s the [Canadian] system was bankrupt, ideologically the system was bankrupt. We see this for example in the *Bi and Bi Commission*, certainly not as a bicultural country, certainly not as a white man's country. But this also coincides with the Civil Rights Movement in the United States, where the pressure was on for a second reconstruction. And it is key to think of Trudeau and John F. Kennedy in terms of the parallels. Where both of them were personalists in terms of their ideologies: Roman Catholic, left-wing personalists. The same ideology that produced Martin Luther King, that produced many of the leading leftist leaders, people who gave the world a universal declaration of human rights, people who fought against nationalism.[148]

For many the American Dream had become a fragmentary nightmare, first with the death of John F. Kennedy, and then when James Earl Ray gunned down Martin Luther King Jr. only one day before the Liberal leadership convention on Thursday, 4 April 1968. The surge of violence and chaos in American cities following King's assassination shared front-page headlines in Canadian newspapers with the convention victory of Pierre Trudeau.[149] Multiculturalism and Trudeau's notions of the Just Society presented an opportunity to negotiate disorder and fragmentation by embracing difference and trying to come together as a holistic group.[150] Of course, while we can say that many aspects of official multicultural policy are noble, for many—especially Black folk—we have yet another reframing of Canada as Canaan, with all the promise yet ultimately the failure of the nation-state to truly enact such values. Instead of backing emerging Canadian solidarity groups or the Black Liberation movement, the governments led by Trudeau (1968–79; 1980–84) expressed sympathy towards South Africa's apartheid regime. In 1982, the Canadian government contributed 4.91 percent of the votes, enabling the Western powers to secure an extremely narrow majority in favour of supporting South Africa's billion-dollar IMF credit.

Unfortunately, multiculturalism is frequently employed as a tactic by those in control of capital to exploit diverse labour and market segments. Proponents promise that universal inclusion will eventually result from the continuous differentiation processes that capital constantly generates for its own benefit. While I think there are things to be hopeful about in Canada, which is the only country in the world with any kind of multicultural policy, I share the concerns of Andrea A. Davis around the "growing mythology of Canadian innocence—the reconstruction of Canadian multicultural citizenship as a new stand-in for a model of contemporary democracy that is assumed to be all-inclusive, nonracist, and pure, even as Black and Indigenous peoples continue to die."[151] Moreover, Rinaldo Walcott, throughout *Black Like Who?*, argues that multiculturalism produces a static heritage that "support[s] identity politics and limit[s] political imaginings and possibilities," that "locates specific cultural practices in an elsewhere that appears to be static," and that makes "others adjacent to the Nation, not quite citizens."[152] Walcott continues to provide nuanced critiques of state-sponsored multiculturalism, while also acknowledging that multiculturalism "provides avenues for living with difference that do not always have to obey coercive state power. Thus, the idea of multiculturalism allows for forms of social relations that take difference as central to human existence, not as a problem but as a set of creative and non-coercive ways to approach living life to its fullest potential."[153] My position, akin to the fader on a DJ mixer, resides in the middle, mirroring Walcott's approach as both political critique and theoretical hope. Chapter 4 delves into these discussions.

Truly multicultural citizenship remains a noble goal, even as Canada falls short of achieving it. For many of us, Canada is the only country we have, so we must critique it and work to make it more just, especially for those who are deeply affected by its legacy of genocide and white supremacy. Cultural anthropologist Renato Rosaldo emphasizes social belonging and individual agency over state recognition and political involvement when defining citizenship; my approach to both citizenship and multiculturalism aims has a similar focus. My ambivalent stance on multiculturalism reflects both the policy's inability to improve the tangible conditions of Black and Indigenous lives in this country and the complex multicultural environment we currently inhabit. For, as Jean-Luc Nancy points out, multiculturalism exists wherever we find culture, which is essentially everywhere on this planet: "Every culture is in itself 'multicultural,' not only because there has always been a previous acculturation, and because there is no pure and simple origin [*provenance*], but at a deep level, because the gesture of culture is itself a mixed gesture: it is to affront, confront, transform, divert, develop, recompose, combine, rechannel."[154] I very much like Nancy's conception of multiculturalism as an understanding of how culture (and essentially remix) functions.

Shared values often hold a community together, and in this regard, the lack of a cohesive narrative has the potential to make the Canadian community unique. Lacking as it does a singular homogeneous narrative, Canada remains a space of constant immigration, exodus, acculturation, and change.[155] In chapter 5 I will apply the term "discordant democracy" when speaking to one's civic responsibility to embrace and negotiate dissonance. Also, community is hardly limited to the space in which one resides, as evidenced in the split identities and communal affiliations of the various poets' soundings. Rather, the poets in this book challenge the pervasive narratives of collective belonging via "diaspora sensibilities" in order to overcome, as Walcott puts it, "the problem of locating oneself solely within national boundaries . . . in the contradictory space of belonging and not."[156] It is around the "contradictory space" that Black writers in Canada create a common culture that is syncretized from a plurality of communities. Community is not inherently static; it is always changing and becoming, as Jean-Luc Nancy argues: "Community without community is *to come*, in the sense that it is always *coming*, endlessly, at the heart of every collectivity."[157] As with the ice cream vendors described by Vincent Andrisani, the sound of the poets in this book endures despite shifts in history and the influence of external power structures. They sound off against Canada's history of exclusion with the intention of creating a better future.

A Sonic Map: From Analogue to Digital

Each chapter of *Soundin Canaan'* opens with a specific listening, followed by a short history of a musical genre. This approach is intended to provide those readers who might not be particularly familiar with the music applied to the poetry discussed with a basic understanding of how the various musics are used by the poets. First, the music and poetry combine to provide a framework for how a certain poet uses a particular music genre (or multiple styles—usually the case) to sound their central ideas. Second, the music is there to provide its own account—somewhat outside the scope of the book proper—of how history, resistance, and forms of citizenship are embodied in sound. It is hardly a comprehensive history of any of these "genres," as each musical medium could easily fill entire books, as they often do. Furthermore, instead of intense musicological analysis, I provide sketches—many from literary sources, since this is a work of literary scholarship—to weave a tapestry that weds music and literature to the broader web of the African diaspora. These sketches may help initiate readers who might not be acquainted with the broader contours of the music (or with some of the intersecting matrices between poetry and music). The intention here is to guide the reader to an understanding of how citizenship is performed, just as with a musical performance. The genres—or *styles*—are loosely defined here as blues and folk vernacular, jazz, reggae and dub poetics, hip hop, DJing and remix, and musical improvisation broadly conceived. Often, I make a stylistic or essentialist choice to attribute a primary musical style to a poet—for example, opening the George Elliott Clarke chapter with blues history rather than jazz—because it fits the musical narrative being told besides clearly articulating a poet's sonic counterpoint. We can call Louis Armstrong a jazz musician first and foremost, but he easily and often incorporated or played blues, swing, and traditional pop music. The same goes for every poet here. Furthermore, I realize these are only brief sketches of some of the musical undertones in the texts. I would also argue that these concomitant musical *styles* dance together in a tradition of rupture and fluidity where past forms or styles inform our understanding and conceptualization of present forms.

> Nas and Muddy Waters

Hip hop music, for example, relies heavily on the innovations of earlier musical genres. Nas's song "Bridging the Gap" is a great example of how hip hop absorbs and is indebted to prior African American musical forms. The track samples Muddy Waters' "Mannish Boy," and Nas's lyrics demonstrate an appreciation of the musical forms and artists that came before him: "Did it like Miles and Dizzy, now we getting' busy / Bridging the gap from the blues, to jazz, to rap / The history of music on this track." Such is Guthrie P. Ramsey's central argument in *Race Music: Black Cultures from Bebop to Hip-Hop*, where he suggests that if we begin to see how bebop in the 1940s epitomized the quintessential Afro-modernist expression of Black urbanity, we can better understand how the musical styles most closely aligned with hip hop represent "the urban contemporary" for the current generation.[158] The present musical landscape is always engaged with the past in an ongoing and often improvised conversation.

So, while I strategically rely on generic prefixes of music to categorize our basic understanding of how they are used by the poets, the reality is that even the poets themselves often, if not always, conflate these forms. For example, M. NourbeSe Philip describes how the poems in *She Tries Her Tongue, Her Silence Softly Breaks* "can be seen to be working in the jazz aesthetic—word jazz, perhaps—where different themes are working with and against each other."[159] Christopher Small calls for more open pedagogical models, stating that "the big challenge to music educators today seems to me to be not how to produce more skilled professional musicians but how to provide that kind of social context for informal as well as formal musical interaction that leads to real development and to the musicalizing of the society as a whole."[160] Music and poetry will always have didactic value because they continue to teach us to be more aware about how we listen.

Lingold, Mueller, and Trettien elucidate that sound does indeed have a politics: "it can be gendered and racialized, used both to liberate people from and reinscribe determinative social categories. Sound has ethical implications and can help to build community or, conversely, to torment prisoners. It can elicit fear as easily as it produces longing or nostalgia. Even what counts as 'sound' or 'signal' and what gets dismissed as 'noise' can differ dramatically across listening practices and auditory cultures."[161] Much of what is considered "noise" should be challenged, as Tricia Rose does in *Black Noise: Rap Music and Black Culture in Contemporary America* (1994), which examines Black cultural production in hip hop, and as Tara Rodgers does in *Pink Noises: Women on Electronic Music and Sound* (2010), which looks at the pioneering work of women in electronic music. Additionally, Dionne Brand, in her essay "Imagination, Representation and Culture," and John Fiske, in "Surveilling the City," have conducted valuable research on how public spaces can be influenced by racial factors.[162] It is important to note that sound isn't always a force for liberation. We can recall instances that are quite different, such as the Nazis using loudspeakers for propaganda. The poets studied here are aware of the racialization of sound and public space, and they self-reflexively use sound/music to challenge easy categorizations of race, identity, citizenship, and how we perceive and engage with their artistic expressions. Therefore, there is not a one-size-fits-all listening approach, as if such a thing were even remotely possible. How one engages with the music of John Cage versus that of Marvin Gaye will require different modes of inquiry and knowledge.

Journalist John Leland argues it was the recording industry of the twentieth century that created the arbitrary separation of music into genres to meet market demands. In the early twentieth century, many Black as well as white performers played a mix of minstrel tunes, ballads, folk songs, blues, and rags. Leland contends that "Black performers became blues singers in the studio, dropping their other master at the door; whites became hillbilly singers. The blues singer, then, was an invention of the studio, and often white record executives."[163] Genres may have been constructed by interests, but they are still useful as tools to examine how a poet employs a style to play within a given format.

The structure of *Soundin' Canaan* progresses from analogue to digital, transitioning through blues, jazz, dub, hip hop, and culminating with DJing and remix. Chapter 1 focuses on George Elliott Clarke's musical (from blues to jazz) and political dedications in his Pentateuch of poetic colouring books. Chapter 2 looks at Dionne Brand's latest books of poetry, *Ossuaries* and *The Blue Clerk*. Both texts invoke Miles Davis, Thelonious Monk, Billie Holiday, Charles Mingus, John Coltrane, and Charlie Parker—jazz musicians who employ disruptive techniques as well as repetition, epistrophe, blue notes, contrafacts, and improvisation in their compositions—and demonstrate the formal and deconstructive approach that Brand takes to remap a historically marginalized yet fluid community of resistance. Chapter 3 offers a reading of M. NourbeSe Philip's *Zong!* as an improvised dub chant that changes with every reading, much in the way critical nuanced improvised performances typically do. Chapter 4 examines the work of Somali Canadian hip hop artist and poet K'naan, whose song of global fraternity, "Wavin' Flag," was chosen as an anthem for the FIFA 2010 World Cup. Chapter 5 examines Wayde Compton's turntable poetics (primarily from

Performance Bond), into which he explicitly incorporates hip hop, quite self-critically describing his use of it as being "largely about the anxiety of the globalization of hip-hop." In the conclusion I revisit the central themes of citizenship, identity, and resistance in the context of Black Canadian poetry, music, and literature. This chapter delves into what a new transnational listening community could potentially sound like, foregrounding Black and Indigenous voices as central to the emergence of a more equitable and just community.

My use of music serves as an in-the-moment antiphon and a disruptive pedagogical approach aimed at delving deeper into poetry and challenging systems of oppression in Canada and beyond. Through music, I unpack Clarke's complex perspective on nationalism and multiculturalism, Brand's vision of a flexible and globally oriented citizenship, Philip's compelling dub chant that encourages active sonic participation, K'naan's music as a force for both sonic and corporate multiculturalism, and Compton's remixes as an opportunity to reconsider citizenship and community in the context of Vancouver's historical and present-day Black community. The mix is informed by interviews with Clarke, Compton, Philip, Cecil Foster, d'bi.young, and others. By the end of the book, I hope that readers will gain new insights into a group of influential poets and, hopefully, be able to hear and more fully *feel* the complexity of Black literary and cultural production in Canada.

REMIX

The book has four primary goals:

1. To challenge and recover the historical significance of Canaan as a symbol of freedom while also envisioning a more just future for all.
2. To bridge the gap between different academic fields by demonstrating the interconnectedness of poetry and music and their profound influence on society.

3. To provide theories for analyzing music and Black Canadian poetry in the context of citizenship while also emphasizing the importance of close readings to appreciate the artistic form and skill of the poets under study.
4. To illustrate how readers, listeners, and remixers actively sound citizenship both within and outside the poems and songs.

Everyone who mixes a variety of texts together is creating a mix, just as the DJ often digs into the historical archive. However, this archive is not stagnant; rather, anyone can remix, remake, reshape, and re-edit a piece of recorded history, creating their own mix. Early hip hop DJs and youth from aggrieved communities did just that when they repurposed the turntable to create an art form that expresses the creative possibilities of liberation, becoming artist activists ("artivists") in the process.[164] We find resonance with the do-it-yourself dialogic mentality of urban youth in the work of Paulo Freire. Freire was a Brazilian philosopher, perpetual educator, and a significant theorist of critical pedagogy, best known for his seminal work *Pedagogy of the Oppressed*, in which he argued that "the oppressed unveil the world of oppression," ultimately transforming themselves and eventually "all people in the process of permanent liberation."[165] Perhaps these are lofty ideas for any book to attempt, but Freire's dialogical ideal of pedagogy—that students should have an equal opportunity to express their opinions with their peers and instructors—is an opportunity to co-perform meaning and engaged citizenship. While this is a literary work focused on the reading of poetic texts through the musical contours inherent in the poetry, it is also a reminder that in the process of liberating our society, critical reading and deep listening is an important step. The explored poets provide a portal to imagine another world.

The selected poets, as we shall see, are writing, sounding, perhaps even singing, about the very resistance and need for greater citizenship status I argue for, and, with an ear towards history, re-sounding the upheavals of the past to imagine a better future. I began with a focus on a loosely constructed approach to Canada's long anti-Black history and then moved to look at Black Canadian writing and the larger ideas of the book.

"Sonic citizenship" as an improvised form of Blackness can work against the malaise of capitalist apathy through a re-engaging of the poetic, which in turn can re-engage the political. Once again, I emphasize the value that music and the larger DJ methodology of *Soundin' Canaan* can play in reinvigorating the active nature of critically nuanced and engaged practices by treating history not as an artifact but as a living elastic fabric of social consciousness. Music as such runs the risk of de-politicizing or de-historicizing the material I engage with, but it does so with an eclectic hope to challenge fixity in all its forms: there is no one citizen, no one community, no one concept of the nation, no one DJ mix. And so, I argue that DJ methodology is not ahistorical; rather, it reflects an understanding and dedication to the past as well as the need to effectively sound and blend such histories into the present. If anything, a cerebral DJ methodology is a multifarious engagement that re-sounds the past to make the present more palpable and immediate. This spirit, of a DJ remixing the past, is taken up in the next chapter as we shift melodies to George Elliott Clarke's shantytown vernacular and formalized poetics—mixing blues and jazz phraseology—and place it against the larger literary canon. Clarke's Pentateuch of colouring books—*Blue, Black, Red, Gold,* and *White*—provides an ekphrastic poetics that remixes and blackens the canon. You can't conceive of Canaan without first tossing the canon into the fire.

#

DIALOGUE AND DISSONANCE

"Jazz washes away the dust of everyday life."

—ART BLAKEY quoted in Ward, *Jazz*, xxi

By way of a coda—an extended cadence, the last part of a piece of melody, "the implication being of some addition being made to a standard form or design"—I want to provide a few thoughts in relation to how I view beauty (aesthetic) and politics (rhetoric) in this book.[1] Art can affect us rhetorically or aesthetically, and I believe the writers in this book do both. The music in the poetry allows for greater aesthetic appreciation of the work, and more radically, it sounds revolutionary ideas concerning social justice. This recalls what poet and theorist Fred Moten maintains in *In the Break: The Aesthetics of the Black Radical Tradition*, which examines both Black performance and Black radicalism, arguing that the two concepts are mutually constitutive to the point of proximate inseparability. In hearing the text, we are moved to consider the social issues of a poem, whether those are citizenship, displacement, belonging, or the meaning of being Black in Canada. We can, of course, choose to be affected only aesthetically by a work and ignore its rhetorical connotations. On a purely aesthetic level, I can enjoy Handel's *Messiah* without being moved to believe in God's grandeur. Similarly, we can feel the power of jazz as it "washes away the dust of everyday life." We can enjoy Black CanLit on the same terms, although when we do both our appreciation and understanding is greater.

The aesthetic concerns beauty and is sensational and deeply personal. Rhetoric regards meanings and ethical relations and is external and social. Literature contains aesthetic and rhetorical elements and uses pathos to invoke an emotional response from the reader. Hence, the rhetoric of Harriet Beecher Stowe's *Uncle Tom's Cabin* drew American readers into the anti-slavery movement and helped fuel the American Civil War, and Amiri Baraka's poem "Somebody Blew Up America" drew so much public indignation that he was removed from his post as Poet Laureate of New Jersey.

There is a connection between aesthetics and rhetoric—how a poem sounds can be instrumental in conveying its meaning. In Langston Hughes's *The Best of Simple*, the character Simple connects the rhythm of bebop to police brutality: "that old club says 'BOP! BOP! . . . BE-BOP! . . . beaten right out of some Negro's head into them horns and saxophones and piano keys that plays it."[2] As Dionne Brand stated in her 2006 Gustafson lecture at Vancouver Island University, "I thought then, and still do, that poetry was/is some kind of perfect speech, some way at getting at the core of things . . . some kind of honest submission to life," and went on to say that, for her, this often meant "tending to the wretched and brutalized consciousness of oppressed peoples."[3] This echoes Aimé Césaire, who said, "*la Justice écoute aux portes de la Beauté*" (Justice listens at beauty's door). Rhetoric (politics) and aesthetics (beauty) are two distinct discourses, but I think when read together they produce fuller understandings in the quest for meaning. Such is my intention, which is why I've interviewed many of the poets in *Soundin' Canaan* in acts of joint meaning-creation between me, the text, and the poet's intent. Poetry is, as Langston Hughes defined it, "the human soul entire, squeezed like a lemon or a lime, drop by drop, into atomic words."[4] Poems resist: we have to labour to convince others that a work does something, and that something in *Soundin' Canaan* is a poetics that aesthetically integrates music to move readers into the underlining social consciousness and communal engagement from which the poem materializes. Again, citizenship is sounded.

For critic Northrup Frye, poetry was about form and did not reflect life but rather "a world of its own."[5] I admit, too often writing on Black writers focuses entirely on their radicalism, rather than on aesthetic beauty or an emotional response to a work, which is another reason I dedicate a great deal of textual space to musical form as one aesthetic pathway into the poetry of George Elliott Clarke, Dionne Brand, M. NourbeSe Philip, K'naan, and Wayde Compton. Musicalizing the literature is one technique to ensure that we hear the sonic contours in the text both as aesthetically pleasing and as a rhetorical strategy that encapsulates diverse notions of citizenship and identity in Canada. I suggest that Canadian poetry—specifically Black Canadian poetry, and Black Art more generally—is most fully represented when we consider both the aesthetic and rhetorical applications of a given work, especially when we regard those aesthetic and rhetorical possibilities as never closed, in the same way that identity, citizenship, and community are always changing. Daniel Fischlin, Ajay Heble, and George Lipsitz state that "the Western art tradition teaches us to expect and savor narrative and aesthetic closure" while by contrast "the improvisatory art of aggrieved communities prepares us to resist closures, to enjoy interruption, syncopation, and indeterminacy."[6] The full appreciation of art—the beautiful and the non-literary values we attach to it—is an improvisatory leap of faith since we are dealing with the play of words (or sounds, or images, etc.) to envision a more inclusive society: truly, a work of meaning and beauty combined. Work in contemporary literary aesthetics acknowledges that it is faulty that "teachers and critics assume that in order to discuss the aesthetic value of a literary text one must treat it as an autonomous object and isolate it from non-literary values and disciplines. The result is an ironically self-fulfilling judgment: literary aesthetics becomes identified with nineteenth-century notions of art for art's sake and mired in fruitless arguments about the possibility of art's autonomy."[7]

I am reminded of a modernist debate between Harlem poet Claude McKay and W.E.B. Du Bois on the nature of art and propaganda, another reframing of the arguments in this coda. McKay felt that incorporating the New Negro propaganda of the time would hinder his art and stifle the development of what he viewed as a true Black literary tradition. By contrast, Du Bois argued that "whatever art I have for writing has always been for propaganda, for gaining the rights of Black folk to love and enjoy. I don't give a damn for art that is not used for propaganda."[8] Propaganda here essentially means rhetoric, influencing a society towards some cause or social action. Propaganda, for Du Bois, is the very soil that grows art. Similarly, in 2007, poet Amiri Baraka spoke in Guelph, Ontario, and recalled that the entire Black Arts movement was a merging of aesthetic and rhetorical practice, explaining

> that our art—if it were relevant—had to help our people gain food, clothing, or shelter. We saw it as absolutely functional in that sense. And the question is: Can you make a song about feeding people that's beautiful? Can you make a song about building a house that's striking and aesthetically powerful? Maybe you can't do that, but that's what we wanted to do. We didn't want to separate social function from the aesthetic function. We wanted to unify those. And we still do. I still do anyway.[9]

Baraka's and Du Bois's desire to merge rhetoric and aesthetic encapsulates my hope for how the theory in *Soundin' Canaan* functions, since theory should be about providing prospects for future thought and even social mobility. My notion of the self is thus primarily social: we have rights and are most free when we learn to sound together. The poets of *Soundin' Canaan* find eloquent, challenging, and beautiful ways to articulate this meaning.

Chapter 1

BLUES VERNACULAR AND "HARMONIOUS DISSONANCE" IN GEORGE ELLIOTT CLARKE'S COLOURING PENTATEUCH: *BLUE, BLACK, RED, GOLD,* AND *WHITE*

"Good poems should rage like a fire
Burning all things, burning them with a great splendour."

—IRVING LAYTON,
A Red Carpet for the Sun, "Esthetique"

"Bebop was about change, about evolution. It wasn't about standing still and becoming safe. If anybody wants to keep creating they have to be about change."

—MILES DAVIS, Miles: *The Autobiography*, 394

Listening: Miles Davis, "Blue in Green"

Miles Davis, "Blue in Green"

Many consider Miles Davis's *Kind of Blue* to be the greatest jazz record of all time. It is indeed one album you will find in most people's collections who have at least a passing interest in jazz. While such rankings and value judgments are not very useful, the album remains a watershed moment in jazz and music. Miles had moved away from the hardbop style that had defined his playing to experiment with modality, giving each performer scales to work with in their own style, allowing for more creative freedom and improvisation.♭ It was, in part, what led to Coltrane's expanded modal approach in his solo career to follow. As Bill Evans writes in the liner notes to *Kind of Blue*, in allusion to the spontaneity of Japanese visual art forms, "the painter needs his framework of parchment, the improvising musical group needs its framework in time."[1] We find a similar modal framework in George Elliott Clarke's poetic work, as he mixes traditions and styles.

The poem "Bluing Green" (from the "Black Eye" section in Clarke's *Black*), named after the recording "Blue in Green" from *Kind of Blue*, is a piece with a measured and film noir–esque presence. It is an excellent example of cannibalization—of mixing and consuming traditions—which is why the poem begins by posing a question (as a statement) on the ramifications of such practice: "'The problem with jazz is miscegenation'?" The inverse, as the poem shows, is true: the *power* of jazz is miscegenation, meaning mixture. Miles Davis, like Charlie Parker, Duke Ellington, and Louis Armstrong before him, had a knack for mixing and reappropriating classical music, showtunes, and anything really, all within the larger nexus of jazz. The ten-measure melody for "Blue in Green" is incredibly modal, drawing

---

Liner Notes

♭ What a cast! Miles Davis on trumpet, John Coltrane on tenor saxophone, Julian "Cannonball" Adderley on alto saxophone (he sits out "Blue in Green"), Bill Evans on piano, Paul Chambers on double bass, and Jimmy Cobb on drums. You can listen to the playlist for this chapter here: https://open.spotify.com/playlist/5DcsjLzr28cDhdfBQJJPws. On another note, I've remixed "Blue and Green," which you can listen to here: https://bit.ly/3onNWKm.

in Dorian, Mixolydian, and Lydian modes, much like how Clarke draws various modes of Davis's persona and musical composition into his own poetic presence. We get a Miles Davis-sounding line like, "So that, if I failed, a motherfucker could / Smash me in the face with my trumpet," followed a little later by a line that sounds like it could only come from Clarke: "Don't I crave a cinematic albescence— / Like lightning rum scorching the throat."[2] The poem's attention to racial mixing, to the risk that poetry will accede into whiteness, is complex, as it has long been speculated that the white pianist Bill Evans actually wrote—or least very likely co-wrote—the sketch for the composition.[3]

Clarke creates a bit of a fabricated misnomer when Davis calls "E." (Bill Evans) a "Jive motherfucker, messed-up-looking white / Boy" who "plays too much *D* natural on *E*-flat blues."[4] The two musicians did clash at times—both suffered serious bouts of heroin addiction—but the fact remains that one of the great things about Bill Evans and Miles Davis was their ability to incorporate different styles (in Eurological and Afrological traditions) as well as both white and Black musicians into their circles. As Davis says in his *Autobiography*, it is completely false that he asked Evans to leave the band because he was white, and such speculation deeply hurt both Evans and Davis; he insists, "I don't go for that kind of shit; I have always wanted the best players in my group and I don't care about whether they're black, white, blue, red, or yellow."[5] Evans was a major influence on Davis, introducing him to European classical music. More important than the speculation about who wrote "Blue in Green" is the ability of the larger group (which, as mentioned, included a young Coltrane) to come together to improvise a sketch into something much larger. Clarke wholly gets this, as "Bluing Green" becomes a poem about how the inauthentic act becomes the authenticity, for "We are only as pure / As the blue inside green."[6] When mixed, blue and green make cyan: the colour of deep water, and cyanide. Under the poem is a black-and-white photograph of two dolls: one Black, one white—a poetic multicultural mix.

This chapter focuses on George Elliott Clarke's musical (particularly with a focus on jazz and the blues music that came before it) and political dedications in his Pentateuch of poetic colouring books: *Blue* (much *à la manière* of Miles Davis), *Black* (much *à la manière* of Malcolm X), *Red* (much *à la manière* of Charles Mingus), and *Gold* and *White* (both of which have expanded casts and are much *à la manière* of Clarke on Clarke). While I devote particular attention to *Blue*, the other colouring books are examined as singular works and in relation to the larger colouring project. In mixing styles, and often appropriating or parodying musical and poetic traditions, Clarke creates an interpretive space for his poetry to function as improvisation. Given that Clarke was one of the first to write in a substantive way about African Canadian literature, particularly within a Canadian nationalist framework and with a concern to anthologize and meticulously historicize his material, I devote some attention to unpacking his nationalism. I find his poetry often complicates his nationalistic frameworks, as he has a cosmopolitan passion for fusing forms to create complex remixes—hence, the blue in green.

I. Blues Lyricism

Blues and Folk Vernacular

> "There is no true American music but the wild sweet melodies of the Negro slave."
>
> —W.E.B. DU BOIS, *The Souls of Black Folk*, 7

> "Canada suffers from the same 'solidarity blues.' A primary measure of a social movement's validity, after all, is the degree to which society's most marginalized and dispossessed are part of and genuinely reflected in the social vision proposed by the movement."
>
> —DAVID AUSTIN, *Fear of a Black Nation*, 12

While Clarke incorporates as much jazz phraseology as he does blues lyricism, the blues is a good place to open our discussion of Clarke's poetics. In fact, such a blues reading of his poetry is the overarching framework used by Nigel Thomas in his exploration of Clarke's *speakerly* text, *Whylah Falls*. Thomas contends that "blues music and music-making by the characters, not to mention the music, often blues-jazz inspired, engendered by Clarke's own subtle word combinations, furnish a considerable part of this work's texture."[7] Blues music and folk vernacular provide formal strategies for thinking through the value that canon formation and the deformation of canons play in the national Canadian and larger diaspora narrative. The blues (like the colour blue) is a word that signifies Blackness, as separation, translation, and survival. Most modern musics owe something to the blues (and to the spirituals preceding it), a music that began primarily in African American communities in the nineteenth century "Deep South" of the United States.

In terms of form, the blues comprises work songs, spirituals, field hollers, shouts, chants, and ballads, among other styles. However, it took some time before the blues were as ubiquitous and cross-cultural as they are today. As the Du Bois epigraph elucidates, and as James Weldon Johnson accurately predicted, "the day will come when this slave music will be the most treasured heritage of the American Negro."[8] A good place to start to understand the spirituals is W.E.B. Du Bois's seminal *The Souls of Black Folk,* a collection of essays on race that champion his metaphor of the veil (a manifestation of the colour line) and his theory of double consciousness: "this sense of always looking at one's self through the eyes of others, of measuring one's soul by the tape of a world that looks on in amused contempt and pity."[9] Du Bois's revolutionary *Souls* anticipates not only the New Negro Movement but also contemporary Black American culture (as well as diasporic African culture) and remix through its unique pastiche of forms. Through a "mix" of the spirituals notation that opens each chapter and his unique articulations of the veil and double consciousness, Du Bois's *Souls* shows how remix is an inherent form of political engagement in African American literature and the blues.

Alexander G. Weheliye provides a valuable rereading of Du Bois's *Souls* from a techno-auditory standpoint akin to disc jockeying as an art form of contemporary (Black) musical culture, looking at how Du Bois, like a DJ, is able to blend together "history, eulogy, sociology, personal anecdote, economics, lyricism, ethnography, fiction, and cultural criticism of black music . . . Du Bois's textual practice emphasizes the fissures in the mix in the same manner that hip hop DJs call attention to their mixes through the rhythmical scratching of records, a result of being played with and against the groove."[10] Weheliye's argument demonstrates how blues music and folk culture are hardly static or perennially folksy.♭ For, as Robin D.G. Kelley instructively points out, what is commonly thought of as "'folk' culture is actually bricolage, a cutting, pasting, and incorporating of various cultural forms that then become categorized into a racially or ethically coded aesthetic hierarchy."[11] The past is neither stagnant nor dissociated from the contemporary moment.

<small>Mammie Smith, Ma Rainey, and Bessie Smith</small>

The blues are at the roots of much music: it is pervasive in jazz and provides the foundation of rhythm and blues. The twelve-bar blues progression can even be heard throughout rock'n'roll. Some early innovators of the blues are W.C. Handy (known as the Father of Blues), Bessie Smith, Gertrude "Ma" Rainey, Mamie Smith, Lead Belly, Robert Johnson, and too many others to list here. What is interesting about this tentative list is how prominent women blues figures were in the creation, innovation, and dissemination of the

---

♭ One recent example of a DJ mixing the blues in a hip hop format is Montreal DJ and consummate innovator of the art of DJing Kid Koala (Koala opens our listening for chapter 5). Koala's *12 Bit Blues* (2012) remixes the blues using an SP1200 sampler and turntable. Over three days Kid Koala cut up and reassembled the bed tracks for *12 Bit Blues* without the aid of sequencing software, often playing each part in real time, before finally returning and adding cuts. *12 Bit Blues* is postmodern blues music, ripped and scratched, and squeezed from a near-tragic lyricism at the edge of the crossroads where new meanings are forged. Kid Koala's practice is also a reminder that the blues continue to be used by artists in all sorts of improvisatory ways. The blues have always been about making it work with what you have on hand. "12 Bit Blues" can be found on the chapter's playlist.

blues—female vaudeville blues singers were eminently popular in the 1920s. For example, Mamie Smith was the first African American to record a blues record, in 1920; her second record, "Crazy Blues," sold 75,000 copies in its first month.[12] The blues, and the spirituals before them, have always been a popular and enduring music, performed across time and gender lines. Ma Rainey and Bessie Smith represent, as observed by Angela Davis, a "black working-class social consciousness"; moreover, they "foreshadowed a brand of protest that refused to privilege racism over sexism, or the conventional public realm over the private as the preeminent domain of power." So, in tandem with its often bawdy nature, the blues genre was, Davis concludes, "responsible for the dissemination of attitudes toward male supremacy that had decidedly feminist implications."[13] The blues genre helped materialize a classical African American canon of music (a formal counter-canon to the European classical tradition), one that provided potent standards off of which other artists could riff, beginning with the early spirituals.

Case in point: the Negro Spirituals "Swing Low, Sweet Chariot" and "Go Down Moses" have been covered on thousands of albums, with everyone from Louis Armstrong to Etta James, Duke Ellington, Johnny Cash, Parliament, The Grateful Dead, and hip hop groups Bone Thugs and Harmony covering the former, and everyone from Grant Green to Fats Waller, Archie Shepp, and Will Smith on the sitcom *The Fresh Prince of Bel-Air* covering the latter.♭ The blues have the power to connect people across diverse backgrounds and time periods, and represent, as Black liberation theologian James H. Cone argues in *The Spirituals and the Blues*, "the power of the song in the struggle for black survival—that is what the spirituals and blues are about." They also exemplify, as Cone declares, "unity music: black existence affirmed through a communal context."[14] This communal articulation of shared social existence in the blues sounds a citizenship that transcends the spurious markers of race, asserting cultural, individual, and communal survival against the hardships faced in

<aside>Louis Armstrong, Etta James, Fats Waller, and Archie Shepp</aside>

♭ There are too many covers to add the playlists, but I've added a few choice selections.

the New World, primarily but not exclusively by African Americans. The blues, like the spirituals before them, are about community, humanity, citizenship, and survival in the face of the horrible legacy of slavery—the blues articulate a painful truth.

This painful yet playful truth is why Langston Hughes describes the blues as *Laughing to Keep from Crying* (the title of one of his collections of short stories and a delta blues classic from Joe Callicott). In his autobiography, Malcolm X, while reflecting upon his younger self before he joined the Nation of Islam, describes how Billie Holiday ("Lady Day") "sang with the *soul* of Negroes from the centuries of sorrow and oppression. What a shame that proud, fine, black woman never lived where the true greatness of the black race was appreciated!"[15] Such an existential ethos is central to the blues, but it is also vital to the Black experience in the Americas, which is why blues music and expression are a fit style for writers across the diaspora working in poetry, song, and prose. The seemingly simple structure of the blues allows for immense feeling and vocal intonation. Cone testifies that you "don't study to write the blues, you *feel* them."[16] This is not to say that the blues lack complexity in performance, or that they cannot be imitated, as I argue that Clarke is a master riffer not only of blues, jazz, and folk idioms, but also of multiple poetic traditions. Furthermore, the blues function iteratively in Canada in a similar—yet unique—fashion as the playful yet painful truth Hughes and others articulate. Yet the blues invite significant stylistic innovations across borders. Blues are about grit, voice, tragedy, and personal loss and are equally about liberation and revolt. Such signifiers are why the blues are so semiotically charged for African Americans—as Houston A. Baker Jr. contends, "The sound is the sign"—but this is not to say that the blues are only about suffering, revolt, and personal catastrophe, for they are regularly about humanity and understanding, a fact that has been lost on many white music critics and musicians over the years.[17] For example, Ma Rainey, in August Wilson's play *Ma Rainey's Black Bottom*, says: "White folks don't understand about the blues. They hear it come out, but they don't know how it got there. They don't understand that's life's way of talking. You don't sing to feel better. You sing 'cause that's a way of understanding life."[18]

A Blues Matrix: Clarke's Signifyin(g) Poetics

> "No matter how comically meticulous /
> My canvas is the blues."
>
> —GEORGE ELLIOTT CLARKE, "IV Confessions," *Black*, 38

Clarke models his creative voice in relation to a variety of artist-intellectuals across borders (with personal anecdotes), and this allows for his poetry to be read in the same way that Baker reads the blues (articulated first in the intro/overture): as a matrix that continually serves as a web and point of input and output for play and creative impulses "in productive transit."[19] The matrix metaphor befits Clarke's poetic colouring books—*Blue, Black, Red, Gold*, and his latest in the continuum, *White*. His poetics consists of criss-crossing inputs and outputs that combine the rhythms of gospel and blues and shantytown vernacular within the highly aesthetic poetic tradition of Western literature. Clarke riffs on nearly every literary tradition—he has a particular reverence for and mastery of African American and Black Canadian traditions, and the larger European canon—in order to create a dazzling, loud, raucous "poetics of arson": a poetics of arson because it sets fire to past traditions so as to create new ones from the ashes.[20] Furthermore, the blues metaphor, given the large amount of poetic dedication in Clarke's texts, offers what Baker terms "phylogenetic recapitulation—a nonlinear, freely associate, nonsequential meditation—of species experience," reminding us that blues help give shape to life, even if that shape is an improvised association upon a standard rhythmic pattern.[21] The blues are perhaps not all that different from jazz: as Ellison writes, much of (American) life is "jazz-shaped."

We can read Clarke's poetry—although within a specific Black/African Canadian context—as critics read Langston Hughes and his shifting registers of deformative folk sound. Amiri Baraka calls Hughes "*the* Jazz Poet" and "one of the first writers to seriously consider the blues as a laudable and important part of American culture."[22] Furthermore, Hughes was able, through his collaborations with blues and jazz musicians, to show that Blackness was boundless,

Langston Hughes

without limits, and allied with music.[23] Clarke's poetics highlight the cosmopolitan—yet fiercely regional—articulation of his own Blackness, which "is not just skin colour, but a polysemous consciousness": a consciousness that like Hughes's own poetry is marked by divergent traditions, sudden improvisational nuances, broken rhythms, traditional formats, and punctuations of riffings, giving voice to the poetry and music of an evolving community.[24] In much the same way that Ezra Pound, in "How to Read," talks of melopoeia as a poetry on the borders of music, Clarke's own poetry straddles this border. The intermediacy of Clarke's *infrapoetics* (a term introduced in the intro/overture) acknowledges signifying as a central component of Black poetics.

There are few books as insightful on the signifying tradition as Henry Louis Gates Jr.'s *The Signifying Monkey: A Theory of African-American Literary Criticism*. First published in 1988, the work is a landmark manifesto about the African American practice of signifying, which Gates uses to examine an interplay among African American writers, particularly Ralph Ellison, Richard Wright, Zora Neale Hurston, and Ishmael Reed. Gates relates the Black signifyin(g) tradition to the double-talk, mischief, play, and deceit of the Monkey in these narratives, yet it is, as Gates describes, "difficult to arrive at a consensus of definitions of Signifyin(g)." This evasion of clear unitary definitions is the greatest strength of such a tradition, for it allows for more interplay, intertextuality, and awareness of form, emphasized not just in the literature but in the literature's relation to the well of music, such as the jazz riff, which "is a central component of jazz improvisation and Signifyin(g) and serves as an especially appropriate synonym for troping and revision."[25] We hear such techniques throughout African American literature: in the opening sermon of Ellison's *Invisible Man*, the unnamed narrator riffs on Dostoevsky's *Notes from Underground* and parodies Melville's passage in *Moby-Dick* about the "'Blackness of Blackness'"; Hughes's *Ask Your Mamma* incorporates the Dozens (a game common in African American communities involving spoken word combat between two contestants, where participants insult each other until one gives up); Paul Laurence Dunbar's line "I know why the caged bird sings" from his poem "Sympathy" is turned into the title of Maya Angelou's first autobiography; and Lorraine Hansberry's *A Raisin in the Sun* opens with a reference to Hughes's poem "A Dream Deferred." These are but a few examples among myriad Black signifyin(g) traditions that signify on the very act itself, for the tradition, like the prison chain in Ellison's *Invisible Man*, "signifies a heap."[26]

Clarke's poetics display the same signifying practices, speaking not only to his brethren and sistren across the border, but often very directly to a congregation of Black Canadian writers (Wayde Compton, Dionne Brand, Dany Laferrière, and Lawrence Hill, to name a few) among other Canadian figureheads (Pierre Elliott Trudeau and Irving Layton, to name but two). In fact, there's no stopping Clarke from imagining and signifying an African American bassist, Charles Mingus, as Canadian, as he does in *Red*—riffing within a tradition that welcomes and encourages such play. Reworking the algorithm of *signified/signifier*,[27] Clarke's poetry, like the two trickster figures Gates invokes, Esu-Elegbara and the Signifying Monkey, is a double-voiced discourse about itself, "because it always entails formal revision and an intertextual relation, and because of Esu's double-voiced representation in art."[28] Similar to how signifying in blues and jazz is characterized by pastiche, Clarke's poetics, as well as his own chronicling of an African Canadian tradition, searches for truth and does so through a lyricism that is not afraid to blur borders and cross literary lines, which Clarke argues the diversity of selected writers do in *Eyeing the North Star*, his first collection of contemporary and historical African Canadian works: "Theses writers avoid nothing. They speak the raw blues of truth, no matter how raucous, hideous, odious, bitter, or sore."[29] I hear the same "raw blues of truth" in much of Clarke's early poetry (1978–1993).

In Clarke's *Lush Dreams, Blue Exile* (a collection of his poetry from 1978 to 1993, published in 1994) we see/hear/witness the same engaged signifying poetics that we see/hear/witness in much of Clarke's work. An early poem, "Watercolours for Negro Expatriates in France," is full of African American references (Du Bois, Josephine Baker, Lead Belly, Richard Wright, Ellington) in convoy with European or American writers (Eliot, Hemingway, Stein) who accentuate music and poetry as a border-crossing practice—an engaged form of citizenship:

John Coltrane

"You have heard Ma Rainey, Bessie Smith. / You need no passports."[30] Clarke's poem provides a modelling of "sonic citizenship," for although the expatriate is technically without citizenship status, citizenship (as a sonic metaphor) should be conferred as a mosaic of identities and cosmopolitan allegiances, especially for those who are exiled or hold immigrant status. Such immigrant status reflects the experience of those Black Loyalists who arrived in Nova Scotia in 1783 after the British lost the American Revolutionary War, then repatriated to Sierra Leone in 1792. A tentative citizenship in flux was the reality for those freedom seekers who followed the North Star into Canada, emphasized by Clarke's poems dealing with Africadian[♭] history, such as "Halifax Blues" or "Hymn to Portia White."[♯] This history comes to life through Clarke's Africadian-infused blues and odes to Africville and Canaan land: "to this birchbark Canaan, to this Nova Scotia"; or, "beautiful Canaan of stained glass and faith."[31] Clarke's spiritual remapping (within Nova Scotia) through ancestral modes and various diasporic traditions is described by Wayde Compton as a poetic syncretism and a "necessary act of making culture" and ultimately community.[32] Some of the signifying poetics are even inadvertent: "Violets for Your Furs" riffs on A.J.M Smith's line "a loaded violet / ... in your fur," which Clarke mentions to Anne Compton was an unintentional resonance: "I didn't know about that echo. I read Smith a long, long time ago. If I read that line, I completely forgot about it. In fact, what I was referring to with that title was a jazz standard of the '50s, John Coltrane's, who is one of my jazz heroes."[♮][33] Signifying poetics allow for expansive references, and for Clarke these signifying practices extend beyond the page and into performance.

♭ Much of Clarke's work explores and chronicles the experience and history of the Black Canadian community of Nova Scotia, creating a cultural geography that Clarke refers to as "Africadia."

♯ White was an Africadian blues singer and Clarke's great-aunt.

♮ Coltrane performed "Violets for Your Furs" on his 1957 debut, *Coltrane*. Originally a 1941 song written by Matt Dennis, with words by Tom Adair, it was made popular by Frank Sinatra on his 1954 album *Songs for Young Lovers*.

It's worth noting that a formative part of signifying in the African tradition is oral and that performance and community are central to Clarke's desire to speak to his community, however broadly defined. The discography presented at the back of *Lush Dreams, Blue Exile* (like the one in *Whylah Falls*) is reflective of the matrix that Clarke draws from (a wide range of albums are drawn into the mix, including Miles Davis's *The Man with the Horn*, Glenn Gould's *The Goldberg Variations*, Anthony Braxton's *Four Compositions*, Prince and the Revolution's *Purple Rain*, and Africadian artist Faith Nolan's *Africville*, among many others).♭ Clarke emphasizes that signifying is less a textual medium than an oral one that resonates most profoundly in auditory spaces and soundings. Like Langston Hughes, Clarke wants to be sounded in multiple formats, and he shares his need with Anne Compton to speak to his local (mostly Black) community beyond a (European) traditional written framework:

Miles Davis, Glenn Gould, Anthony Braxton, Prince, and Faith Nolan

> In the spring of 1986, I was invited to take part in a fund-raising event put on by the Black Cultural Centre of Nova Scotia. I was the only poet on the program. Everyone else was a performer. I was there as the poet. I read in the way I had been taught to read in the university, which is very formal and very Atwood-like in terms of being very plain, no emotion, just straightforward recitation. But this was in front of an audience of my peers, of my own community. So people started yelling at me: "Get off the stage." It was very direct: "You're boring. Go home." The people didn't want to hear some dry shit . . . but luckily I had just written a piece, "Love Letter to an African Woman," which is in *Whylah Falls* (58–59), and I read that, and they loved it. The people got quiet and they started to say, "Preach it! Testify! That's it brother!" And the applause at the end was rich. It was intense. And I said to myself, I will never write again anything I cannot read before my own community.[34]

♭ Faith Nolan's music is not available on Spotify at the time of this writing and so I've included a link to her song about Viola Desmond (a focus later in this chapter) here: https://www.youtube.com/watch?v=yNui_-yBsgM.

In the way that blues represent culture at a crossroads, much of Black Canadian poetry plays with form and uses voice and performance as signifiers of communal affiliation. It is through this communal association that Clarke sounds his blues citizenship: blues because his poetry articulates a painful truth while also celebrating a larger kinship with past and present writers that seeks out liberation and gives voice to his own experience as an Africadian. At much of the heart of Clarke's work is a dedicative kinship as he unapologetically revises tradition.

II. Blackening the Canon, Singing Canaan

Emotion Recollected in Hybridity: Clarke's Dedicative Poetics

Clarke's ability to signify and engage with multiple canons and writers is an act of homage: a form of dedicative sampling. When I asked him about his dedicative poetics, he responded that homage and dedication function as acts of creative kinship:

> It's important for me to recognize forbearers, ancestors, artistic genealogical family and song, because none of us is here solo, or alone in a sense. We all come from a context. There is a genealogical context, cultural context, and there's also an artistic context. And one has many artistic relatives so to speak and you want to claim kinship at least with different folks . . . I'm going to tie this back into jazz and improvisation, and so on, by saying that I think that maybe one of the strongest appeals of jazz as an art form—for many of us—is that it is automatically at its roots: cosmopolitan, multicultural, polyphonic, and all of those notions of diversity and diverse engagements are important to me.[35]

For Clarke, dedication, signifying, and mimicry are forms of active poetics: an engaged citizenship where difference and juxtaposition allow for greater diversity in his work. In *Eyeing the North Star*, Clarke describes African Canadian literature as a species of hybridity: "King James scriptures melded with East Coast spirituals, New Orleans jazz, Bajan calypso, and Nigerian jit-jive."[36] The mixing of Black CanLit is indicative of the coalition of identities that Black Canadians write out of, from the Black Loyalists to the Rastafarian dubbists, and across the diaspora. As Ayanna Black posits, "we [Black Canadian and Black writers] write out of a collective African consciousness—a consciousness embodied in the fabric of oral traditions, storytelling, fables, proverbs, rituals, work-songs and sermons meshed with Western literary forms."[37] Clarke's traces his identity back to the Black Loyalists who settled in Africville and cross-pollinated with the Mi'kmaqs in the area: "They were clear Negro, and semi-Micmac."[38]

Clarke's remixing is akin to blues multiculturalism, challenging any simple reduction of his own Blackness. His dialoguing with other poets, and his declamation of past figures (like Titus Andronicus, the tragic historical and Shakespearean figure), among other hybrid forms of mixed poetics—of blues experience—fit with my own desire to use quotation and signifying to resist simple colonial and binary representations. Clarke, through his own listening to other poets and writers (many of whom are based in Canada), challenges dominant discourses through a polytextured dialogue. Whether he is invoking Dionne Brand in "Bio: Black Baptist/Bastard" (*Blue*) or writing *à la manière de* Miles Davis in "Bluing Green" (*Black*) or attempting to write *à la manière de* Amiri Baraka in "Calculated Offensive" (*Blue*) or writing a poem "In Memory of Derek Walcott (au tombeau de Pound)" *à la manière d'*Auden (*White*), Clarke's mixes interrogate mass culture and reception, particularly regarding academia's valorizing of British canonicity. In many ways, the gumbo concoction of Clarke's poetry and scholarship fits with Paul Gilroy's assessment of Blackness across the Atlantic, which can be looked at as "one single, complex unit of analysis . . . explicitly transnational and intercultural."[39]

Toward a Multicultural Black Nationalism

> Here I am, in my sixties,
> But I announce the 1980s—
> A new Canada, a new Canaan,
> A gilt, sparkling Constitution,
> Sunning a Just Society,
> A rainbow of minorities—
> Multicultural, bilingual, at peace.
>
> —GEORGE ELLIOTT CLARKE, *Trudeau*, 104

The zeal of the Canadian nationalist movement reached a peak during the centennial celebrations of 1967, which helped establish that Canada was *other* to the United States. This anti-Americanism was a response to American neoliberalism and US involvement in the Vietnam War (which lasted from 1965 to 1973); it also served to protect Canada's cultural and national narrative (largely routing/rooting back to the 1951 Massey Report). In the 1960s and 1970s Canada's literary community fought against the American cultural, economic, and political sphere through works that expressed concern about the destructive superpower (America) and its frightening proximity to us: George Grant's *Lament for a Nation* (1965, which provides a short history of conservatism and an analysis of Canada's changing place in the world during the Cold War); Dennis Lee's "Cadence, Country, Silence" (1972, which explores the twofold dilemma of writers who are both colonizer and colonized); Margaret Atwood's poem "Backdrop Addresses Cowboys" (1968, an exploration of North American imperialism); Earle Birney's poem "I accuse us" (1973, a critique of Canada's collusion in the atrocities of the Vietnam War); and the works of many Black Canadian writers who were fighting for the right to even *have* a literary presence, especially in a Black Canadian context, such as Liz Cromwell's *Jungle Tea Poems* in 1975, and the works published in Harold Head's 1976 anthology, *Canada in Us Now*. Much of the fervour for Canadian nationalism was a response to the Vietnam War, but it was also a time of revolution and anti-imperialism, manifested in North America in the sixties crusade for social equality, as represented so well in Bob Dylan's social change anthem, "The Times They Are A-Changin'." The energy of sixties counterculture was funnelled into the literature, and new forms emerged—sound poetry, concrete poetry, folk music, pop art, free jazz—that helped launch what we now call postmodernism and critical theory (feminist theory, queer theory, Black studies, etc.).

_{Bob Dylan}

By 1960, Indigenous people had won the right to vote in federal elections without losing their status rights. Yet, for all the human rights gained in the 1960s, of which we are now benefactors, there were many great losses in the struggle for new civil liberties. The Vietnam War is a case in point: more than 20,000 American draft dodgers moved to Canada, with many staying on even after the war. Canada was, as poet Frank Davey writes, "in some important ways an 'un-American' place."[40] Such migration recalls the "freedom seekers" who made their way underground to Canada, as well as the United Empire Loyalists (including those American Blacks who fought on the British side) who found their way into Canada after the American Revolution. Canada's national narrative and people have always been in constant flux. Thus, Canada has always lived the blues in the tragedy of trying to negotiate difference, especially for those who are pushed to the margins or denied the full political benefits of citizenship. The world was changing and Canada's sense of its place as a peaceful nation was largely in contrast to America's more openly confrontational politics and civil unrest, which culminated in Memphis on 4 April 1968, when Martin Luther King Jr. was assassinated. Around 150,000 people attended King's funeral, a global wake-up call to the injustices in the world (including the Vietnam War and the struggle for racial equality), which Pierre Elliott Trudeau outlined in his vision for Just Society. Clarke sums up these tensions in his dramatic poem, *Trudeau*: "This April 1968: Two days past, Martin Luther King / Was shot through his throat, just for dreaming / Of a truly Just Society— / Exactly what Canada must be."[41] With the loosening of immigration restrictions under the cosmopolitan (yet staunchly nationalist) Trudeau, as well as a growing middle class and the opening of the Trans-Canada Highway in 1962 (which made travel from St. John's, Newfoundland, to Victoria, BC, by car, possible), the unified national narrative of Canada was solidified. Yet this narrative, although projected as multicultural by Trudeau, was largely exclusionary and dramatically white. Clarke's anti-imperialist African Canadian nationalism emerges from this backstory.

Notwithstanding his cosmopolitan poetics, Clarke's critical thinking often fits within a nationalist framework. As Clarke contends, largely as a defence against critiques levelled against his nationalist stance, "if I am a cultural nationalist, I embrace that sign with a *cosmopolitan* passion."[42] Clarke argues in *Odysseys Home* that there is not only a deep history of African Canadian literature but also a sense of nationalism around Black Canadian literature. Since *Odysseys Home*, a large trove of archived materials by Black Canadian writers has come to light, and many of the resulting anthologies have carried Clarke's emblazoned approach into exciting, diverse, and contemporary excavations of Black writing and history in Canada. But does an archive alone constitute nationalism? Yes, and no. The archive constitutes a sense of shared heritage, history, and belonging, but nationalism is an act of imagination as well as, like multiculturalism, an act of faith. Many theorists have critiqued nationalism because the nation is often defined by those who wield power—akin to a kind of fascism—but Clarke's nationalism, like Richard Iton's "geo-heterodoxy," in its "capacity to imagine and operate simultaneously within, against, and outside the nation-state," largely diverges from the current model of nationalism: "This nationalism enacts a counter-influence to the pervasive identification of Canada as a northern, white, wanna-be empire, a pseudo-imperial self-image which reduces blackness to the status of problematic and pitiable Other."[43] In *Odysseys Home*, *Eyeing the North Star*, and *Directions Home*, Clarke uncovers an African (and diasporic) presence in Canada that dates back to 1605, naming early Canadian texts such as John Marrant's *Narrative of the Lord's Wonderful Dealings with John Marrant* (1785), Josiah Henson's *Life of Josiah Henson* (1849), which prepared the way for Stowe's *Uncle Tom's Cabin*, Mary Ann Shadd's *Condition of Colored People* (1849), and John William Robertson's *The Book of the Bible Against Slavery* (1854), and naming

M.E. Lampert as the first African Canadian woman poet. Clarke maintains that African Canadian literature and culture is no mere echo of African American literature and culture. For example, works presented in America are often engaged with differently when they are presented in Canada—witness the sharp responses of Clarke, NourbeSe Philip, and others to *Show Boat*, *Huckleberry Finn*, and the *Into the Heart of Africa* exhibit at the Royal Ontario Museum, which was vehemently rejected as flagrantly and viciously racist.

Clarke's choice to frame Black literature and resistance in Canada as distinct from that of the superpower across the border (much like Atwood's claim for Canadian literature more broadly in *Survival*) is a response to a history typically ignored by historians and scholars. By framing Black Canada as resistive and *other* to the United States, Clarke draws on the universalism of Black Nationalism in an explicitly Canadian context (specifically regional and different in each province), and he does so to work against the notion that to be Black and Canadian is "to suffer the erasure of *Canadian* as a legitimate expression of black identity."[44] Clarke's *Directions Home* succeeds his critically acclaimed *Odysseys Home*, a work that began mapping the tremendous depth of African Canadian literature upon Clarke's revelation of "the existence of a canon of texts dating back to 1785."[45] *Directions Home* responds to its own call with fifteen diverse essays on Black Nova Scotian and West Indian Canadian literature. The collection expands the map begun in *Odysseys Home* by considering national, bilingual, and historical perspectives from multiple trajectories of African Canadian literature and history, showcasing a multiplicity of texts. Clarke includes everything from poetry to autobiography, church histories, and slave narratives. Like George Grant, Clarke upholds the essentialist view that "no minority culture can articulate or preserve itself without endorsing a degree of nationalism."[46] Of course, Black Canadian writing is diverse, and many writers rightfully think of themselves outside a Canadian nationalist framework, preferring various diasporic or regional identifications or altogether rejecting Canada as being foundational to their identity.

Even deciding what constitutes a literary starting point in Black Canadian literature has generated contention. Clarke has celebrated the long literary tradition of African Canadian literature as a framework for African Canadian nationalism, whereas M. NourbeSe Philip has argued that when she began writing in Canada she felt there wasn't much of a tradition, certainly not a modern nationalist one, as she tells Nigel Thomas: "George Elliott Clarke and I disagree on this, and he has critiqued me on this: the feeling that when I began writing here in Canada, there was no body of literature by African Canadians ahead of me to follow or not follow; to write with or against, as there exists in the US or Britain."[47] Philip goes on to talk about the beauty of written sermons in Nova Scotia, among other early traditions, but for her they do not constitute a literature, and certainly they do not foster a sense of nationalism.

More complicated is that Clarke believes it is possible to have it both ways—you can adhere to nationalism *and* be diasporic. In his interview with Anne Compton, Clarke outlines his Red Toryism (like Grant's own conservatism and garrison against globalization) and describes how one needs both revolution and tradition, "as long as it's not oppressive, because it's a way of defining one's existence, as a group, as a people. So there is this Janus-faced approach one has to have, or one should have, as a poet." Compton responds to Clarke's strong nationalist position by asking, "Doesn't that very nationalism, at the same time, make it difficult for the Maritimes to have, and to express, its uniqueness? You can't have it both ways." To which we get a depiction of the kind of nationalism Clarke has in mind: "I think you can have it both ways. There's a difference between nationalism and patriotism, love of one's own place . . . I was looking at an anthology of love poems, and John Clare was there. It gladdened me that he was there. Clare's work is very local. I love the fact that he is willing to celebrate the woman who lives across the field."[48] Clarke's nationalism is a patriotic one, but unlike that of the early sixties Black Nationalism of the Black Panthers and their forebears Malcolm X and the Nation of Islam, his love does not just avow specific regional histories—it also thinks of a nationalism alongside, or as part of, the Canadian multicultural landscape, a landscape that Pierre Trudeau, one of Clarke's complicated heroes, had in mind for the Canadian mosaic.[49] As Clarke told the *Toronto Star* after becoming the Poet Laureate of Toronto, "Toronto has become a magnet for immigrants around the world and migrants from other parts of the country because it offers so many opportunities to get ahead, and to live together in something like harmony ... I'd like to be one of the voices summoning us to recognize the great dynamism of our diversity."[30] Although it is important to critique nationalisms that exclude or limit cultural difference, Clarke's interest is in a nationalism that counters global and local superstructures that continue to erase the history of African Canadians and their long-standing presence in Canada. Moreover, Clarke's desire for counter-canonicity, it is an act of reclamation: a homecoming for those who have been branded as marginal to the nation, or the literary canon.

Blackening the Sonnet and Canoning the Canon

> One of the strange conditions of being Black Nova Scotian is that one is colonized in three different ways—by British culture, by American, and also by Canadian. We have to tussle with the Canadian, as well ... So, part of my strategy as a writer, in responding to my status as the scribe of a marginal and colonized community, is to sack and plunder all those larger literatures—British, American, Canadian, French, African-American, Caribbean—and to domesticate their authors and their most famous or noted lines. In other words, my acts of homage are acts of damage.
>
> —GEORGE ELLIOTT CLARKE in conversation with Anne Compton, 143

Take the sonnet and think of how many diverse incarnations it has had over the years. For example, while Harlem Renaissance and Jamaican-born poet Claude McKay (who was born in Jamaica) often utilizes the sonnet form, he inflects and effectively blackens it via language, tone, meter, and subject matter.♭ The point is that the form (a sonnet, or a jazz rhythm) may have universal appeal, but the subject matter is often intensely regional.

Working against a tripartite colonization (British, American, Canadian), Clarke riffs on established English literary forms, which for him are "acts of damage," with the goal of blackening the Western literary tradition and thereby asserting agency, in particular where Black voices have been historically absent. Clarke uses nationalism as a conservative ideology that privileges order and cultural difference. His desire to blacken inherited traditions and to establish an African Canadian canon is motivated by the political fact that no Black canon has taken root in Canada.[51] For Clarke, the establishment of the African Canadian archive is a reminder of the long history of people of African descent in Canada, as well as a tactic to locate historical lacunae and deliberate omissions with the goal of creating a sense of unity (national pride) around the history of Black people in Canada. As reflected in *sankofa*, a word in the Akan language of Ghana that refers to excavating the past to conceive of the future, Clarke reaches into the archives of the past to imagine a more equitable future for

---

♭ See McKay's "If We Must Die," which uses the sonnet form to call together a Black mass into unified action against lynching and racist violence. While the poem is contained within the "little song" of the sonnet, the form allows for it to be readily memorized and reappropriated for reciprocal poetic action. The poem is McKay's response to the Red Summer of 1919: some seventy lynchings occurred that year, and racial violence reached an apex after a young Black boy swam across the segregated section of a lake in Chicago and was subsequently murdered. After the volta, the opening "if" (1) of the poem becomes a "must" (8) as the poetic speaker switches metrical modes from iambic to trochaic, providing a rolling rhythmic sense of the need for immediate communal action: "Oh kinsmen! We must meet the common foe / Though far outnumbered, let us show us brave" (9–10). The switch from iamb to trochee meter was common among Harlem Renaissance poets (see Cullen's "Heritage" or Chicago poet Gwendolyn Brooks's "The Anniad"), and it indicates how Black modernism revises form through revision. The very action/form of the poem itself is a revision of the sonnet's typical lyrical voice, traditionally asserted through a distinctive "I" speaking to a beloved; rather, the poem speaks to the communal folk class, albeit a masculine group of "Kinsmen!"

Black people. By using the sonnet form in much of his poetry (along with other conventional poetic forms in *Blue, Black, Red, Gold,* and *White*), Clarke engages with multiple writers and histories across cultural lines to create a complex mix that keeps Blackness wide open, like jazz.

Clarke's strategies recall Houston A. Baker Jr.'s in *Modernism and the Harlem Renaissance*, where Baker argues that "the blending of ... class and mass—poetic mastery discovered as a function of deformative *folk* sound—constitutes the essence of black discursive modernism."[52] Building on Amiri Baraka's notion of the "changing same"—his term for the interplay between tradition and individual talent in Afro-American music—Baker designates the *mastery of form* and *the deformation of mastery* as Black strategies of resistance and subversion. Essentially, these terms are biological masks, elusive constellations, and the difference between the two forms is like the one between a praying mantis (mastery of form) and a gorilla (deformation of mastery). Baker elaborates: "The mastery of form conceals, disguises, floats like a trickster butterfly in order to sting like a bee. The deformation of mastery, by contrast, is Morris Day singing 'Jungle Love,' advertising, with certainty, his unabashed *badness*—which is not always conjoined with violence. *Deformation* is go(uer)rilla action in the face of acknowledged adversaries."[53] So while it could be argued that Claude McKay does not remodernize the sonnet, that he simply uses it exactly as Shakespeare did and for exactly the same purposes, I would contend that he does in fact newly engage with the sonnet by effectively blackening it, mastering the form.[54] Comparatively, a poem like Amiri Baraka's "Black Arts" charges forth like a gorilla, unabashedly announcing its *badness*. Like Derek Walcott's (a major influence on Clarke), Clarke's sonnets display a *mastery of form* and a *deformation of mastery*. In his 1998 interview with Anne Compton, Clarke defends his relation to the larger canon and his negotiation with the master tropes, genres, and languages in which he writes and which he works against: "Another point to make about the canon is that it is our canon too. Even though it was imposed on us, it still belongs to us ... Perhaps we can take these models and blacken them ... In order to survive, in order to maintain some specificity for ourselves, we have no choice but to try to claim it for ourselves, to pretend that Shakespeare comes from Weymouth Falls or that Virginia Woolf comes from North End Halifax. I mean, why not?"[55] Clarke here is expressing the value of blackening the canon, as an act of writing back to the Empire as well as creating an "authentic" or "new" voice.

Ezra Pound and Derek Walcott become ideal models for this new poetic voice, particularly Walcott, for his ability to code-switch between traditions. Clarke describes his gratitude to Walcott: "I thank you for pioneering a way of blackening English, of roasting syllables upon the righteous fires of your anger and your love until they split and crack. You cannibalize the Canon and invite your brethren and sistren to the intoxicating, exhilarating feast."[56] Gates—revisiting Houston A. Baker Jr.—echoes Walcott's notion, describing "black English vernacular" as "a sign of black difference, blackness of the tongue. It is not surprising that the vernacular is the source from which black theory springs."[57] Through poetic remix, Clarke blackens English and places himself within the poetic tradition that he has been instructed in as both a poet and an academic, writing back to Empire and the canon.

Much of Clarke's work expresses an elegiac longing for a Black Canadian history that has been neglected. Clarke helps bestow a voice for the unsung, such as the "chalk-poisoned black men who watched gypsum / Choke off roses," in much the same way that early hip hop music bespeaks an unwillingness by certain members of an urban minority to be rendered voiceless by a dominant population.[58] An astonishing aspect of Clarke's *Odysseys Home* is the way it remaps the African Diaspora, with an approach that challenges (or, perhaps, opens up) Paul Gilroy's transnational approach: "Hence, his *Black Atlantic* is really a vast Bermuda Triangle into which Canada—read as British North America or Nouvelle-France or even as an American satellite—vanishes."[59] In this sense, Clarke is interested in translating the Black experience across the diaspora with a particular specificity, arguing for regional Blackness within different Canadian provinces: "I will, to my dying breath, say that black Canadian writing is as regional as Canadian writing in general."[60]

Clarke's notions of Black Canadian writing and identity are both regional and global, and from his perspective this "makes for a far more heteroglot, far more diverse, far more democratic community . . . than you have with African Americans."[61] This goes back to Clarke's desire to work against the idea that Black Canadians do not have a distinct history. He works against the notion that "Brit professors and cracker cops harrumphed, in perfect / Sneering grammar, again and again, 'You have NO history.'"[62] In dialogism with other marginalized Black writers across the diaspora, Clarke's poetics formulate a case for Black history (and African Canadian history) and poetry alongside the existing canon that suppressed Black voices by presenting them as metaphorically inferior to "white" ones. Having set the canon on fire, from the ashes Clarke underscores music as a unifying element across the diaspora, integral to national identification, canon formation, and poetic form.

Incendiary Music

> "Make every lyric a work of treason, / A Criminal's code, an arsonist's song."
>
> —GEORGE ELLIOTT CLARKE, "To X. X.," in *Blue*, 44

Like "Purple Haze" trailblazer Jimi Hendrix, or the young firebrand Archie Shepp, whose fire music ignited the 1960s free jazz scene, Clarke's poetics can be thought of as incendiary music that ignites the personal, interpersonal, and communal through song. Clarke describes how he "became a songwriter—a lyricist—before [he] became, indelibly, a poet" and how he "couldn't sing and couldn't read music and didn't play any instruments, but still wanted to be close to song."[63] I asked Clarke about his role as a musician/songwriter in relation to his poetry, and he related his love of music to his early experiences in the Baptist church:

Well, I am a frustrated musician. And singer for that matter. And one of the most traumatic incidents of my adolescence was when I was 12. And I was sent by my parents to join the Baptist church choir, and I got sent home the same night, because the choir director said, "No, we can't use you . . . you go home." So that was . . . it was a memorable experience because I was convinced I couldn't sing. And I probably can't sing. On the other hand, I feel that impulse towards song, and towards music, and I'm finding now in my life that when I come to read work, I find myself moving more towards that song style, speaking, singing kind of together at the same time . . . Some preachers, or testifiers, in the black church tradition, present their sermons in exactly that way . . . I grew up in that tradition, and there's a sense in which the sermon is supposed to be chanted, almost—almost chanted as much as it is spoken. And there's room for the audience, the congregation, for the antiphonal response.[64]

Procol Harum and Peaches and Herb

In his autobiographical *Where Beauty Survived*, Clarke recalls the broad auditory background he heard growing up, mashing Mozart and Motown, Procol Harum and Peaches and Herb, and performing his own versions with his brothers to create street corner versions of the hits.[65] Thus, just as it is for Barbadian Canadian writer Austin Clarke, music largely structures and thematizes Clarke's work, what he describes to Thomas as a jazz structure: "You know, the basic structure with someone taking off on a solo performance. The improvisations, the riffs. So we have the universals, but we also have the particulars. I have seen this fluidity, not just in jazz but also in calypso and gospel music . . . in each new setting it changes form."[66] The fluidity of Clarke's style, rooted in Black disaporic musics, provides an entry point to Clarke's writing process, even if his poetry feels more formalized than free.

Oscar Peterson

While Clarke is interested in a poetry that emulates jazz and blues improvisation, his poetry often reads as incredibly structured vernacular; nevertheless, it is in playing upon the old standards with new creations that Clarke creates a bricolage of styles, often stealing or parodying musical and poetic traditions.[67] In doing so, Clarke creates an interpretive space for his poetry to function as improvisation—as an incendiary music that both pays homage and sets fire to prior traditions. Thus, Clarke can sing Nova Scotia in *Whylah Falls* with "bass blue notes," and then imagine Oscar Peterson (known as Robertson in Clarke's *Trudeau*) describing Pierre Elliott Trudeau as an iconoclast who's as unpredictable as free jazz: "Unpredictable as free jazz. / From *Native Son* to *Invisible Man*, / He shifts like ectoplasm—or Peter Pan. / His life *is* his art; a canvas / Shimmering black-and-white contrasts."[68] Clarke's opus is open to revision like jazz, mixing styles, histories, materials, and cultures together to enact an oral fusion: "Jazz: It is women who open / The gates to Canaan or Eden"; "Jazz is indelible rainbow *aquarelles*"; "Jazz is multiculti-Aboriginal-Semitic-Afro-Asian-Caucasian; "Yes, jazz is black-market, black-magic Music: / Its Voodoo fuses Malcolm X and Confucius."[69] The numerous references to musicians and orators resonate with Clarke's own Baptist upbringing and reflects his desire to be sounded, rather than simply read.

As Clarke tells Anne Compton, "For me, poetry is not only a printed form, a printed art. It is also an oral art, and it should always be. The two should never be separated. One should have a poem that reads silently as well as it does vocally."[70] Clarke has a point, for rhyme is an ancient form of both poetry and music, yet much of contemporary poetry disavows rhyme—and lyrical voice—as outdated and unsuited to contemporary verse on the faulty pretence that (post)modern poetry must challenge all subject positions. Of course, many European poets' desire to kill tradition differs greatly from that of a Black poet who desperately needs tradition, especially when one's ancestors barely survived the Middle Passage. Clarke told McLeod and me that working directly with jazz musicians on "multicultural relationships in Quebec City circa 2000" inspired him to work more with rhyme:

> And the interesting thing for me, working with D. D. [Jackson] on that project [Québécité] is, that we first began to work on it, I sent him basically free verse material and he rejected it. And said I need rhyme! I need rhyme! Now, if you're coming from any kind

of contemporary school of Canadian poetics rhyme is something you don't do. [Laughs]. It's like, no rhyme. We do not do rhyme here! Alright, this is modernism—in fact, it's post-modernism! We just don't touch it. We don't like it, we don't understand it, and we disavow it because we know it's stupid. Rhyme is ridiculous. Right? So it was really interesting that that project and D. D. in particular forced me to work with rhyme. And I found it very liberating actually.[71]

Bob Dylan, Leonard Cohen, Neil Young, and Joni Mitchell
Clarke goes on to recount that his early experiences with poetry were through trying to write songs, further influenced by his listening to the poet-songwriters of that era: Bob Dylan, Leonard Cohen, Joni Mitchell, Neil Young, and others.[72] For Clarke, "this is the way poetry was supposed to be produced—in the context of song."[73] The hybrid—music and literature, text, and voice—has always been a part of Clarke's poetic drift, reading Atwood alongside Blake, Cohen alongside Dante, and with Dylan as his base.[74]

Like Paul Lawrence Dunbar's, Clarke's poems are musical, although they are not nearly as solecistic as Dunbar's. Clarke writes many sonnets because the form, like a song, suits a direct message and style, making the words effectively present and resonant for readers. Clarke's use of iambic pentameter in his sonnets matches the da-DUM (rhythm) of a human heartbeat, a pulsing similar to that found in the bass line of many jazz standards. As Clarke told me when I interviewed him for the *Malahat Review*,

> poetry exists in the rhythm of pulse and breath; it is "mind-forged" (Blake) language given vocal (originally) expression in tune with the pace of breath and the beat of the heart. The cadences are related to the sounds conjured by the arrangements of tongue, teeth, lips, and lungs. Poetry is organic technology, a physical art—as much as is dance, save that its calisthenics are performed by abstract characters or organically by the movement of the mouth. In any event, it is the cheapest art and thus the most portable, for it can be memorized and taught to others.[75]

Clarke's incendiary poem-songs (they burn down traditions to create new ones from the flames) reject the simple segregation between song and poem—although the formalism of some of the work certainly makes it feel page-bound—with the same fierceness with which Ginsberg, Creeley, Amiri Baraka, and others largely changed the literary academy: they rooted their poetry in the people, making it akin to modern forms like rap.

Clarke describes rap—the decisive poetic form of our generation, as I argue in chapter 4—as the popular movement closest to the Beat Generation, with its ability to fuse song and poetry: "Rap and calypso and reggae, all these forms of popular music have moved very close towards a 'conscious poetics,' while at the same time trying to reach a mass audience."[76] Rap is a complex fusion of orality and postmodern technology, and while I've argued that Clarke uses traditional forms and can write rather formally, he equally can be read as innovative for his open approach towards newness, innovation, and risk-taking. He appears in fine form on "Storm" with Canadian rapper Shad. To read, to hear, and to *feel* Clarke, we need the combined listening skills of the musicologist, the historian, the performer, the citizen, and the poet.

Shad and George Elliott Clarke

III. George Elliott Clarke's Poetic Colouring Pentateuch: *Blue, Black, Red, Gold,* and *White*

Colouring in an Epic

Blue, Black, Red, Gold, and *White* are stand-alone works that share similar ideas, such as the Roman Numeral series (which began in *Blue* and continues in *Black*), "Self-Portrait" poems (three to date), and a familiar cast of poet inspirations like Ezra Pound, Allen Ginsberg, Derek Walcott, and key figures such as Miles Davis and Malcolm X, who both appear (almost like muses) throughout the books.

In "Cool Politics: Styles of Honour in Malcolm X and Miles Davis," Clarke contends that "X and Davis illustrate, despite their flaws, the possibility for the revitalization of non-sexist and life-enhancing chivalric-martial concepts such as virtue, gallantry, and honour, all of which can be used to 'fight the powers that be.' But my other major reason for wishing to reactivate these concepts is that they continue to motivate many black males, including intellectuals."[77] Clarke works against the reification of these figures into "Warhol-like pop idols," as well as the phallocentrism and violence associated with X and Davis that led to them being blamed—like modern-day rappers—for the various ills for which young, Black-delineated youths in urban environments are often held responsible. Rather, as protean figures of cool styling, X and Davis become, as Clarke contends, exemplary and archetypal champions for young Black males to model themselves after in spheres of religion and music, "spheres in which the masterful and the triumphant exude confidence, poise, purpose, style—in short, 'cool.'" These modes of behaviour, within visions of justice that determine masculine ideals, while problematic at times (such as Miles Davis's physical abuse of multiple women, explored further in the subsequent chapter), provide masculine codes (and signs of the "cool") in a manner that "might assist survival." Given that Clarke's poetic trilogy dually interrogates and embraces various styles of Black masculinity, Davis and X, among other figures, are important signifiers for Black creativity, and given that I agree with Paul Gilroy, and others, that race is not episteme, Davis and X are global signifiers—in Canada, even—of radical thought and alternative possibilities for creative citizenship.

For Clarke, X's and Davis's principles are vaguely manifested as a fluid Black dialogue even as they have been suppressed by the pages of history. It is within this negotiation of traditions, of written and oral culture, and of a diversity of speakers that Clarke asserts an "ethics of antiphony"—a kind of ideal communicative moment in the relationship between the performer and the crowd that we find in blues, jazz, hip hop, and other Black diasporic musics. Paul Gilroy contends that "black music cannot be reduced to a fixed dialogue between a thinking racial self and a stable racial community ... The calls and responses no longer converge in the tidy patterns of secret, ethnically encoded dialogue."[78] In creating an assemblage of poetic voices, Clarke sets himself up as witness, DJ, and cultural translator.

This very polyphony and cosmopolitan Blackness, as well as the common aesthetic qualities of each work, is what links together the elements of Clarke's colouring oeuvre. On a large-scale reverberation, *Blue, Black, Red, Gold,* and *White* are laid out with similar sections (each collection contains different representational aspects of its colour). Furthermore, stylistic similarities echo throughout: each collection contains figures who make reappearances and then exit stage left (for instance, Ezra Pound, Miles Davis, Pushkin, Mao, and Malcolm X); sonnets, blues poems, and other traditional verse poems appear; the dedicative poetics and signifying strategies remain the same; blues and jazz vernaculars and "cool" stylings soundtrack each work; all contain visual images (photos); explanations and inspirations are outlined in each work; and a consummate concern with beauty appears in each book, as Clarke's concern is "to recognize beauty when you see it and to not be afraid."[79]

Clarke displays his concern with beauty in his choice of epigraphs. In *Blue* there is an epigraph from Keats, "*What the imagination seizes as Beauty must be Truth*" [italics in original]. In *Trudeau* we get a quotation from Pound, "beauty is difficult." In *I&I*, an epigraph from Pain Not Bread, a poets' collective that includes Roo Borson and Kim Maltman, starts off the book: "This world is too beautiful to be true, and too beautiful not to be true." In *Red,* we get two more epigraphs: one from Frantz Fanon, "I stop there, for who can tell me what beauty is," and one from Ezra Pound, "Beauty must never be explained." In *Gold,* "Beauty ... is the sole business of poetry" (from Robinson Jeffers) and "*na kelu'lk we'jitu* (I find Beauty)" (from Rita Joe). And in *White* we get several. Clarke's preoccupation with beauty in his work connects with Romantic intervention:

> What is beauty? What is truth? The age-old concerns. I think the Romantic intervention, which said, "we have to make art out of some understanding of beauty," and also a political art out of some understanding of beauty, remains germane, remains absolutely de rigueur for artists and writers today. The question has not been answered yet [laughs] ... Maybe it can't be answered in any kind of final way or final satisfactory way. So that's really what I'm pursuing.[80]

It is this search for beauty as truth that makes Clarke's poetics (particularly his colouring books) so provocative and engaging. The poems in each book suit their elemental colouring. For instance, in *Red*, Clarke is concerned with the representational possibilities of the colour red, citing Mao as an influence. In Mao's poems and lyrics, and in Chinese lyrics more generally, the lyric is a translation of *t'zu*, which is a particular style of poetry written to fit a melody. And while we need to be careful not to reduce Clarke's Africadianness to Chinese poetry, thinking of Clarke's poetry as entwined with multiple senses—namely, the visual and the auditory—takes us to the heart of Clarke's engaged practice. Listen: *"Art* neutralizes our pain / til only strong *Beauty's* left."[81]

Blue Lyrics

"Blue is John Coltrane—immortal Coltrane—
recording *Blue Trane*"

—CLARKE, "I. I, 111," in *Blue*

John Coltrane

With an icy blueness and a Black-blues lyricism, Clarke dabs his poetic brush in a sinuous palette of blues: indigo, ultramarine, and cobalt walls, with filaments of sapphire, azure, and blue-red veins. Expansively put, *Blue* confounds its own blueness. Perhaps nowhere in Clarke's large poetic catalogue is the blues matrix more apparent than in *Blue*: a work in five poetic spectrums ("Black Eclogues," "Red Satires," "Gold Sapphics," "Blue Elegies," and "Ashen Blues") that combines the rhythms of gospel and blues and shantytown vernacular with the highly aesthetic poetic tradition of Western literature. Rhapsodic in its composition, *Blue* performs poetic difference: with virtuosity, Clarke navigates the alteration between the self and the other within the subjectivity of one poetic voice.[82] Mixing the British poetic tradition and Black vernacularism with the music of blues and jazz, Clark explores, parodies, and interrogates the aesthetics of poetic history through interpretative renditions (reminiscent of an extended jazz solo). Clarke's self-reflexive, often self-aggrandizing approach to the politics of poetic representation allows him to assert a mixed identity (like the wild yet well-spoken Caliban of Shakespeare's *The Tempest*), and—often ambivalently, through negation—to challenge dominant discourses of the Western literary canon.[83]

Clarke's challenging of dominant discourses involves a syncretism of forms, such as when he infuses the traditional sonnet with blues rhythms in the opening poem of *Blue*. "Negation," from the "Black Eclogues" section,♭ opens the collection of poems with Clarke painting himself as other (turning xenophobic fear to poetic advantage), describing himself as a "Denigrated, negative, a local / Caliban ... Nofaskoshan Negro," thus creating a marginalized space to perform poetic surgery: "To take apart poetry like a heart."[84] "Negation," like many poems in *Blue* (and elsewhere), uses the sonnet form to emphasize the ideas of succession, resistance, and reclamation. Clarke's accentuation on the consonants "n" and "m" in the opening lines, "*Le nègre* negated, meager, *c'est moi*: / Denigrated, negative," does more than stress the beat. These lines play with the French etymology of *nègre*, which can pejoratively be reduced from Negro to "ni**er." Working against the grotesque and racist assertion of the word, Clarke aligns with the reclamation of *nègre*, particularly negritude as used by Fanon, Césaire, and others. Although this process can be overwhelming and grotesquely assertive, it is important to recognize that Frantz Fanon and Aimé Césaire—respectively in *The Wretched of the Earth* and *A Tempest*—use negation/*négritude* in order to renounce colonial connotations, reclaim identity, and usurp imperialism in all forms through a series of inversions and dialectics.[85] The opening poem of *Blue* establishes that Clarke will negate and master received traditions and identities, editing in a hybrid poetics with an improvisatory spirit.

♭ The opening section of Clarke's *Blue*, "Black Eclogues," is an allusion to the three major works by Latin poet Virgil. The works are dramatic and mythic interpretations of revolutionary change in Rome between 44 and 38 BC. In staging the opening of his work with this title, Clarke suggests that his poetry dramatizes poetic and historic change.

Miles Davis   While it might be hard to read the poems in *Blue* as similar to jazz in their improvisation techniques—regard here Miles Davis's *On the Corner*, which fuses electronic and synthesized funk with modal jazz—it does help to frame the type of tactility and freedom that Clarke's visceral poetry attempts to represent by fusing blues, jazz, and folk rhythms with Africanist and British poetic traditions. Furthermore, we can think of Clarke's editing and poetic processes as part of the performance, similar to the ways in which Teo Macero's editing in Davis's *On the Corner* and *Bitches Brew* is central to those works as bricolage. In blending the oral within the textual (using heavy amounts of alliteration and internal rhyme), Clarke congruently highlights the form of the page-poem, as well as the phonetics of sound poetry, to create a listening experience that marries song with text.[86] Clarke's poetry aspires to the status of oral narration/song. Clarke describes that "[his] strength[s] as a poet, whatever they are, derive from the sonic universe of African American verse and song."[87] As popular song often weaves multiple instruments, voices, and chords into a sonic holism, so does the poetry of *Blue* through epigraphs in an intricate web of dialogism and negation.

Through negation, *Blue* interrogates Blackness/whiteness as politically and culturally constructed categories. In appropriating voice freely, Clarke describes his ability to explore a heteroglot Blackness, illuminating the complex nature of Black identity in Canada, riffing on Shakespeare's *Twelfth Night*: "In Canada, some are born black, some acquire blackness, and others have blackness thrust upon them."[88] Clarke uses this variety of styles to create an in-between, hybridized identity, which is formed through his understanding and appropriation of British, American, Black, and white voices. Clarke invokes a plurality of voices to create an intentionally troubling, often ambivalent approach to otherness, ultimately making the past more resonant, notably in his poems that detail the history of Africville.

Africville is one of the earliest Black communities in Canada, located on the south shore of the Bedford Basin in Nova Scotia. Despite the promise of Africville as a safe haven—a Canaan—the Black settlers there were treated with persistent prejudice and were "assailed by bureaucrats and politicians desiring either to rid Halifax of a so-called 'segregated ghetto' or to hijack precious waterfront property for industrial use ... a village which was condemned, again and again, as a 'slum' before it was finally condemned to die."[89] In 1964, the land in Africville was expropriated for industrial use, and within five years the residents of Africville had been relocated and their homes demolished. Ana Maria Fraile-Marcos writes that the treatment of Africville and its residents "underlines Canadian hypocrisy regarding the management of race and difference."[90] Thus, it is the work of scholars, poets, and activists to commemorate and reimagine these communities so that they may exist more fully in the present. The original site of Africville was declared a National Historic Site of Canada, and a replica of the Seaview Baptist Church (demolished in 1969) opened as a museum in 2011. When Black Loyalists and refugees were given land in 1783 and 1812, they were not given any title/deed, a deliberate oversight that was only addressed in 2017. The Nova Scotia government has since announced funding to help people from five historically Black communities to gain legal ownership of land that has been in their families for generations.[91] These acts of repatriation are important, as "commemorative events in relation to Halifax's Africville" have facilitated a "surge of interest in African Nova Scotian History" and an "outpouring of attention to New Brunswick's Black populations."[92]

There is a rooted desire in Clarke's work to have ignored histories sounded in the present, and this includes the early history of Africville. In poems like "African Petition (1783)," "1933," "Bio: Black Baptist/Bastard," and "Antiphony," Clarke provides historical accounts of Canada's mistreatment of Black folk. It is no coincidence that the most historical poems in *Blue* immediately follow "Negation," a poem that reclaims poetry from a Black perspective. In these poems Clarke bears witness to Canada's own tumultuous history and malignant treatment of Black and African Canadian people. "Africadian Petition (1783)," which directly follows "Negation," comes out of the American Revolutionary War (1775–83) and deals explicitly with the Black Loyalists (the Nova Scotians/*Nofaskoshans*) who settled in Africville after the Revolutionary War. Clarke works with actual phrases extracted from letters written by Black Nova

Scotians after they settled in Sierra Leone in 1792, except he imagines these Black Loyalists writing to the colonial powers in Nova Scotia. The poetics are controlled (written almost entirely in quintains), and the language is solecistic, capturing the everyday voices of those who are angered by the lies of a government that promised them prosperity: "We's Dis Gusted by govvermint, / Discomfotable . . . You forgit us, so we be Nothing— . . . your Cownsil's muddying Lyes?" Throughout the poems in the "Black Eclogues" section of *Blue* I am reminded of Caribbean American writer and civil rights activist Audre Lorde's statement and title of one her essays, "Poetry Is Not a Luxury." What is poetry to those who are simply trying to survive? Clarke suggests that these early African Canadian experiences are the stuff of poetry and that their "salvos of pain and rough joy" sound a blues truth.[93]

"1933," the poem that follows "African Petition (1783)," concerns two historical dates—not only 1933 but also 1917, the year of the Halifax Explosion. On a December morning in 1917, the SS *Mont-Blanc*, a French cargo ship loaded with wartime explosives, collided with a Norwegian vessel, the SS *Imo*, in the Narrows, a shipping channel connecting Halifax Harbour to Bedford Basin. The cataclysmic explosion destroyed one square mile of the city's North End, killing 2,000 people and injuring another 9,000. Africville, just north of the explosion, dodged the brunt of the explosion, but the small, frail homes there were heavily damaged—still standing but essentially in ruins. Hugh MacLennan's canonical *Barometer Rising* (1941), which is centred on the Halifax Explosion, skips over the devastating effects this explosion had on the already neglected Africville. Clarke uses the event—through a stanza-long hypotactic description of the "rancid, gamy houses . . . left-over dying / from '17's Explosion" to tell the story of "Indigo Sampson," a "pop-eyed drunkard" who allegedly killed two white boys. On 19 July 1933, the bodies of two young brothers were found a short distance apart by the railway tracks that ran near their home on the outskirts of Halifax. After an inconclusive coroner's inquest—they had very likely been killed by a train—the police and RCMP arrested Daniel Perry Sampson, an Africadian First World War veteran, for the murder of the two boys. Clarke's poem details the racism surrounding the event and reimages the incident as "two white small boys who accost him, zestfully, / as 'n-i-g-g-e-r.'"[94] The casual execution of Sampson at the end of "1933" reflects the casual displacement of African Canadian people, which provoked a violent response to their disempowered position on the part of some African Canadians (see Clarke's *Execution Poems*); furthermore, the poem hinges on the advent of the Second World War and the casual killing of Jews and racial others by the Nazi regime. Clarke's poems, for all their Tarantino-esque revisionism, concern historical witness, working explicitly with a *"History* [that] fell upon us [African Canadians] like the lash." At the end of "Bio: Black Baptist/Bastard," he writes: "Listen closely: I am trying to cry / That's my condemned blood on the page."[95]

Performing a Calculated Offensive

In 2012, Gaspereau Press reissued *Blue*. In reviewing the work for the *Chronicle Herald*, critic Philip K. Thompson expresses his fear that much of Clarke's resistance borders on "hate speech" (a claim I will investigate from a different angle in *White*). Thompson claims:

> Despite vocabularic genius, and his personal kindness and warmth, there is a Malcolm X violence in some of the more powerful racial rants, which properly decry horrific treatment of blacks in America (and even "Nofaskosha") but sometimes approach "hate speech" toward the white race. For some readers, regardless of colour, these poems may cross the line. Anger is legitimate poetic expression, but unhealed anger between races through the millennia causes great destruction still.[96]

Set aside Thompson's spurious reading of race, his equating of Malcolm X with violence, his choice not to focus on the love poems for "white" women, and his lack of understanding of how irony/parody functions in *Blue*. Let's focus instead on what led Thompson to make such a (mostly misguided) claim. Thompson does not even commit to commenting on which poems border on "hate speech," although he is likely referring to poems such as "Miles Davis: An Autobiography," whose title indicates a clash with an original host voice, or "Calculated Offensive," a poem with a clearly ironic title, and one of Clarke's most virulent—and polemical—poems in *Blue*. Having assigned "Calculated Offensive" as a poem for close reading to my own students, I can see how a few students in the mostly white class might assume that Clarke hated white people. Clarke, of course, does not hate white people, and Thompson's tired trope of reverse racism, which fails to correlate racism with power or to differentiate between representation and reality, is far too literal.

In *Blue*, Clarke uses troubling language in an active way to challenge his reader to engage with the poem. In "Calculated Offensive" he places diverse poetic practices (English and African American/Canadian) in juxtaposed dialogues (tossing European praxis into a poetic fire in order to blacken it), often with corporeal manifestations that are intended to offend many of his readers: "Put Europe to the torch / All of Michelangelo's dripping, syphilitic saints, / all of Sappho's insipid, anorexic virgins."[97] Sure, there is virulence here, but there is also a musical play with language. Notice the clever rhyming of "syphilitic" and "insipid." Perhaps most elusively, Clarke weaves his voice of poetic otherness though engendered imagery, moulding poems of the type that are composed "when two sick melodies fuck," referring to Davis's own mixing of classical and jazz traditions, as well as Black and white musicians (such as Bill Evans) in his group.[98] The visceral and violent imagery in "Miles Davis: An Autobiography" often deconstructs masculinity (while affirming its creative and social milieu vis-à-vis an archetypal character such as Miles Davis) by performing gender in its most sadistic and primal constructions of social hegemony. Clarke describes a type (not the only one) of rhythm he craves in "L'Assassinat" (Miles Davis) as a "Roaring whore whose left eye was / Ripped, who took three skull fractures, a cracked / Jawbone, whose cussed clit was severed . . . because of evil love."[99] The reader encountering Clarke's viscerally engendered language will undoubtedly question its function, wondering how the paradox of "evil love" functions didactically. Clarke often plays with race or gender to draw attention to the various vicissitudes of constructed identities.♭ Clarke performs/lampoons and draws energy from the proximity between masculine bravado (such as in Davis's writing) and a creative spirit of resistance.

Clarke's often hyperbolic poetry is exemplified by the elegy for Japanese writer Mishima Yukio, who committed ritualistic suicide (*seppuku*) in 1970. The poem "II. i" helps flesh out the practice of listening and performance as an inherently embodied act. By performing double articulation, relating a corporeal pun on the act of *seppuku* (which involves gutting oneself), as well as poetry as an embodied intuition, Clarke's poem constructs and negates the physiognomic act of poetry within its destructive potential: "the agitated, salacious fire / of *Poetry* in the gut."[100] We are left feeling *Blue* in the pits of our guts, as an embodied act of listening, highlighting that all poetic constructions of identity are in flux, constantly fleeting and changing in the construction of "new." Paralleling Miles Davis, Clarke breaks away from previously defined traditions, while still relying on their form (such as the sonnet) to create more complex identities. In the liner notes of *Bitches Brew*, Ralph Gleason argues that "electric music is the music of this culture and in the breaking away (not breaking down) from previously assumed forms a new kind of music is emerging."‡

This newness challenges modernity's attendant disavowals of the past in favour of a poetics that not only traverses but embodies the past. Hence, one of Clarke's poetic idols, the modernist *par excellence*, Ezra Pound, becomes "unsavoury Pound, who liked / to put 'negros' in

---

♭ Clarke contemporizes this notion, writing a sixteen-line variation of the sonnet in support of trans rights and pronouns. The poem, "Pronouncement on Pronouns" (from *White*) is a riposte to attacks on Transgender nomenclature (particularly by the likes of Incel celeb Jordan Peterson), and supports identity as fluid: "Transgender's transgressive because it frees / *Masculine* and feminine, as *they* please." Clarke, *White*, 101.

‡ This sentiment is echoed by Miles Davis in his *Autobiography*, where he argues that electric instruments have nothing to do with bad or good music: "All these purists are walking around talking about how electronic instruments will ruin music. Bad music is what will ruin music, not the instruments the musicians choose to play" (295).

lower-case (in their place)." Clarke extracts a blues truth from an onerous canon that plays with the words and prejudices of dead white men even as he feels indebted largely to that tradition. "Onerous Canon" is suitably dedicated to Derek Walcott who, like Clarke, blackened the canon he inherited, while making room for Black voices to be heard, as Walcott (like Clarke), performs with "a veriloquous, unadulterated voice, / extracting black blues from a yellowed Oxford."[101] The dedications in *Blue*, and the poems written in *à la manière de*, are telling signs that parody is at work, which is why we need to be careful when reading Clarke not to judge him (as a preacher of hate) too quickly without knowing the history a given piece draws from, and for what purpose.

For example, a poem *à la manière de* Malcolm X, or Miles Davis, without sampling their style (lodged with Clarke's own poetic persona) would fall rather flat. Writing *à la manière de* Amiri Baraka in "Calculated Offensive" lets us know that there is a certain countercanonicity and Black Arts Nationalism at work in the poem; it also lets us know that Clarke is riffing on a tradition that Black folk in the New World were forced to learn at the suppression of their own. Baraka's poetry provides a good example of how poetry can move through blues and jazz to Black chant and graphic sound. As M.L. Rosenthal wrote, "No American poet since Pound has come closer to making poetry and politics reciprocal forms of action."[102] For Baraka, art was a weapon of revolution. Like "Somebody Blew Up America," Baraka's poem "Black Art" provides an *Umwalzung*—that is, revolution—through a complete overturning of prior poetic systems, enacting one of the most ferocious Black chants ever to appear on the page.[b] While we should condemn Baraka's anti-Semitism, which

---

[b] Baraka is one of the most important poets and music critics of the twentieth century: full stop. The controversy and backlash over his public reading of his poem "Somebody Blew Up America," as well as some of the homophobic, anti-Semitic, and misogyny of his middle period poems, often overshadow the incredible firebrand prowess and construction of Baraka's cerebral and polemical thinking. Baraka lived a very tumultuous life and his poetry and social activism reflect that. While most of his poetry isn't available on *Spotify*, you can listen to "Black Art" on YouTube: https://www.youtube.com/watch?v=Dh2P-tIEH_w

sadly the poem has in abundance, "Black Art" provides an improvisatory chant in the form of a free jazz poem.[103] Baraka's poetic violence disavows lyric voice in favour of a gruffer, more militant poetics: "Poems are bullshit unless they are / teeth or trees or lemons piled / on a step ... Fuck poems ... We want 'poems that kill.' / Assassin poems." The onomatopoeic chanting machine guns are informed by the free jazz tradition (he performed this poem on different occasions with improvising musicians) as the language itself often breaks down into Black chant, into anacrusis, into the very sounds of violence enacted upon the poem: "Airplane poems, rrrrrrrrrrrrrrrr / rrrrrrrrrrrrrr... tuhtuhtuh tuhtuhtuh tuhtuhtuh / ... rrrrrrrrrrrrrrrr ... Setting fire and death to / whities ass."[104] Hardly an indictment or appraisal of the poem's content, its form, along with Baraka's opus, altered the course of African American literary culture. It didn't merely blacken the canon: it blew it into a million pieces.

Ultimately, compared to Baraka's "Black Art," Clarke's "Calculated Offensive" is timid; it is certainly less violent, and certainly it is not racist "hate speech." Rather, it challenges anti-Black racism through parody and an extremely furious male voice; furthermore, one must remember that poetic violence (the burning of a canon) is a perfectly natural response to the very real violence Black folk faced at the hands of crude slave masters, colonizers, and imperialists. Both poems retain the need to establish counter-canons (for Baraka it was the establishment of a Black Arts movement) that can be defined without non-Black sources. Counter-canons can, as Gates writes, "*create* a tradition, as well as to define and preserve it."[105] All canons are by nature exclusionary, but sometimes that exclusion is a response to historical omission. Essentially, Baraka, using the pronoun "we" throughout "Black Arts" to connect to a larger Black community, searches for "a black poem / And a / Black World. / Let the world be a Black Poem / And let All Black People Speak This poem / Silently / or LOUD."[106] The full irony of the opening line of Clarke's "Calculated Offensive," "To hell with Pound! / What we desire is African: / Europe is so septic, it seeps poisons," is hypocritically felt, along lines of parody, in the "Red Satires" section, where Clarke reads Pound at his tomb (with an analogous picture of Clarke at Pound's tomb, reading his [or Pound's] cantos in deep contemplation), sifting his "*Cantos*, pound for pound, / To ferret out fresh, untainted measures."[107]

It is in these contradictory moments that the reader might be tempted to denounce Clarke's approach as a totalizing principle that prevents him from having to clarify ethically grounded statements. However, Clarke does not believe that abrogating a form, especially if inherited, is necessarily totalizing, saying that the sonnet form is in fact postcolonial, and asking, "now what can we do with it?"[108] Essentially, Clarke, like Baraka often did, is free to adapt, revise, and combine traditions. If Clarke's poetry carried an ID card it would read something like, "Multicultural Jazz Man." Not that such polyphony allows Clarke to evade critical engagement of or criticism for his choice of language, for it is such contradictions in *Blue* that make our reading of his poems engaging, calculatedly offensive, and often confrontational.

Kevin McNeilly describes Clarke's poetry as an "enticing tangle of contradictions and confrontations, things like a vicious delicacy or a brutal lyricism."[109] When I asked Clarke about his confrontational poetics, I unintentionally asked him to defend himself as poet:

> I still feel, or at least I felt at the time I was working on *Blue*, especially, that if there is such a thing as a Canadian poetics, an Anglo-Canadian poetics, that it was still a little bit sedate, a little bit. And that's despite the interventions of Michael Ondaatje and Irving Layton, etcetera, etcetera. And, I felt, maybe wrongly, at that point in my life in the 1990s, and maybe because of the fact I was in the United States – land of the free, home of the brave, blah, blah, blah, blah – that it was ok to strike out and attempt a more visceral, a more vivid, a louder, a more gruff, a more in your face kind of poetic . . . But the experience of writing *Blue*, in particular, was an effort to break away from what I had considered an imprisoning mode of discourse that almost insisted on politesse – on being polite – in our poetry . . . I had an audience here that might question or might be bothered by some of the things I chose to write. But . . . that was the whole point: particularly, *Blue*, *Black*, and maybe a little bit of *Red*. Saying: "Yeah, we can claim this space."[110]

Clarke goes on to say that as a Black poet he should be allowed "to speak forthrightly out of the cultural traditions that are important to [him]" and to inject that voice, sensibility, and musicality into Canadian poetry.¹¹¹ What is ultimately misguided about Philip K. Thompson's review of *Blue* is that he reads Clarke *too* literally, falling into the clichéd stereotyped camp that Black poets write straightforward performance pieces, when in truth there is a lot of play, revision, and high intellect, even in Clarke's most offensive (and calculated) poems. Furthermore, using the sonnet and European traditions as he masters them, or effectively blackens them, creates an aesthetic that allows for both cerebral and performative engagement. Clarke's aesthetic is both neoclassical and postmodern, a quasi-improvisation and quasi-stylized vernacular, composed of 60 percent Miles Davis and 40 percent Wynton Marsalis.♭

Such experimentation among forms (European and African American/Black /Canadian) situates *Blue* as work of constant revision that could be accused of diluting poetic purity. Similarly, Miles Davis's rock/jazz fusion record *Bitches Brew* was viewed by neoclassicists upon its release "as selling out jazz's cultural dignity and musical seriousness to the prurient vagaries of a craven popular music business eager to cater to the worst longings of the youth culture market."¹¹² Clarke explores poetic authenticity in *Blue* with modernist priorities in his melding of different traditions, echoing Pound's notion to "Day by day make it new / cut underbrush, / pile the logs / keep it growing."¹¹³ Clarke told me that Pound remains important to his continued desire of "making it new":

> Pound is inescapable because he created the modern syntax, the modern grammar, the modern diction, for expression in English-language poetry, and he did it by transplanting into English the "best practices" of the best authors from the half-a-dozen

---

♭ Wynton Marsalis is often viewed as a traditionalist whose style reflects and attempts to preserve neoclassical approaches to jazz, while Miles Davis is generally viewed as a jazz innovator, whose own music was infused with high levels of hybridity, especially in the later part of his career.

languages that he knew the innards of. Despite—or to spite—his anti-Semitism and other vile prejudices, Pound was actually multicultural—an aesthete—who long-ranged through other *langues* to import into English their strengths of brevity or clarity or impiety, thus creating Imagism out of his scholarly "Orientalism" and Vorticism (the literary form of Cubism) out of his Esperanto poetics. One of the strengths of the Pound corpus is—as it is in Bob Dylan's different output (or that of Miles Davis or David Bowie)—variety. Pound can turn out a sestina of medieval cannonades, a lily-delicate haiku, a *film noir*-spirit, Laforguean quatrain, and/or a Latinate long poem of loosened blank verse (*vers libéré*), not to mention straightforward songs and prose-poems. He didn't only follow Confucius in saying, "Make it new," but was always "making anew" and trying new forms.[114]

Clarke then describes how his work *Canticles* (inspired by Pound's Cantos) is a "stereophonic collage" of characters, and indeed it is as he weaves an epic catalogue of voices including Hannibal, Harriet "Moses" Tubman, Marie-Josèphe Angélique, and Phillis Wheatley, and revises and reworks history with the powers of a firebrand poet in full control of his craft. In *Blue*, we see the early working of such cataloguing in poetic approach and speech.

In his poem "Nu(is)ance," which is dedicated to Wayde Compton, Clarke asserts that his poetic aesthetic is at least doubled—"Jabbering double-crossing doubletalk"—and that he would "rather stutter a bastard's language / Only spoken in gutters, a broken, / Vulgar, Creole screech, loud with bawling, slurring" because it is "literal, guttural *Poetry*."[115] In claiming his (and Compton's) poetic technique as a cross-fertilization of languages, code-switching between forms, reduced even to auditory screeches, Clarke assembles and gathers new forms of poetic vernacular. The epigraph to Wayde Compton is apt, given that Compton's work creates poetry out of a variety of styles, the same way that turntablism assembles a polyvocality of voices in hip hop. Home, for Clarke, is both a diasporic experience that cuts across borders and a rooting in the specificity of a Black/Africadian context.

Like Baraka, Clarke often uses the collective "we" as a rhetorical device to draw in or exclude the reader depending on their ethnicity or political identification.[116] However, because his work encompasses both the history of Black Canadians and their relation to the poetic canon (or his uneasy relation to it), academics and a larger listening audience are brought into Clarke's ambivalent negotiation of poetic traditions. Like an antiphon—the ritual responsory by a choir or congregation, or the call and response in music—Clarke's poetics respond to both history and literary canons. In "Antiphony" the works of canonized poets such as Wordsworth, Yeats, Chaucer, Shakespeare, Milton, and Hopkins are reduced to dusty, purposeless words that lack direct antiphony because they no longer participate in the dialogic method that Clarke's speaker invokes.[117] "Antiphony" is a calling back on educational colonization that "bash[es] grammar into gravel" with a speaker that pronounces "tragedy was our slavery."[118] This aspect of witnessing evokes the DuBoisian idea of double consciousness (Clarke as Black poet and academic working within and outside the literary canon) and redresses academicized literature by throwing words into a poetic fire and reshaping them with an outstretched diction directed towards a larger community. The epigraph to Austin C. Clarke, the first Black writer to publish a novel in mainstream Canada, is an antiphonic moment that highlights Clarke's imperative to speak to a community with markedly anti-racist principles.

Like the poem "Blank Sonnet" (from *Whylah Falls*), "Antiphony" utilizes a call-and-response technique, with Clarke at the centre as witness, to juxtapose stark images of perceived whiteness and Blackness with the English poetic canon. "Blank Sonnet," which emulates the traditional Shakespearean sonnet form, collapses on itself as the antithetical love letter because it becomes the very thing it renounces: beautifully crafted love poetry that evokes a quasi-Blackness from its flames. Xavier, the speaker of the poem, desires the "slow, sure collapse of language / Washed out by alcohol" rather than the cadenced verse of English poets.[119] Similarly, "Onerous Canon," dedicated to Derek Walcott, highlights the anxiety of influence that Clarke's poetic project confronts, as well as Walcott's, and that of Black writers in general. The poem situates archetypal poets of the Western canon (Yeats, Keats, Claire, and Pound) in defamilarized positions that compromise their authority: "whiny, beseeching Keats, / who should've drunk some *Alexander Keith's*." However, "Onerous Canon" is occupied less with the anxiety of influence, than with how an ambiguous abrogation of poetic figures can function to render Clarke's voice as distinctly and uniquely Other. By negating the voices of canonized poets, "(Auden in the margins, / Eliot, Yeats, and Pound in the dungeon)," Clarke creates an ambivalent space (his voiced fused with Walcott's) that allows him to interrogate the act of writing from a space of Blackness within a tradition of whiteness, remixing both polarities.[120]

Antiphony in Clarke's poetics—like the poem of the same title—anticipates the response of the reader, as well as a symbolic larger Black community whose voices have been suppressed intentionally by mainstream society. Toni Morrison describes the practice of antiphony as that "which symbolizes and anticipates," which is what Clarke does when he responds to the call of Black Nova Scotians who couldn't care less about British poetry.[121] For the labourers and gypsum miners described in "Antiphony," Shakespeare meant nothing, for how could he? Rather, "Shakespeare came down to us as *Black Horse* beer," reminding us of Lorde's refrain: poetry is not a luxury.[122] The fact that the poem uses imperfect iambic and much alliteration and inner rhyme accentuates the musicality of a seemingly quotidian people whose unrecorded traditions prove just as musical as any that have been written down. As Clarke told *Canadian Literature*, "In the poem, I question the value of my allegiance to British poetry when my community has been illiterate—and exploited and oppressed by British imperialists and their Canadian descendants."[123] Clarke's investigation of his dual inheritance as a poet and the more *blue* vernacular of his Africadian inheritance—he uses improvisation as a strategy to find synthesis between the two—are together what make the conversation between divergent cultures most fruitful in *Blue*, and elsewhere. As Clarke writes, "I also, suddenly, heard all those countrified, Negro voices as Miltonic, Shakespearean, bluesy, epic, classical, and simply, lyrical."[124] Clarke is no L=A=N=U=A=G=E poet, as his desire to pen poems like songs is ultimately a hope to respond to and be heard by his community.

Such poetic antiphony is why in one moment Clarke can write a bawdy blues poem about interracial sex, "À Dany Laferrière," *à la manière* de Sade, that speaks, "Christ, I'd rather torch a Church and sink in Hell / To sink in her just once, that blond slut . . . Her ass, her white panties winking swank cunt," and then write a sweet sensual poem that connects beauty to poetry, akin to how Coltrane plays, in "Naima:"♭

John Coltrane

> Naima. . .
> Lawd, have mercy,
> Lawd, have mercy, gal.
>
> Either our Poetry closes
> aflame—
>
> or
>
> a-flowering.[125]

Clarke's poetics closes "aflame" or opens "a-flowering"—both tell us something about the poetic act. By weaving a plurality of voices (in both Eurological and Afrological traditions), Clarke challenges us to relisten to history. It is through close listening that we make sense of the ambivalent, seemingly inconsequential moments in *Blue*. In this sense, listening as a sense is described by Jean-Luc Nancy as "always to be on the edge of meaning."[126] In negotiating meaning in *Blue*, we participate as listeners in making sense of the act of sense-making. These moments of sense-negotiation are tactilely represented on the

---

♭ "Naima" is a ballad composed by John Coltrane in 1959 from the album *Giant Steps*. The piece was named after his wife at the time, Juanita Naima Grubbs. Compared to the other pieces on *Giant Steps*, "Naima" is particularly restrained, comprised of a slow melody with a brief piano solo.

page: "A pen burns paper." However, as with any listening practice, Clarke's final words in the collection acknowledge the transitory nature of all human expression with a polemic finish and inevitable rise from the flames: "Every poem is its own pyre, flamboyant, / The smoking words laying waste to *Time*."[127] To return to some of my students' own confused readings of "Calculated Offensive," it should be noted that for the few students who felt either hurt or confused by Clarke's poem, the majority found the poem, along with *Blue*, engaging for the fiery nature of Clarke's nuanced poetics. The calculated offensives and antiphonic moments in *Blue* are, like every book, a closing and an opening: Clarke's *Blue* somehow manages to open "a-flowering" even when it closes "aflame."

Black Power

"and I know how various yet unchanging / Blackness is"

—CAROLYN M. RODGERS, "What Color Is Lonely," 266

Black is the colour of coal, of humanity, of ebony, of the outer limits of outer space. It is the opposite of white finality. The poems in *Black* (told in eight sections riffing on "black") are bold, brash, and boisterous and continue many of the ideas in *Blue*. Again, we encounter poems about poetry and Blackness, and the Roman Numeral series continues (IV–VII). Miles Davis reappears, and Clarke reads another poem at Pound's tomb. Yet the collection gets a little more personal than *Blue*, and, given that Malcolm X is one of *Black*'s central symbolic figures, the lyricism is surprisingly less vicious, the offences softer. Nevertheless, *Black* begins with a hanging ("George & Rue: Coda") that picks up from *Execution Poems*, dedicated to the hanging of George and Rufus Hamilton in 1949. Established early in *Black* is a concern again with re-examining history—for example, the racism, poverty, and vindictive justice system is more central than the Hamiltons' actual crime—as well as a musical play with language: "The Two young Negro men, unhinged, / Swing lazily to a bluesgrass,

Dixieland tune."[128] While *Blue* focused more on the past, influenced by Clarke's experience growing up in the 1960s in Nova Scotia and living and teaching in the United States, *Black* feels more confessional (George and Rue were his cousins). In all five colouring books (with more on the way), Clarke manages to capture the experience of a Black man's political and personal indignation at the injustices of history. He also pauses often—equivalent to a musical fermata—to appreciate the accumulated beauty of art over the (p)ages. In *Black* we hear the many musics of Clarke: the Black neo-Protestant Baptist, influenced by gospel; the expert listener of African American musics; and the operatic classicist who writes librettos.

Aside from the musicality in the colouring books, there are unique emotional resonances in the realm of each colour. *Blue* might be canvassed on censorship, *Black* on race, *Red* on the erotic, *Gold* on wisdom, and *White* on making more explicit the connection between beauty and justice, and all the colours together create an irresolute epic like Pound's own *Cantos*. As Clarke told CBC Books in 2013,

> I have tended to write narrative poems, narrative collections, and plays and libretti for operas. Those projects have tended to dominate most of my output ... But I also find myself writing the nature poems, the love poems, the political poems, the historical poems, and then the question is, what do I do with them? They don't belong in the projects, so these colouring books, as I'm now calling them, just seemed to be the right place to put them ... I'm not a painter, I'm not an artist, but colours speak to me in a literary and psychological way.[129]

Furthermore, I think we can expand Baker's blues matrix to include the semiotics of colour and the criss-crossing impulses between the colours that bleed into each work. The colours, like the blues music Baker draws from, are indeed powerful for their freely associative and open models of representation: Black is too expansive to be any one thing; certainly, it defies the confines of skin colour. Like Robin Kelley does with his notion of "infrapolitics"—the circumspect struggle waged daily by subordinate groups who function beyond the visible spectrum—I reintroduce my borrowing of the term to discuss what I term *infrapoetics*, a discursive and creative language practice that challenges centre/margin positions. *Blue, Black, Gold, White,* and *Red* (the colour that scatters the least of the visible spectrum of colours) operate beyond the visible end of the spectrum to take poetic voice into "new" territory. Black, and Blackness, for all its visibility and nuanced shading, often remains static—or worse, invisible.

<small>Black Star</small>   Historically, being raced as Black has been akin to invisibility or colourlessness, like Ellison's Invisible Man, or Yasiin Bey (then Mos Def), who animates this reality when he raps, "I'm dark like the side of the moon you don't see." Consequently, in *Black*, Clarke declares that his "'belonging' carries an asterisk, one shaped like a—ragged—maple leaf," painting himself as "A sort-of African-American and a so-so English Canadian, I read Irving Layton through the lens of Jean Toomer—without jive, without apology. The blackness of my English be that of ice."[130] Although he defines his citizenship in a Black Canadian nationalist context, he brazenly mixes traditions and writers (here an outspoken white Canadian poet with a Harlem Renaissance writer) and presents poetry with a tongue that "cannibalizes all other tongues . . . it even fucks up Black English badly."[131] The poem "Language," whose first section is appropriately dedicated to hip hop wordsmith Wendy "Motion" Braithwaite, provides resistance, parody even, in order to challenge the margin/border that Clarke, as a Black academic poet, feels confined by, and so he spoils "Her Majesty's English."[132] Like the Caliban of "Negation" (*Blue*), Clarke's speaker takes on "Creole verse" and "second-hand grammar" in order to assert a space where hybridity—historical humour even—can transcend reified cultural borders.[133] Furthermore, the near-sonnet poem "Letter to a Young Poet" chastises a young poet for wanting to write love poems, since *"Poetry* eats its lovers alive."[134] Clarke prefers a confrontational love ("All true songs acknowledge *Pain,* / But *Love* is everything") in the warring of his poetic psyche, one that can reclaim language and poetic positioning.[135] Similar interstices are used by Césaire in *A Tempest*, as Caliban negates Prospero's power through his reclamation of identity and naming: "Call me X.

That would be best. Like a man without a name."¹³⁶ As with Malcolm X, whose own act of renaming was an act of reclamation, Clarke's Blackness is recuperative and expansive.

As he does in the multipage poem/universe dedicated to *Blue* (most explicitly in "I. i"), Clarke provides a nuanced reading, once again in the Roman Numeral series, beginning with the negated and the darkest, most racist, and codified representations of Black:

> Black is black and black and black
> Black is a *nègre* nigger, a *negrita* nigger, a *schwartz* nigger
> Black is a mulatto, sambo, negro, quadroon, octoroon,
> Black is Africa, as photographed by Leni Riefenstahl¹³⁷

The reference to Leni Riefenstahl, the German photographer who filmed the propaganda film *Triumph of the Will,* and whose bold colour photographs of Africa (and African peoples) were international bestsellers, alludes to a prime example of the anthropophagic (cannibalizing) lens through which racists often dilute Blackness. While many praised Riefenstahl's photographs, Susan Sontag rightly criticized them as further proof of Riefenstahl's "fascist aesthetics."¹³⁸ Clarke then negates such fascist renderings of Blackness by providing more expansive semiotic representations, such as a bawdy line to blues singer and Black feminist Bessie Smith, before taking us into a combative realm where Wynton Marsalis is pitted against Miles Davis: "Black is Bessie Smith's black bottom you are invited, politely, to kiss / Black is Wynton Marsalis trying desperately to equal Miles Davis."¹³⁹ Black, as "IV. iii" indicates, is hardly a single entity, and such creative kinship and inventive improvisation upon the Blackness of Blackness works against the sometimes subtle intricacies of racism. As in "I. i" in *Blue,* where Clarke reflects on his own penned blueness, "Blue is *Saltwater Spirituals and Deeper Blues; Lush Dreams,* / *Blue Exile;* and *Blue* / Fatal, foolhardy poetry," *Black* continues Clarke's poetic cataloguing: "*Black* is the future of *Blue* / Black is *Whylah Falls, Beatrice Chancy, Execution Poems,* and *Black—* / Choirs of light."¹⁴⁰ Clarke's choosing to end "IV. iii" by referring to his works as "Choirs of light" contests the Enlightenment model of lightness as good and Blackness as evil by stating that Blackness is actually most luminescent.

The mixing of colours—within each colouring book—fits the resonant and redolent remix that happens in Black music, which for Clarke is central to his own poetic identity. In *Black,* the "canvas is [still] the blues," but it is more representationally squawk-like and dissonant—at times—than it is in *Blue*: "This voice, my very own, / Be a saxophone disrupting sirens."[141] The internal rhyme between "own" and "saxophone" ties jazz, identity, and poetic ownership together, much like the clever homophone that connects aesthetic and identity in the poem: "By iambs / (or 'I am's')."[142] In the same poem, in section II, "The Canon," Clarke once again smashes and praises canons (Chaucer, Milton, Donne, Blake, Baudelaire, Hopkins, Li Po, Thomas, Toomer, Walcott, etc.) with his rhetorical hammer, in order to establish that a good poem (sounding rather Barakian), "stabs like a dagger now, / Explodes later like a grenade." Such blending between music, identity, history, and poetic self-representation makes Clarke's poetics engaging, for Clarke contends that "every good song is ambivalent"—such is also Baker's argument for the power of discursive Black modernisms.[143] While the overarching architecture of *Blue* is more blues than jazz in *Black* the design is more jazz, and while hardly free jazz, it is, under Clarke's pronouncement, a jazz model that allows him to speak freely, to be representationally as unbound as possible: "Composing a jazz of randomness—just like / Our never-finished lines, leaping from direction / To direction: a *vers libre* architecture."[144]

While the sonnets in much of Clarke's work, or even his formal vernacular, might make it feel as if his poetry is page-bound, Clarke's compositional poetics are actually quite varied, as are his writing styles—he writes jazz librettos, for heaven's sake![b] Clarke's ability to

---

[b] Clarke's librettos are *Beatrice Chancy* (libretto 1998; verse-play 1999), *Québécité,* and *Trudeau: Long March, Shining Path.* Many of Clarke's works have also been produced as plays, often in international/multicultural settings. Notably, in 2002 *Whylah Falls* was translated into Italian and staged in Venice. Joseph Pivato describes the irony and international prowess of the work being performed in Italy, as "the Italian chorus sang

sample different styles (his poems in the colouring books range from sonnets to *vers libre*, blues, "uta" [Japanese verse form], decima, translations, and sestina, among various other samplings and paratextual referencing) makes him a master DJ, reviving and reworking the past, selecting samples from varied sonic crates; Clarke contends that the "the poet is / A gardener in a graveyard."[145] While the anxiety of influence is enough to frighten many people away from pursuing poetry, for Clarke it helps drive his poetic persona. Clarke leans into T.S. Eliot's often-quoted claim, blurring the line between immaturity/badness and maturity/goodness: "Immature poets imitate; mature poets steal; bad poets deface what they take, and good poets make it into something better, or at least something different."[146] Clarke's ability to remix disparate traditions opens his work as improvisational, as mixed, as bluing green.

As colours blend in *Black*, so does Clarke's poetic identity. Clarke's experience as an Africadian poet acknowledges the plurality of voices that historically have comprised Nova Scotia's mixing: immigrants, refugees, West Indian, African American, and Indigenous people. In *Black*, Clarke describes his racial mixing in relation to his own defamiliarization as a Black Mi'kmaq poet—his bluing green: "I am, I guess, strange, foreign, Negro" ("À Bellagio"); "Indo-Gypsy, mocha-black Mi'kmaq;" and most personally, in a "A Discourse on My Name": "*George* is English / *Elliott* Scottish, and *Clarke* Irish. / Of course, this makes it a misnomer, / For I am an Africadian— / A Black Nova Scotian of African-American / And Mi'kmaq roots."[147] As Clarke contends in his essay on "zebra" poetics, "all African diasporic writing, African-Canadian literature engages the symbol and the image of the mixed-race black because this figure violates the

---

jazz, blues, and spirituals in an ornate Venetian theatre named after Carlo Goldoni." Joseph Pivato, introduction to *Africadian Atlantic: Essays on George Elliott Clarke*, ed. Joseph Pivato (Toronto: Guernica, 2012), 9. Lastly, Clarke told me in an email that "If [he] ever got to do another opera libretto, the subject will be the imagined meeting of Brown, Hendrix, and Miles Davis: The trio had actually been on the cusp of collaboration before Hendrix's untimely death" (Clarke, personal communication, 2012). In that case, we can only hope he writes another libretto.

sanctity of racial polarities, thus reminding Africans and Europeans of the white-initiated sexual violence against black women that ensured the sadism of slavery."[148] With this in mind, the images of Black women by photographer Richard Scipio that appear in *Black* (and many in colour in *Illuminated Verses*) are semiotic acts that attempt to reclaim the black female body, still sexualized, but with the intent to work against "white-initiated sexual violence." These images illuminate Blackness, and work against elect whiteness, which is likely why Clarke's *Illuminated Verses* took eleven years to find a publisher willing to include the "unclothed black feminine" presence.[149] The feminine is often under attack in *Black*, through phallocentric Black presences, but such mixings—bluing green—like Miles Davis's presence in the colouring books, animate the risk and danger of mixed performances.

Miles Davis's representational power (like that of Trudeau and Malcolm X) in Clarke's work is immense, particularly because of his consummate skill as an improviser who blends traditions (and colours), and for his brash and outspoken nature. As Davis says in his autobiography, "I've always liked honesty and can't stand people being any other way." The tonal language of his music and speech—his ability to use *motherfucker* to compliment someone or simply as punctuation—speaks to the kind of freedom—*vers libre*—that Clarke strives for in his work. Miles Davis's occasional vulgarity makes him an even more lucrative figure for complex representation and negotiation, for Davis could make incredibly tender music and then—to put it bluntly—go and beat the crap out of a woman: "I thought that I was still in my Ferrari, so I told her, 'Bitch, what are you doing in my goddamn car!' And then I slapped her and ran out of the building." Conversely, while in Paris, Davis learns what love is from Juliette Greco, who is "the first woman [he] loved as an equal human being;" Paris, and Europe more broadly, teach him a kind of freedom the pre-civil rights United States cannot: "I had never felt that way in my life. It was the freedom of being in France and being treated like a human being, like someone important."[150] Clarke does not whitewash the power of violence to instruct his readers on historical injustices, even when they are tinged with misogyny as in Davis's case, or in the inclusions of such as figures as Mao, Malcolm X, Titus Andronicus, and Marquis de Sade.

Working in the in-between space between love and hate, violence and beauty, Clarke told me that polyphony is akin to sexuality (and violence):

> Polyphony is akin to sexuality, for there is always a sublimated and sometimes an explicit violence in coitus, a metaphysical violence that is both marriage and transgression, but such is a source of pleasure too (if gendered in troubling ways at times). Penetration is both assault (especially if unwanted) and union; but I don't just refer to the phallus here: tongues, fingers, the clitoris, nipples can all figure in the union of bodies or the violation of a body by another (or others). Polyphony is no different: the merging of voices is also a brouhaha, a riot, a confrontation, whose pleasurable effects would result from a harmonious dissonance. However, if polyphony is viewed as violent, as having disrupted alleged harmony or the public peace (and quiet), that transgression reveals the repression that is uniformity or the oppression that is silence . . . Behind every comedy, there is Sade; within every tragedy, there is the Joker . . . History is a constant (violent) argument over power—contending devils, and I think that such turmoil is always embedded in even sedate literary texts, if often unheard. It is the function of authorial polyphony to strip away "ideas of order" (Stevens) to get at the hubbub, shouts, cusses, sounding under the surface of censure, censorship, "civility." Yes, to hear the "libertine" within the "libertarian," but also within the "prude" and the "slavemaster."[151]

This "harmonious dissonance" sums up Clarke's poetics well. Iteration remains a big part of his poetics, and while literary polyphony could descend into "hubbub" quickly, Clarke finds valuable resonance (what he's usefully termed "harmonious dissonance") by including noise, discord, and playful asides. In fact, some of my favourite moments in Clarke's poetry are those cacophonous parts he edits in.

In the section "Black Ice," mixed-race and Blackness are examined through the revolutionary spirit and assassination of radical Malcolm X, as well as a poem about the assassination of John F. Kennedy, whose tragic death is fit subject for "pure poetry": "a head-shot president / spilling a brain-matter rainbow / over a backseat of flowers."[152] Clarke draws from the political fervour of the 1960s around American and Canadian nationalism, the assassination of two Kennedys, Malcolm X, and Martin Luther King Jr., and the rise of robust Canadian Prime Minister Pierre Elliott Trudeau. Malcolm X is a powerful figure who is repeated in each colouring book, especially in *Black*, and with good reason. As Black activists became more radical in the late 1960s with groups like the Black Panthers, Malcolm X and his teachings were part of the groundwork upon which they built their movements. The Black Power movement, the Black Arts movement, the international adoption of the slogan "Black is Beautiful," and the current Black Lives Matter movement all have roots in Malcolm X. The resurgence of interest in Malcolm X among young people in the 1980s and early 1990s, and again post-2010s, was fuelled, in part, by his use as a cultural icon by hip hop groups such as Public Enemy. In many ways, Malcolm X was Marcus Garvey's ideological heir. Clarke describes the former as being ironically no less "wary of mixed-race blacks," quoting a 1963 interview with Barbadian Canadian novelist Austin Clarke, where X describes how the white man always rejects mixed-race marriages, and that "as far as we are concerned, as long as we can tell that you have black blood, you are one of our brothers and when you get in that borderline . . . then it's best for you to get some papers, especially nowadays, because you are going into an era today where the color of your skin might. [*sic*] Save your life."[153] Clarke points out the icy realpolitik nature of X's response, which fits with much of X's own problematic views on race as articulated in *The Autobiography of Malcolm X*.

Notwithstanding Malcolm X's early, somewhat redacted views on race, and his sexist belief that "a woman's true nature is to be weak," X, as Clarke pens, "forced us to be beautiful for the first time."[154] Particularly relevant in X's growing consciousness was his more complex reading of race, which hinged racial experiences upon oppression, arguing that "the white man is *not* inherently evil, but America's racist society influences him to act evilly." Thus, X became a man who worked to, as he put it himself, "destroy the racist cancer that is malignant in the body of America."[155] Clarke chose to write two poems focusing on the assassination of X. The first of these, written *à la manière de* Clément Virgo (a Black Canadian filmmaker), displays the cinematic presence of the death scene, as well as the potential once again for pure poetry "from the holes in the orator's chest, / his multiplied mouths." Following the poems on X's assassination is "IX/XI," which serves to remind us that history continues to repeat itself and that we need to continue to visit the thinking, the violence even, of radicals like Malcolm X in order to understand how to break cycles. "IX/XI," which fittingly mirrors the letter "X," is a gravitas poem comprised of five-line stanzas that explores the cyclic nature of violence, including the global catastrophe from the ruins of 9/11: "History shook that city that said, '*History* is history.' / A Malcolm X prophecy came to a fiery, smoking life / In a King Kong apocalypse of planes hitting towers." New York is part of a lineage of exploded cities that in Clarke's poem include "London, Hiroshima, Baghdad, / And Halifax, Nova Scotia, on December 6, 1917."[156] From this epic cataloguing of violence and historical destruction, *Black* challenges us to imagine a better society.

We have a responsibility to change the world for the better. Toward the end of his life, Malcolm X realized this potential, challenging the widespread belief that he was driven by hatred of white people. In the epilogue to *The Autobiography of Malcolm X*, Alex Haley describes how X left a mostly white college student body and told Haley that the "young whites, and blacks, too, are the only hope that America has ... The rest of us have always been living a lie."[157] Clarke's desire to tell the truth, often through a lie, is where the personal and historical often meet and where change is possible in *Black*. In Clarke's own "Autobiography (II)" he describes himself as "[a] buck-toothed, loud-laughing, so-called poet: / Ink on my hands like bomb residue."[158] This sly and somewhat self-deprecating line completes the earlier reference that a good poem "[e]xplodes later like a grenade." Furthermore, the final poem in the collection, "Will," contemplates the poet's own funeral scene, which is more salubrious than tragic:

"Let there be music—lots, *lots*! . . . Let poetry be read . . . Burial must be at Maplewood Cemetery, / In Windsor, Nova Scotia, / Right beside my mother, / And someone, please, plant Lombardy poplars nearby."[159] Underneath the poem—growing—is a picture of a flower, recalling the line in "Naima" (*Blue*) that poetry opens "a-flowering." And so *Black* begins with arresting images of death (an execution) and closes with the poet's own death. From the modal representations of identity to the *infrapoetic* sounding that makes citizenships more visible, *Black* embodies transformation.

infraRedpoetics

"Beauty must never be explained."

—EZRA POUND quoted in Clarke, *Red*, 7

So states the Ezra Pound epigraph (placed beside another epigraph about beauty, from Fanon) that prefaces George Elliott Clarke's *Red*. In his third colouring book, Clarke follows Pound's maxim with a collection of poems that again challenge convention and open the poetic possibilities of red: the colour of blood, rubies, communism, anger, fire, and roses. *Red* (composed of twelve sections), through an *infrapoetics,* continues to make the hidden, the forgotten, the downtrodden, the bass notes, more visible and audible. In *Red*, Clarke's words pop with the punctuated scarlet elegance of a Duke Ellington tone poem. The poems brazenly and blazingly incorporate the mixed Odyssean waters of sex-infused pre-Christian Rome, the crimson violence of *Titus Andronicus*, the rhetorical syncopation of James Brown, the metaphysical cadence of Pushkin's verse, and the insurgent politics of Mao Zedong and Malcolm X. And Clarke's collection crescendos with its reimagination of the great African American jazz bassist Charles Mingus as a Canadian. For all these diverse voices and characters, Clarke's poetry is candidly self-reflexive. He identifies as part Aboriginal, as a *"noir 'peau rouge'"* whose "typed face glows" like "a portrait etched in lye."[160] Homage remains important in

Red, as Clarke dedicates this collection to his polymath father, William Lloyd Clarke, whose artwork appears on the cover of *Red* and throughout the volume (his parents are honoured in many of his works). In "Taxi," the reader is situated in his father's Halifax cab, where Clarke's father speaks with "suave grammar / And stunning puns . . . fathering a son / Who could credibly be crowned a *poet*." In the poem his father drives white passengers around who read Clarke's father under drab clichés of a Black working man who is "not expected to sire any bard." In the final stanza, Clarke (the poet) enters the poem (enters history) and "taxi'd a book into their hands, / And spoke almost as graciously, graceful, / As my unparalleled father would have."[161] The clever usage of "taxi'd" as a verb is the type of wordplay Clarke assumingly inherits from his father, along with his grace (although his father could be harsh, as his memoir *Where Beauty Survived* makes apparent). Clarke implies that he is where he is because traditions include more than those who are privileged enough to publish poems. With every colouring book Clarke gets a little more personal and reveals more about his own history; such is the path of an aging poet looking back on his work. There is a less militant presence in *Red* than in its predecessors, and even though the context is different from the initial usage of the sixties feminist rally cry, "the personal is political," there is an absorbing political and cosmopolitan presence in *Red*. *Red* is more international in scope than *Blue* or *Black*: we get personal poems like "Going to Halifax," as well as poems set in Mexico, France, Italy, and the United States, an approach that will be expanded in *Gold* and *White* through translations of living poets. Red has a wide gamut of personal associations for Clarke, who is part Aboriginal ("Afro-Metis," he asserts); also, in *Red*, Malcolm X, who was known as Detroit Red in his twenties, returns as a presence.

This *infrapoetically* expansive territory is aptly displayed in Clarke's "Other Angles," an epic catalogue of red's representational possibilities. Yet, different from *Blue* and *Black* is that the colour catalogue doesn't appear as part of the Roman Numeral series, which seems to have reached its conclusion in *Black*. The poem "Other Angles" ranges from the scatological "[r]ed is a bloody shit" to Clarke's own, red-infused poetic catalogue:

> Red is Aboriginal and African and Chinese and Cuban
> and Nova Scotian
> Red is *George & Rue, Illuminated Verses,* Trudeau: Long March /
> Shining Path, *Blues and Bliss, I & I,* and *Red*—
> Poetry in the blood.

Again, red, and *Red*, like the other poetic colours, absorbs traditions and self-reflexively considers Clarke's own oeuvre. Red is a "tongue accustomed to corruption" that draws other works into the matrix of its signifying potential. The poetic catalogue also functions antithetically to an ordered epic catalogue, since red can represent everything from Red Label scotch to a "fragrant flaming violent Klansmen barbecued on a blazing cross."[162] Part of the work happening in the colouring books amounts to an opening where boundaries are explored, exploded, in favour of creative expression. As Miles Davis once said, "I always thought that good music had no boundaries, no limits to where it could grow and go, no restrictions on its creativity ... And I always hated categories. Always. Never thought it had any place in music."[163] Clarke suggests the same for "good" poetry. Like any fiery, fervid artist dedicated their *techné*, Clarke unapologetically makes polyphony and contradiction a poetic act.

In "Poor Imitation," Clarke quotes Miles Davis as a proxy—and perhaps parodic—voice that asks, "*Why should some motherfucker make me feel bad because of their ignorance?*" [italics in original]. The poem explores the racial/poetic misreadings that the poet encounters at home and abroad. In Havana the poet is Cuban, while in Canada he is "comfortably / American in every café, / but suspiciously Arab at every airport."[164] Within these in-between spaces, Clarke avows a heteroglot African Canadian identity that "muck[s] up black and white states," for "*Negro* experience transgresses all borders."[165] In "Malcolm X: The Last Interview," Clarke imagines that Malcolm X gave a final uncensored and improvised interview to James Baldwin immediately before he was assassinated, speaking in a terse blues-prose: "The blues are my only language— / each elegant, crisp text."[166] Playing once again with the standard figures, notably Malcolm X, Clarke continues to create new spaces of play using similar tropes. This is executed more than in any other poem in *Red* when Clarke reimagines African American jazz bassist, improviser, and composer Charles Mingus as an "Africadian" poet/musician. Engaging in an act of mythopoetics, Clarke compares Mingus to the mythological figure of Odysseus and also to *Ulysses*, the Roman name for Odysseus, as well as the name of a Tennyson poem and a novel by James Joyce; Clarke writes, "Your bass sounds like a typewriter / Punctuating *Ulysses*, / Or like a shotgun puncturing Odysseus."[167] These lines highlight the phonetics of sound poetry through sibilance (or alliterative paronomasia), creating a listening experience that synchs song with text and mythopoeia.

"Charles Mingus: An Autobiography" (notice Clarke's ongoing affinity for mixing personal truths with imaged acts) is largely a manifestation of a freer poetics that crosses borders: "But you are as free as music." Even though the poem is carefully composed in tercets—giving it a Dantean epic quality—the poem is about resisting confinement through play and revision. The poem is dedicated to Ayanna Black—a Black Canadian feminist, jazz poet, and arts advocate who passed in 2009—as homage becomes a way to live on, as songs and poems often outlive the more temporal body. Through an extemporaneous approach to living, the Halifax-born Mingus takes "Jazz lessons with dark rum— / 'Mmmmmmmm, well, uh huh....' / Fuck ideas." Ideas keep the dialogue stagnant, so Clarke's Mingus pulls off "a *beaucoup* blues *coup*, suh!"[168] The homophonic echo and internal rhyme between "*beaucoup*," "blues," and "coup" demonstrates Clarke's ability to play with words in the way that Mingus played with convention; he often put major sevenths with minor sevenths, played a fourth away from the key, and things like that long before it was called avant-garde, which is largely Clarke's point: that he himself is Mingus, participating in a tradition of riffing long before postmodernism called it so. Useful, from Mingus's autobiographical *Beneath the Underdog*, is his conception of "rotary perception": "imagine a circle surrounding each beat—each guy can play his notes anywhere in that circle and it gives him more free space."[169] Clarke's poetic colouring books are about dancing within the circle of his larger works, creating more room for experimentation and potentially greater improvisation.

Charles Mingus

James
Brown

    Clarke's vernacular formalism constricts his poetry at times, but upon listening to Clarke read his work that pretension diminishes, for Clark wants his poems to sound and, as he told me, have a *"speakerly," "performance-orientated"* quality to them.[170] In *Red* we get plenty of poems that succeed in both, often simultaneously. Some poems are sonnets ("Veil'd Devil"), others are bawdy and raucous blues with clear blues structures ("First Light Blues" and "Tomcat/Pussycat Blues"), and some are straight-up pop songs, such as the poem "James Brown's Rhetoric," syncopated exclusively from a sampling of actual James Brown song titles to form a five-stanza poem/song. The last poem in the collection, "17, 34, 51," reads like a folk ballad as Clarke contemplates how he has been a poet for two thirds of his life: "Two thirds my life a poet, I / Gleam—like a portrait etched in lye . . ."[171] The ellipsis at the end of the poem indicates that Clarke will assuredly go on being a poet, and, as *Red* makes clear, an international one at that.

    There is an internationalism at work in *Red*, in part due to Clarke's popularity as a poet outside of Canada, as well as his praxis of writing poems on the go in hotel rooms or cafés. Some poems once again translate Blackness, except that in *Red*, Blackness is *negritude* gone global, as Russian poet Alexander Pushkin's verse and character in translation/transculturalism make various appearances, writing in the spirit of Blackness: "A white-faced Black Russian, and vigorous— / Verse as rigorous as a "nigger" is—" who writes "Rudely bittersweet or sour, sickly dour."[172] If *Blue*'s poet-spirit is part Pound, part Walcott, and *Black*'s is part Toomer, part Layton, then *Red* is certainly part Pushkin, part Mao. In "À Bellagio (III)," building on a sequence started in *Black*, Clarke continues his corruption of language in the service of poetry: "I's still a black bastard bastardizing English. / There is no freedom outside Poetry."[173] Clarke's bastardizing poetic praxis remains a response to historic silences.

    In the poem "Looking at Alma Duncan's Young Black Girl (1940)," Clarke provides a serious examination of Duncan's painting and asks, "Does painter Duncan tell herself, '*Negresses are so much stronger / than we white ladies*'? / Maybe." Clarke's blurred impression imagines what the young Black girl's life might have been like; he edits in details—for example, she's "studying jazz lingo— / to backtalk and lindy hop"—

and reminds us that (to echo Lorde again) "Her world isn't poetry / (Negroes can't afford that yet); it's potatoes." Edited in are important figures of Black history, from Malcolm X (who shouts, "There is no accidental lyricism") to Angela Davis and Rosa Parks (women the girl might become), dedicating the poem to Viola Desmond (the pre–Rosa Parks of Canada, who gets her own poem in *White*). Clarke's reading is sensitive to the era of the image, as he attributes Duncan's "signature of crayon and ash" to the "lightning of prophecy."[174] History continues to teach us lessons if we are willing to listen.

We are left feeling *Red* as an embodied act of listening to beauty, even when it's corporeally violent and ugly: "Exeunt omnes with the two cadavers— / Throats split like vaginas."[175] As with much of Clarke's work, the moments when we feel beauty eclipsed by brute violence—as in the case of Clarke's stage directions to *Titus Andronicus* in the section titled "Red Arsenic," complete with an epigraph from Mao Zedong—are opportunities to ask what's happening and why. Clarke's fearless project to materialize difficult poetry makes beauty productively complex in *Red* (and in the colouring series), and the poetry worth reading, listening to, digesting, and rereading. Clarke's search for beauty is like Amiri Baraka's, who, when asked by Saul Williams in 2004 the function of the artist, responded, "I believe what Keats and DuBois [*sic*] believed: Truth and beauty . . . There's no sense in being an artist except to tell the truth and to make the world more beautiful than it is."[176] Sung full-throated by a master in full control of his craft, the poems in *Red* make the world more beautiful.

White Gold: Unprecedented Beauty

> "O! Let my true colour(s) beam!"
>
> —GEORGE ELLIOTT CLARKE, "Whitewash"

Clarke's latest collections in the colouring series—*Gold* (2016) and *White* (2021)—continue his exploration of "harmonious dissonance" in relation to beauty (and justice) and include a familiar cast, with appearances by Malcolm X, Miles Davis, and Ezra Pound. In *Gold* we get a jazzy riffing on Austin Clarke's "When He Was Free and Young and He Used to Wear Silks" and a range of dedications, notably to Italian jazz, blues, pop composers like Piero Piccioni and Ennio Morricone, and political activists like Rocky Jones (and Joan Jones in *White*), all penned with Clarke's signature risky bravado. *White* expands the range of dedications to include elegies for Leonard Cohen and Gord Downie, justice-focused poems on Emmett Till, Viola Desmond, and COVID-19, poems about blues and jazz figures such as Thelonious Monk and Portia White, and translations of other poets' poems into English, and offers a suite of nine poems—"Nine Scribes Lives"—that are written to be sounded (almost rapped) aloud. Even a seemingly page-bound poem like "Abandonment" (from *Gold*), written *à la manière de* Saint-John Perse (a French poet and diplomat) and based on a repositioning of Finnish folklore *vis-à-vis* heterosexual relationships, leaves room for improvisation. As Clarke told me, during a live performance in Italy at the time, he took "the line, 'She's a bad woman will make a bad wife, a bad mother,' and repeated it several times, stressing and elongating 'bad' to 'baaaaaaaaad'—in a sense, thus, applying James Brown pronunciation to *Kalevala* diction, and the audience went craaaazzzy!"[177] Having seen Clarke read his poetry many times, I can imagine Clarke moving and swaying to the rhythms of the elongated words, embodying the sounds like Monk did at his piano.[♭] All of Clarke's poetry aspires to song, as poetry is indeed cadenced and, as Clarke suggests, hints at song. In *Gold* and *White* Clarke continues to play with form and song: we get villanelles, sonnets, poems in *terza rima*, and blues-and-jazz-and-pop-infused poems for readers to unpack like a DJ working through an archive.

Gold consists of ten sections, and given that *Blue* was written mostly in the 1990s, and first published in 2001, we do see the wisdom ("Wisdom" is also the name of the penultimate poem in the collection) that comes

---

♭ In 2015 I arranged an improvised performance with Clarke, a bassist (Darin Nicolle), and a pianist (James Darling). In this video you can see how carefully Clarke listens in the moment and embodies his words: https://www.youtube.com/watch?v=Q6FOMhc1tpw.

with time. Gold shimmers (like speckled words), as does the beautiful cover to the collection, complete with "AU" inside the jacket of the book: a physical manifestation of gold. Clarke opens the collection by reminding readers that the colouring books are efforts to write outside the lines to connect moving dots, and *Gold* continues that tradition while also being a colour he carries in his skin: "even if I am not, alas, formed of such mettle."[178] While Clarke remains subversive, in *Gold* (and perhaps even more so in *White*), we get the sense that he is particularly aware of his poetic legacy.

In "Golden Moments" (a euphemism for orgasm) we get the range of gold and *Gold's* metaphorical possibilities, from "Malcolm X, Iceberg Slim, Miles Davis, and Dorothy Proctor- / Mills" to Clarke's own works "*Directions Home* and *Traverse*; *Illicit Sonnets* and *Extra Illicit Sonnets*."[179] Uniquely, the colouring series absorbs, catalogues, and recatalogues (from the other colouring books) historical figures and Clarke's own works of poetry and scholarly work (itself concerned with cataloging). Hence, Clarke's work echoes epic and canons his output with a cosmopolitan approach towards canonization and commemoration. His poetics (orgasmic and harmoniously dissonant) take numerous forms in their mixedness, such as the blues poems "Venus: An Anatomy" (in ABA), "Oreo Blues," or "Mariangela E La Seduzione," written in the manner of Ennio Morricone, which mimics the "moans" and pop eroticism of the song it uses as its base. At other times, Clarke's dedications are more virulent, such as when he writes back to history in the style of Mao Zedong in "How Europe Underdeveloped Africa." The poem rereads Walter Rodney's 1972 book of the same title, whose premise describes how colonial regimes in Europe intentionally underdeveloped Africa. As Clarke raps, "Cancel all bullshit blandishments: / *History* is Europe playing 'blackface.'"[180] Clarke's concerns are largely historical and international, but the regional and the local remain key to understanding his concerns around citizenship and cosmopolitanism.

In the section "Gold Coast," which begins his dedications to other poet laureates of Toronto (expanded in *White*), his focus is acutely on Toronto. In "Toronto Tantra" he makes his cosmopolitan poetics clear:

Ennio Morricone

> Each nationality is mouthfuls of accents-
> as cosmopolitan as the cosmos.
>
> It is Toronto's *modus vivendi,*
> right?
>
> To compose a Commonwealth
> courageously gorgeous
> where every citizen conspires
> like jazz musicians,
> improvising beauty.[181]

From his locale of Toronto, Clarke emphasizes how citizenship is sounded, and he does so with an understanding of his own identity as mixed—a living history.

In *White,* Clarke continues to write back to nation (his "Letter to Canada" riffs on Ginsberg's 1956 poem, "America"), and in "Living History" he speaks of his various identities—"African," "Canadian," "Africadian," / Eastern Woodlands Métis"—and asks, "how can [he] be Afro'd, Canuck, and free?" The question is prompted by an incident where Clarke, with his family and young daughter, on Christmas, of all days, is asked by a "drunkard," "What's your *Slavery Identification Number?*" Citizenship remains an important marker of both inclusion and exclusion and one that functions in relation to whiteness where *Liberty, Justice,* and *Equality* are "just, rich, white folks' words?"[182] The question mark is integral, for Clarke writes a living history that shimmers like gold on his skin while refracting and absorbing whiteness. A truly *just society* must include all the colours of the spectrum.

White is the opposite of Black. It represents contradiction in that it can symbolize enlightenment from one angle and oppression from another. Or, purity and innocence from one viewpoint or sterilization and isolation from another. White can also signify death and/or mourning and the ancestral spirits: the ghosts of the past (a living history) haunting the present. White light can encompass any hue on the visible spectrum, so in the context of the colouring books it can absorb and provide critical shading to the other colours. And white is also the other half of George Elliott Clarke (where White is also a family name). The poems in *White* (told in twelve sections that play with white and whiteness), Clarke's official "fifth 'colouring book' / (rejigging sojourns in *Blue*, *Black*, *Red*, and *Gold*)," encompass this mix and the inherent contradictions of whiteness.[183]

In "Whitewash"[♭] (a reference to the whiting paint) Clarke writes, "White is Nobel Peace warmongers: Kissinger, Obama, Aung San Suu Kyi," and then names his own contradictory statement and controversy: "White is 'Maybe I will, maybe I won't,' quoting a once murderous poet."[184] This is (very likely) a reference to a planned (and then cancelled) talk where Clarke said he might or might not read from the work of Steven Kummerfield. In 1995, Kummerfield (then Stephen Brown) and his friend Alex Ternowetsky murdered Pamela George, an Indigenous woman (and aspiring poet), near the airport in Regina. Clarke's planned talk at the University of Regina—titled "'Truth and Reconciliation' versus 'The Murdered and Missing:' Examining Indigenous Experiences of (In)Justice in Four Saskatchewan Poets"—was cancelled due to the outrage Clarke caused when he said that he might or might not read from Kummerfield's work. Clarke had known Kummerfield since 2005, but he was unaware of his past crime when he befriended him (and supported his work, which has since been removed from the parliamentary website). While Clarke's talk was intended to explore larger questions of social consequence, his choice to perhaps read from Kummerfield's poetry in the context of the lecture was problematic and, at best, very misguided, even if Clarke was being a little flippant. It reminds us that art cannot escape accountability or the social relations from which it springs. Clarke has since apologized for the suffering his statement caused, and his very brief reference here in a poem about whiteness (perhaps referencing his unintended whitewashing of history) speaks to the ugly things—the other side of beauty—that his work confronts. He has since dealt with the cancelling of his talk and his side of the story in

---

♭ Listen to Clarke read his poem: https://www.youtube.com/watch?v=_i3M0dChJfI

his poem *J'Accuse*: a fourteen-part book dedicated to victims of violence, including Pamela George.

Thus, *White* contains a broad spectrum of ideas and artists and is the "collateral damage to poetry." In relation to his own work, "*White* is *The Merchant of Venice (Retried), The Motorcyclist, Locating Home,* 'Settling Africville,' *On / Entering the Echo Chamber of Epic, Canticles I (MMXVI) & (MMXVII), These Are the Words, ¶ / Canticles II (MMXIX) & (MMXX), Portia White,* / and *White*— / sanctified— if spectral—illumination / *O! Let my true colour(s) beam!*"[185] Clarke's poetic output is nothing short of unbelievable, and his scholarly work often sits comfortably beside his poetic work. Echo remains part of Clarke's process as he repeats, reworks, and remixes key themes and ideas and his dedications to musicians (such as Portia White and Thelonious Monk).

Portia White

The references to Portia White go back to Clarke's early poems (see "Hymn for Portia White" in *Salt Walter Spirituals and Deeper Blues*), and for him she symbolizes Black excellence and the crossing of borders both real and spiritual. As he writes in *Where Beauty Survived*, "in coming to idolize Portia White as a supreme Black-woman relative who escaped—partially—the boundaries of race, gender, and class, I glimpsed the possibility of creative contradiction, everywhere resident in colour imagery. I could peer into the dark heart of whiteness, or note notions of *Black Beauty* as being equivalent to *Snow White*. More yin-and-yang than polar opposites."[186] Portia White (1911–68) was Clarke's late great-aunt as well as the first Black Canadian concert singer to garner international acclaim. In *White* he writes another hymn for Portia White—a song of praise that is strophic and metrical in nature—describing her as "our glory, we, each freed slave: / The North Star is your lustrous grave / Portia, oh Portia White— / Voice like silver and skin . . . like . . . night . . ."[187] The references to the North Star, slavery, and perhaps Canaan land place her in the realm of Harriet Tubman, and through her voice she provides a metaphorical crossing into freedom. The ellipsis at the end of the poem is telling too, as the hymn trails into silence and longing. Portia White broke barriers barring her from the white classical world, and it is in this mixing—more yin-and-yang than opposites—that we get a window onto Clarke's mixed approach to Whiteness and Black excellence.

In another dedication, Clarke honours, in ballad form, genius innovator Thelonious Monk (explored more in the next chapter) and the disowned Rothschild, Pannonica de Koenigswarter. Pannonica de Koenigswarter (aka Nica) was one of the leading patrons of jazz (referred to as the "bebop baroness"), who befriended many of the giants of that music, and some twenty-four songs were written for her.♭ Charlie Parker died in her apartment. But it was Thelonious Monk's music that truly amazed her: "Fingers conjuring hallelujah ... Blues licks ooze outta the keyboard." She first heard "Round Midnight" on the radio by a then unknown Monk and listened to the song over and over again. Eventually she would meet him and become the biggest supporter of his music, bankrolling many of his endeavours, writing the liner notes to his 1962 recording *Criss-Cross*, and even taking responsibility for his marijuana possession in 1958, which led to her spending several nights in jail. She was present up until Monk's last moments and sat beside Monk's wife, Nellie, in the front row at his funeral in 1982. Clarke's poem explores their relationship and uses it to explore themes of miscegenation, patronage, race, music, and art. Was her support a way to escape "her white lady's burden?" Or was it about sex and, as Clarke alludes to, sadism? Or "were the pair like his keyboard—a coal seam punctuated with lilies?"[188] It was, as I read the pair and Clarke's exploration of them, a reciprocal relationship, more yin-and-yang than opposites. In fact, it recalls the negotiation we see in many of Clarke's poems as he takes on a dual performance as artist and patron of poetry. Clarke resists a clear binary between white and Black while exploring the contradictions and power dynamics between a rich white woman and an underappreciated Black genius. Monk wrote the song "Pannonica" for her, and it's a spellbinding and enchanting recording with some dissonant notes (the A section ends with

Thelonious Monk

♭ There are too many to name, but a few include Sonny Clark's "Nica," Horace Silver's "Nica's Dream," and Kenny Dorham's "To Nica."

a chord a half-step from where it started), yet it feels harmonious. Whether they were lovers or not—Clarke's poem is full of sexual innuendo—they managed to traverse borders of race and class and found freedom in art.

Many of the poems in *White* feel politically urgent, whether Clarke is writing about COVID-19 or Viola Desmond. In his poem to Viola Desmond—another ballad—Clarke celebrates her legacy. Desmond sat in the "whites only" section in a theatre in Nova Scotia, yet she was not charged with creating a disturbance or sitting in the whites-only section of the theatre (there was no actual law); rather, the authorities insisted she hadn't paid the extra fee for a downstairs ticket—a ticket she was never allowed to buy. She spent the night in jail with male prisoners, was fined $26 for failing to pay the extra 1 cent tax, and, as the story goes, left her white gloves on and sat upright all night long. Her audacity to challenge racial segregation in Nova Scotia helped Black Nova Scotians seek full citizenship status. Desmond challenged how a Black woman was supposed to behave in society by choosing to sound off against the racism of her time. This happened "nine years before / Rosa Parks sparked the Civil Rights crusade / States-side, a century past Civil War." Clarke connects her act as one that combines justice and beauty, evidenced in part by the long arc of history, as "Sis Desmond" can be found on the ten-dollar bill (replacing genocide-architect and Canada's first prime minister, Sir John A. Macdonald):

> As an entrepreneur, she sought *Value*
> And *Profit in Beauty*, Sis Desmond did,
> But she courted *Justice* because it's true—
> *Beauty* turns ugly when *Justice* is hid.
>
> . . .
>
> From two cents to ten dollars, an increase
> Of 50,000 percent.[189]

Desmond was given a royal pardon and remains a symbol of resistance and the essential right of citizenship for all.

In another poem, "Towards a Declension of 'Unprecedented,'" Clarke deals directly with the many injustices of the pandemic as they relate to socio-economic and political life and what is deemed "non-essential," such as bookstores, as opposed to "essential," such as liquor stores, as well as the overuse of the term "unprecedented" to describe the realities of the crisis. Clarke sees such overusage of the term as an evasion of the historical realities that have persisted from slavery to George Floyd:

> "COPVID-20," unprecedented
>
> in revealing the Ku Klux Klan Kop plop his knee
> atop a black man's neck, so breath stops). Unprecedented
> is how abuses thought long out-of-date are brought up-to-date.
> So poets must be street-corner oracles, unprecedented![190]

Clarke reminds us that words are weapons—Baraka sought poems that explode like grenades—and that it is the poet's job to tell the truth in the pursuit of beauty and justice.

William Carlos Williams wrote that "It is difficult / to get the news from poems, / yet men die miserably every day / for lack / of what is found there."[191] We could learn much from reading poems. Indeed, such an approach to life (much of which can be found in Clarke's colouring books) would be truly unprecedented. The colouring books succeed—despite and because of all their scatting across historical time frames—in thinking through the issues of belonging, citizenship, and the role of the poet as a discursive trickster and community builder. Clarke tells Nigel Thomas that community should be an act of mixing, border crossing, blurring traditions, and starting new conversations, "because a community is not just one thing; it's a whole bunch of discourses that are taking place"—it's a full spectrum of colours, "the scorching, searing brand of a rainbow."[192]

REMIX 1

<small>Burt Bacharach</small>

Speaking with rapper Shad on the CBC Radio show *Q*, Clarke spoke enthusiastically about poetry as the soul of the arts. His statement that "if you have access to your own heart, your own mind, your own soul, and you feel the pressure of inspiration because of joy or unfortunately sorrow, you are very likely to end up speaking something like poetry" was an inspiring pronouncement of the organic and universal nature of poetry.[193] He clarified this statement to me by referencing Hal David and Burt Bacharach's "What the World Needs Now Is Love": "That song comes to mind in thinking about why the world should need poetry. It is the first civilizing art, for it is the basis of scripture, whether inscribed or chanted. It conjoins imagination and emotion; so, for so long as human beings dream, recall, and/or have feelings, they/we will always invent poems."[194] Thus, in listening carefully to Clarke's poetics we find song and come to a fuller understanding of beauty and justice—a beauty that can, as Dostoevsky and others have claimed, change the world.

Blue, Black, Red, Gold, and *White* affirm an identity/citizenship that is in flux, creating a poetry formed in the spaces between culture, poetry, and history. Clarke plays upon an inherited standard and ascribes difference, analogous to Thelonious Monk and Miles Davis and to poets Ezra Pound and Derek Walcott. The difference that Clarke asserts is not simply generic, but rather a highly didactic difference formed in resistance to the dominant poetic and Eurocentric tradition that subjugated his own voice. Clarke's primary role as a poet is one who listens carefully to history and invites his readers to listen to his own thinking, often through direct invocations.

Clarke challenges us to listen to his own discursive listening practice: "Listen: An unflinching clarity will issue in the only legitimate / response: scabrous, scatological, flamboyantly raw poems"; "Listen: his lies hiss / Mussolini's lines;" "Listen: Rainwater cries, 'Red October!'"[195] Such direct invocations to the reader to "listen" appear frequently in Clarke's work. As Katherine McLeod offers in "Listening to Multi-Vocality in George Elliott Clarke's Jazz Opera *Québécité*," "Listening, as a critical practice, fundamentally alters the interaction between audience and text from passive to participatory."[196] Thus, as readers, we enact "sonic citizenship" when we listen carefully with Clarke across vast traditions and within the sensuous feast of sampled musics. For Clarke, meaning is never closed, and despite what seems like a closed nationalism, he states, in his early anthology, *Eyeing the North Star*, "I testify: African-Canadian literature has always been international."[197] There will always be historical gaps, Clarke is aware of this, and as much as he establishes canons for understanding Black Canadian writing, he acknowledges the very nature of flux of such histories.

Even Clarke's early works, like *Saltwater Spirituals and Deeper Blues* (1983), display a self-reflexive concern with the poet's role in history and emerge from a tradition of Black Nova Scotian music, literature, orality/preaching, and various arts of home-grown expression. In *Whylah Falls* Clarke fuses the African diasporic with the European Hellenistic and Judeo-Christian traditions, while in the poetic colouring books he re-examines those fusions to assert a poetics that can be adequately thought of as a representation of multiculturalism. Clarke's poetic and musical sampling opens his poetics up to polyphonous soundings. My DJ approach is hardly an evasion of the critical and historical work happening in Clarke's poetics, for I agree with Clarke's point, in reference to his cosmopolitan nationalism, that you can have it both ways: it is, after all, largely the premise of this book to proudly straddle and confound borders to speak to the kind of engaged citizenship that I contend poetry models. Similarly, Clarke explores and explodes genres, writing novels, operas, poems, criticism, various musical styles, and orature, and even creating/uncovering some new works/genres.

Read *vis-à-vis* the blues matrix we can understand Clarke's poetry as an ongoing dialogue in unity with a fractured community holding on to and revising tradition. Through an *infrapoetics* Clarke looks deep into the past and provides a blues truth that is often buried, forgotten, or needing to be (re)sounded. For all the repetition and blues-jazz riffing in the texts, Clarke always makes the past and music his own, a testament to his poetic talent. His Pentateuch of colouring books illuminates Clarke's own progress as a poet in search of beauty and a more expansive community. The colouring books reflect his dramatic ascent as one of Canada's most prolific poets. His poetry and music aspire to the divine: "Subtle blues, supple blues . . . But worms can't eat music. / It exists like light— / Up in the air, divine— To be divined / Like tears / Dissolved in the snow."[198] We can only speculate on what the next colours will bring—Clarke tells me Green and then Brown will complete the series—but certainly music will be the force that moves the works in his pursuit of beauty and justice.

"Sonic citizenship" (a bottom-up listening approach), like jazz, incorporates difference, and by inviting us into the mix Clarke continues to expand our concept of citizenship, not just in his poetry, but also by providing literary maps of African Canadian literature—sadly often omitted elsewhere—in works like *Odysseys Home* and *Directions Home*. Canada's literary landscape, like Clarke's blues poetics, is boundless. We now turn to Dionne Brand's "outer space sounding" in her poetic work, *Ossuaries*. Brand, through the mobility of Yasmine, rewrites the performance(s) of improvised jazz musicians in order to subvert Western traditions, much like Clarke does, but from the perspective of a Black radical feminist. As Lorde makes even more clear, "for women, then, poetry is not a luxury. It is a vital necessity of our existence. It forms the quality of the light within which we predicate our hopes and dreams toward survival and change, first made into language, then into idea, then into more tangible action."[199] Let's listen as Brand's ideas in *Ossuaries* (and later in *The Blue Clerk*) manifest into language and then call us into action.

Chapter 2

LISTENING TO A LISTENING: THE DISRUPTIVE JAZZ POETICS OF DIONNE BRAND'S *OSSUARIES* AND *THE BLUE CLERK* (A CALL TOWARD FREEDOM)

"in order to draw a map only the skill of listening may be necessary."

—DIONNE BRAND, *A Map to the Door of No Return*, 18

"I not only entered the music but descended, like Dante, into its depths."

—RALPH ELLISON, *Invisible Man*, 9

Listening: John Coltrane, "Venus"

_{John Coltrane, "Venus"}

John Coltrane is best known for his work on albums like *Blue Train* (1958) and *A Love Supreme* (1964), but his later works, notably *Interstellar Space* (1967/1974), are some of his most exciting and rewarding listens.♭ I first heard about *Interstellar Space* when reading Dionne Brand's *Ossuaries*. Since I haven't seen the album in the wild since, it was quite serendipitous that I found the original vinyl a few weeks later at Kops Records on Queen Street West in Toronto. Shortly after that, I spent part of an afternoon having tea in Kensington Market with Dionne Brand, who was at the time advising me on the trajectory of my thesis. Since then, I've listened to *Interstellar Space* many times, and it remains (much like Dionne Brand's work) challenging and rewarding. While Dionne Brand invokes and samples many jazz artists, it is Coltrane's work that remains redolent. Given that I already have a listening dedicated to Coltrane (in the overture), it might make more sense to focus on Charlie Parker, Thelonious Monk, or Charles Mingus, who also appear in Brand's work, but Coltrane's "outer space sounding" really gets a hold of you if you welcome it.

Nowhere in Coltrane's oeuvre is space, particularly cosmological, as a theme more present than in *Interstellar Space* (recorded in 1967), released posthumously in 1974. Coltrane and drummer Rashied Ali are the only musicians on the recording, on which the almost folksy "Venus" appears, which Brand references in her works *What We All Long For*, *Ossuaries*, and *The Blue Clerk*. In "Venus" Coltrane alternates quiet moments with sections of great intensity, showing off his phenomenal technique and ability to improvise without the need for chordal instruments. Salim Washington argues that with a recording such as *Interstellar Space*, "Coltrane was able to play more freely than ever before, dipping into his unconscious and streaming consciousness to produce works that were at once primal and unsettling

---

Liner Notes

♭ You can listen to the playlist for this chapter here: https://open.spotify.com/playlist/1femY0yRTZHrCAat59EP2m

as well as intricate and dense."¹ The way that Coltrane and Ali play off each other recalls how Brand and her central character Yasmine in *Ossuaries*, or how Brand and her Clerk in *The Blue Clerk*, or even the reader and the text, improvise together to create meaning. Unsettling, like the musical undertones of "Venus," Brand's *Ossuaries* challenges a clearly definable self or community and uses the central character of that text—Yasmine—to create a more expansive notion of identity, expanding what it means to be a citizen sounding across geographical and metaphorical borders.

This chapter looks at Dionne Brand's *Ossuaries* and offers connected thoughts on *The Blue Clerk*. Both texts invoke Miles Davis, Thelonious Monk, Billie Holiday, Charles Mingus, John Coltrane, and Charlie Parker—jazz musicians who employ disruptive techniques as well as repetition, epistrophe, blue notes, contrafacts, and improvisation in their compositions—and demonstrate the formal and deconstructive approach that Brand takes to remap a historically marginalized yet fluid community of resistance. Like the jazz artists *Ossuaries* and *The Blue Clerk* invoke (Charlie "Bird" Parker and Coltrane being at the epicentre of each work), the texts can be read as extended jazz solos that assert a poetics of dissent, difference, and disruption, thus opening new spaces of possibility for the globally defined citizen.

I. Jazz

> Jazz is a mode of democratic action, just as the blues is a mode of deep, tear-soaked individuality. Charlie Parker didn't give a damn. Jazz is the middle road between invisibility and anger. It is where self-confident creativity resides. Black music is the paradigm for how black people have best dealt with their humanity, their complexity, their good and bad, negative and positive aspects, without being excessively preoccupied with whites. Duke Ellington, Louis Armstrong, and Coltrane were just being themselves. And for whites interested in the

humanity of the "other," jazz—a purely American
form—provides them with examples of sheer and
rare genius.

—CORNEL WEST, *Hope on a Tightrope:*
Words and Wisdom, 102–3

Cornel West, ever the evocative writer, champions jazz as a powerful reaction by Black folk, as well as an expression of humanity. As with the previous section on blues music, it is hardly possible within the scope of this book to define and outline the entire history of jazz. Rather, I hope to provide context for how jazz is broadly conceived in *Soundin' Canaan*, as background that might prove useful when encountering a jazz text, such as Dionne Brand's *Ossuaries*: a jazz text, largely for its incorporation of jazz artists and jazz phraseology, which allows Brand and her central character, Yasmine, to move between the past and present and think through the improvisationally defined global citizen. Jazz, like the blues, is a distinct musical form, prominently of African American origin, that emerged in the United States in the early decades of the twentieth century. Similar to the blues, jazz incorporates, adapts, and subverts other musical elements, with early influences including "African and European music, American folk music, marching band music, plantation songs, spirituals and gospel music, minstrelsy, ragtime and the blues."[2] Jazz is defined by its ability to amalgamate other forms, along with the music's broader techniques, which include various rhythmic properties, from swing and syncopation to complex harmonic languages, as well as an overarching focus on improvisation.

Jazz artists took various instruments, in the way that DJs would later repurpose the turntable, to make a new (often improvised) music that would have very likely confounded the inventors of those instruments. African novelist Chinua Achebe poses useful rhetorical questions in his essay, "Colonialist Criticism," that surge to the heart of the matter:

> But, in any case, did not the black people in America, deprived of their own musical instruments, take the trumpet and the trombone and blow them as they had never been blown before, as

> indeed they were not designed to be blown? And the result, was it not jazz? Is any one going to say that this was a loss to the world or that those first Negro slaves who began to play around with the discarded instruments of their masters should have played waltzes and foxtrots? No! Let every people bring their gifts to the great festival of the world's cultural harvest and mankind will be all the richer for the variety and distinctiveness of the offerings.[3]

Achebe uses the example of jazz to articulate his right and need to use the Western novel form to express the experience of African people. Achebe's argument, with its cross-cultural and anti-colonial positioning, describes how African Americans utilized the instruments they had access to that enabled them create a music that was uniquely their own: a music contributing to the "world's cultural harvest," growing and taking root in a variety of musics, cultures, and soils. This is not to argue that jazz is not about tradition—far from it—but it is a tradition that can be modulated, although never possessed, once learned. As Ellison argues, "For after the jazzman has learned the fundamentals of his instrument and the traditional techniques of jazz—the intonations, the mute work, manipulation of timbre, the body of traditional styles—he must then find 'himself,' must be reborn, must find, as it were, his soul."[4] Hence, jazz is about finding alternatives to dominant modes of being. As Daniel Fischlin, Ajay Heble, and George Lipsitz contend, improvisation is a means to speak free of constraint, to assemble alternative communities, and improvisation provides a critique "of dominant structures of thought."[5]

Jazz finds space to reinterpret the self and dreams the future in meaningful ways. Jazz was one of the first musical styles to break away from monolithic conceptions of performance; it created music that was hard to emulate. Jazz encourages its performers to take chances, to step out on the ledge, and to blow freely, without restriction. In the previous chapter, we saw how George Elliott Clarke adapted blues and jazz to play with language, worry the line, and envision the self/citizen in relation to a larger community. Jazz remains an important stylistic innovation not only for music but for poetry as well, as Charles Olson in an interview once claimed: "Black Mountain Poetics" did not define the postmodern for the decade of the 1950s, for "there was no poetic. It was Charlie Parker."[6] Furthermore, there were entire movements in African American culture that linked poetry and music/jazz together, evidenced in the work of the Last Poets, and poet-musicians like Gil Scott-Heron. This is not to conflate jazz and poetry as unequivocally homologous, but it is to acknowledge that the two forms provide a thickness of meaning not possible in ordinary language. Such innovations, depending on one's initiation, can make music-inflected poetry challenging to read, but as Clarke argues in his reading of the highly skilled Black Canadian/American jazz poet, Frederick Ward, "difficulty in poetry is akin to dissonance in jazz."[7] Ward is a crucial example of how poets writing about or living in Canada have used jazz in literature to speak about their experiences.

Jazz music has a long history in Canada. The earliest jazz musicians heard in Canada were from the United States and appeared around the mid-1910s on vaudeville stages across the country. For example, the *Canadian Encyclopedia* describes how the Original Creole Orchestra, which "was a New Orleans ensemble that included the cornetist Freddie Keppard, toured the Pantages circuit in western Canada in 1914 and 1916, and Jelly Roll Morton, the self-proclaimed inventor of jazz[,] worked in Vancouver cabarets as early as 1919 and as late as 1921."[8] There are a number of excellent books that trace the diverse history of jazz in Canada, including the many informative books on the subject by Canadian jazz historian Mark Miller.[9] Miller's excellent work covers a wide range of material from numerous historical moments, Canadian jazz personalities (Oscar Peterson, Kenny Wheeler, and hundreds of others), and various jazz beginnings in Canada. Simply stated, there are long traditions in Canadian jazz, as well as Canadian jazz musicians who have inspired or rivalled various American jazz musicians as formative influences for young Canadian musicians. And while jazz is now part of the music curriculum at many schools, jazz in Canada for a long time, as in the United States, was often viewed as a danger and a perversion not only of music, but of morals, as Sarah-Jane Mathieu contends in her book, *North of the Color Line*: *Migration and Black Resistance in Canada*,

> Freddie Keppard

1870–1955. Despite, or because of, this threat, jazz thrived in most Canadian cities.

In Winnipeg, a jazz ensemble appropriately named the Porters' Union Band was made up of porters, masons, and Garveyites. Montreal, as Grizzle describes in *My Name's Not George*, was an important hangout for porters—"Paris of the North," or "Harlem of the North"—with the most popular joint being Rockhead's Paradise, which was opened in 1928 by former porter Rufus Rockhead.[10] Mathieu writes that, largely because jazz was thought to be a threat to institutions of whiteness, and especially because jazz often flourished in crowded urban areas were young people gathered, popular belief and law "concurred that jazz, drugs, and alcohol, presumably peddled by black porters and entertainers, jeopardized white Canadians' morality and white womanhood in particular."[11] Jazz, while it represented freedom and mobility for many, was often viewed by mainstream media as a threat to the nation's morals because of the dances it inspired and the racial intermingling that sometimes happened. The *New York American* reported around this time that "moral disaster is coming to hundreds of young American girls through the pathological, nerve-irritating, sex-exciting music of jazz orchestras." Such rhetoric about the deleterious effects of jazz were common in its early days. In 1900 a commentator in the American magazine *Etude* wrote that "the counters of the music store are loaded with this virulent poison which, in the form of a malarious epidemic, is finding its way into the homes and brains of youth to such an extent as to arouse one's suspicions of their sanity."[12] Esi Edugyan in her novel *Half-Blood Blues* examines the notion that jazz and those who played it were parasitic to Nazism. Her narrator, Sid, states with satire:

> Jazz. Here in Germany it become something worse than a virus. We was all of us damn fleas, us Negroes and Jews and low-life hoodlums, set on playing that vulgar racket, seducing sweet blond kids into corruption and sex. It was a plague sent out by the dread black hordes, engineered by the Jews. Us Negroes, see, we was only half to blame—we just can't help it. Savages just got a natural feel for filthy rhythms. . . We was officially degenerate.[13]

This sort of moral panic around jazz and miscegenation was hardly limited to Nazi Germany. Jazz novels set in Canada dealt with the same fears of the corrupting potential of jazz.

Morley Callaghan's novel *The Loved and the Lost* (1951) grapples with this notion of moral disaster, dealing as it does with the relationship between Blacks and whites in Canada and the anxieties that surround miscegenation. Set during the early 1950s in Montreal, the novel primarily concerns young, inscrutable Peggy Sanderson, who unabashedly consorts with both white and Black men in jazz clubs. In the novel, jazz is a space of danger but also one where interracial possibility is displayed. As we will see, jazz, as a creative force, in *Ossuaries* emphasizes the music's potential to cross all sorts of physical and psychological borders. It is important to note that in the pages of *The Loved and the Lost*, any interracial possibilities are planted strongly between the "peaceful pure whiteness of the snowbound city" and the "Nigger nightclubs" within the city.[14] It is as if, as Toni Morrison narrates in *Jazz*, "just hearing it [jazz] was like violating the law."[15]

Or just reading it: Chicago poet Gwendolyn Brooks's influential poem "We Real Cool" (1960), with the rhyming lines "We / Jazz June. We / Die soon," was occasionally banned simply because it mentioned the word "jazz."[16] And few literary trials were more incendiary than the 1957 obscenity trial over Allen Ginsberg's poem *Howl*, Part I which contains various references to jazz.[b] Additionally, the Brooks example reminds us that women (and non-binary and trans) poets and musicians have been subjected to marginalization and policing both from mainstream critics and within the larger literary spheres to which they belong. In the early days of jazz, the very notion that there could be women jazz instrumentalists was ridiculed. A 1938 editorial in *DownBeat*, under the headline "Why Women Musicians Are Inferior," stated, with clear misogynistic and racial parody, that there

---

[b] Also worth mentioning is the 1969 broadcast controversy in Finland, where a group of three actors read Ginsberg's *Howl* with jazz music specially composed for radio broadcast. The broadcast led to a criminal investigation by the Helsinki police because of the poem's alleged obscenity, particularly its references to homosexuality.

"should be women in jazz, but there is not. Why is it that outside a few sepia female[s], the woman musician never was born capable of sending anyone anywhere but to the nearest exit . . . You can forgive them for lacking guts in their playing but even women should be able to play with feeling and expression and they never do it."♭ The same pressures that faced women jazz instrumentalists often faced women writers. For instance, Brooks's powerfully blunt poem "The Mother," which deals with abortion, was nearly removed from the collection *A Street in Bronzeville* by the editor of the collection, Richard Wright. Wright argued it was not a fit subject for poetry, yet Brooks did not back down, assuring him it was. I argue that Brand and Philip continue to find new ways to articulate jazz on the page.

Still, I have not answered what jazz *is*, and I doubt that I could even if I devoted this entire book to that question (as others have done). Perhaps jazz, in all its ubiquity, tells us that it doesn't matter what it is, so long as the music continues to inspire people around the world. Thus, to return to my challenge to definitions that opened this book, we are reminded that definitions are useful in drafting strategies to clarify our objects/subjects of study, but they are hardly carved in stone. As bassist and writer William Parker reminds us, definitions are mutable and context-dependent and often don't translate into the real world: "Who cares what jazz is? Jazz is nothing. If jazz enlightens us and uplifts us, then it has value; if it dulls us and makes us less alive, then it

---

♭ In April 1938 instrumentalist Peggy Gilbert responded to *DownBeat*'s "Why Women Musicians are Inferior" with her own comment on the era's infamous discrimination against women musicians. The article was published, but much to her irritation, *Down Beat* renamed it "How Can You Blow a Horn With a Brassiere?" Nevertheless, Gilbert became a noted advocate for women instrumentalists. Furthermore, *DownBeat*'s argument holds little weight considering there were incredibly talented women jazz instrumentalists working at the time. Among the most influential was Mary Lou Williams, who was revered for her compositional skills by jazz artists like Benny Goodman, Duke Ellington, and Louis Armstrong. In the 1940s, Williams would inspire a whole generation of bebop artists, serving as a mentor to Thelonious Monk, Charlie Parker, Miles Davis, and Dizzy Gillespie, among many others. A few Mary Lou Williams songs can be found on the playlist.

has no value. Ask a starving child, 'What is jazz?' The child might say jazz is a hot plate of food."¹⁷ I don't want to expel definitions completely from the literary garden, for I think they have instructional value, especially if we make an effort to recast them, but Parker's example of how language is sometimes disconnected from the *real* is a valuable reminder that if jazz, or poetry, is to mean anything it must account for the divide between experience and aesthetic intangibility. Jazz is not just about sounds, or how words appear on a page; it is also about how those sounds and/or words function as tools to uplift and enlighten people who are willing to march to a different beat. In *Ossuaries*, Brand does just that. She looks at the complexities of our age and with a jazz sensitivity that grabs us from the first loaded note.

II. "History Will Enter Here"

> "My body is history, fossil, passé."
>
> —DIONNE BRAND, "I Used to Like the Dallas Cowboys," in *Sans Souci*, 128

> "I want nothing that enters me / screaming / claiming to be history"
>
> —DIONNE BRAND, "I Am Not that Strong Woman," 123

Ossuaries, an urgent long poem, as well as a vital listening of the modern crises of culture and ideas, concerns a revolutionary protagonist named Yasmine, who is on the run after robbing a bank. The text charts Yasmine's personal history over some thirty years and deals explicitly with history as a story to be reworked and recovered. In much of Brand's work, from *No Language Is Neutral* to *A Map to the Door of No Return*, history is a distortion that requires the poet's careful understanding and reworking. History can also be a great burden, particularly for people who have been subjected to or ruptured by its imaginative and corporeal machinations. Reflecting the *ostranenie* effects of poetry,♭ the poetic notation and explication of history in Brand's work is often disjunctive, disruptive, and free from linearity. Fred Wah, in his essay "Strang(l)ed Poetics," views jazz, with its open-endedness and its free-moving lines, as an aesthetic model suitable to the *ostranenie* effect of avant-garde poetics: "Certainly the jazz model of a freely moving line playing off of and against the bound chord progressions showed me the delight of distortion and surprise."[18] It is precisely this free movement of ruptured lines throughout time that *Ossuaries*—as well as *A Map to the Door of No Return*—encompasses in its sounding, tracing the absences of untraceable absences: "It was a rupture in history, a rupture in the quality of being... Blacks in the New World Diaspora... signified the end of traceable beginnings."[19] Jazz artists create new lines of play upon a standard, "reshap[ing] time"; similarly, to live in the diaspora entails an act of constant self-creation: "To live in the Black Diaspora is I think to live as a fiction—a creation of empires, and also self-creation."[20] In writing against the oppressive violence of history, Yasmine attempts a renaming, an opening up of the historic, much like "the arms wide as Olaudah Equiano."[21] Like the slave narrative of Equiano, which provides a voice for "the poor creature [who is] cruelly loaded with various kinds of iron machines," including an iron muzzle to prevent speech, Yasmine and the unnamed narrator provide a voice to the historically silenced.[22] This widening of history to a genealogy of lived communal experience, this writing against a written history so as to avow an upward mobility to a community that has been immobilized, is a generative act of opening up space. As a poet, Yasmine renders her own history palpable by tracing its various subversive inscriptions from an underground position to enact a citizenship that is poethically♯ bound

---

♭ Defamiliarization or *ostranenie* (остранение) is the artistic technique of persuading the audience to see familiar things in an unfamiliar or strange way to enhance perception of the familiar; essentially, the process or result of rendering unfamiliar (OED).

♯ "Poethical" is a useful neologism that combines ethics with poetics. It comes from Joan Retallack's *The Poethical Wager* and is a term "that beckons towards the reader for help" (62).

in the enactment of rereading and relistening—of a citizenship freely and extemporaneously moving across borders.

Yasmine works against simple constructions of linear narratives that prioritize the Hegelian process of dialectics; she participates in what Kamau Brathwaite terms *tidalectics*, which provides an Africanist model for thinking about history and which provides a cyclical approach to history rather than a linear one (this is taken up more fully in chapter 5). As Edward Said discusses in *Orientalism*, we are products of historical processes to date, which have left in us numerous traces, without a precise inventory. Therefore, there is importance to creating historical inventories, especially for minority and disenfranchised subjects, who must work through the traces of imperial domination, gender, race, and class. The jazz strategies that Brand and Yasmine apply in *Ossuaries* are acts of historical recovery. Yasmine's jazz-sounding and circular narrative is a process that works through her, responds, and creates her own subject position. In this fashion, repetition, a type of circulation, is one of the central tools of the jazz performer and improviser; it allows the performer to connect to a larger global community while permitting, albeit from a liminal space of difference, critiques of power structures, even while the unequivocal grip of history asserts itself: "history will enter here."[23] In moving between various geographies (Algiers, Cuba, Canada) and periodic crises (most topically, the Iraq War), Yasmine asserts a politics of dissent, of timeless struggle, and claims a difference in relation to Western historiography, thus also rewriting herself as an improvised Other.

Ossuaries moves freely from "Bird" to Monk to Mingus, to the far-out regions of Coltrane's free jazz. Rather than a static written or recorded historiography, the text and recorded media insist on being sounded and listened to. The eruptive and beautiful outerspace keening of Coltrane's playing on "Venus" reflects the notion that there is value in a history of disunity—a disunity that Yasmine tries to recover through her own mnemonic jazz historiography. Figuratively, this is a history that can never be fully recovered, for as Sharon Morgan Beckford has argued, "New World Africans' history is one of adoption: slaves being adopted into a new family, left without a full history."[24] Brand (Yasmine) turns this disunity into an opportunity to respond to the silences of history through acts of historical reimagining and careful engagement. Hence, as playwright Suzan-Lori Parks argues, history is always open to rewritings, especially in cases where the disenfranchised have been written out of history. Challenging written history and a dominant centre through remix, Park says: "Since history is a recorded or remembered event, theatre, for me, is the perfect place to 'make' history—that is, because so much African-American history has been unrecorded, dismembered, washed out, one of my tasks as playwright is to ... locate the ancestral burial ground, dig for bones, find bones, hear the bones sing, write it down."[25] I like this notion of digging up bones (a fitting comparison, given that an "ossuary" is a container for bones), which reminds us that the jazz historiography participates in a polyrhythmic archaeological digging up of the repressed bones that consume Yasmine. Nevertheless, despite such containment, *Ossuaries*, and Black Canadian literature more generally, is about recovery, and doubly so for Black women.

Marlene Goldman describes how the body of a Black woman is often a figurative symbol of oppression, one that "signal[s] 'a form of memory that is lived only through the body.'"[26] Furthermore, as Brand suggests, to live in a Black body is to embody a history situated as a sign of particular cultural and political meanings in the diaspora: "They remain fixed in the ether of history."[27] The philosophy of dualism sees the mind and body as separate; yet the mind and body are *in*divisible, for the physiological and psychological confront the past and present through embodied experiences. As Christina Sharpe adeptly puts it, "history for Brand [is] written on her flesh, as an optic that guides her way of seeing, understanding, and accounting for her place in the world."[28] Themes of exile and diaspora reverberate throughout Brand's work, in which we often encounter women who resist colonialism and oppressive spaces and find freedom in flight and change. In *Ossuaries* this is reflected in Yasmine's constant need to be on the run to wherever "the sonorous oceans took [her]." The ocean and water metaphors throughout the text recall the trauma of the Middle Passage, as Yasmine thinks of "the deepest suicidal blue waters," "'shipping out' ... like this passages continuum ... as if we could exhume ourselves from these mass graves."[29] Water in *Ossuaries* is both assault and healing, for even though "she's not coastal," like sediment washing Yasmine's past along with the larger injustices of history (such as slavery) ashore, Yasmine is able to take control of her own destiny.[30] As Katie Mullins details, in her reading of Brand's short story collection *Sans Souci*, "it is only when one has the power to feel pain, to confront a violent and oppressive history, that one can gain the power to heal." Furthermore, in a rather salient reading of Brand's relationship with the body and history, Mullins elaborates: "By making the bodies of black women sites of inscription for past, present, and possible future events, these bodies ultimately assume an overwhelming . . . power that is liberatory for black women who re-claim their past."[31] As an ossuary is a container or room in which the bones of dead people are placed, the larger metaphor of an ossuary contains history, as well as sediments, repositories, and traces of bones to be recovered and made into inventory.

The notion of the container represents Yasmine's confinement in and subjugation to the boundaries of a world that compels her to rob a bank. The structure of *Ossuaries* illustrates the notion of containment, in that the long poem is divided into fifteen different ossuaries, or containers. In "Ossuary XI" the world is described as a giant Ossuary.[32] History as containment is even more fixed for those who remain haunted by the past (see NourbeSe's description of the *Zong* massacre as "hauntological" in the next chapter). Brand's writing complicates Northrop Frye's question, "Where is Here?," which in the context of the African diaspora alludes to dislocation and loss. Leslie Sanders writes that "for those who came in chains, history is a haunting"—it is "hauntological." The poet's task, then, "is to render history palpable, trace its inscription in and through personal narrative in order to unfold its wider significance."[33] Because history resides in language, Brand's dealing with the language of history—of historical inventories, many of which are extremely oppressive, and which appear throughout *Ossuaries*—is about confronting lived genealogy. In "Ossuary XI" Yasmine sits in a museum and reads/contemplates Jacob Lawrence's *War Series*, particularly "victory," which actually "looked like defeat," even though history might paint war as glorious for the victors. Lawrence[b]—a beloved African American painter, whose paintings Yasmine reads like poems, engulfed in their "stanzaic and raw elations"—envisions what war actually looks like in his gouache *War Series*: "their painter knew the rimlessness of any hopes."[34] No history is impartial, just as no language is neutral. The speaker of Brand's *No Language is Neutral* writes herself into a canon that fails to see her:

> History will only hear you if you give birth to a
> woman who smoothes starched linen in the wardrobe
> drawer, trembles when she walks and who gives birth
> to another woman who cries near a river and
> vanishes and who gives birth to a woman who is a
> poet, and, even then.[35]

From an underground space, and against a history of oppression, Yasmine engages with the recurring catastrophes of the contained world. Against the impossibilities of living and loving congruently the jazz soundings in the text provide a way through the chaos into a space where inventory can be recollected, and where hope for the future, however faint, is possible.

III: Ossuaries

Writing Jazz

> "But the chaos is always resolved into order ... the trumpet calls, the ensemble answers, comforts, screams out its tight collective protest against the (white) withholding world."
>
> —KAMAU BRATHWAITE, "Jazz and the West Indian Novel," 277

---

[b] Lawrence referred to his style as "dynamic cubism," although by his own account the primary influence was not so much French art as the shapes and colours of Harlem.

> Bud Powell, Max Roach, Duke Ellington, Count Basie, and Mary Lou Williams

In the introduction to his work *A Poetics*—a title that recalls Aristotle's *Poetics*—Charles Bernstein asserts that *"poetry is an aversion* in the pursuit of new forms, or can be."³⁶ While Bernstein's statement is imbued with a tone of negative capability♭ and modernist sentiment, it serves as a reminder that poetry, or art for that matter, is at its best an alacritous and polemical pursuit of "dissent" that seeks out alternative possibilities. Dionne Brand's long poem *Ossuaries*, like Charles Mingus's jazz tone poem "Pithecanthropus Erectus"—a meshing of sumptuous and disparate sounds, rich in sonic adventurism, which Brand intertextually references—is an ekphrastic sounding for freedom amid the ruins of an often oppressive world. Jazz, given the exigencies of the political, cultural, and sonic soundscape from which it was shaped, is the paragon modal—in the jazz sense♯—to score *Ossuaries*. In her essay "Jazz" (from *Bread Out of Stone*) Brand describes how jazz and literature were part and parcel of her developing consciousness when she was growing up, reading literary classics while listening to jazz on the radio: "This is where I end up each night with Bud Powell, Charlie Parker, Max Roach, Duke Ellington and Count Basie. This music has a cool quality. Makes me feel older and more intelligent than I am at nine or ten . . . I read *Little Women* to Miles Davis, *Wuthering Heights* and *The Year in San Fernando* to John Coltrane and *Lady Chatterley's Lover* and Mills and Boon Romances to Mary Lou Williams." Listening at the radio, Brand asserts, "jazz and literature melded into big people's lives, a life I was going to have."³⁷ Both jazz and literature are sets of arranged sounds, and given her experience with jazz music at such a young age, it is only natural, improvisational even, that Brand would make use of music

---

♭ By way of a gloss, the concept of negative capability comes from poet John Keats. It is a theory that describes the capacity for accepting uncertainty and irresolution in life and was applied by Keats primarily to his analysis of Shakespeare.

♯ Rather than a model, I am using modal to refer to modal jazz—as discussed in the prior chapter in regard to Davis's *Kind of Blue*, and a kind of jazz that uses modes rather than chord progressions—to emphasize the emotive and improvisational framework of Yasmine's character and Brand's larger structural goals.

to articulate the consciousness of her characters, as well as her own critical thinking.

After all, as Brand asserts in "Jazz," jazz artists' "gift of improvisation is their open invitation for joining and resolution, their proposition for oneness and union, but I feel that their proposition hasn't been risen to, appreciated or paid back."[38] In this way, *Ossuaries* not only pays these artists back by using their artistry as a laudable poetic form for the global oppressed citizen (particularly Black and queer women) but also employs jazz as a metaphor for a "coming community" that is able, through improvisation, to function along a contingent axis of meaning across different spheres of race relations, music, time, and possibility. Fischlin, Heble, and Lipsitz urgently link musical improvisation to social rights, outlining how "both rights and improvisation call into being what [they] call an ethics of cocreation, an understanding that all things are interconnected co[-]creatively."[39] Blackness, for Brand in *Ossuaries*, is always in process, co-creative, interconnected, freely malleable and open-ended, and socially minded, and it far exceeds categories of the biological or the ethnic. To borrow from Rinaldo Walcott's description of Blackness, Brand's *Ossuaries* functions in an in-between space where politics and ethics refuse "the boundaries of national discourses. To be black and at home in Canada is to both belong and not belong."[40] Thus Yasmine, the central character of *Ossuaries*, is a (presumably African American) woman who lives an underground life (like Dante, Dostoevsky's narrator in *Notes from Underground*, and Ellison's unnamed protagonist before her) of constant malleability and movement—belonging and (un)belonging at times—as she crosses tangible borders (Algiers, Cuba, New York, Canada) and anachronistically weaves through time *vis-à-vis* the text's sonic jazz *verbings*.♭ In *Ossuaries*, Brand once again writes about the experience of the refugee and takes the issue of belonging—or not belonging, which can be positive at times—up to complex boundaries that challenge any simple understanding of identity or community within a

---

♭ *Verbings*, because the jazz not only helps aestheticize the text, but it also actively pushes it forward.

globalized framework. Yasmine is exemplary of the ebb of globalization and is *par excellence* the world citizen who, like a jazz artist, is always responding to change. As a result, like the work of the jazz artists invoked throughout *Ossuaries* (Charlie "Bird" Parker being at the epicentre of the work), Brand's text can be read as an extended jazz solo that draws improvisation from the margins of history to assert a poetics of dissent, difference, and disruption, which emboldens the rights of a shifting community that has been othered.

<small>Coltrane and Charlie Parker</small>

Brand's direct invocation of jazz artists Miles Davis, Thelonious Monk, Charles Mingus, John Coltrane, and Charlie Parker♭—musicians who themselves employ disruptive techniques in their compositions, as well as repetition, epistrophe, blue notes, contrafacts, and improvisation—highlights both the formal and deconstructive lexical approach that Brand takes to remapping a historically marginalized community onto a parallel present, thus creating a fluid community of resistance. This community of repetition and difference recalls what poet and scholar Amiri Baraka calls the resistive, anti-simulacrum power of bebop: the "willfully harsh, *anti-assimilationist* sound of bebop."[41] *Ossuaries*'s antiphonic calling upon a musically and historically displaced community, through constant interplay and musical intertextuality (a polyphonic layering), opens the text to multiple interpretations from its readers; thus, it enacts within its own unfolding a listening praxis that is ethically grounded in the possibilities of a better future. Jazz, as a methodological reading lens, provides a creative articulation for the possibility of a more inclusive future; as bell hooks declares, "African American performance has been a site for the imagination of future possibilities."[42] The text, read as a call towards freedom—like Coltrane's *Ascension*

♭ Pivotal jazz figures appear elsewhere in the work of Dionne Brand— notably in her novel *What We All Long For*—including artists such as Miles Davis, the Art Ensemble of Chicago, Thelonious Monk (particularly his "Epistrophy," which is an important recording in *Ossuaries*), John Coltrane (particularly his "Venus," which is also one of the key jazz recordings that animates *Ossuaries*), Ornette Coleman, Billie Holiday, and Cecil Taylor, among others. I've added a few of these artists to the playlist.

or *Interstellar Space*,♭ and like Parker's improvised and groundbreaking use of rhythmic dissonance in songs such as "Ornithology" and "Ko-ko"—offers the reader an opportunity to hear the world anew, even if it is *vis-à-vis* an eruptive, often discombobulated and fissured warning "to a fatal future."⁴³

In fact, the act of listening, metaphorically enacted as an extended jazz solo, becomes a central trope of *Ossuaries* as the text weaves in and out of diachronic and synchronic temporalities. This asserts a poetic politics that values difference yet also looks for hope in subversive political manifestos (often with Marxist tendencies) ‡ and innovative jazz cadenzas to provide a theoretical framework to cope with the anxieties of existing in a globalized and often alienating (and xenophobic) world, particularly for Brand's global citizen and protagonist, Yasmine. *Ossuaries*' remix of genre allows for multiple passageways into the text, challenging its readers to participate in an archaeological digging up of the repressed bones that consume Yasmine: she says, "I was caged in bone spur endlessly."⁴⁴ The provocative dialogics conjoin with jazz as an interpretive form for Brand's own jazz-like poetics. Brand's approach to her long poem *Ossuaries* is reminiscent of an extended jazz solo: the only concrete punctuation marks in the text are commas, and the text does not even end with a period, suggesting that its enactment persists even after we put the book down. Furthermore, the play between the narrator (who is very possibly a version of Brand herself) and Yasmine, who take turns soloing over each "Ossuary" (what I presume to be Yasmine on the odd numbers, the narrator on the even), adds to the antiphonic quality that draws the reader into the performance. While Brand's poetry often reads as

---

♭ These are some of Coltrane's most improvised and avant-garde works with a direct political context. Fischlin and Heble argue that Coltrane's 1965 collective improvisation for *Ascension* can audibly be heard as a sonic approximation of the spirit and the movement that has historically animated the narratives and struggles of African Americans. "The Other Side," 26.

‡ The text references the work of Karl Marx (particularly *The Eighteenth Brumaire of Louis Bonaparte*) and Friedrich Engels (particularly *The Origin of the Family, Private Property, and the State*).

an incredibly structured vernacular (each chapter opens with one tercet and then continues with five on each page), only deviating from the tercet form twice,[45] in many ways so does improvisation, in that it allows you to create compound spaces of play and revision over former models. The inclusion of Coltrane's free improvised "Venus" in the acknowledgments is perhaps an entryway into the text: "Venus" is a sounding of space that literally takes us beyond the space of the poem and into "unknown galaxies."[46] As Brand notes in "Verso 14" from *The Blue Clerk*, "the tercets are like Rashied Ali's drums, consistent, sheltering, pushing: the three lines are completely steady."[47] The text is controlled and free, as well as virtuosic in its ability to simultaneously be both. Readers are drawn into the text's sounding and what Yasmine herself describes as a "violent syntax and the beginning syllabi of verblessness."[48][♭] Readers less familiar with jazz might find the references to jazz texts and artists disorienting, but such disorientation helps assert the poetic marginality of the text in relation to more popularly consumed genres, as well as its resounding call for freedom to a global community of fragmentary—possibly exiled, or on the run—listeners.

The question of whether *Ossuaries* is a jazz poem—or an avant-garde poem, for that matter—is more generatively focused by asking how it participates in the jazz form, and how it utilizes jazz (as an avant-garde manifesto and motif) to assert its difference. Brand continues to provide an inventory (much like her prior work, *Inventory*) of the tumultuous horrors of the modern world, and jazz is one of the strategies she uses to soundtrack her approach. *Ossuaries* not only contains a jazz structure but also employs jazz in theme, as identity, history, culture; and Yasmine's own fractured narrative skips and jumps like a soloist over the chord progressions of the tercet. Jazz is the sonic zeitgeist of the twentieth century, appearing in everything

---

[♭] Numerous avant-garde poets have employed the disjunctive jazz form and content in their poetics: Amiri Baraka, Charles Simic, Michael Harper, Yusef Komunyakaa, William Corbett, Al Young, Robert Creeley, Jack Kerouac—who applied improvised jazz licks to his poetics—and countless others.

from the "Jazz Age" writers such as Fitzgerald, and the Harlem Renaissance writers such as Ishmael Reed with his boisterous/cutup jazz fantasy, *Mumbo Jumbo*, to texts by Beat writers like Jack Kerouac and more contemporary texts like Toni Morrison's *Jazz*. In *Jazz*, for example, Morrison uses jazz as a larger metaphor for the lifeblood of the city: "It pulls him like a needle through the groove of a Bluebird record. Round and round about the town. That's the way the city spins you."[49] Brand's novel *What We All Long For* describes the city using comparable jazz-influenced language: "Yes, that was the beauty of this city, it's polyphonic, murmuring . . . that gathering of voices and longings that summed themselves up into a kind of language, yet indescribable."[50] Despite the fact that *Ossuaries* employs some of jazz's most important—as well as lesser known—pieces, like Coltrane's "Venus," it is easy to mistake Brand's writing as overly traditional and formal, especially since there are but two deviations from the tercet in *Ossuaries*.

One critic, Lynette Hunter, applies misguided criticism that not only reads Brand's work under a neat modernist guise but also elevates her to the level of a sociologist whose politics are effective because her work is traditional: "Politically the most assertive of the three writers discussed here [Brand, Claire Harris, and M. NourbeSe Philip], Brand is poetically the most traditional."[51] Comparing the political utility of Black women writers against one another is unproductive; moreover, Hunter's labelling of Brand as overtly traditional overshadows Brand's innovations and interest in contemporary dilemmas—in finding new ways to speak and challenge authority. Brand's work is indeed innovative, and aesthetic and social dissent are inseparably and strangely harmonious. Timothy Yu defines the analytic power of the avant-garde as that which "reminds us that the aesthetic and the social are inseparable . . . defined as much by a distinctive kind of community as by its revolutionary aesthetics."[52] The blending, the improvising even, of tradition and innovation, of revolutionary politics and aesthetics, is effusively articulated throughout Brand's *Ossuaries*, her most fully realized jazz sounding.

Ornithology: New Languages

> "Charlie Parker tears through the night. A heavy, humid Tristes Tropiques kind of night. Jazz always makes me think of New Orleans, and that makes a Negro nostalgic."
>
> —DANY LAFERRIÈRE, *How to Make Love to a Negro without Getting Tired*, 9

Charlie Parker Like Charlie "Bird" Parker, a great improviser invoked directly and symbolically throughout the text (see pages 45–46, 70, 144–45, and 160–61), *Ossuaries* challenges notions of canonicity (what fits) by constantly rewriting itself. What is not written in *Ossuaries*, the in-between spaces of silence, as well as the palimpsestic reverberations throughout, are apostrophic callings towards the malleability of any singular interpretation. Like Bird's "Ornithology," one of the acknowledged sources in the appendix, which is a contrafact—that is, a newly created melody written over the chord progressions of another song, in this instance the standard "How High the Moon"—Yasmine constantly writes over herself. Parker's "Ornithology," which remains one of the most popular and frequently performed bebop tunes, is emblematic of the jazz tradition; furthermore, Charlie Parker afforded writers—particularly marginalized writers who related to the dissonant notes, repetition, and energy in "Bird's" emotive and evocative playing and revising of tradition—more innovative modes of expression to emulate in their writing.

In the spirit of Charlie Parker, *Ossuaries*, along with its extemporal and on-the-go Yasmine, wobbles like a blue note, a worried or unsettled note that is sung or played at a slightly slower pitch than that of the major scale, for expressive tension: "being there out of her elemental America / unsettles her, untethers her." Brand wields disorder, paradoxically, as an unsettled ordering, packing her lines with energy and freedom, expert control, replete with repetitions and cadences that articulate the cacophonous history of Yasmine, who is "discomfited" and whose own lyrical "I" is fissured as an ambivalent "slippery pronoun."⁵³ The disharmony of the text recalls a larger tradition of dissonance in jazz; for example, Duke Ellington equated dissonance in jazz with the African American experience: "Hear that chord. That's us. Dissonance is our way of life in America. We are something apart, yet an integral part."⁵⁴ Under this rubric, the jazz modal offers an aesthetic form to animate the revolutionary and discordant nature of Yasmine. As Yu asserts in *Race and the Avant-Garde*, "racial others [such as Charlie Parker] offered an escape from Western aesthetics, serving as a source for the revolutionary breakthroughs that have characterized the twentieth-century avant-garde."⁵⁵ Yu's assertion of racial otherness as aesthetically radical reminds us that the form of jazz and the politics of dissent are inseparable in a text such as *Ossuaries*. Form and content are interrelated, interdependent, and interactive. Yet *Ossuaries* is also unique in creating soundings that engage in a critical reading praxis of its own sounding: it is aware that it is a text built around other texts, and aware of itself, from its opening moments, as a "looking back," a reflection upon its own unreadability.⁵⁶

Ossuaries, swimming within the language currents of incomprehensibility, asserts its untranslatability throughout: "each bone has its lost dialect now, / untranslatable though I had so many languages"; "here she is a polyglot"; "so first the language she would never quite learn." Despite these challenges, "we listen."⁵⁷ Essentially, the text, in reading itself, intimates that no single or authoritative reading is possible; rather, it provokes intersecting possibilities that are consonant with the assembling qualities that typify readings of the long poem, as well as improvisatory and avant-garde performances in jazz. In *On the Edge of Genre*, Smaro Kamboureli makes the compelling argument that "the inclusiveness of the long poem does not presuppose a harmonious interrelationship among its mixed literary kinds, nor does it necessitate a complete cancelling out of their idiosyncratic generic elements."⁵⁸ Kamboureli's reading of the inclusive, yet often disruptive, assembling of the long poem is distinctly the pursuit that compels the meta-narrative unfolding between the narrator (unnamed), Yasmine, the speaking text, and the reader, and this happens within a space of contrasting interpretations that assemble and disassemble generic prefixes. Beyond jazz, several genres push and pull against readings of the text, such as the mock-epic, not only in encompassing and critiquing epic form,[59] but also in Yasmine's own purgative journey towards redemption in the hope for a better future. *Ossuaries* does more than play upon the epic form, as a jazz improviser plays upon a standard; in calling the epic form into recognition it doubly subverts the epic form and meaning while paying homage to the epic's inherent referentiality.

The most direct epic at hand in *Ossuaries*, as I read it, is Dante's *Divine Comedy*, whose form is also built around a variation of the tercet (*terza rima*), and whose own speaker, like Yasmine, struggles to redeem his lost love amid the depths of hell while living in the present. In many ways, Dante Alighieri, as poet and citizen, and poet and traveller in his text, provides a poignant counterpoint to Brand and her Yasmine. Both Dante and Yasmine are exiled (Brand can be read as a self-exiled poet from her own Trinidad), and like Dante, Yasmine must find a new language to express her epic travel into an underground while struggling between the occupations of living and loving. In "Ossuary III," Yasmine tells us that to live and love are simultaneously impossible: that we can only truly do (or perform) one at a time: "lived and loved, common oxymoron, / if I have lived, I have not loved, / and if I have loved, I cannot have lived."[60] Yet Yasmine is no Dante, and certainly she is no Beatrice, being closer to a Charlie Parker figure of a jazz underworld, whose love is moved by dissent: a dissent that is a descent like Dante's (or Ellison's nameless protagonist in *Invisible Man*) into the uncharted realms of inward and outward revolutionary action. These Dantean allusions, within the shifting jazz intertextualities, allow *Ossuaries* to be read as modelling a reading practice where disparate traditions are read in relation to and against one another, moving the text into an expressive reappropriation of history:

> this genealogy she's made by hand, this good silk lace,
> Engels plaited to Bird, Claudia Jones edgestitched
> to Monk, Rosa Luxemburg braids Coltrane
>
> as far as she's concerned these names reshaped time.[61]

The genealogy the text constructs, reading jazz giants in relation to feminist activists, invites the type of play that happens in both political and jazz arenas.♭ Furthermore, the above passage reveals that in *Ossuaries* the discordant jazz textuality is inseparable from the discordant political textuality: Yasmine's dissent and her embodiment of multiple *topoi* function congruently within a variety of social and aesthetic margins. This remixed approach is played out as Yasmine and the narrator trade off between each "Ossuary," often blurring the lines of who is speaking. As readers and listeners, we are challenged to untangle the polyphony of voices presented to us.

In describing harmolodic music, avant-garde jazz musician Ornette Coleman states, "The kind of music we play, no one player has the lead," signifying that meaning is a patchwork of disparate speaking voices.[62] Aldon Lynn Nielsen asserts that "harmolodic music destroys the conventional view of the relationship between melody line and background musician."[63]♯ The issue of who is speaking is overshadowed by the impulse to listen, which ultimately defers absolute meaning or ending. *Ossuaries* does not preclude ending, but rather suggests "new" possibilities for movement that are largely antithetical to modernist innovation, yet that fit within a radicalism that invites critiques of the past. Even though Brand's poetic form in *Ossuaries* contains (the way an ossuary contains a skeleton) highly formalized vernacular (the tercet formalism of the poem perhaps seemingly an odd choice for innovative delivery), it is also spontaneous. *Ossuaries* mirrors jazz's

<small>Ornette Coleman</small>

♭ Claudia Jones (1915–64) was a Black Nationalist, political activist, and communist in the United States. Rosa Luxemburg (1871–1919) was a Marxist theorist, philosopher, and political activist of Polish Jewish descent who became a naturalized German citizen.

♯ Harmolodics is the musical philosophy of Ornette Coleman and is associated primarily with the jazz avant-garde movement, although many of its implications extend beyond these limits. Coleman defines harmolodics as the incorporation of one's physical and logical components into an expression of sound. Applied to the particulars of music, harmolodics means that "harmony, melody, speed, rhythm, time and phrases all have equal position in the results that come from the placing and spacing of ideas." Coleman, "Prime Time for Harmolodics," *Down Beat* (July 1983): 54–55.

unpredictable history of improvisation and innovation, even within a perceived standard. Brand displays virtuosic delivery upon the received standard of the tercet. Her poetics are not quite the "make it new" that Pound has in mind, although the concept of making it new is hardly a solely Euro-poetic construct of modernism.[64]

Brand's Yasmine displays a scathing cynicism towards some of the exclusionary practices of modernism, using Miles Davis as a signified phallic and misogynistic innovator and as a counterpoint to the positive portrayals of other jazz artists in the text.[b] In the previous chapter I mentioned Davis's innovative virtuosity. However, for Yasmine, Miles Davis is also an oppressive force, like that of her male comrade and lover, particularly for his misogynistic views, which are displayed openly in the title of Davis's *Bitches Brew*. With a political reverence for Fanon and an abhorrence of Davis, Yasmine muses, "Miles's 'Bitches Brew' on the stereo and Fanon / like a double-edged knife in her teeth . . . the thin mean horn she hated / . . . the cynicism and who gives a fuck trumpet."[65] Davis is certainly one of the great jazz innovators of the twentieth century; however, Yasmine troubles this reading of Davis and searches for a "music still unheard."[66] Using jazz, *Ossuaries* does not provide agency to the past over the present so much as it looks toward the freedom the future may hold.

Returning to the jazz poetics this chapter uses as a model/modal for critical practice, as well as the recognition of emotive confession the text enacts in its own reading, this chapter reads *Ossuaries* as a search for new grammars, for new symbolically coded speech. William Harris writes, "It is not an improvement or modification of available techniques that the black artist requests; rather, his call is for an entirely new grammar."[67] Like the work of fellow Afrosporic (Trinidadian Canadian) poet M. NourbeSe Philip, the grammar of *Ossuaries* might aptly be described under what Philip terms *kinopoeia*: "*the kinetic quality of language which . . . is best exhibited by those vernaculars that combine the African with (in this case) English.*"[68]

---

[b] In her book *Mad at Miles*, Pearl Cleage makes the argument that she was not able to listen to Miles Davis's softly muted trumpet without hearing the muted screams of the women he blatantly abused.

Throughout the text, Yasmine is forced to speak a "new sign language" in order to regain mobility, to regain voice and agency, in the same way that the poem asserts an anarchistic approach to received standards, paralleling jazz's value in the repetition of difference.[69] In the changing of forms, in the reworking of language through the acknowledgment of its limitations, and in her "dim-lit ambiguous" stanzas, Yasmine, along with the narrator, values constant transmutability, trying to balance the cultural and the anarchistic.[70] Parallel to Charlie Parker, Yasmine rejects static traditionalism as she improvises the self. Parker ideally represents another "order" beyond the realm of the popular: Parker was notorious for turning his back on his audience while he soloed. It's not that Yasmine or Parker don't reproduce tradition, it's that they break the mould of expectations, which is why it is ridiculous that so many of Parker's improvised solos have been transcribed for "exact" performance and popular consumption. The various repetitions in *Ossuaries*, and there are many, are always performed with a difference.

Epistrophy: Repetition with Difference

> "There is no Negro *problem*. There is no Southern *problem*. There is no Northern *problem*. There is only an American *problem*."
>
> —LYNDON B. JOHNSON, "The American Promise," March 15, 1965 (emphasis added)

The above epigraph, taken from then President Lyndon B. Johnson's call for Congress to remove the barriers that prevented all Americans from voting, besides being a response to the torrid and entropic civil rights movement, is an epistrophe: an emphatic device that places emphasis on the last word in a phrase or sentence. The device is also used by Thelonious Monk—as it is by Brand throughout *Ossuaries*—in his song "Epistrophy," a composition built on thirty-two bars that does not follow the standard AABA form, as bars 9 to 12 are a repeat

Thelonious Monk

of 5 to 9, and bars 13 to 16 repeat bars 1 to 4.♭ Monk's "Epistrophy" undoes and repeats itself, much like Yasmine's constant writing over herself in a perpetual undoing: "to undo, to undo and undo and undo this infinitive."⁷¹ This undoing, within the infiniteness of the infinitive, is also a redoing, a series of repetitions that address the reader by way of redressing meaning. The formal technique of epistrophe, functioning somewhat like an antistrophe (the return to a movement), is a direct reference to the song "Epistrophy," by Thelonious Monk, which is acknowledged while putting its maxim into praxis: "I've got no time, no time, this epistrophe, no time, / wind's coming, no time, / one sunrise to the next is too long, no time." "No time," ironically, is repeated time and time again, highlighting the form of epistrophe, which is the repetition of the same words at the end of successive phrases, clauses, or sentences, which is precisely how it functions in Monk's imbued, emotive, and disruptively timed playing. Time and disruption are crucial to the jazz allusions in the text, as the text's localities shift in and out of time, trying to escape the grips of history with epistrophic urgency and a constant yearning for newness: "or are we still slaves in this old city, / back then, back then, always back then."⁷² Brand's use of epistrophe recalls how variation and repetition are integral in jazz.

Henry Louis Gates Jr. elucidates, "Repetition of a form and then inversion of the same through a process of variation is central to jazz."⁷³ Thus, repetition is always different in each of its sonic iterations, an idea supported by Jeffery T. Nealon, who states, "African-American traditions have deployed 'repetition with a difference' as a key concept in maintaining a vibrant culture on the margins of the American mainstream."⁷⁴ *Ossuaries* is full of repetitions, but they are not merely a technique of asserting rhythmic permeations that affirm Blackness, for Yasmine is not necessarily semiotically charged as a purveyor of African American culture (her name is after all Arabic and Persian in origin), so much as she signifies difference: the rep-

---

♭ "Epistrophy" was once even called, as Robin D. G. Kelley details, "Iambic Pentameter," which suits the cadenced meter of Monk's composition. Kelley, *Life*, 564.

etition of the violent gazes throughout the text signifies Yasmine's alterity to hegemonic culture. It is precisely her somatic and linguistic differences that alienate Yasmine as she travels abroad. While in Havana, as a foreigner who is doubly alienated, culturally and grammatically, Yasmine can only live "on rations of diction, / shortened syntax," a partial language that turns her, in her viewing and anthropophagic (cannibalistic) consumption by others, into a scopophilia♭ of alterity, into language itself: "she became allegorical, she lost metaphora." Yasmine is anthropophagically consumed as an "other," as a "specimen, / at the anthropometric spectacle," "in the museum of spectacle," recalling the dehumanizing processes of colonization, slavery, and subjugations of difference.[75] Difference with repetition becomes a theme of *Ossuaries*, one that challenges us to consider how Yasmine fits within the social vicissitudes of various resistive cultures, such as jazz, African American culture, and globalized alterity; furthermore, her repetitions provide the framework for her various flights across time and space to assert a polyphonic identity (free, yet contained with the container of each poetic ossuary). When Brand evokes and uses the form and spirit of Monk's "Epistrophy," it is no mere simulacrum of the piece, but rather an interpretation that includes difference, emphasizing Yasmine's extemporal identity.

♭ *Scopophilia* is derived from Greek and refers to the "love of looking"—generally, one's deriving pleasure from looking at someone. The term has been used by psychoanalysts, such as Jacques Lacan, and was borrowed by cinema psychoanalysts (such as in Laura Mulvey's "Visual Pleasure and Narrative Cinema") of the 1970s to describe pleasures in spectators when they watch films (men as the active looker and women as the passive observed). Furthermore, theorists such as bell hooks have taken up the term as a mechanism to describe racial othering.

Pithecanthropus Erectus: De/constructing the Self

"It's not only a question of color anymore . . . It's getting deeper than that. I mean it's getting more and more difficult for a man and a woman to just love. People are getting fragmented, and part of that is that fewer and fewer people are making a real effort anymore to find out exactly who they are and to build on that knowledge . . . We create our own slavery."

—CHARLES MINGUS qtd. in Hentoff, liner notes, *Pithecanthropus Erectus*

"Without ever leaving the ground, she could fly."

—TONI MORRISON, *Song of Solomon*, 307

Charles Mingus

The title cut of Charles Mingus's classic *Pithecanthropus Erectus* is one of his most powerful pieces: a four-movement tone poem depicting humankind's evolution from pride and success to hubris and slavery and finally to ultimate destruction. The piece is held together by a recurring theme and is fragmented by chaotic interludes as humankind's spirit sinks lower. Aside from evolution, the song's title, which roughly translates as "Upright Ape Man," refers to Mingus and his upright bass. In *Ossuaries*, Mingus's "Pithecanthropus Erectus" parallels Yasmine's own sense of false security and her struggles to escape her own oppressive past. Attempting to escape the oppressiveness of "back then" (which can be read as a historic racism that exists as right now), Yasmine, to paraphrase Larissa Lai, yearns for a parallel present that without constant struggle is unattainable, because of all the accumulated errors—the accumulated bones—that now make her, and us, who we are.[76] Yasmine's yearning is also a yearning for the possibilities of a better future, a desire to escape the oppressive structures even within her own revolutionary sphere, as her male comrade and lover claims, "'You're nothing, Yas, / I made you something by fucking you, / other than that, you're nothing.'" Momentarily she can only find solace and escape this temporality through the movement of music, imagining, "as if she should hear instead Monk's / 'Crepuscule with Nellie,' its deliberate / and loving notes scoring her back"; and later,

> Charles Mingus recovers her, 'Pithecanthropus
>
> Erectus,' and he does, then she was
> three and her mother lifted the needle on the record,
> the rushing out and out her feet tingling[77]

These movements and moments of the jazz manifestos that score Yasmine in and out of time exemplify how the text constructs itself in relation to memory. Memory, together with the liberating dissent that encompasses the political vernacular of her jazz musings, is in many ways the type of poetic flight the text enacts. The deep anguish produced by Yasmine's constant failures within her insurgent politics leaves her a disenfranchised global citizen; furthermore, it sets the stage for her performative flight from the law in a poetic narrative of movement through borders that are personally delicate as well as politically charged. The notion of flight as a return to, as well as an escape from, a disjunctive present towards a communal narrative is a common fictive motif of Brand's poetic writing. Moreover, as Leslie Sanders argues, "slaves flying back to Africa people the folklore of the enslaved Caribbean and North American."[78] Charlie "Bird" Parker melodically moves through the text as a representation of expressive (and at times excessive) flight and freedom; similarly, the poet's (whether Brand, Yasmine, or the unnamed narrator) own bird-like flight can be read as palimpsest—as an articulation of the repetitions that come in acknowledging difference. Yasmine's difference is even more potent given that she defies and confounds gender and machismo, largely taking over the action in the robbery, "newly awakened to her violence." For while there are moments when history forcefully enters the text, the bank heist, and her subsequent movement across geographical borders, is one instance in the text where "history will see."[79] Her unforgivable Blackness and gender bending is possibly why her comrade, six ossuaries earlier, attempts to control her through sexual violence. As in Toni Morrison's *Sula*, Yasmine defies all expectations of what a Black woman is supposed to be. She is travelling dangerous grounds; as Nel warns Sula: "You can't do it all. You a woman and colored woman at that. You can't act like a man. You can't be walking around all independent-like, doing whatever you like, taking what you want, leaving what you don't."[80] Like Sula's feminism, Yasmine's extends beyond gender and race; her various dissents/descents are acts of defiant citizenship that resist the structural systems of oppression.

As the narrator describes, Yasmine is on the side of the marginalized: "Yasmine knows in her hardest heart, / that truth is worked and organized by some, / and she's on the wrong side always."[81] It is from the position of being on the wrong side, what Daniel Fischlin and Ajay Heble describe in jazz as the "other side of nowhere," that Yasmine can speak from her informed global position as "a body out of time, moving at a constant angle" like a discordant note, arriving wherever "the sonorous oceans" take her.[82] Fischlin and Heble describe how Dave Douglas and Charles Mingus herald the improviser as a site for locating resistant critiques, "iterative consciences that directly address injustice, the meaning of democratic values (often in so-called democratic spaces where those values have been forgotten or lie dormant), and the transcultural importance of these sorts of resistances."[83] Yasmine fits within this continuum of the global improviser, moving freely across borders while using the various tropes of jazz to articulate a global sounding, like Mingus's "erectus / [with its] fierce bright timbals," which ventures most outwardly towards an "outer space sounding." Brand, through the mobility of Yasmine, rewrites the performance(s) of improvised jazz musicians to subvert Western traditions. This results in a contractual edifying of the destructive *and* generative potentialities of constant self-creation in the face of horrifying atrocities and auto-critiques that signal "the inabilities to live."[84] It is through the destructive genesis of rewriting, repetition, remix, and translation that Yasmine (and by extension the

> Dave Douglas

readers of the text) is drawn into the text's disruptive poetics—into its jazz undertones—and into the politics of the exiled individual in relation to utopian hopes for a "coming community," perhaps a socialist community, as Yasmine is markedly Marxist.

For example, Engels's *The Origin of the Family* and Marx's *The Eighteenth Brumaire* (see "Ossuary IV," where Yasmine reads them at the same time) serve as reminders that the future cannot be built upon the past, but that the past with its proclivities towards injustice contains many of the answers leading to a more utopian future. While the constant ruptures and eruptions of gloom throughout the text might signal that *Ossuaries* is hardly concerned with utopian principles, its undertones are "sincere explosions" forewarning of ecological destruction—much like Mingus's "Pithecanthropus Erectus"—leading toward the eradication of the individual, indeed life itself: "she reads later that Mingus said the last movement / suggests the 'frantic burst of a dying organism.'"[85] Yasmine's constant rereading and her perpetual feelings of displacement underpin the notion of a disruptive or "inoperative community" (Nancy), which is always potentially a "coming community" where people do not belong to this or that universal, but to a "whatever" category.

Individuals and, by relation, the societies that connect them together, have no single essence, and therefore, as Giorgio Agamben insists, "the point of departure for any discourse on ethics is that there is no essence, no historical or spiritual vocation, no biological destiny that humans must enact or realize." Rather, as humans discursively practise the act of being human, we are always striving toward a "coming community," where people do not belong to this or that universal, but to a whatever category: "the coming being is whatever being." In *The Coming Community*, Agamben attests that the whatever simply belongs, since it is the condition of belonging itself. We exist as possibility, and it is the possibility of the whatever "itself being [taken] up without an identity [that] is a threat the State cannot come to terms with."[86] In the same way that the disruptive musical practice of Black creative musicians created an *anti-assimilationist* musical soundscape, so too does "sonic citizenship," at its theoretical core, enact anti-assimilative challenges to the state, for the nation-state can no longer represent any single unified ideology. Agamben argues that the "whatever" simply belongs, since it is the condition of belonging itself. Furthermore, he explains, the Latin word for whatever, *quodlibet*, refers to an expression that emphasizes not merely "it does not matter which," so much as "being such that it always matters," as well as to a polyphonic piece of music in which several melodies are combined in an often playful mode.[87] In this way, like Agamben's theory of the "whatever," Brand's *Ossuaries* deconstructs normalizing concepts of all-inclusive communities in favour of a community to come.

In the way that jazz—an undeniably American music—is rooted in a variety of Pan-African soils that often incorporate African elements and a thematic return to Africa,[♭] Brand's Yasmine moves through multiple spaces as she searches (although often impossibly) for some sense of permanence (of community) even while abhorring such fixity: "how to say I wish for permanence, / then I cast it off as dullness, stupidity, / then wish again for certainty."[88] As Sanders argues, "a diasporic consciousness, by definition, imagines itself rooted in an elsewhere, or believes that rootedness, and so safety, is elsewhere possible."[89] This space of elsewhere possibilities, of transitory hope, produces a culturally transnational narrative, a craved movement, where Yasmine is constantly reinventing herself, wanting to fly like a bird (musically like Charlie Parker), yet is immobilized by such deceit: "in other people's passports, / in mathematical theorems of trust / in her vigilant skin and feathery, feathery deceit."[90] Yasmine's translation between passports, temporalities, and various localities becomes a performance, enacting or enunciating cultural communication and promoting multiple levels of shifting perspective via dialogue. Conceptually, cultural translation read through Yasmine's various diasporic flights across time is productive because it prescribes an

---

[♭] Abdullah Ibrahim (formerly Dollar Brand), who was born in Cape Town, has many songs/albums that thematize Africa (see *African Sketchbook* and *African Marketplace*); Randy Weston, who was born in Brooklyn and incorporates many African elements into his music, eventually settled in Morocco. I've added a few tracks from each to the playlist.

ethical responsibility to reading and theorizing literature within the framework of cultural specificity and shifting perspectives of modernity. On the ground, as readers, we consider the shifting and multiple perspectives, as deep bass notes ripple through the text, disturbing notions of subjectivity, particularly any simple acceptance of the self/lyrical "I."

Venus: Outer Space Soundings

> "I'm playing intergalactic music, which is beyond the other idea of space music, because it is of the natural infinity of the eternal universe ... Music is a universal language ... The intergalactic music is in hieroglyphic sound: an abstract analysis and synthesis of man's relationship to the universe, visible and invisible first man and second man."
>
> —SUN RA quoted in Jost, 181

Sun Ra, who thought of himself as much a scientist as a musician, used space, music, and improvisation as ways to escape the material world and to contemplate cosmic realities. Similarly, John Coltrane used improvisation to develop spirituality and contemplate the divine. Aptly, in 1966, when Coltrane was asked what he would like to be in "ten or twenty years," he responded, "I would like to be a saint," which is fitting since after his death the African Orthodox Church canonized him as Saint John William Coltrane.[91] Space: physical, intergalactic, spiritual, and cosmological for both Sun Ra and Coltrane, was a way to transcend the earth for, as Ra's trumpet player Phil Cohran put it, "You had to think space. Had to expand beyond the earth plane."[92] Coltrane's "Venus" provides a powerful metaphor of space as transcendence; this is present throughout *Ossuaries* as Yasmine improvises in each space while trying to move beyond the limits imposed upon her. Furthermore, the cosmos itself is not stable, and rather than the spiritual impetus of Coltrane's search for the

_{Sun Ra}

divine, Brand incorporates improvisation as survival; poetically, the space metaphor challenges simplistic notions of identity: the "I" of the text.

In *Ossuaries*, the lyrical "I" is a contested site full of narrative multiplicities and contradictions, as the narrator in the second Ossuary exclaims, "I, the slippery pronoun, the ambivalent, glistening, / long sheath of the alphabet flares beyond her reach." Here, and elsewhere in the text, the unnamed narrator (which I have suggested might be a performative enactment by Brand of her poet-self), the "I" of the text, is muddled within Yasmine's own sounding, highlighting that the ambiguity of identity, even while claiming an "I," is the reality of the exiled, or globally defined, jazz poet and citizen. In describing the ambiguities of a solidified personality, of the failures of language to describe the multiplicities of identity, the unnamed narrator of *Ossuaries* reminds us that truth in the text is indiscernible from the falsities of language, thus emphasizing that the unreadability of Yasmine is what defines her ability to exist outside of language, outside of determinate sign systems, blowing freely like "the Venusian winds"—a reference to Coltrane's "Venus."[93]

In Brand's novel *What We All Long For*, Coltrane's "Venus" represents both the tender feelings the character Oku feels toward his love interest, Jackie, as well as the uncertainty of the boundaries and spaces that lie between them: "And he played her 'Venus' more times than he could recall because he felt that tender, that undone with her, that out in space, that uncertain of boundaries, and that much in peril if she didn't love him back."[94] Brand's *Ossuaries* plays with the uncertainty of boundaries and states that community and identity are processes continually made, unable to be totalized by universalizing language or globalization. Fischlin and Heble argue that the "very tensions operative in improvisation as a social practice are those that are at stake in the making of community as an ongoing and dynamic interrelational practice."[95] In viewing Yasmine's identity as an unfixed metaphor, as movement, as bluenote, as contrafact, as perpetually reread and relistened to, we move into an understanding of community as fiction (as narrative), of self as fiction, of history as fiction, of fiction as history, of the reader as woven into the fabric of meaning. Yasmine sounds herself into the type of community in which she would like to belong, finding individual freedom while desiring a larger cosmological community.

In challenging dominant culture while striving toward a personal freedom of mobility, Yasmine embodies many of the resonances of improvisational practices in jazz and Afrological practices more generally. Nathaniel Mackey describes the drive of Black music, most focally in free jazz, as an aesthetic striving toward an individual and collective freedom:

> During the sixties, assertions were often made to the effect that jazz groups provided glimpses into the future. What was meant by this was that black music—especially that of the sixties, with its heavy emphasis on individual freedom within a collectively improvised context—proposed a model social order, an ideal, even utopic balance between personal impulse and group demands.[96]

Mackey's description of the collective individuality of an improvised jazz context speaks to Yasmine's own "sonic citizenship," which is defined both in her ability to improvise individually as well as within the groups and cultures of each topographic surrounding in which she finds herself, always rereading her "disorderly" self and each "constellation of bodies." Her enactment is spatial, travelling via sound, as her very name is interpellated musically: "Yasmine, some long-fingered horn player, / could blow confessions over those two cool syllables." That cool horn player blowing confessions is Yasmine, who is in many ways that "anonymous bird": a Charlie Parker enactment improvising a painful truth as we listen.[97] Yasmine is that very enactment of historicized sound. As listeners, how can any of us read without considering the listening of our own listenings?

The text demands that we move beyond a logocentric definition of reading as a discovery of the inherent meaning of a text and into a reading that produces multiple meanings in the act of (un)reading and (re)listening. *Ossuaries* values repetitions of difference over repetitions of sameness. For a moment, like the moments when we become lost within the free-moving lines of a piece of music, we embody the book, "for a book asks us to embody, which at once takes us across borders of all kinds."⁹⁸ In listening to the performance of the text, of the polyphonic confessional nature of *Ossuaries*, we become a part of the book's various musickings. Every listening act is a reopening of space, a space of translatory possibilities, and one of "sonic citizenship," as we listen along with Brand/Yasmine, who models a citizenship beyond borders. Thus, listening/translation can be an opening process, one that enacts a fluidity between borders (real or metaphorical). As readers we enact translation via listening continually as we read and reread a text. *Ossuaries*, replete with listenings of listenings, is a call toward an engaged reading praxis that invites participation in a tapestry of different and shifting world views and epistemologies. If *Ossuaries* moves along any linearity, it propels itself toward the possibility of a better, perhaps more just, more freely moving globalized community (with communities of difference within communities of difference). *Ossuaries* has intertextual references to Karl Marx's *The Eighteenth Brumaire of Louis Bonaparte* (it appears in the acknowledgments), a text that states, "The social revolution of the nineteenth century cannot draw its poetry from the past, but only from the future. It cannot begin with itself before it has stripped off all superstition about the past"; Brand similarly engages directly with the confrontations (wars and injustices) of a shifting present. We need to invent tools to meet the changing demands of the present. Like the music of Sun Ra, which proposes outer space as a more just place,♭ and like Coltrane's *Interstellar Space*, *Ossuaries* constantly invites the possibilities of a "music still unheard," ultimately presenting the present as a place that is ethically challenging to live in: "who could have lived each day knowing / some massacre was underway."⁹⁹

♭ Ajay Heble argues that "outer space functions for Ra as a metaphor for possibility (or perhaps for performing the impossible), for alternatives to dominant systems of knowledge production, and that this was particularly important for aggrieved populations sounding off against systems of oppression and racist constraint." Heble, "Destinations Out: Towards a Jazz-Inflected Model for Community-Based Learning," *Improvisation, Community, and Social Practice* (2012), 1.

Nevertheless, the speaking text announces, "I do, I do / anyone, I'm not unique," implying a collaborative guilt and a sincere approach to the responsibilities of being a citizen every day of one's life (and the burden that comes with perpetual struggle).[100] While Yasmine steps into "another country, another / constellation of bodies" and becomes part of the commonplace ennui of killing chickens on a Maple Leaf farm in Canada, we are reminded that despite some of Yasmine's best efforts it is difficult to completely escape the periodic crises of the modern world.[101] Nevertheless, Yasmine continues to imagine the future with a global consciousness, just as Coltrane framed "his music as an act of transnational imagination."[102] Ultimately, like the sonic undulations of the text, the Marxist musings, and Brand's (and Yasmine's) constant relistenings of jazz, there is always hope.

BREAK:
The Blue Clerk

//

We get extended conversations about Coltrane's "Venus," and about a host of other writers, philosophers, jazz musicians, and artists, in Brand's long prose poem *The Blue Clerk*. The work stages an intense conversation between the poet and the Blue Clerk, who is the keeper of the poet's discarded pages. At one point, Brand discusses Charles Mingus's seminal *Pithecanthropus Erectus* as "a work of political philosophy," and the clerk nervously asks, "You aren't thinking of translating, are you?" Rejecting a Eurocentric approach to conventional philosophy, Brand asks the reader to listen to, translate, and take seriously Black cultural production. For it is in jazz and poetry that we can reject homeostasis and move into what Brand calls "the heterogenous qualities of life."[103]

Nowhere is this more apparent than in her engagements with "Venus" in *The Blue Clerk*. Poet Kaie Kellough contends that the tension between the author and the clerk is like the tension between

Coltrane and Ali on *Interstellar Space*. In "Verso 14" Brand provides a close reading of "Venus," describing how "the drums serve as pacing for the horn, but it has its own investment in this state of things . . . the drums played by Rashied Ali, structure the horn and are in turn structured by the horn. Coltrane works on the first declarative syntactical unit." The poet ventures out to describe the in-the-moment conversation between Trane and Ali as two "travellers going out to an unknown," much like the conversation that Brand/the poet and her clerk are having, and by extension, the reader. We are called to pay attention—to listen—so that we too may enter a "more lucid, open state of being at the end." Through "Venus" Brand invites the reader to participate in a meaning that is irresolute, for like "Venus," "You don't know when it begins, and it ends yes and you say, but it doesn't conclude."[104] This conversation between the clerk and the author mirrors the one between Coltrane and Ali and invites us, as readers, co-creators even, to listen to the complex relationship between Black music and literature.

Kaie Kellough asks us to consider two useful questions in relation "Verso 14": "How do writers connect to the same movement toward freedom that we hear in free jazz?" and "How do form and freedom structure one another?"[105] *Ossuaries* and *The Blue Clerk* do more than collect; they also open spaces of possibility. Improvisational jazz music, like poetry, can work against traditional timekeeping, and Brand—like Philip and Compton—makes more space for Black avant-garde practices to work against narrow generic understanding. Thus, Brand writes back to historical silences and lacunae. In "Verso 40.5" she writes: "Summary. There is a photo of Monk and Nellie and / Coltrane. It is not possible for me to describe the five / centuries it took to record this image."[106] The image is not shown in the text, but I show it here (see Figure 2.1). The photo is the product of the five centuries behind Monk, Coltrane, and Nellie, encompassing the massive contribution of Black cultural production in North America, which has not been taken as seriously as it should, which also speaks to the erasure of Black artists and writers in literary institutions.

Listening to a Listening

Figure 2.1 Monk (left), Nellie (middle), and Coltrane.

Brand acknowledges that it is impossible for language to contain the depth of the image or the emotional capacity she feels in those centuries of Black innovation and perseverance. As she writes at another point in *The Blue Clerk*: "Sundays are a bad time for the author. Just the sound of Billie Holiday alone accounts for this. Eleanora Fagan can break any Sunday in two."[107] The mere sound of Holiday's voice—her sounded pain—opens an emotional connection that wounds Brand. Hence, the image of Monk, Coltrane, and Nellie carries meaning that speaks beyond words: it contains the past and a portal to future possibilities. As Brand writes in her 2018 lecture, "The Shape of Language," in reference to Coltrane's *Interstellar Space*, the music speaks "out and beyond the time that we live . . . it's like Coltrane blowing into a future . . . I often think that is the job of Black artists to blow out of the time that we live in. It's like sending word to some place where it may be understood in the future."[108] Brand's engagement with the past suggests this much, and she invites us to not only listen, but to truly hear and *feel* the revolutionary potential of Black music and creativity.

Billie Holiday

REMIX 2

Brand's *Ossuaries* is a jazz sounding of deep listening. American accordionist, electronic innovator, and improvising musician Pauline Oliveros defines "deep listening" as "learning to expand the perception of sounds to include the whole space/time continuum of sound—encountering the vastness and complexities as much as possible."[109] Brand recalls much and "edits in" plenty in *Ossuaries*, just like her Yasmine, whose deep listening is so overwhelming that she finds it hard to even mourn as she watches the "powdering towers," referring to the World Trade Center on 9/11, fall before her eyes on "the grey blood of television": "her whole existence was mourning, so what?"[110] It is precisely this type of "editing in"—from the epic cataloguing to the modern-day existential crises of the text—that would impress poet-critic Charles Bernstein: "What interests me is a poetry and a poetics that do not edit out so much as edit in: that include multiple conflicting perspectives and types of languages and styles in the same poetic work . . . A poetry—a poetic—that expresses the states of the art as it moves beyond the twentieth century, beyond the modern and postmodern."[111] Brand's *Ossuaries* is a poetics of recollection, of constant movement that, like jazz, edits in forms (other genres) to defer absolute authority. It is from the rubble of fallen towers that we must, as Yasmine does, go on living, even loving.

As with Philip's *Zong!*, Canada does not figure predominately in *Ossuaries*, although it is in Canada, on a Maple Leaf farm, that Yasmine finishes her journey. Canada's presence at the end of the text sustains a dialogue within a Canadian national space that speaks to the larger contours of globalism and transnationalism: Canada practises the same exclusionary practices as other nations that divide the wealthy from the poor, and the citizen from the immigrant. However, cities within national boundaries tend to confound ideological borders, as the various cities Yasmine travels to serve as opportunities to rediscover the self, proving moments where origins become intricate and blurred. Brand imbues the city as a *whatever* space, a place of possibility, polyphony, and forgetfulness, as "a place where the old migrants transmogrify into citizens with disappeared origins who look at new migrants as if at strangers, forgetting their own flights. And the new migrants remain immigrants until they too can disappear their origins."[112] *Ossuaries* problematizes origins, and it uses the globality of music[113] as an example of how easy border-crossing can be, since it is music, especially African American music, and culture, that, as Brand says, "pervades the lives of people of all backgrounds in North America." Music connects the various fragmented *Ossuaries* (or contained songs) together to sound more inclusive communities, while serving as a tool in the text to redress colonial racism and Western neoliberal ideologies. Jazz is an improvisatory gift because it brings together people of different backgrounds, making space for community, however tangled. Jazz "leaves you up and open and in the air and this is the space that some of us need, an opening to another life tangled up in this one but opening."[114] Such an opening is possible through deep listening.

Revolutionary undulations permeate the sonorous textures of *Ossuaries* and *The Blue Clerk*. From actual revolutionaries, to theorists of the revolution, to the jazz manifestos that swing the notation of the texts, we are called to listen, and then listen again. Beyond that, like the insurgent soundings of the text, and the glaring inequalities that subjugate (yet do not defeat) Yasmine, and the author in dialogue with the clerk, we are called to act—a broadly conceived *enactment*—in the struggle for greater citizenship rights for all people on a local, national, and global scale. Brand challenges us to think critically about the function of art and to consider the implications of our soundings. Such an engagement is a push towards social justice and a collective calling to imagine different futures in the now. Now is the time indeed to speak truth to power. To quote Fred Moten (riffing on a Fred Hampton quote about racial power) in conversation with Stefano Harney, and speaking to those on the sidelines, "The coalition emerges out of your recognition that it's fucked up for you, in the same way that we've already recognized that it's fucked up for us. I don't need your help. I *just* need *you* to recognize that *this shit is killing you, too*, however much *more softly.*"[115] It is also a call for us to orient ourselves—as DJs, listeners, sonic citizens, and improvisers on the edge—to the music and poetry of the everyday realities of oppressed peoples and to help bend the moral arc of the universe a little closer towards justice.

This bending towards justice continues in the next chapter, which focuses on dub poetics and chant in relation to NourbeSe Philip's *Zong! Zong!* sounds an improviso imperative, especially in a transnational and Afrosporic context. Through dub chant, Philip stretches the boundaries of the form's aesthetic to reveal and revel in the poetic possibilities of recovery and improvisatory citizenship(s).

Chapter 3

DUB POETICS AND IMPROVISED CHANT IN M. NOURBESE PHILIP'S *ZONG!*

Listening: Lillian Allen, "I Fight Back" and "The Subversives"

Dub is renegade art and rebel music. As dub poet Lillian Allen affirms in "De Dub": "We believe that art in itself is symbolic and although it can play a major role in people's lives and in social and political movements, it cannot change the structure of social relations. Our work extends beyond merely creating art; we take our poetry and our conviction into the community."[1] Poetry, at least idealistically—and I extend this analogy to music—is a form of citizenship and community that is active and urgent; it is where ideas are wrangled with, shaped, dreamed up, and brought (or birthed) into the world.

Lillian Allen is a founding mother of dub poetry in Canada, and her first two albums won the Juno Award for Best Reggae/Calypso Album (for *Revolutionary Tea Party* in 1986 and *Conditions Critical* in 1988).[b] Allen is a trailblazer in the field of spoken word and dub, and

Lillian Allen, "I Fight Back," and "The Subversives"

Liner Notes

[b] Both "I Fight Back" and "The Subversives" from *Revolutionary Tea Party* have been added to the playlist for the chapter. Allen continues to push boundaries, so I've added a more recent track as well, "We Stories" from

her album *Revolutionary Tea Party* is a good starting place for getting into her music and poetry as she translates her diasporic experience into "new forms." As she dubs in "The Subversives," "I break from your sentence / write a paragraph of my own / create new forms / space." In "I Fight Back" she reminds us that "Here I am in Canada / Bringing up Someone Else's Child," yet they label her "Immigrant, Law-breaker, Illegal, Minimum Wager / Ah no, Not Mother, Not Worker, Not fighter / And I Fight Back." In the song, and throughout her work, Allen calls out institutions of oppression and discriminatory practices in Canada that are often rooted in slavery. We are collectively called to fight back and gather in revolution and love. As we will see this chapter, dub is an innovative Caribbean/immigrant art form, and it is also an articulation and performance of citizenship rights, often across borders and through cross-cultural connections to diasporic communities.

While this chapter focuses primarily on Marlene NourbeSe Philip's groundbreaking long poem *Zong!*, I spend some time looking at dub poetics. I take this approach in part because dub poetry has been neglected in CanLit and there are aspects of the music/movement that inform Philip's work. While *Zong!* is not explicitly a dub poem—it resists such narrow categorization—I do feel there are aspects of dub, Caribbean, and Afrosporic culture that provide a way into understanding some of Philip's thinking and broader concerns. The final part of this chapter provides a reading of *Zong!* as an improvised dub chant (and turntable mix) that changes with every reading, much in the way critical nuanced improvised performances often do. While Philip might be more apt to see her poem in the jazz aesthetic, the multiple echoes (the dubs of the drowned African voices) in *Zong!* allow it to fit within multiple contact zones of sonic, oral, textual, and multimodal traditions.[2] Furthermore, even though *Zong!* is not directly about Canada, the text is rooted in the transatlantic slave trade, which is very much part of Canada's own imperialism as a colonial satellite and settler colony.

Anxiety (2012). You can listen to the playlist for this chapter, here: https://open.spotify.com/playlist/4mKodztloMkFHRRglByruz.

I. Reggae and Dub Poetics

> "Dubin dubin / dubin dubin / de people dem a dub in de street."
>
> —MUTABARUKA, "Dub Poem," *The Mystery Unfolds*

Mutabaruka

Reggae

Reggae, a precursor of dub poetics, is integral to the performative poetry scene in Toronto, beginning in the 1970s and into the present moment, in which reggae and dub continue to develop and thrive. My discussion of reggae will be brief, because the main focus of the first half of this chapter is on how dub poets, chiefly in Toronto—with a particular emphasis on the "mother" dub poets—create a complex understanding of global communities, sounding polyphonic citizenships, plural identities, and iterative resistances with an attuned diasporic consciousness. From there, I adapt the dub consciousness as a viable tool for sonic engagement and resistance in M. NourbeSe Philip's long poem, *Zong!*.

Reggae, as a musical genre, form, or style, first developed in Jamaica in the 1960s. The term reggae is sometimes broadly applied to all Jamaican dance music, but in fact it refers to a distinct aesthetic style of music that evolved out of ska and rocksteady, albeit strongly influenced by African American jazz and rhythm and blues. As poet and reggae historian Kwame Dawes articulates in *Natural Mysticism*, reggae's arrival signified "a pivotal and defining historical moment in the evolution of a West Indian aesthetic." Dawes offers that it was the emergence of reggae in the late 1960s "that provided Jamaica (and the Caribbean region) with an artistic form that has a distinctively postcolonial aesthetic." Reggae is postcolonial in the sense that its subversive lyrics (and forms) are a political response to the cultural legacies of slavery, colonialism, and imperialism. Reggae absorbs other forms, and it is not afraid, Dawes tells us, to "change and be changed, it is not reluctant to examine itself and try to stretch the limits of the aesthetic."[3] In addition, as media theorist Dick Hebdige illuminates, the Jamaican concept of "versioning"—that is, democratic revisioning—is at the heart of most African American and Caribbean music: "They're just different *kinds* of quotation. And that's the beauty, too, of versioning. It's a democratic principle because it implies that no one has the final say. Everybody has a chance to make a contribution."[4] Moreover, "versioning" involves thinking through how citizens adapt to a society that is itself always changing. Reggae's adaptability and open aesthetic have made the music particularly popular among urban populations: you will find reggae and its diverse offshoots in nearly every metropolis on the planet.

> The Wailers, Jimmy Cliff, and Eric Clapton
>
> The Maytals
>
> Lee "Scratch" Perry

The *Dictionary of Jamaican English* (first published in 1967) tells us that reggae is a modified spelling of "rege," as in "rege-rege," a word that means rags, ragged, or a quarrel or row—an argument. As a musical term the word first appeared in the 1968 rocksteady song, "Do the Reggay" by Toots and the Maytals. As with the blues and jazz, there are long-running debates about how the term originated. Reggae music is typically played in 4/4 time because the symmetrical rhythmic pattern of the music is most suited to that pattern. Perhaps reggae's most notable feature is its offbeat rhythms: staccato chords, typically on a piano or a guitar (or both) on the offbeat measures, frequently referred to as the *skank*. A standard drum kit with a highly tuned snare drum (to give a timbales type of sound) often blasts out the *riddim*, a basic pattern that is used repeatedly by different artists. Reggae became popular among Western audiences mainly through the music of The Wailers (a group started by Bob Marley, Peter Tosh, and Bunny Wailer back in 1963), the 1972 film *The Harder They Come*, starring and featuring the music of Jimmy Cliff, and Eric Clapton's 1974 cover of Bob Marley's "I Shot the Sheriff." Reggae is always revisiting and dubbing over itself, rooted as it is in a central aesthetic of change and variation upon a repeated rhythmic pattern. We encounter the dub aesthetic in quintessential dub organizer Lee "Scratch" Perry's consummate capacity for improvisation, which never truly settles down, as he articulates in his song, "African Hitchhiker": "I am an alien from outer space / And I got no home and I'm living in my briefcase." Reggae has found many homes as it has evolved: its echoes can be heard in hip hop and rap, dancehall, raggamuffin, reggaeton, and other fusions.

Reggae music is often intensely political and concerns freedom and redemption; much of it narrates the Middle Passage and slavery and contests colonialism. It is also music with a strong message of love, unity, and community, a message that is spread through the embodied practice of dance. As Marley calls to us in "Roots, Rock, Reggae," dancing is a way to feel liberated. Thus, Reggae is a celebration of life's potential realized and enacted in loving practice. Dawes articulates, "dancing is not simply an act of recreation, but a statement, an articulation of reality."[3] Reggae, like most musics, allows one to effectively bend time and cross-national boundaries, to enter an ideal category where unity and allegiances can be formed across the fictitious borders of nation-states. Dub, as a palimpsestic aesthetic, is at the heart of the postmodern articulation of reggae music, yet dub poetry stands apart as a unique articulation for Black Canadian and Afrosporic poets who sound a citizenship locally and globally engaged in the communal space where poetry and music can dance together.

_{Bob Marley and The Wailers}

Dub Poetics

> "Dub poetry is just another chapter in a long succession of dynamic innovative forms which includes the griots of Africa, slave narratives, the dialect poetry of Paul Lawrence Dunbar, the Baptist church preacher. There are the blues poets—Langston Hughes and others of the Harlem Renaissance . . . black American jazz and blues with their poets of the sixties, Jamaican DJs and then dub poets and black American rap . . . bringing out the dynamism of the word has always been part of black culture and lifestyle."
>
> —CLIFTON JOSEPH quoted in Lillian Allen, "De Dub," 18–19

Clifton Joseph rightly contends that the separation of musical styles is largely fiction, for Black creative expression finds unity and cross-pollination in a vast "sound painting" of influences across the diaspora. Brenda Carr contends that "dub should be understood in a continuum with diasporic oral, musical, and popular culture performance practices including (but not exhausting) gospel, jazz, blues, r&b, ska, calypso, rapso, megasound system DJs, reggae, and rap."[6] Essentially, dub can absorb any musical style provided that it fits its aesthetic purposes. More concisely, dub poetry is a form of performance poetry with a West Indian aesthetic and origin. It evolved out of dub music in Jamaica in the 1970s, comprised of spoken word pieces over reggae rhythms and Nyabinghi traditions.[7] Unlike the Jamaican form of "toasting" (a significant stylistic influence on hip hop), which also featured spoken word performances, but improvised, often in chant, to the music of the dancehall DJ, a dub poet's performance is usually pre-written and prepared. Spoken or chanted with the background of reggae rhythms, or *a capella* or *ital*, and using Jamaican Creole/Patois, dub poetry effectively blends African and Caribbean, oral and griot traditions with more standard approaches to poetry and performance. Dub performances were created by removing the vocals from side A of a record with a dub machine to create a B side containing a rhythm/instrumental track, often amplifying the bass and drums. Traditionally, dub poets have been closely aligned with DJs as they reanimate and sound the past in the present through a performance atop a tentative original.

Linton Kwesi Johnson

Jamaican-British dub poet and activist Linton Kwesi Johnson provided an early prefiguring of the dub-poet-DJ when in 1976 he wrote: "The 'dub-lyricist' is the dj turned poet. He intones his lyrics rather than sings them. Dub-lyricism is a new form of (oral) music-poetry, wherein the lyricist overdubs rhythmic phrases on to the rhythm background of a popular song."[8] The influence of reggae is readily apparent in Johnson's poem "Reggae Sounds," from the 1980 album *Bass Culture*:

> Shock, black double down-beat bouncin'
> Rock-wise tumble down sound music

> Foot drop, find drum blood story
> Bass history is a-movin' is a-hurtin' black story.

Johnson was an early progenitor of dub poetry, but it was Oku Onoura, inspired by "the 'vibes' of the deejays," who first coined the term "dub poetry."[9] Living in Jamaica in the late 1960s, Onoura was influenced early on by a mishmash of African American popular musics and trends. He read and listened to The Last Poets and Gil Scott-Heron as well as the poetry of Langston Hughes—as did proto-rap and hip hop artists in the late 1970s and early 1980s in the United States. Christian Habekost writes that Onoura "sees dub poetry as a form of poetry that can absorb and incorporate any kind of black musical rhythm."[10] In a 1986 public discussion, Onoura defined dub poetry as "to take out and to put in . . . It's dubbing out the little penta-metre and the little highfalutin business and dubbing in the rootsical, yard, basic rhythm that I-an-I know."[11] Just as Pound resisted the tyranny of the "goddam iamb," dub poetry often resists what Edward Kamau Brathwaite refers to as "the tyranny of the pentameter," although classical dub is often carefully structured around a chorus and metered rhymed verse.[12]

Traditionally, "Jamaican Creole is the *natural* language of dub poetry," and while dub poets often privilege reggae music, nearly all forms of African American and Afro-diasporic music are used in the performance of a dub poem as the mode continues to evade a single homogenizing definition or approach. For me, what binds dub most explicitly to reggae is not so much the metrical rhythm but the fact that dub poetry, like much reggae, "began as, and remains, *rebel* poetry."[13] This is not to say that dub poetry eludes any possibility of definition. d'bi.young anitafrika, a renowned Canadian dub poet and dub monodramatist, thinks through dub vis-à-vis her own mother's manuscript on dub, which identifies the four major elements of what, for her mother at the time, was an emerging form: music, language, politics, and performance.[14] Dub, as such, bridges the personal and the political, and as d'bi developed her own understanding of dub she added four more elements—"urgency, sacredness, integrity, and self-knowledge"—for a total of eight. "I then renamed the earlier elements of music, politics, and performance to rhythm, political content and context, and orality."¹⁵ For d'bi.young, the principles of dub poetry—self-knowledge, orality, rhythm, political content and context, language, urgency, sacredness, and integrity—combine to comprise "a comprehensive eco-system of accountability and responsibility between my audiences and me. Each principle in the methodology challenges me to not only be self-invested but to (re)position to the centre of my micro and macro communities, being both accountable and responsible (able to account for and respond to these communities)."¹⁶ d'bi.young told me that "the community is a big, big thing, because the community has raised me."♭¹⁷ Similarly, Dawes writes in his poem, "Holy Dub": "This poet is a griot in search of a village."¹⁸ Dub poetry has the power to link disparate communities together—like a grand multicultural dub mix—through lines of solidarity.

Numerous dub poets opt to leave dub elusive, with some of the biggest names in dub poetry referring to their work as poetry (full stop) rather than as a subset of music or poetry. For example, dub pioneer Mutabaruka contends, "My poetry is just: poetry." This is echoed by Jean "Binta" Breeze, who notes: "I'd rather say I am a poet and write some dub poems than say I am a dub poet."¹⁹ Breeze and Mutabaruka's defensive responses reflect their desire to be taken seriously, as dub poets—particularly in print—have often had to justify themselves against negative critiques of the form. Victor Chan contends, quite falsely, that dub poetry does not reflect any "subtlety of approach, anything that is inward looking, musing, quiet, reflective, tender, delicate, or registering a complexity of position or feeling."²⁰ Even those who write carefully about reggae, dub, and performance poetry have critiqued the form. In his introduction to *Voiceprint*, Gordon Rohlehr writes about both the potential and the failure of

Jean "Binta" Breeze

♭ I suggest seeking out some live performance videos by d'bi to see her work in practice. In her radical interdisciplinary performances, she addresses issues of gender, sexuality, race, class, and the human experience. You can view a 2013 performance and interview between d'bi and myself here: http://www.improvcommunity.ca/content/dbiyoung-anitafrika.

dub poetics: "Dub poetry at its worst is a kind of tedious jabber to a monotonous rhythm. At its best it is the intelligent appropriation of the manipulatory techniques of the DJ for purposes of personal and communal signification."[21] Similarly, Kwame Dawes, a reggae/dub poet himself, acknowledges some of the limits of dub poetry, particularly how the "back-beat rhythm lends itself to anapaesthic and iambic rhythms which have become too easily stereotyped meters for the 'dub poem.'"[22] Defying Chan and others' recalcitrant claims about dub, the best dub poets, like top-tier performers/innovators/writers in any medium, are able to extend dub's form to new soundings, which I will argue M. NourbeSe Philip does in *Zong!* even though the poem is not strictly a dub poem. Furthermore, all genres have those who master its aesthetic and those who mimic or appropriate the form—surely there is a palatable distinction between Charlie Parker and Kenny G despite them both falling under the rubric of jazz? And however valid critiques of dub—or any poetic form—may be, dub remains a powerful aesthetic challenge to Western paradigms of poetic validity while allowing for complex diasporic identifications.

Dub, as Carr points out, "reframes the logic and assumptions of Western cultural gatekeepers who have asserted the incompatibility of political and aesthetic categories," enacting "dub-aesthetics-in-the-diaspora."[23] Furthermore, these dub aesthetics, as Habekost contends, are shaped by Jamaican Creole/Nation Language and a rhythm/*riddim* that allows poets to pick words over a distinctive musical beat. *Zong!* is dub, at the level of language, just as at the core of Philip's *She Tries Her Tongue, Her Silence Softly Breaks* is a dub chant: "and english is / my mother tongue / is a foreign lan lan lang / language/ l/anguish."[24] For "dread talk" and Creole—a mishmash of languages and vocal inflections—is, as Afua Cooper asserts, "the language of the poor, the downtrodden, those who continue to resist and resist and resist."[25] Thus, women in dub are the doubly downtrodden. For gender is, as David Austin argues, "a double whammy" and the "burden of black women" in search of a mother tongue.[26] Women in dub continue to expand dub's repertoire to include not just familial concerns—which they do—but also a wide poetic spectrum that incorporates but is hardly limited to love, sex, spirituality, and other diverse concerns that speak to the experience of being gendered in Canada, or the larger diaspora, dubbing down not only white supremacy but also the sexist manifestations of societies that often place women, especially women of colour and trans women, at the bottom of the social hierarchy. As Cooper insists, "almost from its inception, women were bringing new agendas and new voices, different sounds and riddims into dub."[27] Cooper names Queen Nanny, an Akan Jamaican Maroon warrior princess leader, anti-slavery fighter, and Black liberation warrior and strategist, as an inspiration for women dub poets; she also cites dub poet Faybiene Miranda, who co-published a book of poetry with Mutabaruka in 1976, and Louise Bennett, one of the first women to write down her dubs. Women dubbists (I am being somewhat essentialist with my language here to make my point) were integral from the onset, and it's not just that there are a significant number of women in dub, but there are at least as many women dub poets as men, especially in Canada: a fact that cannot be ignored.

[margin: Louise Bennett]

Toronto, like Jamaica and England, has a high concentration of dub poets, many of whom are founding mothers of the Canadian dub poetry scene and legacy, including Lillian Allen, Afua Cooper, d'bi.young, Ahdri Zhina Mandiela, and, I would add, NourbeSe Philip (with an asterisk).♭ The poetry of these dubbists articulates new forms of space on the page and in performance, enacting Black (and Afrosporic) individuation from the mother-poet perspective

---

♭ I use "with an asterisk" to emphasize that Philip's belonging in any tradition remains liminal, as she does not neatly fit within the L=A=N=G=U=A=G=E poetry tradition, or within dub poetry; this is, I think, how Philip wants it. While Philip's work is very much part of the African Caribbean aesthetic, she describes that she does not do performance poetry, although "performance, albeit unrealized, is very much part of my work." Performance is as Philip states, "the completion of poetry. Without it poetry is the sound of one hand clapping." Furthermore, Philip describes her non-literary sources as the poets of the Caribbean, "the calypsonians like the Mighty Sparrow, Kitchener, and Calypso Rose, and the Rastafarian prophet-musicians—Bob Marley, Peter Tosh, Jimmy Cliff and others." Philip, *A Genealogy of Resistance*, 118, 131.

(a perspective that is only partly explanatory given the current gender diversity of the field). Of the eleven poets anthologized in Cooper's book of women dub poets, *Utterances and Incantations*, seven live in Canada and all are Afro-diasporic. This mother-poet perspective provides an idealized womb-metaphor for the birth cycle of growth, regeneration, and wisdom heard in the sounding of women dub poets' chants, in their utterances and incantations, and in their "'multiplying tongues.'"[28] That there are many women in dub poetry is revealing, especially when we consider dub's origins in the 1970s and the number of Caribbean immigrant women who have used the form to articulate their experience of emigrating to Canada. Dub is an immigrant art form: it is an articulation and performance of citizenship rights, often across borders and through cross-cultural connections to diasporic communities. Just as dub borrows from technology, removing sounds from recordings, and then adding to them, a vast number of Caribbean Canadian women were removed—whether by forced exodus, choice, or economic imperative—from one society to another, irrevocably changing themselves and Canada in the multi/cultural exchange.

Kristen Knopf, using Lillian Allen as her example—who met Oku Onuora in Cuba in 1978 and shortly after began working with dub in Canada—contends that dub enacts the possibilities of multicultural performance: "For the first two albums she received a Juno Award. Her dub poem 'Colors' is a piece that propels us directly into the way multiculturalism is reflected in most of Allen's dub poetry ... expressed through the various colours in which the lyrical subject is dressed, on the other hand it poses the question of who subdues/marginalizes these colours/cultures."[29] This give-and-take and push-and-pull of multiple influences and cultures, as well as gendered experiences, is what allows dub to function as a powerful articulation of womanist-informed diasporic encounters. Diaspora is an involuntary scattering or migration of people, and dub is a direct manipulation of those experiences into what Allen calls "new forms." Furthermore, women dubbists continue to evolve dub poetics in a Canadian context, most dramatically, perhaps, in dub theatre.

An early example of dub theatre in Canada is Ahdri Zhina Mandiela's chimerical *dark diaspora ... in dub*: a theatre piece composed wholly from dub poems that integrates choral vocals, dub *riddims*, drums, choreographed dance, chant, and elaborate costumes. *dark diaspora* proclaimed a new era in dub, one that was continued by other dub theatre practitioners such as d'bi.young.[30] *dark diaspora* openly acknowledges its indebtedness to Ntozake Shange's experimental choreopoem *For Colored Girls Who Have Considered Suicide / When the Rainbow Is Enuf.* The diasporic experiences, as articulated through dub, in the dub play are uniquely "African" as well as Black Canadian and could have only ever been conceived in the consciousness of a Black woman living on Turtle Island / in Canada. *dark diaspora* charts the experiences of Black women from Africa through the Middle Passage and into the New World, exposing the dark irony of a country like Canada trying to turn brown or "raw" sugar into "refined" white sugar, since the raw element of the African or diasporic experience can never be erased. As the choreopoem "afrikan by instinct" in *dark diaspora* makes clear, "diasporic black *canadians*" are "afrikan / / by instinct / / afrikan," as the speaker searches for "my own tongue" and reminds the audience—parenthetically—that "(slaves do have beginnings)."[31] *dark diaspora* concludes with a dubbing of the pro-Black James Brown chant: "say it /say it / say it / say it loud / i'm black / & i'm proud / say it loud."♭[32] Is this a facsimile Blackness copied from America?—if so, only partly and with intent. Dub draws lines of affiliation: once we move out of the cultural and into the cross-border (musical) associations we realize that dub, at its heart, is a way to write over the language of the colonizer. Such a writing-over allows dubbists, as Cooper contends, to "not only [act] Kali- and Demeter-like, but [to] constantly [strive] to be like Maat, the Kemetic (ancient Egyptian) deity of order, harmony, balance, justice, compassion, and righteousness."[33] These dubbists reshape the disharmony of the world, for, as Dawes writes, "You've got to sing those songs just to keep on keeping on," as difficult as it might be to sing, let alone to find an appropriate voice and language to speak in.[34]

♭ See the playlist for Chapter 5 to listen to Brown's "Say it Loud."

II. Black Chant: Searching For a Mother Tongue

"To love! is to resist."

—M. NOURBESE PHILIP, *A Genealogy of Resistance*, 29

Worrying the Line

In an interview with Nigel Thomas, M. NourbeSe Philip describes, from a Caribbean perspective, how "language is central to the way we are, to the way we be, to use a Black expression, the way we interact with our environment and others."[35] Language can afford mobility, resistance, and self-awareness, yet it can also be used as a form of oppression; for dub poets, it is unequivocally the former. As Yvonne Brown testifies, English is a language that has been changed in a multiplicity of ways by those who have had the King's English forced upon them: "They bend it in all sorts of ways. Expressed in dub poetry, in reggae, in calypso, the whole thing. They make that language work and they bend it out of shape ... we have a good time making it deviant!"[36] It is this notion of deviance, of troubling the line between standard language and coded speech, that empowers many Black poets and musicians across the diaspora to work against a standard mode of operation. And, as we shall see, this bending of language in a diasporic context provides a conceptual framework to read the aesthetic qualities of Philip's *Zong!* I contend that the dub aesthetic is informed from the rhetorical implications of being outside what is considered standard. Dissonance is not simply something unmusical—there wouldn't be jazz institutes or hip hop festivals if it were—rather, dissonance can provide a valuable metaphor for Black creative expression and experience, and it is a valuable mode for contesting and reshaping standard Western notions of proper language and harmony. As Ajay Heble notes in *Landing on the Wrong Note*, dissonance remains an important strategy for aggrieved populations to sound off against systems of oppression.

Clifton Joseph

In my paper "Disruptive Dialogics," I contend that "[Thelonious] Monk's style, or even his public persona, can be read as a negotiation of dissonance with the intention to disturb the naturalized order of knowledge production, thus creating a disruptive poetics that challenges hegemonic listening approaches to jazz and its dialogically intertwined manifestations."[37] While Monk has provided an endless fountain of poetic inspiration for poets in America (Amiri Baraka, Al Young, Charles Simic, Michael Harper, William Corbett, Yusef Komunyakaa, Dave Etter's Well You Needn't, and Art Lange's The Monk Poems, among others), he has equally been an inspiration to a variety of Black Canadian and Afrosporic poets. Everyone from Fred Booker to Frederick Ward, Clifton Joseph, Wayde Compton, Dionne Brand, and Hope Anderson, and many others, have drawn inspiration from Monk, and often in a Canadian context. As Fred Booker, a singer-songwriter-poet born in Cleveland, Ohio, who immigrated to Canada in 1966, writes in "Can You Dig That?": "Thelonious Monk . . . names rolling off my tongue / easier than / 'William Lyon Mackenzie King' / ever did."[38] Clifton Joseph, one of Canada's most revered dub poets, ends his first collection, *Metropolitan Blues*, with an elegiac poem that pays homage to Thelonious Monk, who died one year before the work was published. The poem ends with an affirmative and iterative "MONK LIVES" for two full pages and was recorded as a jazzy-dub poem on his record *Oral/Trans/Missions* (1990).[♭39] Monk's tipping meters and peculiar chords attract poets who want to represent dissonance through a jazz orthography on the page; we can ask: What does Monk tell us about dub poetics?

Of course, Monk was not a dub poet, but his negotiation of multiple forms in both the classical and jazz tradition and his stylization of those forms into new modes of playing and approaching rhythm—of making it new—is a reminder of how Black artists have subverted, and continue to destabilize, oppression while improvising upon a

---

♭ Dear Reader: the humble author wants to point you to a 2013 remix he made of Monk's "Epistrophe" and "Round Midnight," which features parts of Joseph's poem, "A Chant for Monk": https://djtechne.bandcamp.com/track/epistrophe-in-the-tradition.

standard to make tradition meaningful in the present moment. Ajay Heble advises that "oppression, after all, is itself a space of dissonance, for it means being out of tune with naturalized assumptions about social structures and categories."[40] Through rhythmic alteration and angularity, poets working in the Black tradition—the "Afrological"— are able to use negation of form and language to challenge the Western epistemic order of knowledge production, not just at the level of music, but also at the level of language. Even Monk's titles become verbal nouns, evidenced in Monk's songs "Rhythm-a-ning" and "Jackie-ing," for resistive identity formation is largely about using words differently, or bending them like notes. To my ear and logic, this strategy makes perfect sense, since as Philip describes in *Genealogy*, "to speak another language is to enter another consciousness. Africans in the New World were compelled to enter another consciousness, that of their masters, while simultaneously being excluded from their own ... The survival of African musical art forms probably owe their success and persistence to the fact that they were essentially non-verbal art forms."[41] These non-verbal art forms manifest in coded speech, to the datum of drum playing, to the dubbing over of English through new modes of speaking, writing, and performing.

Clare Harris expresses the desire to change language, to make it dance, in her long poem, *Drawing Down a Daughter*, which scatters "words sentences paragraphs drawing down a daughter / / she scrambles after." The poem uses just about every device of verse poetry (poems, prose, narrative)—*sans* strict meter and line breaks—to create a literary collage of the narrator's past (Trinidad) and present (Calgary) and her pre-birth experiences as she prepares a birth gift for her daughter. The challenge of finding an appropriate gift is most explicitly confronted and emphasized in the narrator's knowledge that the English language is oppressive; the best advice she can give her daughter is to shape this enforced language so that it may dance and sing.[42] Harris lets her daughter know that she can find an identity even in a language that is not explicitly hers by making it dance/sing—by dubbing over it. The entwined orthographic representation of dance/sing through a glissando of fragmented words is a feat of finding the beat in dissonance, for as James Baldwin has said, "Negro speech is not a question of dropping s's or n's or g's but a question of the beat."[43] As Philip makes manifest, New World Africans, in their deforming and fusing of English and African dialects, were able to create a new language full of rhythm. Philip contends that "the linguistic rape and subsequent forced marriage between African and English tongues has resulted in a language capable of great rhythms and musicality." Philip terms this new speech "*kinopoeia*," [italics in original] which combines the African with the English to create a new speech that can reclaim "i-mages" (drawn from the Rastafarian practice of privileging the "I") in the construction of oneself: "*the kinetic quality of language which I believe is best exhibited by those vernaculars that combine the African with (in this case) English*" [italics in original].[44] This kinetic quality is essentially what dub exemplifies, an ample ability to duppy the past and manipulate a present to create more meaningful "i-mages" of the self and the African diasporic community.[45]

<small>Oku Onuora</small>

In worrying the line—challenging normative ways of acting and speaking—poets and musicians across the diaspora continue to transpose lines of power by disturbing the popular notion of what is right/ *white*. In an interview with *Empire*, NourbeSe Philip uses as an example how dub poet Linton Kwesi Johnson uses a dub beat to fragment sound and ideas to then put them back together, akin to what she is doing with her poetry: "Refashioning it so that it can carry what you want it to say: managing the brutal history that casts a long and deep shadow around the language." She goes on to describe how we see this hidden meaning in Rastafarian language and its unique orthography, which refashions words to reflect a specific world view—one that resists the language of Empire.[46] James Scott has discussed how forms of resistance among subordinate groups are not always legible for those in positions of power, and how because of this they constitute "hidden transcripts" that intersect with the sphere of formal politics only on occasion.[47] Since dub's choice of clear narrative via Nation Language speaks most directly to the people who need the alternatives a dub poem provides, dub poems are frequently resistive in nature, yet hardly absent of love. In "I Write About," Oku Onuora probes: "You ask: Why do you write so much about blood, sweat & tears? Don't you write about trees, flowers, birds, love? Yes I write about trees – trees with withered branches & severed roots I write about flowers – flowers on graves I write about birds – caged birds struggling I write about love – love for destruction of oppression."♭⁴⁸ In the anger and resistance of a revolutionary poetics (see Audre Lorde's essay on the use of anger) is love for a better future: a more just society.

Many poets in Canada use dub to challenge the image of a multicultural Canada. For instance, in her poem "Oh Canada II," Afua Cooper provides, as Knopf argues, "a postcolonial subversive revision of the Canadian national anthem":

Canada
of genocide you are accused ♯
why is it your jails are filled with Black men
why is it your prisons are filled with Native men
what are your intentions Canada
that you seek to bound us so⁴⁹

Dubbists like Cooper, Mandiela, d'bi.young, and Lillian Allen, among others, who challenge the whitewashing strategies of Canadian imperialist history, appropriate their adopted tongues through acts of rhetorical alteration and linguistic combat in order to reclaim a silenced voice. In doing so they provide greater citizenship status for the dispossessed. If the voice sounds militant, resistive, and confident—yet tinged with love—it is because these dubbists have historically had agency stripped from them. Left "tongue / dumb," they must find new ways to dance and sing.⁵⁰

♭ Oku Onuora has remained consistent in his political views and his use of dub/Rastafarianism as a path towards liberation, evidence in his 2016 poem/song, "Yesterday, Today, Tomorrow."

♯ The line "you are accused," as I hear it, recalls Earl Birney's polemical poem, "I Accuse Us."

Dub Chant: Searching for Mother Tongue

> English
> Is my mother tongue.
> A mother tongue is not
> not a foreign lan lan lang
> language.
> l/anguish
> anguish
> - a foreign anguish.
>
> —M. NOURBESE PHILIP, "Discourse on the Logic of Language," in *She Tries Her Tongue*, 54

Many Black Canadian cis women, transgender women, and nonbinary poets resist the commoditization of form and voice, using the lacunae and the silences of the historically ancillary Black female body and person to reclaim the "gendered" poet and, ultimately, language itself.[51] Dionne Brand, Claire Harris, and Marlene NourbeSe Philip, among manifold others, write with the intention to revivify an Afrocentric feminist epistemology that acknowledges the value of difference. As Sharon Morgan Beckford avows in *Naturally Woman*, the Demeter and Persephone myth represents the Black women's quest for individuation.[52] The need to reclaim myth is the same need to reclaim the loss of mother tongue.

Philip argues in *She Tries Her Tongue, Her Silence Softly Breaks* that she "set out to destroy the lyric voice, the singularity of the lyric voice, and found that poetry had split. Metamorphosed. Into a multiplicity of voices—the polyvocular."[53] Similarly, Claire Harris, in "Why Do I Write?," argues that the lyrical "I" is charted in her writing with a complex history:

> The response embedded in my "I" is not the disembodied "I," nor is it everyone's "I," both of which are rooted in the faulty and debilitating versions of history, in notions of power and control over both persons and nature central to modern European culture, to

its cult of individualism, and to the Americas. Nor is it the naïve "I" of autobiography. Instead it is the "I" of a specific body, the African body, the female African body, as well as the "I" of the imagined, and selectively structured, narrative context.[54]

Thus, the "I" of the lyrical voice is subverted through the untelling of its various metaphorical and corporeal machinations and reclaimed for the gendered subject.

The linguistic rape (of enforced English) is troubling when read along the space that Black women historically occupy. As Philip tells Nigel Thomas in an interview, "one of the reasons that Black women were brought to the New World was to pacify men . . . Black women's bodies were reaped, very much the way that land is reaped."[55] In North America, Black women have had limited agency over their bodies, exemplified by the raping of Black women by their slave masters, by having their bodies displayed as sexually perverse (think Saartjie Baartman, aka the "Hotentot Venus"), or by pop markets where Blackness is often subsumed or appropriated in acts of minstrelsy by white pop stars.[b] In recent Canadian history, Black women's bodies

---

[b] In *Outlaw Culture* bell hooks examines the blatant cultural appropriation and fetishization of race that appears in Madonna's *Sex* book and in her videos, as well as in her film *Truth or Dare*. Furthermore, she critiques the misogyny and sexist attitudes portrayed in gangster rap as "a reflection of the prevailing values in our society, values sustained by white supremacist capitalist patriarchy" (bell hooks, *Outlaw Culture: Resisting Representations* [New York: Routledge, 1994], 135). Such misogyny, which reflects "white supremacist capitalist patriarchy" (hooks's useful terminology), is hardly a bygone product of nineties music videos. For instance, there were thousands of responses in defence or chastisement of the highly sexualized performance by pop star Miley Cyrus at the 2013 VMAs, and of the overt and provocatively sexual images in her video "Wrecking Ball." While many of these critiques have noted the sexist and patriarchal nature of the music industry, few have focused on the fetishization of race in Cyrus's work, particularly her appropriation of twerking—a sexually provocative dance style created by Black women—and her reduction of Black women (who appear as sexualized props in that performance) as "lewd, lascivious, and uncontrollably sexualized" (Cate Young, "Solidarity is for Miley Cyrus," 2013, https://www.cate-young.com/

were reaped once again by affluent whites for material gain, such as in 1955 with the Domestic Worker Scheme, which was implemented to recruit approximately three hundred women annually from Jamaica, Trinidad, and Barbados to redress a perceived "shortage of labour."[56] Hence, it should surprise few with even the slightest knowledge of Canada's colonial history that Black women's writing in Canada challenges language and gender through a feminism—in search of a mother tongue—that must be of necessity, as dub poet Lillian Allen contends, "anti-colonial, anti-capitalist, anti-imperialist, and anti-sexist."[57] Women in dub show that poetry and feminism are hardly the domains of white people and European aesthetic standards.

As Carr fittingly notes, "Canada, formed of many distinct cultural entities, has to negotiate its complexities and productive dissonances in ways that allow for the m/othering and be/longing of all its citizens with their diverse transnational allegiances."[58] Yet if this m/othering is to work against the othering of Black bodies, we must place value on the importance of stories (not just the ones we tell, but the ones we contest) to create counter-narratives informed by and from Black women. M. NourbeSe Philip's *She Tries Her Tongue* is an exodus that riffs upon the wombs of language, racism, and exile, through the epic rebellion of the father figure—colonialism—in a search for a mother figure, a mother tongue, a reworking of the Demeter and Persephone myth. In *She Tries Her Tongue* the speaker listens acutely throughout history, "the listening / breadth of my walk," as the exiled Persephone searches for "She whom they call mother."[59] For Philip, Canada functions as an adoptive mother country that she holds historically accountable for its injustices and re/birthing: "Canada needs to m/other us. Her very salvation depends on m/othering all her peoples—those who be/longed here when the first Europeans arrived — the Native peoples; as well as those, like the African, who unwittingly encountered History

---

battymamzelle/2013/08/Solidarity-Is-For-Miley-Cyrus.html). As Cate Young states, "the subsequent ignoring of the racial implications of what she did is just the latest incident in the long line of things that shows me as a black woman, that white feminism does not want me, or care to have me."

and became seminal in its development."⁶⁰ Without a mother, or a tongue, the poet is left "tongue / dumb," a figurative representation of the violence enacted upon the slave, who was torn from a real mother, a mother country, and a mother language, often with horrifying consequences for enslaved people caught speaking their native language.⁶¹ Philip drives this point home in Edict II in "Discourse on the Logic of Language": *"Where necessary, removal of the tongue is recommended. The offending organ, when removed, should be hung on high in a central place, so that all may see and tremble"* [italics in original].⁶² For mother-dub poets and for many African diasporic poets as well, to dub over language is to claim a space of resistance where maternity can be representationally, mythically, or communally possible again. Part of discordant and complex citizenship is the ability to maintain, recover, and engage with a mother tongue, especially in a foster-mothered country. A dubbing that connects a disjointed and painful history to a fragmented yet congruent tradition, maintained through the oral transmission of stories, language, and *riddim*, reflects a choice to sustain language as well as a necessity for survival. The strategies of the dub poet reflect the desire to recreate the village, and by writing poems down, calling together a larger reading public, the dub poet enacts a cross-cultural literary bridging between orality and textuality.

NourbeSe Philip remarks that dub poetry's popular culture status and its deep roots in African oral practices have stimulated its crossover appeal between Black and white audiences, enacting what Maria Caridad Casas terms the *playscript*, which is written in *medium*, but spoken in *mode*.⁶³ A dub poet's choice to write down poems, or tell stories in the subjugator's language, is a politicized act of resistance; by changing the intonations and meanings of the English language through grammatical reformation, among other linguistic techniques, such poets enact semiotic resistance. We see this in d'bi. young's poem "foolishness," which undulates between solecistic dialect (via various elisions) and standard English in order to find solidarity and poetic "revolushun": "mi membah when mi did deh a jamaica / ghetto life nevah fun . . . I am di colour of her skin / when she look pon mi / she see herself within ... unity mean finding solidarity /

among our differences."⁶⁴ᵇ We also see this in NourbeSe Philip's reworking of language in her poetry, especially in regard to colonial languages like English.

As Philip articulates in *Zong!*: "Words break into sound, return to their initial and originary phonic sound—grunts, plosives, labials—is this, perhaps, how language might have sounded at the beginning of time?"⁶⁵ And so, we move closer to Black chant, a language in itself, and a force that exists on the edges of orality and literacy—in a space that punctuates silence. There are forces older than writing. Zora Neale Hurston puts this well in *Mules and Men*, saying, "Belief in magic is older than writing. So nobody knows how it started," for magic is like improvised Black chant: "the chant of strange syllables rose."⁶⁶ Black chant is Afro-diasporic postmodernism—not to be chronologically defined—that reminds us, as Aldon Lynn Nielsen points out, how "traditions of graphic reproduction and improvisation are part of an iterative continuum with orality, not secondary or elitist or pale reflection of the spoken."⁶⁷ A dub chant refuses to conform to standard English, as we will see in *Zong!*, and through that refusal, NourbeSe Philip and other dub poets cultivate what Kamau Brathwaite calls "Nation Language," a positive expression he uses to disrupt the hierarchical "bad English" implications of "dialect." This chant or dialect, Brathwaite goes on to say, "may be in English, but often it is in an English which is like a howl, or a shout,

---

ᵇ We see similar strategies of abrogated English in the work of nineteenth-century African American poet Paul Laurence Dunbar, whose poems cover everything from music (his instrument was the banjo), to spirituals, religion, coloured soldiers who fought in the Civil War, race relations in America, odes to Ethiopia (in his *Lyrics of Lowly Life*, 1896), and the American South. His poems are replete with repetitions, abrogative language, neologisms, listenings, religious allusions, and refrains. Furthermore, Dunbar's proximity to poets whose literary blackface defined the meaning of blackface for white culture has led some early scholars and readers to place his work in the minstrel tradition. Even though Dunbar was often embarrassed by the solecistic dialect in many of his poems, he has become the prototype of the poet with two distinct speaking voices. Like many dub poems, his poems seem to break into song when read aloud.

or a machine-gun, or the wind, or a wave. It is also like the blues."[68] Furthermore, there can be no chant without silence, since chant is often a response to historical silences, and a response to the failings of language—written or oral—to express a horrifying past. For how can the enslaved or exiled fully speak if they are left without a language to speak in? This lack of language is poetized in NourbeSe's "Meditations on the Declension of Beauty by the Girl with the Flying Cheek-Bones," which does an excellent job poetizing the challenge of finding the words through a colonizing language, asking "If not" in "whose language / Am I / In not in yours / Beautiful."[69]

On Silence, "Duppy States," and Diasporic Memory

"between notes / composes / the improvise in silence / —a symphony."

—M. NOURBESE PHILIP, *Looking for Livingstone: An Odyssey of Silence*, 46

Silence is an oft-articulated theme by the writer working at the margins. It is the primary topic of Philip's *Looking For Livingstone: An Odyssey of Silence*, which presents a challenge to Western assumptions about the silence of Indigenous populations, as well as a postulation on the empowerment and story of silence. As Philip indicates, "When the missing text is silence, what is the language with which you read the silence? . . . To deal in silence one must learn a new language."[70] Thus, *Zong!*, like *Looking for Livingstone*, finds new language and sound, even in silence, for "Everything has its own sound, speech, or language, even if it is only the language of silence."[71] In *Zong!* it is the untelling of silence, represented in the various manifestations of chant, in which silence becomes audible, challenging us to listen, or un-listen: there is no music without silence. In Philip's *Zong!* the reworking of the legal text ("Gregson v. Gilbert"), particularly in the opening section "Os," exposes the many silences of the legal jargon.

Silence provides pause, allowing the mind of a reader/audience to enter a work. The chant of dub—I've moved to using dub more figuratively here—is a direct response to a history of silence, and as Philip tells Thomas in an interview, "I don't believe that we as a colonized people were ever silent or were ever silenced . . . we have been written in as silences."[72] The challenge is to learn to read the historical silences in order to learn "a new language." Philip's writing of poems that deal explicitly with historical silences reflects her desire to speak out, to re-examine and give a voice to the historically silenced, echoing James Baldwin's call (in a 1970s letter to Angela Davis) to speak out, rather than continue the cycle of silence: "We live in an age in which silence is not only criminal but suicidal . . . for if they take you in the morning, they will be coming for us that night."[73] For these reasons *Zong!* "can only be told by telling. In the many silences within the Silence of the text."[74] Scholar Patricia Saunders, examining *Zong!*, makes the case that "to work through language and silence, language must be destroyed, and 'Ferrum' allows her [Philip] to do this. She calls 'Ferrum' her 'revenge' on language and her 'very own language.'"[75] I emphasize silence here not so much as the antithesis to chant, as silence is the doubling/dubbing of chant—its phantom limb. No chant without silence, and no silence to be revealed without the healing power of chant. Silence, an articulation of historical evasions, can also be a moment of power, for silence, as we shall hear in *Zong!*, can reveal discovery, possibility, and even meditation. As dubbist d'bi.young unveils, "through meditative silence all is revealed. Be sure to ground yourself firstly in an ongoing personal practice of silence and from that place, all your truth (questions and answers and practice) will emerge."[76] In addition, silence is about surrender—"I surrendered to the SILENCE within"—in the hopes of recovering memories apropos a new diasporic consciousness.[77]

While silence is a central tenet of much of Philip's work, there is also a double meaning here as there has been critical silence in CanLit around Philip's work. In part, one might argue that this is because her work is difficult in terms of form and because she is outspoken, but the truth is that there are many white poets whose difficulty and radicalism are celebrated in CanLit. As Paul Barrett writes in "The Poetic

Disturbances of M. NourbeSe Philip," not only is Philip seen as an outsider in CanLit, but what "*is* surprising is the extent to which she is also missing from the contemporary debates that have transformed CanLit."[78] In *Black,* Philip reflects that this is largely because she writes "in the shadow of empire and on the frontier of Silence; I write against the grain as an unembedded, disappeared poet and writer in Canada."[79] It is difficult to label the precise tradition she explicitly belongs in, as she often finds herself exiled from the Black tradition, perhaps much more so than the academic tradition, or by those who write and discuss L=A=N=G=U=A=G=E poetry: "my work does not fit the traditions of Black poetry."[80] Yet what are the traditions of Black poetry and music? I resist calling NourbeSe a dub poet or, on the other end of the spectrum, a L=A=N=G=U=A=G=E poet. In improvising at the margins of multiple traditions (dub, jazz, Euro and Afro avant-garde aesthetics, oral and written), NourbeSe takes the experience of exile/silence—exemplified in form—and makes it sound a complex citizenship routed/rooted in place and poetic language. Philip gives voice/chant to the act of uprooting. It is through escape, through flight—physical or metaphorical—that exiled individuals develop duppy states of mind that aid in survival, resistance, re-routing and rooting, and even pleasure.

The poets in this book share a sense of mixed identity and inheritance; they inhabit compound identities in multiple cultural contact zones, particularly NourbeSe Philip, the central poet of this chapter. As Myriam Moïse announces, "Philip's writing encourages the reader to share her African spiritual quest and her triangular journey from the Caribbean to Canada and back to West Africa. Philip's poetry demonstrates how boundless diasporic spaces can be, as the diaspora displaces home and away, here and elsewhere, thus constantly redefining the limits of its own horizon."[81] Home, like citizenship, is a process to be reworked, akin to dub performance: a postmodern pastiche of past and present. As a poet who often invokes Black chant and creative Black approaches to poetry, Philip tests the limits and elasticity of the dub form, yet she is often exiled from the Black tradition. It is from this perspective that Philip's work is informed, and it is what allows her to engage with the past from a diasporic or "duppy state" of mind.

"Duppy states" is a term coined by Richard Iton to denote the powerful afterlife and persistent mockery of coloniality—its resurgence rather than its remission. It signifies a state that is simultaneously "there and not there." In Jamaican patois, "duppy" "refers to the specter or the ghost that emerges when one has failed to properly bury or dispose of the deceased: therefore, emancipation is haunted by slavery, independence by colonialism, and apparent civil rights victories by Jim Crow."[82] In *Zong!*, the past haunts the memories of the present, as the ghosts of the past are not done with us, which is essentially why Philip describes *Zong!* as hauntological, "a work of haunting" in that the poem is haunted by the spectres of the drowned Africans who were disposed of in the mass grave of the cold, dark sea.[83] Diasporic memory is an act of survival, as diasporic memories recall a past that African people were systemically taught to forget. Scholar Mary Chamberlain maintains that "diasporic memory is a necessarily layered one which links the black experience and provides a cultural continuity with those back home and overseas." She elaborates: "diasporic memories [are a] certain form of memory or post-memory of place or trauma" associated with the forced exodus of Africans to the Americas.[84] The echoes of this collective trauma persist through a collective remembering: in the weaving together of memories across time and the diaspora, the past is dubbed into a present where meaningful counter-memories can be formed. David Scott classifies "counter-memory" as "the moral idiom and semiotic registers of remembering against the grain of the history of New World black deracination, subjection, and exclusion."[85] It is against the grain of history that we, as readers or audiences, along with the poet, are compelled to remember the past.

"Diasporic memories" challenge insular representations of national identity that often devalue difference. For many, a dub is about more than *riddim* and feeling good (although those are important parts), in the way that Carnival is about much more than the party. As Philip argues, "to African Caribbean people, Carnival is much more than a dance in the street; it represents our sense of collective freedom and right to be free."[86] "Diasporic memories" recall traditions and remain powerfully intact in the consciousness of African people across the diaspora. Philip's quoting of Ovid's *Metamorphoses* in the title poem from *She Tries Her Tongue*, that *"All Things are alter'd, nothing is destroyed"* [italics in original], serves as a remembrance of the altercation and alteration that Africans underwent from the Middle Passage into bondage and then freedom.[87] In *Zong!*, Philip's fictional remembering, and improvising (Philip co-writes the text with an African spirit: the cover says, "As told to the author by Setaey Adamu Boateng"), of the *Zong* massacre, within the collective trauma of slavery, provides a resistive dub chant that untells historical silences and reroutes what it means to be a citizen (a sounding person).

LISTENING INTERLUDE

Before I move into the improvised dub chant of Philip's *Zong!*, I want to pause for a moment and listen. Philip composed her text with the ancestors in mind: Setaey Adamu Boteng is the ancestral voice that Philip listened to when she created *Zong!*. Philip was careful in her process to not do harm to those ancestors who lost their lives and were thrown into the ocean to drown. She travelled to Africa and met with elders who might have been ancestors to the drowned, and she entered the work with a profound sense of the task. We too are called to enter into careful relationship with the text as we read, listen, and perform *Zong!*. That is, we are to listen for the music and the pure sound of those voices calling out to us. In an endnote to her brilliant essay "Notanda," which follows *Zong!*, Philip names a number of musical pieces that she listened to while writing—at times obsessively. It is an interesting mix: Van Morrison's *Endless Days of Summer*,[♭] for it "conveyed a sense of loss of something brief, beautiful, and fleeting"; Ali Farka Toure's

Van Morrison, Ali Farka Toure, and Ayub Ogada

[♭] I believe the Van Morrison song that Philip refers to here is "These Are the Days" from *Avalon Sunset* (1989). Interesting, although perhaps little more than observation, the song's line "These are the days, the time is now" recalls MLK's and Charlie Parker's insistence that "now is the time." Time is fleeting, and we have a responsibility to not only enact change in the moment, but perhaps to also find beauty where we can.

"Hawa Dolo," for a similar reason; and Kenyan Luo musician Ayub Ogada, for his music "recalled a memory of what might have been lost to those on board the *Zong*."[88] *Zong!* emerges from these replete listening practices. The text teaches us to listen to the dubs, the echoes, and sonic bones in the deep of the ocean. The work is indeed a chant, calling for collective sounding. We enter into the communal spirit when we read and sound *Zong!*.

III. Voicing the Unvoicable: The Improvised Dub Chant of Philip's *Zong!*

> The sea is slavery ... Sea receives a body as if that body has come to rest on a cushion, one that gives way to the body's weight and folds round it like an envelope. Over three days 131 such bodies, no, 132, are flung at this sea. Each lands with a sound that the sea absorbs and silences. Each opens a wound in this sea that heals over each body without the evidence of a scar ... Those bodies have their lives written on salt water. The sea current turns pages of memory. One hundred and thirty one souls roam the Atlantic with countless others. When the wind is heard, it is their breath, their speech. The sea is therefore home.
>
> —FRED D'AGUIAR, *Feeding the Ghosts*, 3–4

Ebora: "Hauntological" Legalities

Zong! is hauntological:♭ "it is a work of haunting, a wake of sorts, where the specters of the undead make themselves present. And only in not-telling can the story be told; only in the space where it's not told—

♭ See Jacques Derrida's 1993 *Specters of Marx* for the origination of this neologism. Derrida moves beyond ontology towards a hauntology where the figure of the specter from the past remains persistent and contested.

literally in the margins of the text, a sort of negative space, a space not so much of non-meaning as anti-meaning."[89] There is a need to collect the bones of the dead, the drowned Africans who were thrown overboard the *Zong* by the crew allegedly to conserve water and make a legal claim for "goods" lost at sea. *Zong!* is haunted by the *ebora* of the text, *ebora* being a Yoruba word for underwater spirits. The text is also haunted by the legal jargon of the "Gregson v. Gilbert" case, the surviving document of the massacre, which is reworked by Philip—who shows her skills as both a poet and a lawyer—into a language of dub, as Philip inserts collective agency into the remembering of one of the slave trade's most brutal massacres.[90] The *Zong* massacre is a story many people are familiar with; the episode continues to inspire works of literature, including Fred D'Aguiar's *Feeding the Ghosts* (1997), which focuses on the story of an enslaved African who survives being thrown overboard; a detailing of the bizarre legal case by James Walvin in *Black Ivory*; and Margaret Busby's play *An African Cargo*, which was staged at Greenwich Theatre in 2007 and dealt specifically with the 1783 trial.

As the story goes, the *Zong*, a merchant ship, sailed from the west coast of Africa with 470, 442, or 440 slaves aboard, and seventeen crew, and was captained by Luke Collingwood. Due to faulty navigation, the six- to nine-week journey took some eighteen weeks. The navigational error led to a shortage of water and a sickness that ravaged both crew members and Africans. Apparently, to conserve what water remained, and to preserve the remaining African cargo, the crew threw slaves into the sea to drown, a tactic that allowed the owners of the *Zong* to make a legal claim to the insurers for the loss of cargo/goods. At the grotesque sight of watching the "cargo" thrown into the sea, some Africans threw *themselves* into the sea. The total number of the drowned was between 130 and 150, all of whom either were thrown into the Atlantic or jumped in on their own volition or were ordered to jump in against their will; an additional thirty died before landfall in Jamaica.[91] Upon arrival, the owners (Gregson) made a claim to their insurers (Gilbert) for the loss of "cargo," citing a lack of water to sustain the slaves (the "cargo"). When the insurers refused to pay, the ensuing trial maintained that in certain cases the deliberate killing of slaves was in fact legal and that the insurers could be obliged to pay the insurance money. Collingwood's orders were not uniformly popular with the crew. What is particularly disturbing is that during the week of the massacre it rained for two full days, which allowed the crew to replenish their water. Essentially, the massacre had no "logical" reason to continue.[92] Initially, on 5 March 1783, the court ruled in favour of the shipowners. Gilbert still refused to pay, citing that one cannot bring about a loss intentionally. An appeal was heard at the Court of King's Bench in Westminster Hall on 21–22 May 1783. At the hearing it came out that heavy rain had fallen during the massacre, so the case was to be tried again. There is no evidence, however, that another trial took place. *Zong!* riffs on the legal document from the King's Bench hearing. The legal account is one version of what happened, a happening couched in lawful/official language that Philip gradually dislodges through the poetic excavation and untelling of the legal text. Reworking the legal document ("Gregson v. Gilbert"), the story is untold through fugal and counterpointed repetition to create a complex weaving of memories, polyphonies, and cacophonies, which respond to and sound the *Zong* massacre.

At the time, the *Zong* massacre was a touchstone for the abolitionist movement. One abolitionist, Granville Sharp, attempted to have the crew prosecuted for murder (he failed). The *Zong* massacre continues to remind us of the illogical brutality of the slave trade. In 2007 there was a bicentenary commemoration of the end of the British slave trade, during which a replica of the *Zong* sailed down the Thames to the Tower of London.[93] British Romantic landscape painter J.M.W. Turner had the *Zong* in mind when he painted the "The Slave Ship," formally titled "Slavers Throwing overboard the Dead and Dying—Typhoon coming on," in 1840. This brutal moment continues to haunt us; as Christina Sharpe puts it, those Africans who were thrown in or who jumped in "are with us still, in the time of the wake, known as residence time."[94] Philip responds directly to this haunting in her work.

At the time of this writing, Philip's *Zong!* is the most recent of an ongoing series of responses to the historical trauma of the *Zong* massacre. As argued by Veronica J. Austen, this work engages in a nuanced exploration of the question: "Can, or even should, silence be overcome?"⁹⁵ This silence remains in the intangibility of a historical document that in two brief pages turns the murder of 150 human beings into incomprehensible legal jargon. The story's incomprehensible brutality is represented in the poetic medium's reappropriation of legal-speak, even though Philip deeply "distrusts this tool [she] works with—language."⁹⁶ Poetry, however, is a possible site of intervention against the apparent logical order of the legal report, for poetry "push[es] against the boundaries of language" and enables "each poet to speak in his or her own tongue": to find a voice in the cacophonous babel of the *Zong*.⁹⁷ Through "exaqua"—a neologism meaning to bring above the surface of water—Philip is able to rework the "Gregson v. Gilbert" document into a poetic sounding that echoes "those murdered Africans [who] continue to resound and echo underwater. In the bone beds of the sea."⁹⁸

Want of Water

The first part of *Zong!*, "Os," a Latin word meaning bone, and poetically the most conventional section of the long poem, deals explicitly with the underwater bones through the skeleton of the legal case. For example, "The order in destroy" ("Zong! #2" 5) and "to the order in / destroyed" ("Zong! #9" 17) come from "the slaves were destroyed in order to throw the loss on the underwriters," as do "the loss in underwriter" and "the sustenance in want" ("Zong! #9" 17), which come from the case: "the loss in underwriter" and "the negroes died for want of sustenance, &c."⁹⁹ There are prominent manipulations of the source text in the poem, and the riffing, the dubbing of the source text, is reworked to highlight the brutality behind the facade of the legal jargon. In particular, the phrase "want of water" appears throughout the text, copied verbatim from "Gregson v. Gilbert." The text opens in water, as the word itself is interrogated with mantra like percussion, immediately challenging any simple ortho/typographic representation of the case:

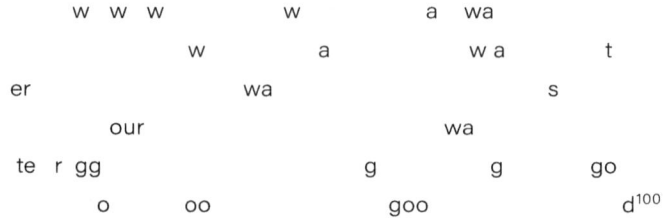

The words on the page undulate like crashing waves, or bodies sinking to the bottom of the poem. It is important to note that in this section no word appears directly under another, an important sounding that one translation of the text misses.[101] Philip, as Kate Siklosi points out, makes use of "the persistent gaps and fragments as a vocal score; when she reads the first passage above, for example, the deferral of the word 'water' becomes an unhurried meditation on the slave's torturous crossing of the Atlantic. The sonority of the sputtering fragmentation is painfully and mournfully delayed, with the letters and phonemes enunciated in long, drawn-out pauses."[102] The single syllable of "wa" becomes a melismatic chant, a heterophonic modulation that uses a few sounds—musical cries—to articulate loss. *Zong!* is an elegiac chant, but it is also a poetic manifesto for the possibilities of historical revisionism: a reimagining of the events of the *Zong* through the poetic excavation of the bones of the drowned.

We are called to chant the poem, and quickly realize in *Zong!* that poetic voice is collective, a force of many voices working against the singularity of the legal case. Each phoneme, as Sarah Dowling argues, "roils and stutters so that the first line of the poem contains only the letters w and a, barely completing the first syllable of the first word."[103] The poetic text/speaker(s) work at that which is nearly impossible to speak. In 2012, in Toronto, I heard Philip read *Zong!* as part of an AvantGarden reading series.[104] In her reading, the opening poem and phoneme "wa" was enunciated by Philip, slowly and elongated and in the order it was written, while she had around fifteen others read the poem in non-sequential order, echoing or dubbing her words, a reverberation that erased the origin of clear beginnings or

Figure 3.1 Philip and musicians improvising along with a reading of *Zong!* on November 29, 2013. Photo: Paul db Watkins

endings.♭¹⁰⁵ Philip's desire to read this way dates back to her figuring out innovative modes to read *She Tries Her Tongue*, which she explains to Nigel Thomas reflected a "need for a choral collective voice. I ask the students to come and read with me."¹⁰⁶ The soundscape we entered at her reading was cacophonous, but also mantra- and chant-like—horrifically beautiful. To chant the poem together is an act of collective survival. The graphical possibilities of the written text, the various morphemes and phonemes, became realized in the performance of them, taking us into the unreality and corporeality of the haunting events that transpired when Collingwood ordered the Africans thrown overboard. "Os" concerns water, the thirst for water, the repetition of being surrounded by water, and yet lacking water—of being engulfed by the legal language of murdered "goods." Throughout the opening section of "Os" we are

---

♭ You can view excerpts of live performances of *Zong!* here: https://www.youtube.com/watch?v=zLlUFzrhyAg&t=572s

surrounded by a sea of words that cycle back over the legal case trying to find truth in the untruth of what transpired, squeezing out a blues lyricism that thirsts for some answer; "the truth is" of the legal case becomes "the truth was," and the opening poem's asking of whether the water *was* good challenges the essentializing of the assured "is."[107] We are in the past, reworked in the present, where the legal language is repeatedly used to highlight the thirst and drowning of the murdered Africans: "negroes of no belonging"; "came the insurance of water"; "negroes exist / for the throwing"; "a sea of negroes / drowned / live / in the thirst" (Philip, *Zong!*, 29, 30, 34, 35).

The sonic repetition of the legal case provides a context where a singular phoneme from water, the "w," or "wa," proliferates significations beneath the surface to highlight the intangibility of interpreting the legal text and history itself. As Erin Fehskens suggests, "This is fresh and salt water, water as conduit, lack of drinking water, water as grave, and more metonymically, maritime trade as the material foundation of the insurance industry and speculative finance. Water in the poem resists graphic and aural cohesion while demanding repetition."[108] The ebb and flow of water washes over the language of the poem, yet the sediments of the bones rise to the surface. Law and poetry share an inexorable concern with using the right words, yet how can poetry or law possibly express Captain Collingwood's deliberate drowning of 150 Africans, with another sixty dying "for want of water for sustenance."[109] The only way, for Philip, to express the deliberate destroying of humans, considered mere property, is to destroy the very properties of language in the retelling, or untelling, which is why Philip "intentionally mutilates the text.[110] Similar to how Philip moves beyond representations of what New World experiences were for Africans in *She Tries Her Tongue*, we are made visually aware in *Zong!* that Black creativity is never exhausted. The spectrum of Black creativity ranges from silence to shout, as Philip draws from Lindon Barrett's argument in *Blackness and Value* that shout was the "principal context in which black creativity occurred."[111] Shout, and the cacophony of *Zong!*, point to one strategy to make meaning out of the deliberate massacre of 150 people to collect insurance money. In an interview with Myriam Moïse, NourbeSe asks, "How do we make meaning of 400 years of peoples being uprooted, kidnapped and taken half way around the world? To what end? I think we are hardwired as humans to try to make meaning. *Zong!* is an attempt to write, to come to terms with the meaninglessness of so much that passes for life."[112] At times the only way to make sense out of the unspeakable is to improvise a voice that unravels such human brutality.

Zong!: An Improvised Dub Chant

As James Baldwin writes in a 1962 letter to his nephew, "We have not stopped trembling yet, but if we had not loved each other, none of us would have survived, and now you must survive because we love you and for the sake of your children and your children's children."[113] Baldwin emphasizes the power of love to hold familial ties together despite the damaging legacy of transatlantic slavery and its afterlife. As an improvised dub chant, Philip's *Zong!* responds to that painful legacy through a doubling of voices, sound systems, lexical markers, and languages, to emphasize and echo the Middle Passage and the transatlantic slave trade. By contorting historical trauma into the power and love of song, into Black creative survival, *Zong!*, as a dub, is a form of political engagement that chants the transatlantic slave trade to create diasporic voice and agency where history has inserted silence. I've taken dub here (with much liberty) as an extended metaphor for how mixing and remixing is an act that finds resonance in interwoven dialogues across time and space. *Zong!* is a noisy text—full of intersecting dialogues and voices, a riffing on the legal text. All of this is actually an integral part of dub; indeed, Kamau Brathwaite emphasizes the "noise" of dub as in the tradition of African oral performance.[114] The dub, akin to the bass line or the "dread beat," permeates the text. Philip strategically employs dub, silence, and other linguistic elements to highlight the challenge of representing the massacre.

The challenge in reading/sounding *Zong!*—what I call an improvised dub chant—is that we need to improvise the meaning each time we pick it up. I realized after writing a first draft of this chapter that Phil Hall has already referred to Philip's work in a review as "dub chant," not in *Zong!*, but in reference to *She Tries Her Tongue*, writing that at "the book's core is a chant."[115] I've settled on *improvised dub chant* because *Zong!* is not quite dub in the strict sense, yet I've aligned Philip on the boundaries of the dub tradition because I think dub is a useful strategy to understand what's happening or unhappening in *Zong!*. Even as Philip plays with the margins of dub, and ultimately does not belong to a single unitary tradition, dub provides a model that underscores the echoing of the past in the present through a subversive practice of call and response, shout and chant, and does so with a wholly new poetics. I hope this reading does the opposite of simplifying *Zong!*; rather, I expect it provides a context for how we get lost in the *riddim* of the poem and sink into its polyphonic folds. Philip reads her own text more in the classic fugal tradition where the theme is stated and then reiterated in second, third, and subsequent voices, although her reference to African dance-style "crumping" is elusive. Crumping, which NourbeSe describes as a dancing body being "contorted and twisted into intense positions and meanings that often appear beyond human comprehension," serves as another instructive challenge to find meaning in the chaos—to read and hear differently.[116] Despite how the poem is read, "grunts, plosives, labials" combine to form new meanings as words echo, antimetabole, and canon one another—new thoughts and patterns emerge in the multivocality of the text.

While my focus here is on my own interpretation of the written text, I asked Philip about her improvisatory live readings and about what she thought of my reading of *Zong!* as an improvised dub chant. She responded positively that her work is both dub and chant:

> Your question is an exciting one and very generative and addresses some of the questions I myself have—questions that come out of doing these "improvisatory" performances. I should explain that there are two kinds of performances I have been engaged in with *Zong!*. One is the type of collective reading you were a part of and which you mention in your question. In the other type of performance I work with musicians in an improvisatory context. We chose small sections of the text and improvise on

those. The work lends itself beautifully to this process. However, while I don't think that there is necessarily an opposition between the jazz improv process and the multiple echoes of a "duppy performance," or that you're suggesting it, the "multiple contact zones" approach you speak of is what interests and haunts me. For instance, I am very keen to introduce the sounds of techno, scratching and turntabling into the text. Yes, oh very, very yes, it is an improvised dub chant. As it must be, for improvisation is what you are left with once you enter the Zong.[117]

Like improvisation in musical practice, *Zong!* as text and performance embodies creative real-time poïesis, risk-taking, and collaboration: as readers we are called to sound the text, to meditate with and between the various languages (glossing with the aid of glossary). Edited in *Zong!* are improvised performances, incantatory phrases, chanting, stories, webs and threads, the echoes of the undead, languages and sounds, polyphonies, mutilations, *riddims*, silences, legal jargon, and listenings. Indeed, *Zong!* is a resonant reminder that poetic language and history are there to make.

As readers and listeners we are co-performers of Philip's rehistoricizing of the *Zong!* massacre, for as Austen argues, "readers too must perform a balancing act, neither assuming that they can construct an authoritative reading of *Zong!*, nor surrendering themselves to accepting incomprehension."[118] Philip draws from the Rastafarian concept of I and I when she performs *Zong!*, and allows the "the words and word clusters to breathe for the I 'n I ... I 'n I is a Rastafarian expression suggesting a collectivity."[b][119] Without our co-performance, our chanting of the text, the page and history remain inaudible. Philip's desire to "introduce the sounds of techno, scratching and turntabling into the text" is another way into

---

[b] There are a lot of songs in dub/reggae that use this expression. I've added punk/reggae band Bad Brains' "I and I Survive" to the playlist because it speaks to the collective fight against oppression and to this chapter's engagement with survival. The "I and I" is a subject pronoun that is closer to "we" and "they" in English and speaks to collective in relation to the divine.

understanding the construction and mutilation of history taking place, as Philip creates a DJ mix, improvising an African multivocal language mix with English, Spanish, French, Dutch, Patois, Latin, and African languages (predominantly Yoruba and Shona). Philip's choice to leave various words untranslated reflects her concern to preserve cultural context (and language). This technique of selective word choice and fidelity challenges the reader to move beyond the text proper and to consult the glossary and beyond. Moreover, it echoes the confusing reality of being on the *Zong*. Like a detective we return to the glossary at the back to understand how meaning in *Zong!* is multiple.[120] The various intermingling languages reflect the transnational globality of the slave trade, as well as the Babel and Babylonian madness aboard a slave ship.

The poetics of the text emulate and are engulfed in this cacophony, with improvisation being both a necessity to survival and a reflection of the unmediated and random brutality of the massacre. The circular nature of the appearance of many poems highlights how Philip works against linearity: generally, words do not tend to appear directly below other words. Furthermore, Philip often picks random words like Collingwood's throwing of random enslaved people overboard, exemplified in the section "Ferrum" (Latin for "iron"), where words become particularly fragmented, yet another language begins to emerge from the submerged voices of the *ebora*.[121] This apparent randomness transforms mistake into a generative possibility, much like the very name of the *Zong*, which was supposed to be *Zorg*, a Dutch word meaning care. A careless error was made when the name was reprinted, and this carelessness in writing the name of the ship is a reminder that song can manifest anywhere, for Zong is a close homophone to song. Philip describes in writing her compendium essay to *Zong!* that her "fingers would hit an S rather a Z in typing *Zong*. Song and Zong . . . if said quickly enough they sound the same."[122] The improvised dub chant of Philip's text riffs on this critical error and the many errors of human cruelty to find, to make, and to chant song where it seems impossible. Such dubbings appear throughout the text's blood (*sang*) song: "& rum they sang & / sang . . . *le sang*"; the red / cove / *le sang le* / sing *le* song"; all sing / sing / they sang *le* /

sang el / song *le* / song sing"; "sings a / tune a sad tune"; "we / they / drum / a / rude / sound how / they dance / always."[123]

The rud(e)imentary sounds of the text are the natural rhythms of suffering and trauma experienced and resisted through the act of song. Words fall and echo other meanings ("pig" slides into "nig") as the text moves from the provisional "if / if / if / if only *Ifá*" into the whole yet fragmented note of *Ifá*, the Yoruba Grand Priest divination who is silent, as an African King (the *oba*) "sobs again." As readers we are implicated in this chanting, mixed in the italicized question, "*did we decide?*" And while, as the epigraph to the section "Ratio" (Latin for reason) by Paul Célan advises, *"No one bears witness for the witness,"* we bear witness to our own listening of a text too unreal to be told.[124] As Sina Queyras writes, "What right do I have to be witnessing this?"[125] And so we listen to our own listening as Philip "spin[s] a tale / to be / told not / heard nor / read / a story that can / not be / un / told," canoned later in the text: "come the tale / that can / not be / told."[126] As *Zong!* repeats the abject horror over and over we find ourselves chanting, propelled into the grotesque mutilation of bodies at the edges of orality and literacy, in a space that punctuates the silence of history.

Philip breaks words down to emphasize how malleable language and identity are, an example being the metathesis in *Zong!* between slave and *salve*, like a balmy chant healing the slave: "salve the slave / e *salve* to / sin *salve* / slave *salve*." Homophonic and anagrammatic links between otherwise incommensurate terms—like "salve" and "slave," "song" and "Zong," or "if" and "*Ifá*"—show how easily meaning flows into new meaning, where a song "for us" enjambs into a song "for *os*"—for the underwater bones.[127] The text asks us to reflect upon our listening experience by linking the collective "us" to the living memory of the submerged dead with "os." Philip represents chant by showing how words are sounded even against the stagnant and inaudible pages of history and the book. Such breaking down of words into sounds, into phonemes and morphemes and half-utterances, is the only way for Philip to represent the destruction of African bodies and voice aboard the *Zong!*. Philip's linguistic strategy of graphic representation fits with Fred Moten's line of reasoning that voice remains in African American visual art forms, arguing that the cries of Emmett Till and his mother can be perceived in the photographs that were captured at his funeral.[128] Philip's "crumping" of words together breaks them down to return them to their original sounds. *Zong!* takes us directly into the language of "grunt and groan, moan and stutter," and multimodal chant, for it is through such chanting that the text can improvise its meaning, challenging the printed logocentric understanding of language, while asking readers to concede that human experience is fragmented and "broken by history."[129]

Zong! enacts a poetics of fragmentation from a babelian chorus that challenges the reader to unpack its meanings. Thus, in writing this chapter I found that *Zong!* resists straightforward quotation and that an abstracted quotation sounds silent compared to the cacophony of the reading/listening experience of the text proper. Hermeneutic interpretation is defied, with the result that in the cacophony of the many-voiced, the underwriters are underwritten by the palimpsestic and experimental/experiential embodiment of the words crashing together like waves that bend and swell. This dissonance is most apparent in the final section of *Zong!*, "Ebora," where the voices of the underwater spirits mix and mash to form one of the most polyphonic and generatively unreadable poetic endeavours in all of contemporary literature. "Ebora" is an instance of improvised happenstance: Philip's printer for no apparent reason printed the "first two or three pages superimposed on one another—crumped, so to speak—so as to render the page a dense landscape of text" (see figure 3.2).[130]

I don't think we can adequately interpret the dense landscape using traditional scholarly tools. The palimpsestic layering of the light grey text is Philip's painstaking struggle to avoid imposing absolute meaning. We are welcome to see and hear the faded and multiplicitous voices of history's undead, but not unsounded. We are presented with a bombardment of voices that had earlier been silent in the text. While *Zong!* opens with "Os," reworking the bones of the source legal case, it dramatically departs from "Gregson v. Gilbert" in the remaining movements: "Sal," "Ventus," "Ratio," "Ferrum," and "Ebora."

Such dramatic transportation through the myriad voices chanting with and against one another represents Philip's choice to ground the poem in the ungrounded space of pure poetic sound: the black ink

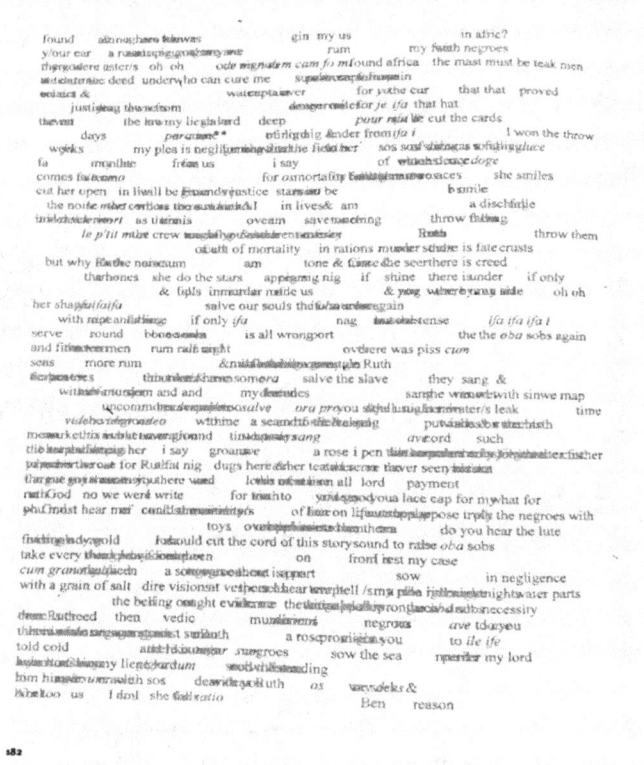

Figure 3.2 Scanned text (182) reproduced with the permission of the author.

speaking back to the blank inaudible page of history. Experimental poetry is the chosen medium—on the page and in performance, as Philip often performs *Zong!* live with improvising musicians—because as Matthew Jenkins argues, an experimental poetics of indeterminate meaning "can be more ethical . . . because it speaks with a language that does not try to control, judge, know, or totalize the Other."[131] Philip describes her desire "to avoid imposing meaning," and how to that end she offers poetry that can "disassemble the ordered [the legal text], to create disorder and mayhem so as to release the story that cannot be told, but which, through not-telling, will tell itself."[132] For Philip, poetry, like improvisation, is "risk taking of the highest order; otherwise known as working on the edge."[133] Philip's poetics combines various mythologies, as well as poetic traditions, to create an intermediate mix where meaning is negotiated at the crossroads: a crossroads that reimagines the past so that we can envision the future. The experimental poetics of *Zong!* animates the many-voicedness of the massacre, but the lyrical is also an important signifier in *Zong!*, as lyric voice and apostrophe sound authorial voices within the waves, even if they are often blended with a white male voice: "the lute sound / to raise / the dead / the died / i hear"; "i pen this / to you / when i am / her / able."[134] The anti-narrative or anti-lyric at work points to the glossolalic scatting required to make history sound, as Philip views the Caribbean "and the entire New World as a site of massive interruptions."[135] The drowned Africans are non-citizens (legally speaking), and by giving them a voice Philip provides them with personhood. *Zong!* is loaded with improvisatory dubbings; how else is Philip, or anyone, supposed to voice the unvoiceable?

Audi: Voicing the Unvoiceable

Philip manipulates epic and lyric traditions to provide a voice to those whose voices have been taken from them. In her poetic archaeology she digs up the bones of the past, saying, "I, too, want the bones." The story that cannot be told, but must be told, is "a metaphor for slavery," because it is the institution of slavery, perhaps more than any other mechanism of modernism, that ignominiously denied people their identities and transformed them into products of capitalist logic.[136] Philip's apostrophic naming, her choice to create and include names for the drowned, which appear at the bottom of each page in "Os," is an attempt to claim that which is irrecoverably lost in the sea of history, a symbolic act of resistance on behalf of the bodies that in legal terms to do not matter. As Dowling asserts, naming is not an address exactly, but it undoes the slaves' anonymity and calls them into some form of lyric personhood.♭ The Africans aboard the *Zong*

♭ Naming remains an important form of identity in Black Canadian culture, as Shad raps, "I've got a good name, my first name came from slave in Babylon, back in the day, rat in a cage / Raised in chains, he trained like become dicta, footnotes, as Philip explains her need to name them: "*The Africans on board the* Zong *must be named. They will be ghostly footprints floating below the text . . . the footnotes in general is acknowledgment—someone else was here before—in* Zong! *footnote equals footprint.*"[137] Kate Siklosi describes how in Philip's recent performances of the poem, she projects the names onto a water table that cycles the names through gurgling water, making it look as if the names are floating amid ocean waves. This adds a well-considered hauntological aspect to the performance, which grounds the names as present and integral to our understanding of the poem. The 150 Africans to whom Philip gives names read like an epic-catalogue roll call, one that poetically accounts for the lost ledger that would have contained their names. What was archived instead was a list of each enslaved person's value, placed alongside a list with fowl and other "goods" to be sold. Thus, *Zong!* destroys narrative and epic form, yet it does so by creating counter-narratives that provide polyvocality and epic voice to the unmitigated loss of an entire group of people's histories, histories that would have included their African names. The new ledger, placed as a glossing at the bottom of the page in "Os," untells the legal case, reworked above the names, while also providing an elegiac song that moves through the text like an undercurrent. Akin to the epic cataloguing of names, the glossary at the back of the text provides, as Fehskens observes, a connective tissue between the various sections, one that enables the reader to decipher repeated words, toggling between glossary and poetry, "infusing the purposefully disordered poetic space with the apprehending, cataloguing powers of definitions. The Manifest provides a fascinating collection of lists, fascinating because of their explicit imbalance with one another."[138] It is this balancing act within the cacophonous poetic form and historical glossing, between ordered and destroyed, that Philip bestrides in order to

---

Rocky, but I mean his brain not boxing." Shad, *TSOL*, "A Good Name." Similarly, George Elliott Clarke in "A Discourse on My Name" pens: "*George* is English / *Elliott* Scottish, and *Clarke* Irish. / Of course, this makes it a misnomer, / For I am an Africadian— / A Black Nova Scotian of African-American / And Mi'kmaq roots." George Elliott Clarke, *Black*, 125.

bestow voice to the historically silenced, and destroyed, in the Zong massacre. Agency is achieved through the polyvocality of song.

Through what Philip calls the "cacophonous representation of the babel that was the *Zong*," the sections of the poem following "Os" chant a series of stories that repeat themselves yet do not want to echo, canon, or retell the details as they unfold.[139] A crew member tells Ruth—a woman who waits on the ship—after reading the Captain's orders, "*do not / read this ruth / it will destroy you*"; this is followed by his intimately declarative statement that "this is me / ant for y / our eyes."[140] The play on words through the clever use of enjambment emphasizes the implications of the order to murder the Africans, by not only directing the text to the crew but also (by the "me / ant" and y / our eyes") implicating "our eyes" as we listen to the horror unfold. Like the elliptical relation between "order" and "destroy"— "the order in / destroyed"—*Zong!* alters meaning to allow readers to arrive at their own conclusions.[141] Philip alters the *Zong* massacre by including voices, particularly those of white male Europeans, that are responsible for destroying people and histories. In "Sal," Philip clarifies that the primary voice belongs to "a white, male, European voice," who addresses his dialogue chiefly to "dear ruth," a character in the Manifest listed under the category "Women Who / Wait."[142] The epistolary form of this correspondence, and the Captain's auspicious order to throw the Africans overboard, together provide contrast with the more plural voices of the Africans in the text, while also working to undo "'authorial intention' [that] would have impelled [Philip] toward other voices."[143]

By embedding, jamming, and crumping the language of the colonizer within the text, Philip compels us as readers to listen even more closely to decipher exactly who is speaking. As Dowling usefully contends, "Philip creates a contrast between different types of vocal utterance in order to break the association of voice with personhood." These expressions with multiple voices remind us of how Philip uses the Caribbean demotic, which has a unique structure. It's not frequently used, and when it is, it's very specific and localized.[144] As Dowling suggests, the Caribbean demotic invokes a moment of capture: "*de men / dem cam fo mi /* for me for / *yo* for *je / pour moi &*

para / mi flee / the fields / *gun bam / bam*," which extends the narrative into the larger history of the slave trade—of which the slave ship is the metaphor and moving extension.¹⁴⁵ As readers, we acknowledge the massacre as a moment of unknowability, yet we must read with the hope that some truth will be revealed in our ethical improvisation upon a history of silence. Philip's sounding of "impossible bodies, slaves whose material traces have been fully lost" is an act of recovery, repatriation, and a moment where mourning itself is purgative and essential not only to the poetic form of the text but also to forging a historical community that cuts across time and space to remember what was lost.¹⁴⁶ It is a powerful text that chants the past to the future.

As Judith Butler opines in *Precarious Life*, we can "reimagin[e] the possibility of community on the basis of vulnerability and loss." She writes that "without the capacity to mourn, we lose that keener sense of life we need in order to oppose violence."¹⁴⁷ Mourning, for the incommensurable loss of people killed in the *Zong* massacre and, by extension, for the larger transnational slave trade, is a moment of close reflection that reminds us of our humanity and of the degradation and countless crimes against humanity during the slave trade. To be an enslaved person was to be ignominiously deprived of one's name, identity, and personhood; essentially, it was phenomenologically to not exist. As Moïse puts forth in her reading of *Zong!*:

> Identity and being are two important concerns in *Zong!*. In the section entitled "Os," and especially in poem # 21, Philip plays on notions of being and not being, thereby questioning definitions of humanity, which leads to the implicit indictment of slavery as a crime against humanity. Absence of being is linked to the oppressive presence of the blank on the page, a visual effect which arguably represents the historical voicelessness of African Caribbean women.

Moïse's reading of *Zong!* summarizes the absence of being for victims of the slave trade and qualifies the poetic form Philip uses in the text as a method that reinscribes *being* back onto the bones of the dead. The dead, the duppies of the text, haunt the present as the bones are retransformed back into sounding beings. This is no simple transmutation, and as transformative as this process is in the text, the bodies are still lost to the sea, a metonymic marker for the image of Empire. By looking at the sea of history, and its sonic sediment in the present, we can engage in the anti-narrative potential of Philip's improvised dub chant. As Marina Warner contends, we must: "for no story, for no past, for the blank [s]pace, for the emptiness of the sea against this terrible charge, this terrible burden, of needing to look at the past and its cost."[148] The duppies of the past will continue to haunt us until their bones are appropriately laid to rest.

Àse: A Genealogy of Possibility

> The past is neither inert nor given. The stories we tell about what happened then, the correspondences we discern between today and times past, and the ethical and political stakes of these stories redound in the present. If slavery feels proximate rather than remote and freedom seems increasingly elusive, this has everything to do with our own dark times. If the ghost of slavery still haunts our present, it is because we are still looking for an exit from the prison.
>
> —SAIDIYA HARTMAN, *Lose Your Mother: A Journey along the Atlantic Slave Route*, 133

As Saidiya Hartman suggests, the past is hardly static: the spectre of slavery haunts the present. Therefore, the stories we tell are crucial to engaging with the palimpsestic past to build a more ethical future. The sea in *Zong!* represents the cyclical nature of history, which swallows up the past while washing the sediments upon the shores of the present. *Zong!* speaks of the wretched sea like Mutabaruka's "Dub Poem": "Dis poem shall speak of the wretched sea that washed ships to these shores / Of mothers cryin' for their young swallowed up by the sea." Dub is effective in framing *Zong!* as the text echoes the past, like the ghosts (duppies, or zombies) in Jamaica who haunt the living because their bodies were not properly interred. At times I felt horrified (haunted) reading/listening to the *Zong* massacre unfold, and couldn't help but feel there was a pedagogical intent in Philip's untelling, so I asked her about it, and she responded evocatively as follows:

> I would say that modernity itself is haunted, isn't it, by the ferocious history or histories of murder, genocide, war and death that brought it into being, no small part of which is the slave trade, and in particular the transatlantic trade. Take, for instance, the speculative financing we live with today, which brought the world financial system to the brink of collapse. The roots of that system lie in the financing practices developed as a part of the transatlantic slave trade. Once we know that then the untold suffering unleashed on the world as a result of those practices becomes not an aberration but entirely understandable, expected and predictable. Ian Baucom's book, *Specters of the Atlantic*, explores this idea of the recurring moment that the *Zong* incident signified. I also think that modern society is steeped in amnesia, which is the flip side of the haunting mentioned above, and is, perhaps, one of its progenitors. This social amnesia is an integral part of the warp and woof of modern society, and I would suggest Russell Jacoby's work by the same name for an exploration of this idea. I am talking here of a cultivated amnesia, carefully nurtured by the media and western capitalist governments, which makes it easy to disrupt bonds of connections and relationships, which, in turn, hurls us into spaces where consumerism trumps all, even as we move irrevocably ever closer towards the destruction of the world as we know it. It is the amnesia that, in part, generates the haunting.
>
> There has to be a hauntological pedagogy, as you call it, to my work because of the erasures of the histories of Africans in the so-called New World. We have been severed from indigenous cultures, names lost, spiritual practices outlawed; there is a sense in which you could say that shorn of all those things that make humans human, we become ghosts of ourselves,

haunted by all that we know we know but can't remember, as well as by what we know we don't know and, simultaneously, spectral beings—duppies, zombies, or jumbies, inhabiting a world that is not truly ours—aware that somewhere out there in a parallel universe there is another world where we could become truly embodied, with embodied addresses, so to speak. When I perform *Zong!* the distance between these two worlds becomes smaller.[149]

Philip's response to my reading of the poem is loaded with the various hauntings of modernity and recalls the devastating effects of slavery on the present, as well as the collective amnesia that continues to, as Philip puts it, "disrupt bonds of connections and relationships," echoing the horrors of the past. Philip's hauntological pedagogy provides a fictionalized poetic rendition of the real and devastating massacre to find an opportunity to reclaim the narrative. *Zong!* provides a counter-history through its anti-narrative, and its haunting is concerned with no less than the inscription and remembering of those erased voices and histories carelessly thrown into the sea of slavery.

Such remembering is an act of historical resistance and pertinently signifies the power of song to recall the past, as Kwame Dawes describes in his poem "Ska Memory": "You told me once to listen to the way / a melody could collect memories, could flesh and swell / and bleed, and though you are long dead, I thank you for it."[150] Hence, the song of *Zong!* is a metaphorical digging up of lost melodies, and even though it is impossible to raise the bones from the bottom of the Atlantic, Philip can, as she insists through the medium of the poem, "re-transform" these bones "miraculously, back into human."[151] The fracturing of history echoed in the fractured indices and aesthetics of *Zong!* is ironically about making history and voice whole again in a context where enslaved people were considered property, like words, recorded in the ledger alongside china and other perishable commodities. So we can ask, what can *Zong!* and the historical recording of the *Zong* incident teach us about citizenship and community in the present? For starters, as a hauntological pedagogy *Zong!* contests the spurious categories of citizenship as a conferred privilege of ownership and extends the ideology of citizenship to include all those who sound or who have sounded—thus making citizenship an inalienable human right. It is the slavers aboard the *Zong* who become less than human in their capitalistic and machine-like culpability while the dead (of the *Zong*) continue to haunt the living and sound a personhood that defies the barbaric practices of modernity and its attendant disavowals of the past. Philip—in her poetry, performances, and public interventions—models a "sonic citizenship" directed at the state and that expands the category of human. While the bones of the dead can never be physically recovered; instead, the repatriation happens when we find a place, as Philip contends, for the bones within ourselves:

> The bones of the undead can find a resting place within us. Each time I perform *Zong!*, it manifests as Ceremony, and there is a sense in which the living and the dead are both interested in the future, albeit in different ways, and here I am drawing on the brilliant essay by the Caribbean novelist, George Lamming, on this subject. Within African cosmologies this is not at all unusual, since the Ancestors, albeit no longer alive, are a living force. When we engage with them they repay us by releasing their grip on us. The grip, I maintain, is because of the haunting, and when released we can be in a more playful relationship with them. They find a resting place with us not necessarily within us, and it is in the remembering that we give them peace.[152]

As readers we provide voice to some of the historical gaps and silences in the text, enacting a "sonic citizenship" that is aware of the need to avow our own identity through a performative adherence to understanding and reworking the past.

What often appears as silence, or a concern with silence, in Philip's work is an improvised dub chant that punctuates the narrative gaps of history with the possibility of what has been left out of the narrative. This dub sounding in Philip's poem "She Tries Her Tongue, Her Silence Softly Breaks" is about "break[ing] the culture of silence / in the ordeal of testimony; in the history of circles" so that she might find voice, where history has only inserted silence, or erasure:

>   . . .Silence
>   Song word speech
>   Might I. . .like Philomela. . .sing
>   continue
>   over
>   into
>   . . .pure utterance.[153]

In *Zong!*, as in *She Tries Her Tongue,* Philip performs and chants agency against a history written by those who have inserted silence where Black voices and histories should be present, sounding. We chant along with the various polyphonies, cacophonies, and shouts in *Zong!*, and while we can never witness for the witness, we can listen. *Zong!* models how we can listen better to consider the effects our reinterpretations of history have on changing the perception of the past, interwoven with the possibilities of our futures. *Àse,* an affirmative dubbing in *Zong!*, refers to a Yoruba concept meaning "may it manifest," which signifies the power to enact change and relates to everything from ancestors, to spirits, humans, animals, rivers, songs, and so on. According to Yoruba consciousness, our very existence is dependent upon *àse*. Through an improvised dub chant Philip incinerates the apparent orthodoxy of the legal text, sings the story that cannot be told, and provides a voice to the bones of the *Zong* massacre to create a future where pure utterance can be possible, doing all this at the edge of new meanings. *Àse.*

REMIX 3

I used dub to examine some of the concepts of this book around community, citizenship, and resistance, particularly using *Zong!* to test the limits of the dub aesthetic. Such adaptability and heightened specificity speak to the unique ability of numerous Black artists across the diaspora to maintain traditions that in many instances date back to ancestral roots in Africa. As Carr importantly insists, "dub aesthetics are deeply community rooted and accountable," and Philip's *Zong!* is about making history and the murderers aboard the *Zong* accountable for their actions.[154] I hope the open nature of music allows readers to draw their own conclusions about how to read or listen to a dub poem. Whether or not *Zong!* is dub in the strictest sense—or, as I argue, a hybrid form of dub chant—dub remains an important aesthetic for interrogating the past to build a more sustainable future.

Symbolically, dub chants are about more than creating poetic music for people to enjoy—although dub is thoroughly enjoyable—because dub is renegade and rebel art. As readers and listeners of dub, we work as co-creators of communities that are more aware of the violence of the past with the intention to build and sound more inclusive communities. Philip's fragmented dub poetics in *Zong!* contest the legal document on which Philip riffs, as words have the power to instrumentally determine people's futures. While a passport might not *actually* define citizenship, legally, in the letters of the law, it does. By altering the "Gregson v. Gilbert" document through a dub chant Philip shows the power of remix to create a more equitable future.

Zong! is not evidentially about Canada, yet the duppies of the text animate the transnational slave trade that is very much part of the nexus of Canada's own imperialism as a colonial satellite and settler colony. In "Interview with an Empire," Philip frames her own work not in relation to Canada but against it, yet within it:

> The space that is Canada is framed by a history of colonialism and racism against the First Nations, African-descended people, the Japanese, the Chinese and South Asians, to name some of the more egregious examples. It is provocative that such a framed space has allowed for works like *She Tries*, *Looking for Livingstone* and *Zong!* to be produced. This is less about the nature of the work or about Canada being a wonderful multicultural haven that we have been "lucky" enough to be let into. That so-called luck has been very expensive for Indigenous people; rather it is about

the fact that the space that is Canada is the sine qua non of the work being produced, although it is not about Canada but rather about a larger history. Empire, colonialism, and racism work like the words on the page framing, or parenthesizing a space within which something life-fulfilling can take place.[155]

Symbolically, we can read *Zong!* as a universal diaspora that includes a Canada still suffering from a collective amnesia about the brutal genocide of the Middle Passage. Philip's reworking of language in search of mother tongue—dub tongue—is symbolic of Canaan as a land to be reworked; as Philip describes, "'We ent going nowhere. We here and is right here we staying.' In Canada. In this world so new. To criticize, needle and demand; to work hard for; to give to; to love; to hate—for better or worse—till death do we part."[156]

The mere fact that Philip writes a text like *Zong!* in the first place, or that Ahdri Zhina Mandiela's *dark diaspora... in dub* is so transnationally political, or that Giller Prize winner Esi Edugyan's *Half-Blood Blues* is about Americans and Afro-Germans and Jews playing jazz in Nazi Germany, is indicative that Afrosporic people's and Black Canadians' historical concerns are as diverse as anywhere else on the globe. *Zong!* is thus an affirmation of the connective tissues and accumulated bones that bind us together in the matrix of a shared creative and egalitarian social existence: it is a sounding for the value of human life and citizenship in the snare of global commerce, slave labour, and historical silence.

As a non-Black scholar who identifies with Black politics and unifying strategies, I find incredible importance in the coalition politics of valuing difference, however wide the gaps might appear. Dub as a mix brings us a little closer to understanding our shared social existence while also challenging the vestiges of colonial practices, which are very much alive even when they remain visibly hidden. Dub, pivotal to the poetic movement in Canada, unabashedly announces these discriminatory practices and hierarchical citizenships by their very name: injustice. We have no realistic alternative but to embrace difference and understand the past.[b]

Zong! is a cacophonous chant in which poetry connects the past and present together to create a more sustainable—and ethically viable—future. *Zong!* is an improvised script, chant, and temple of transformative possibility: a tall yet ineluctable order for poetry. Chanting along with *Zong!*, and the various dub texts discussed earlier, not only challenges the printed logocentric understanding of language but also asks us to concede that poems, like everything else in life, are ephemeral. The ephemerality of life reminds us that we can create more equitable histories and that we can do so with an improvisatory spirit to remix and make new. Canada/*Canaan* remains a project to be remixed, so we turn now to K'naan to listen to how that might sound as voiced from the perspective of someone who came to Canada with many of the same hopes as the "freedom seekers" who followed the North Star with little more than the clothes on their backs, some songs, and dreams of the possible.

---

[b] Lillian Allen's poem, "In These Canadian Bones," from *Psychic Unrest* sums up this immigrant diversity and poetics:

> In these Canadian bones
> where Africa landed
> and Jamaica bubble
> inna reggae redstripe
> and calypso proddings of culture
> We are creating this very landscape
> we walk on. (65)

Chapter 4

WAVIN' THE MULTICULTURAL FLAG: CANADIAN HIP HOP AND "SONIC CITIZENSHIP" IN K'NAAN'S MUSIC

Listening: Shad, "Fam Jam"

Shad's "Fam Jam (Fe Sum Immigrins)" is a throwback and toast to the trials of immigrant experience in Canada.♭ The song deconstructs the faulty notion that immigrants contribute little to Canadian society; it does so by providing potent examples of how immigrants construct the new Canada. It consists of the catchy hook, "Not bad, huh, for some immigrants?" The hook samples Jay-Z's identical line in the track "Otis," which itself was taken from the movie *Scarface*: a film about the perversion of the American Dream. In the Canadian context, the line sounds the possibility of the Canadian Dream within the larger multicultural project. Shad says that working on "Fam Jam" (from *Flying Colours*) "in the city of Toronto offered a daily reminder of the diversity of stories in our midst. This diversity is often and rightly celebrated, but the innumerable stories that comprise our

Shad's "Fam Jam"

Liner Notes
♭ See the video for "Fam Jam": https://bittylink.com/I83. You can find the playlist for this chapter here: https://open.spotify.com/playlist/6y311CJZCRIQbqXOKqRUZL

treasured multiculturalism here in Canada can also hold a lot [sic] pain, as well as some complicated questions around what it means to succeed, and what it means to belong."[1] The feeling of not fully belonging manifests when Shad raps, "Don't turn away the stateless, think of the waste / If one in three refugees is a Lauryn Hill," referring to the Grammy-winning artist who was part of the group The Fugees, a word derived from *refugee* that was a derogatory term for Haitian Americans.

The video for "Fam Jam" offers a celebratory mix. In it, the larger community—family, friends, children—gathers to throw a large party that celebrates diversity. As we will see with K'naan's negotiation between borders and two worlds—Somalia and North America— Shad confronts his own negotiation of borders: "Now when you're Third World born, but First World formed / Sometimes you feel pride, sometimes you feel torn / See my Mother's tongue is not what they speak where my Mother's from / She moved to London with her husband when their son was 1." Shad, who was born in Kenya of Rwandan parents, uses his own story as an example of how much an immigrant can achieve to remove the negative connotations of the word, suggesting that Canada should allow for dual identities and cultural allegiances if it is to be a truly multicultural society.

This chapter focuses on hip hop music as an emblem for "sonic citizenship" and, by extension, on what I term "sonic multiculturalism." While I touch on the pioneering work of Shad (who was raised in Ontario), Michie Mee (born in Jamaica and later moved to Toronto), and others, I most closely examine the work of Somali Canadian hip hop artist and poet K'naan, whose song of global fraternity, "Wavin' Flag," was chosen as an anthem for the FIFA 2010 World Cup. Hip hop is an increasingly global phenomenon, one that provides a global forum though which displaced subjects can negotiate multiple concepts of identity/citizenship. I investigate the possibility of a global citizenship (in part within the ironic confines of doing so through a neoliberal corporate-based promotional anthem) beyond the nation, with a particular focus on K'naan's first two albums, *The Dusty Foot Philosopher* (2006) and *Troubadour* (2009), using "Wavin' Flag" as an anthemic case study.

I. It's Bigger Than Hip, or Hop, or US

Hip Hop Legacies   Mos Def

> We went from pickin' cotton
> To chain gang line choppin'
> To Be-Boppin'
> To Hip-Hoppin'
> Blues people got the blue chip stock option
> Invisible man, got the whole world watching
> (where ya at) I'm high, low, east, west,
> All over your map
> I'm getting big props, with this thing called Hip Hop.
>
> —MOS DEF, "Hip Hop," *Black on Both Sides*

Hipi means "to open one's eyes and see." *Hop*, from Old English, means "to spring into action."[2] Thus, hip hop: an opening. Rap remains a noisy element of contemporary culture. Yet many cultural critics of rap and hip hop culture praise hip hop music for its ability to function as an educational tool, citing Black women, Indigenous rappers, and/or LGBTQIA2S+ rappers as nuanced examples that draw attention to racism, sexism, and the other intersections of oppression.[♭] Yet the media fixate on violence at rap concerts, the criminal use of samples, lurid fantasies of killing cops, homophobia and misogyny, and Black nationalism, often marring more fruitful dialogues.

[♭] I make a distinction between rap and hip hop. Such obfuscation around hip hop terminology is hardly an academic concern, as various MCs (emcees/ masters of ceremonies) engage with these slippages in their lyrics. KRS-One has a song called "Hip Hop vs. Rap" in which he raps, "Rap is something you do / Hip Hop is something you live." [Head to the playlist to hear this song]. To clarify, I use "hip hop" to refer to the musical form and culture and "rap" to refer to mainstream form and the act of rhythmically delivering lyrics, usually to a beat.

Hip hop is a chiaroscuro of social consciousness and mainstream commodification, a chameleon art form that adapts to every environment it encounters, a personal saviour and communitarian mobilizer born out of a disenfranchised youth movement in the post-industrial urban nightmare of America's neglected ghettos. Hip hop's hagiography consists of graffiti writers, breakers, DJs, and MCs, who animate the Black postmodern ethos through raps that contain ad-lib logorrhea, near-assonance, and gritty vocab with gunfire punctuation, announcing with bravado to an oppressive white world that the carcinoid Other has adopted the master's tools and that things will never be the same. Hip hop is without a doubt the most popular and influential musical movement since jazz, and, like jazz, rap (as firebrand Archie Shepp describes) contains a "blues element. It's physical, almost gymnastic. It speaks to you organically. Rap grows out of what young people really are today, not only black youth, but white – everybody."³ᵇ Rap's gruff poetics have captivated me for three-fourths of my life.

<small>Snoop Dogg</small>

I encountered hip hop music for the first time when I was ten years old. I remember bringing home a cassette tape of Snoop Dogg's *Doggystyle*; the album's iconography was brash in its explicit display

---

ᵇ It's particularly interesting to hear a free jazz pioneer continually speak in support of rap music. In an interview with Ollie Bivens for *All about Jazz*, Shepp states, "What youngster in the ghetto is going to be able to buy a saxophone? Of course, they buy records and turntables and they created new instruments. They're making something out of nothing. I'm all for these young people. In fact, I think we have to come over to their side. We should begin to make connections with their lifestyle, their culture and their music. I would love to have heard Coltrane play with Digable Planets or James Brown. Those things just never happened because our people never saw the connection." Ollie Bivens, "Archie Shepp: The Cries of My People," interview, *All about Jazz*, February 24, 2005, https://www.allaboutjazz.com/archie-shepp-the-cries-of-my-people-archie-shepp-by-ollie-bivens. Shepp throws himself into the hybrid jazz-rap mix on his *Phat Jam in Milano* (2005), which features Shepp playing with Oliver Lake, Hamid Drake, Joe Fonda, and rapper/poet Napoleon Maddox.

of "pugilistic eroticism."¹# Aesthetically, the music was smooth, full of funk-infused hard-thumping gangster rhythms. Shortly afterward, my parents found the cassette and took it away; therefore, this experience was also my introduction to the world of censorship. To listen to hip hop is to enter a world of intricacy and contradiction. The music has sparked fierce debates about its validity and effect on its listeners (see Tricia Rose's *The Style Wars*). While mainstream or commercial hip hop music is at times misogynistic or glorifies violence, much of hip hop culture and the larger movement of rap music has formulated its own critiques of sexism, misogyny, and violence. A more productive approach is to examine how misogyny and sexism in gangster rap are, as bell hooks writes, "a reflection of the prevailing values in our society, values sustained by White supremacist capitalist patriarchy."⁴ Hip hop music is hardly representative of one style or movement; rather, it has been used by many aggrieved populations around the world as an oppositional form that reaffirms community ties and challenges dominant modes of discourse.

Hip hop consists of four elements: hip hop dance (notably breaking), urban-inspired art (markedly graffiti), DJing (turntablism), and beatboxing/MCing (rapping). Paul Gilroy, in *The Black Atlantic*, describes hip hop culture as growing "out of cross-fertilization of African-American vernacular cultures with their Caribbean equivalents rather than springing fully formed from the entrails of the blues."⁵ As hip hop scholar Tricia Rose poignantly suggests, "to interpret rap as a direct or natural outgrowth of oral African-American forms is to romanticize and decontextualize rap as a cultural form."⁶

♭ I borrow this term from a bell hooks film titled *Cultural Criticism and Transformation*. On another note, my listening to hip hop music at a young age in a community far removed from the initial movement is hardly a product of the early 1990s, given how pervasive hip hop music is these days. According to a 2005 American study, hip hop and rap music are immensely popular among seventh through twelfth graders, with 65 percent of youths of all backgrounds listening to the music in a typical day. See Donald F. Roberts, Ulla G. Foehr, and Victoria Rideout, *Generation M: Media in the Lives of 8–18 Year-Olds*, KFF publication no. 7251 (Menlo Park: Kaiser Family Foundation, 2005).

While hip hop music certainly incorporates forms of oral storytelling, it is also infused with, and informed by, modern technology: "rap simultaneously makes technology oral and technologizes orality."[7] Friedrich Kittler states that "technology literally makes the unheard-of possible" as the symbolic becomes the *real* and the human becomes the machine.[8] Hip hop is technological and traditional, which is appropriate since the music is an expansive conglomerate of artistic forms and styles that most specifically originated as a street subculture within African American communities in 1970s New York City, predominantly in Morris Heights in The Bronx and later in Latin American communities, and is now a transnational art form.

Hip hop, as Alexander Weheliye argues, has come to define what "it means to be black and 'modern' within a global context and particularly in youth cultures."[9] Hip hop is found almost anywhere on the planet, which is why Saul Williams in *The Dead Emcee Scrolls* declares that "no other music so purely demands an instant affirmation on such a global scale."[10] The global consciousness of hip hop allows the music to be particularly transferable to diverse cultures as a mode of expressive possibility, especially against oppressive systems that attempt to silence marginal voices. Hip hop continues to play a central role in African American, Hispanic, and Caribbean-based musical practices in the US and around the world. Furthermore, hip hop music and rap have been used, as rapper and hip hop historian Chuck D explains, to help "Brazilian kids learn English when school systems failed to bridge the difficult language gap of Portuguese and Patois to American English"; in Africa, South Sudanese musician Emmanuel Jal uses hip hop to heal war-torn African youth; and Indigenous youth continue to use and adapt the form to tell stories of resilience in the face of ongoing genocide.[11] The only condition really needed for hip hop to emerge—whether in Vancouver, New York, Tokyo, Nigeria, Johannesburg, or Rio Janeiro— is an alienated group of young folks looking for a creative outlet. Hip hop provides powerful tools—through beats, voice, and culture—to help the silenced gain a voice and be heard in their own terms (rap was formed as a prophetic language that addresses silence, the silenced, and the state of feeling like a non-citizen).

Signifying Postmodernism and Hip Hop Studies

Houston A. Baker Jr. defines postmodernism in hip hop: as "nonauthoritative collaging or archiving of sound and styles that bespeaks a deconstructive hybridity."[12] Such "nonauthoritative collaging" is useful in thinking about how hip hop remixes the past. As rapper Common states, hip hop carries on the tradition not just of Afrika Bambaataa, "but the tradition of Miles Davis, James Baldwin, Bob Marley, Fela Kuti, too. We are the children of jazz. We are the children of all black art around the globe."[13] Hip hop freely borrows from all genres, with the rapper's lyrics signifying in a postmodern context and musical sampling functioning much like an intertextual reference. David Foster Wallace provides an evocative description of the purely aesthetic and postmodern quality of hip hop:

> Like the drum machine and scratch, sample and backbeat, the rapper's "song" is essentially an upper layer in the dense weave of rhythm that, in rap, usurps melody and harmony's essential functions of identification, call, counterpoint, movement, and progression, the play of woven notes ... until "rhythm" comprises the essential definitions of rap itself: dance beats that afford unlimited bodily possibility, married rhythmically to complexly stressed lyrics that assert, both in message and meter, that things can now never be other than what *IS*.[14]

While Wallace's hypotactic depiction does not directly mention postmodernism, his description of hip hop's deconstructive capacity to create new art with modern recording technologies is (as Wallace mentions elsewhere in *Signifying Rappers*) postmodern.

Hip hop borrows from older signifying traditions, but it is made possible by technological and urban deindustrial conditions. Hip hop uses remix and juxtaposes multiple forms and cultures as it adapts to new environments. When Philip Glass, Steve Reich, John Cage, or Brian Eno—all white minimalist composers of the twentieth century—use sampling and postmodern techniques it is considered art, but when hip hop artists do it (and often better) it is considered less radical and a threat to intellectual property, even though the practices themselves are older than copyright law.

Hip hop innovator DJ Kool Herc, who took many of the music styles of toasting and dancehall with him when he immigrated to New York City from Jamaica, has said, "Hip hop, the whole chemistry of that came from Nigeria, Africa."[15] Hip hop's use of repetition belongs to an African continuum, a continuum that poet Amiri Baraka states is part of "Rhythm and Blues, and the poetry of the real. Rap, as old as how we spoke across space, beating the log"; however, we must acknowledge that hip hop's use of technology also situates it within a North American technological and urban postmodern framework.[16] As Robin D.G. Kelley notes, "hip hop's hybridity reflected, in part, the increasingly international character of America's inner cities resulting from immigration, demographic change, and new forms of information, as well as the inventive employment of technology in creating rap music."[17] Hip hop has always been global and regional, since it was, after all, crafted by a Jamaican (Kool Herc) and then fashioned into new forms—which even included disco and European techno—by a Bronxite (Afrika Bambaataa), who was influenced by the formative experiences he had in his travels to Africa and Europe. So it is unsurprising, to me at least, that hip hop music samples from the massive archive of previously recorded material, establishing a dialogue between the original and its new context. Thus, an artist like K'naan can draw from the full range of the African diaspora, taking sounds and language from Somalian culture and language, fusing them with his North American—particularly Torontonian—experience to create a style of expression that reflects the reality of a globally conscious citizen.

By listening to hip hop lyrics, K'naan was able to teach himself English and develop a sense of global consciousness, demonstrated in his spoken-word piece before the UN High Commissioner for Refugees in 1999 that criticized the UN for its failed aid missions to Somalia. Just as Langston Hughes celebrated the blues for the poetry that is inherent in the music, using the form as a model for his own verse, hip hop's hard-hitting beats (the thumping 2s and 4s and off-kilter timing innovated by J Dilla and others) invite poetry. Hip hop, like poetry, provides artists with a means to articulate their unique experience in the world, speak to injustice, and find pleasure in wordplay. As M.K. Asante states, "No movement is about beats and rhymes. Beats and rhymes are tools—tools that if held the right way can help articulate the world, a new world, in which we want to live."[18] If blues and jazz shape life, then hip hop, for many today, makes life livable.

For scholars, hip hop presents a new field—even if some scholars criticize hip hop for its newness, or as Aldon Lynn Nielsen contends, for being poetically conservative. In *Black Chant*, Nielsen does not include rap within the tradition of African American experimental postmodern poetics that he champions in his text. He does quite the opposite, contrasting the works of these artists, "which have tested the limits of writing and musical languages and have found new things to do with sound and signification," with "the actually quite conservative (perhaps even reactionary) poetic forms of much Rap."[19] Nielsen, in an otherwise masterwork on African American experimental poetics, uses rap as a straw man—which is too bad, since actual poetic analysis of the best of rap lyrics (which doesn't happen in *Black Chant*) fits within Nielsen's aesthetic continuum of poetic innovation. Unfortunately, Nielsen displays his generational bias towards what was hardly a new music in the late nineties when *Black Chant* was written. Just as I am more inspired by youth culture and by Nikki Giovanni getting "Thug Life" tattooed on her arm in support of rapper Tupac (2pac) than I am by a traditionalist who disengages from the younger generation, I am equally inspired by young artists who look to the past to inspire the present generation. Given all the change and improvisation that Nielsen rightfully attests happens in contemporary Black poetry, it is unfortunate that he depicts Blackness in terms of hip hop as uninspired and unchanging, failing to see the music as one facet in the larger spectrum of Black Studies.

Nielsen's point is taken that hip hop's status as the new thing can lead to other fringe poetics being ignored, but what he fails to account for is that rap lyrics did not even have an official anthology until 2011, when Yale released *The Anthology of Rap*. While *The Anthology of Rap* is not without its faults—once again peripheral/underground artists are largely ignored and many of the mistakes in the lyrics are copied and pasted from the internet[20]—the collection provides, as hip hop pioneer Chuck D writes, "the tools to make meaning of those lyrics in relation to one another, to think about rap both in terms of particular rhymes, but also in terms of an art form. Every great literature deserves an anthology."[21] The seven-hundred-page anthology exhibits the vast variety within hip hop and recalls the arguments outlined in my introduction about the dangers and values of canon formation. By the nineties, hip hop had gone global, but by the first decade of the 2000s Nielsen's fears of hip hop as an academic offshoot of Black Studies were confirmed. You can now get a diploma in Hip Hop Studies (McNally Smith College of Music), and hip hop courses are offered at universities in the United States and Canada. Over the past five-plus years I integrated a course with a hip hop forum and live music (https://international.viu.ca/intercultural-hip-hop). Former American president Barack Obama was well versed in hip hop lingo and culture. Welcome to the hip hop planet.

Resistant Communities

Public Enemy

"I'm on the microphone / Saying 1555, how I'm livin.'"[♭]

—PUBLIC ENEMY, "Can't Truss It"

When thinking of hip hop music and culture there is a tendency to focus on the subversive qualities of the music more than on how it is the most commodified music in today's global music market. This is understandable, especially if one is providing a methodology for how hip hop can be used for radical and resistive models of thinking. Hip hop, like other Black musics, hearkens back to the plantation: an institution that yielded returns that compared well with the most outstanding investment opportunities in manufacturing and that helped drive the economic expansion of America, Canada, the UK,

---

♭ The date 1555 is a reference to a group of Africans who were brought from Ghana as enslaved people to London by a London merchant ship.

and other countries that adopted the slave model.[22] Hence, Chuck D in "Can't Truss It" makes the apt comparison between the current music business and the slave model, where mostly white moguls at the top exploit Black musicians. Chuck D even raps that there is a "holocaust... still goin' on." Explaining the song, Chuck D told the music magazine *Melody Maker*, "We don't control what we create. And because of the media, we don't control the way we think or run our lives."[23] Ornette Coleman talks about jazz and capitalism in a similar vein and relates the market system of the recording industry to a system of exploitation: "the problem in this business is that you don't own your own product. If you record, it's the record company that owns it... What I mean is, in jazz the Negro is the product."[24] Both Chuck D and Coleman describe how Black music has been sold as goods and services, much like the production of cotton on a plantation, and thus both icons use their music as an alternative structure to the system in place. The capitalist framework that artists work within highlights that resistance is always multilayered within the push and pull of capitalism. Hip hop artists have always had to deal with market demands, even as the best of the music confounds expectations and provides resistance at the levels of lyrics, organization, and sound.[b]

In *Black Noise*, Tricia Rose provides a complex investigation of the resistive history and musical development of hip hop as an art form working within the politics of culture. Rose's compelling analysis examines rap's language, iconography, diegesis, oral elements, storytelling forms, marginality, and aesthetics in post-industrial America.

---

[b] Black resistance is much older than hip hop. For instance, the notion that enslaved people were passive victims of slavery is patently false. The complex organization—with and without the help of whites—of the Underground Railroad is one example among many of "freedom seekers" resisting slavery. Even on the plantation, Black folk created and maintained their own religious observances without the supervision of their white oppressors or ministers. Today, spirituals survive as a testament of freedom seekers' will to transcend victimization. Lastly, the notion that enslaved people did not fight back is also untrue, evidenced most popularly by Nat Turner's Rebellion. Nat Turner and his followers killed nearly sixty whites.

She describes hip hop as "a cultural form that attempts to negotiate the experiences of marginalization, brutally truncated opportunity, and oppression within the cultural imperatives of African-American and Caribbean history." Importantly, Rose maintains that the critical force of hip hop "grows out of the cultural potency that racially segregated conditions foster." Essentially, hip hop is resistive because it prioritizes Black and marginal voices that have been pushed to the boundaries of urban America, which is why much of hip hop music is fuelled by anger yet sustained by fluidity, or what Rose refers to as *"flow, layering,* and *ruptures in line."* Rose puts forth the idea that in hip hop, visual, physical, musical, and lyrical lines are set in motion and broken abruptly with sharp angular breaks, yet they sustain motion and energy through fluidity and flow: "rappers speak of flow explicitly in lyrics, referring to an ability to move easily and powerfully through complex lyrics as well as of the flow in music."[25] Thus, just as bebop focused on playing fast and displaying instrumental virtuosity to confound white markets and assert difference, the linguistic and sonic collisions in hip hop lyrics and performance denote similar mastery.

K'naan, "Somalia"

Hip hop provides an avenue for aggrieved communities to challenge the patriarchal conquest of language, recontextualizing standardized English to assert identity against a perceived standard. In his song "Somalia," K'naan challenges the notion that education is only a product of institutional learning by asserting how hip hop not only helped him learn English but also facilitated his escape from the physical and psychological prison of poverty:

> Do you see why it's amazing
> When someone comes out of such a dire situation
> And learns the English language,
> Just to share his observation.
> Probably get a Grammy without a grammar education.
> So, fuck you school and fuck you immigration!

Through hip hop K'naan defies his immigrant status as one who has newly arrived in Canada and uses his lyrical skill to connect with those in "the slums and in the Native reservations" ("Somalia").

Furthermore, K'naan uses English against the very system that would impose Standard English upon an immigrant as a test for citizenship. By transforming English, possessing the language "as a space of resistance," hip hop artists use linguistic manoeuvring to resist and spatially impose themselves upon the terrain that has been forced on them.[26]

No surprise then that there are thousands of references to slavery by rappers, who locate their verbal boomerangs of resistance against such historically oppressive systems. Talib Kweli asserts, using rap battling—verbally outwitting an opponent through linguistic means—how his own resistive raps stem from being ontologically situated in a country where his ancestors were sold into bondage: "I was sold to a sick European by a rich African battlin' / Middle Passages, I can't go back again / Battlin' years of denied history, lies and mysteries / Wives with misty eyes watchin' their husbands be beaten viciously."[27] Shad relates the crazed infatuation with Blackness to the roles he is expected to perform as a Black man in Canada, viewing those roles as a form of mental slavery: "With mental slavery, the shackles is loose / And it's hard to cut chains when they attached at the roots."[28] This resistance in politically conscious hip hop contests the judgments placed upon the music and culture and upon the rappers who resist not only language but history as well. Hence, the anger in hip hop is often perceived as inaudible noise—Rose aptly titles her hip hop manifesto *Black Noise*—with the subtonic bass and hard-hitting drums couching lyrics in a grenade thrown directly into the mainstream's values. The noisiness of hip hop music—which was initially heard as outlaw music before it was largely commoditized—is an affront to those who guard the keys to what is classified as serious music. That is the same confusion as slave masters encountered around the spirituals, which to them was "unmeaning jargon."[29]

In his seminal work on the Association for the Advancement of Creative Musicians, *A Power Stronger Than Itself: The AACM and American Experimental Music,* George E. Lewis describes how—in reference to the AACM's experimental music—"the criticism of the new music as 'just noise' can be seen as a holdover from antebellum days, when the music of black slaves, as historian Jon Cruz notes,

Talib Kweli
Shad

'appears to have been heard by captors and overseers primarily as noise—that is, as strange, unfathomable, and incomprehensible.'" In fact, the AACM, whose history Lewis vigorously outlines, "developed new and influential ideas about timbre, sound, collectivity, extended technique and instrumentation, performance practice, intermedia, the relationship of improvisation to composition, form, scores, computer music technologies, invented acoustic instruments, installations, and kinetic sculptures."[30] While at least metrically different from the sounds of the AACM, hip hop music too afforded the disenfranchised alternative methods and strategies to assert their own version of freedom and what qualifies as sound. As Heble, Fischlin, and Lipsitz put it: "One person's 'noise' is another person's sophisticated signifying system," even if it does sound like "unmeaning jargon" (Douglass) to many white listeners.[31]

MC Lyte

The vehement reactions to much of rap's sexism, misogyny, and homophobia deny the vast existence of accepted sexist social practices that endow the male gender role, especially since such heterosexual, heteronormative, and misogynistic behaviours are often propagated by mainstream culture and media as acceptable. More productive analysis focuses on how rap music affronts popular reception and even provides a voice for artists, who use the hip hop medium to fashion new expressive possibilities. "When I was young," MC Lyte recalls, "I was like, how else can a young black girl of my age be heard all around the world? I gotta rap."[32] True, the recognized dearth of women or openly queer, trans, and non-binary MCs in the mainstream is troubling, but any movement is larger than how it is popularly received.♭ This is hardly unique to hip hop.

♭ Some queer, trans, and non-binary MCs include DijahSB, Angel Haze, Katey Red, Quay Dash, Medusa, Lil Nas X, and Deep Dickollective.

One of hip hop's didactic functions is to trouble, to worry the lines, and to engage in radical sonic protest. We hear this in NWA's anti-police brutality anthem "Fuck tha Police," which drew the ire of the FBI, and which repeats the title phrase multiple times in the chorus.♭ The song's violent and anti-authoritarian message provokes response by claiming, and with some reason, that the Compton police can kill minorities with impunity. Rather than simply dismiss an intentionally provoking song, it is better to look at the ethos that creates anger toward the establishment in the first place. This recalls Curtis Mayfield's defence of the honest depiction of poverty and social violence in blaxploitation films; Mayfield believes that "the way you clean up the films is by cleaning up the street. The music and movies of today are the conditions that exist. You change music and movies by changing the conditions."[33] While the song is explicitly American in context, it is important to remember, as Robyn Maynard writes in *Policing Black Lives*, that "most know, for example, the names Trayvon Martin and Michael Brown as victims of anti-Black police violence, but could not . . . recite the names of Andrew Loku, Jermaine Carby, or Quilem Registre."[34] Hip hop speaks to these conditions and often crosses borders, which is why hip hop can take root across the border in Canada and thrive, finding many listeners who locate community in the resistive, multicultural, and anti-assimilative sound of the music.

NWA

As this book has shown, there is a long tradition of resistance in Canada. As discussed in chapter 1, in 1946, nine years before the Rosa Parks protest, Viola Desmond sat in a "whites only" section in a theatre in Nova Scotia and was charged and spent the night in jail. We can call this an early hip hop moment in Canada's history: a hip hop moment and one of "sonic citizenship" because Desmond was willing to create a social disturbance to assert her right to equality. In "Towards a

---

♭ "Fuck tha Police" appears on the group's 1988 album, *Straight Outta Compton*: the song portrays a mock court scene, in which the police department is put on trial. The song itself has been translated into other media and genres and was covered by the alternative rock group Rage Against the Machine.

Methodology for Reading Hip Hop in Canada," Rinaldo Walcott rebukes George Elliott Clarke's claim, as he reads it, that Black Canadian culture is fundamentally conservative and suggests as an alternative that "black Canadian culture is far more insubordinate than it is often given credit for."[35] Desmond is one example of many of these resistive (hip hop) moments in Canada's history, and hip hop remains prevalent for youth expression in Canada, as both a global signifier of citizenship: hip hop functions as a cross-border anti-oppression movement, even as it gets resold into the bondage of the current market system.

II. Hip Hop Canada

Singing Fools, Main Source, Dream Warriors

Michie Mee

There is a long history of hip hop culture and music in Canada—far more than I could ever cover here.[36] Much of that history dates back to the late seventies and early eighties, with Mr. Q's "Ladies Delight" in 1979, the not so great, but overtly political, "The Bum Rap" by the Singing Fools in 1982, and the first French rap song, "Le Rap-à-Billy" by Lucien Frencoeur in 1983. In the late eighties and early nineties a few Canadian acts, such as Maestro Fresh Wes, Main Source, and Dream Warriors, enjoyed some international success. There was also a significant recording titled *Jamaican Funk—Canadian Style* (1992) by Canada's first notable female MC and hip hop pioneer Michie Mee (with production from L. A. Luv). Michie Mee was born in Jamaica and later moved to Toronto, and the Jamaican (dancehall, reggae, dub) sound is particularly evident on the single and in the colourful video for "Jamaican Funk (Canadian Style)," yet for some reason—especially given that one of the editors is Canadian—no Michie Mee lyrics appear in *The Anthology of Rap*.[b] Nevertheless, Mee's impact cannot be underestimated: in 1985, at the age of fifteen, she performed on stage with Boogie Down Productions, and she was the first rapper to sign a deal with a major US record label in 1988.

---

[b] While this song is not available over Spotify, I've included a link to the song and music video, here: https://www.youtube.com/watch?v=ObqLwv7UtP8.

Mee's work continues to showcase Canada—as Maestro Fresh Wes and others did—as a nexus of hip hop originality and diversity. Mee opens her track "Canada Large" (from *Jamaican Funk*) by celebrating Canada as a gateway of possibilities for the young artist: "Step off, you wanna know where I come from, Canada." She then moves on to list local neighbourhoods in Toronto, particularly her own area of Jane and Finch, and raps, "Looking for Jamaicans, Toronto's got nough." "Canada Large" is a celebratory anthem for hip hop in Canada, which Mee contends is distinct from the American scene, largely because of Toronto's Caribbean identity.[37] Michie Mee's music negotiates multiple identities and national frameworks, particularly an American art form (hip hop) with her own Jamaican background and a Toronto-based positioning. Hip hop has always embodied "sonic citizenship"; it challenges where one resides, recalling Eric B and Rakim's hip hop mantra: "It ain't where you're from, it's where you're at."[38]

Not that place is unimportant in hip hop—otherwise, rappers wouldn't always be calling out their home towns. However, it is hip hop's ability to draw together various fractured communities across national boundaries that makes it a global art form. As Mark Anthony Neal insists, "I maintain that the emergence of hip-hop . . . was representative of a concerted effort by young urban blacks to use mass culture to facilitate communal discourse across a fractured and dislocated national community."[39] Rap today is more globally assimilated yet still fiercely regional, which is why hip hop fits local grassroots movements. Rinaldo Walcott contends that "what is at stake in Canadian hip hop is a refiguring of an elaboration of the urban landscape of Canada and by extension the urban landscape of North America—black and otherwise."[40] In Canadian hip hop, narratives of belonging and unbelonging resist the simple reductions of multiculturalism and ask us to reconsider the scope of anti-Black racism, the nation-state, and geographical boundaries. Early hip hop pioneer Maestro Fresh Wes's 1989 "Let Your Backbone Slide" was the first Canadian hip hop single to break onto the US Billboard chart. But it is his track "Nothin' at All" (1991) from his follow-up album that

Maestro Fresh Wes

Rascalz

directly looks at Canada as a country inundated with racism. Despite this, Wes rightly celebrates Black excellence.

By 1998, hip hop in Canada was hyperaware of its own national borders, evidenced in the various events that impelled the anthemic and collaborative track "Northern Touch" (winner of the 1999 Juno for Best Rap Recording), which launched Canadian hip hop as a resilient art of determination. "Northern Touch" featured MCs from across Canada (Rascalz, Checkmate, Kardinal Offishall, Thrust, and Choclair) and was intended to bridge the regional on a national front so as to display Canada's diversity: "all the way from T-dot [Toronto] to the Van City [Vancouver] all stars." Connecting Vancouver to Toronto and the larger hip hop nation, "Northern Touch" is, as Walcott suggests, "a sound that announces the indelible pleasure of the in-between."[41] The previous year, the Rascalz had won the 1998 Juno for Best Rap Recording for *Cash Crop*, but they declined it, as the rap award was not televised with the other awards. The Rascalz issued the statement that the award was "a token gesture towards honoring the real impact of urban music in Canada."[42]

By the following year, hip hop had gone mainstream in Canada. This time the Juno Awards televised the Best Rap Recording, which rightfully went, given its critical impact and sales, to the Rascalz for "Northern Touch." Additionally, the Rascalz performed "Northern Touch" live during the ceremony. "Northern Touch" celebrates Canadian hip hop's ability to function across regional borders while maintaining local specificity, dually negotiating the larger milieu of global hip hop aesthetics and politics, as "Canadian hip hop is forced to be more double voiced than most."[43] Given that hip hop is an immigrant art form, it makes sense that many of Canada's major hip hop artists have negotiated various locales of citizenship and multicultural identity: k-os (locales as disparate as Toronto and Trinidad), Shad (born in Kenya of Rwandan parents and raised in Ontario), Michie Mee (born in Jamaica), Maestro Fresh Wes (of Guyanese parents), Kardinal Offishall (raised by Jamaican immigrant parents), and K'naan (born and raised in Mogadishu, Somalia).

In "Bakardi Slang" (from *Quest for Fire*), Kardinal Offishall breaks down T-dot as a unique space—Black difference has made Toronto one of a kind:

Ya'll think we all Jamaican, when nuff man are Trinis
Bajans, Grenadians and a whole heap of Haitians
Guyanese and all of the West Indies combined
To make the T-dot, O-dot, one of a kind

Contrast this unique make-up with Offishall's "Everyday (Rudebwoy)" (2005), which speaks directly to Kardinal's experience as a Black man in Toronto: "So where I rest I'm stressed by the 5-0 (Here we go) / Cops drive around the turf, lookin' for someone to search / With they flashlights checkin' in my dashboard (Whatchu lookin' for?)." Hip hop Canada remains a space both to celebrate difference and to speak out against oppression. Hip hop communities readily disavow skin colour in favour of more diverse notions of community and hip hop aptitude,[44] which is why white artists like Buck 65, Classified, and D-Sisive (who won the 2013 Juno for Best Rap Recording) are considered important Canadian hip hop emissaries, along with a slew of bilingual, mixed-race, and other non-Black artists who've been making hip hop music in Canada for some time. These artists include bilingual and interracial Montreal trio Laymen Twaist (popular in 1990); the large political rap collective Sweatshop Union; Japanese Canadian Kish; Chinese Canadian turntablist Kid Koala; Japanese, white, Black, and mixed-race rap group Swollen Members; the hip hop–influenced jazz group The Shuffle Demons; mixed-race rapper Eternia; and a wide variety of French artists, including multilingual soul–jazz–hip hop super group Nomadic Massive and the separatist rap group Loco Locass, whose 2004 single, "Liberez-Nous des Liberaux" (Liberate us from the Liberals), scrutinized the Quebec government and became an unofficial separatist anthem. Hip hop in Canada allows for cultural collision and is effective in articulating marginality, poverty, and injustice, particularly in its adoption by Indigenous artists.

> Kardinal Offishall
>
> Sweatshop Union, Eternia, Nomadic Massive, Loco Locass

> War Party, The Halluci Nation, Snotty Nose Rez Kids

Indigenous groups like War Party, Tru Rez Crew, Kinnie Starr, Winnipeg's Most, Mob Bounce, The Halluci Nation (previously A Tribe Called Red), Snotty Nose Rez Kids, and others, effectively articulate the struggles of Indigenous life within the borders of Canada (on Turtle Island). War Party's first album, *The Reign,* put Indigenous rappers on the Canadian hip hop radar. Their song, "Feelin' Reserved," was the first major Indigenous hop hop music video to get rotation on Much Music; War Party also won the Aboriginal Music Award for best rap album in 2000. Though many important Indigenous artists are making politically charged music in Canada today, it has been truly incredible to watch the rise of Haisla Nation duo Snotty Nose Rez Kids. Their album, *Trapline,* is full of deft lyricism, raw truths, and unique beats that mix classic hip hop with trap. In the music of War Party and Snotty Nose Rez Kids there is no romanticizing of life on the reserve, which is depicted instead as a place of intergenerational trauma that shows the effects of settler colonialism. By transforming spaces like the reserve into places of power, and by tapping into traditional culture—for example, The Halluci Nation's fusing of electronic and hip hop music with customary chant and drumming, creating a style referred to as "powwow-step"— Indigenous artists and groups bring Indigenous narratives directly into the mainstream. Shifting dispositions of power, hip hop creates a collective space where contemporary issues of injustice along with ancestral forces are negotiated on a popular stage—the precise negotiation I hear in much of K'naan's protest poetry.

Few Canadian hip hop artists (other than Drake) have had the level of international success that rapper/ poet K'naan has, and few Canadian hip hop songs are as well-known as K'naan's song of global fraternity, "Wavin' Flag." This chapter is but one of a number of resolutely scholarly pursuits to examine K'naan's oeuvre. K'naan was born in Somalia in 1978 and grew up in the violent capital of Mogadishu until the Somali Civil War broke out in 1991. Thirteen-year-old K'naan first settled with his family in New York, before moving with them to Toronto's Rexdale neighbourhood, where there is a large Somali community. As he raps on "Coming to America," a

> K'naan, "Coming to America"

track about his continual exodus and eventual post-"Wavin' Flag" settlement in America: "Mogadishu was my cage . . . T-dot to the motherfucking dot B / And the Rexdale lobby . . . I'm tired of always going through barriers . . . So I'm coming, coming to America."[45] How appropriate then that K'naan's birth name (Keynaan) means "traveller" in Somali, which holds homophonic reverb with Canaan. Calling himself the dusty foot philosopher, K'naan rhymes: "They call me dusty cause my feet have been through a lot / The wisdom of my survival that's just due to Allah."[46] Like the themes of improvisation, resistance, and citizenship status that tunnel through *Soundin' Canaan*, K'naan's music tenaciously affirms the self and community in the face of injustice and immigrant status. K'naan's musical and poetic roots are deep: his aunt Magool was a well-known Somali singer, and his grandfather, Haji Mohammad, was a poet. Through listening to hip hop records—which his father, living in America, sent him in Somalia—K'naan learned English and began to use hip hop as a weapon to fight oppression: "Music is my ammo, I'm ready for battle."[47] Building on the political energy of the 1999 incident where K'naan spoke before the UN's High Commissioner for Refugees, critiquing the UN for its failed aid mission to Somalia, K'naan's debut record, *The Dusty Foot Philosopher* (2005), presents lyrics about the nature of injustice and hope, complemented by production that draws from K'naan's diasporic background with elements of Somali music, hip hop, and world music. Certainly, in K'naan's music, "consciousness and craft combine."[48] Through his rap poetics of protest, K'naan raises hip hop to a global signifier of citizenship status.

K'naan, "The Dusty Foot Philosopher"

K'naan, "Better"

III. K'naan: Wavin' the Multicultural Flag

Dusty Foot Troubadour: Hip Hop as Protest Poetry

K'naan, "Coming to America," "Dusty Foot Philosopher," "Better"

My poetry hails within the streets
My poetry fails to be discrete
It travels across the earth and seas
From Eritrea to the West Indies
It knows no boundaries

—K'NAAN, *Dusty Foot Philosopher*, "Until the Lion Speaks"

"[W]hen a man is denied the right to live the life he believes in, he has no choice but to become an outlaw."

—NELSON MANDELA, *Long Walk to Freedom*, 256

K'naan, "Until the Lion Speaks," "Take a Minute"

Having been declared less than a full citizen by the South African government of the time, did Nelson Mandela have any choice when resisting that system other than to become an outlaw? Politically an African Nationalist and a democratic socialist, Mandela spent twenty-seven years in prison for his unrelenting activism against apartheid. It is figures like Mandela and Gandhi who, through their words and deeds, inspired K'naan to write politically charged rap songs like "Take a Minute": "How did Mandela get the will to surpass the everyday / when injustice had 'em caged and trapped in everyway? / how did Gandhi ever withstand the hunger strikes at all? / didn't do it to gain power or money if I recall / It's the gift, I guess I'll pass it on / Mother thinks it'll lift the stress of Babylon."[49] K'naan's first two albums, *The Dusty Foot Philosopher* and *Troubadour*, reflect his role as a poet who has witnessed and resisted much to get to where he is today. As a rap troubadour, K'naan uses his "surviv[al] [of] such violent episodes" in his past to create "medication out [his] own tribulations."[50]

K'naan's rap protests both heal and confront the malaise of bloodshed that haunts his old home of Mogadishu, as well as the violence he witnessed in Toronto's Rexdale community, condemning those who use hip hop to glorify violence without truly experiencing hardship. These struggles take place at the level of language in K'naan's lyrics. Given that language is a site of struggle, bell hooks writes that the "oppressed struggle in language to recover ourselves—to rewrite, to reconcile, to renew. Our words are not without meaning. They are an action—a resistance. Language is . . . a place of struggle."[51] K'naan uses language to negotiate an internal struggle with his own past and current more privileged position, resisting the "murders [who] hold post in [his] old home."[52] Given the post-industrial anti-oppression format that hip hop affords, and given how it emerged as remarkable protest music in the endless tundra of homogenous pop music that consumed the 1980s, it is no surprise that K'naan uses the medium as the quintessential weapon to renegotiate cultural space, synthesizing tradition with postmodern rap.

K'naan draws from American hip hop resistance and his own Somali background, using rap as poetry, which Gates contends functions as "the art form par excellence of synthesis and recombination." This synthesis and recombination creates spaces in which one can apply resistance through new creations or hybridization. The lyrics and sonic qualities in rap as "signifying in a postmodern way"—even though the lyrical structure of rap is quite formal. It is the lyrics, as *Anthology of Rap* editors Adam Bradley and Andrew DuBois contend, which allow for formal analysis, distinguishing between end rhymes, internal rhymes, and effective enjambment, to notice the caesural pauses within lines, along with a host of other formal elements used in poetic analysis. I appreciate the efforts of Bradley and DuBois to establish rap's poetic tradition within the larger African American and Western poetic heritage, but I disagree with their notion that to "read rap lyrics in print . . . is most often to restore them to their original form."[53] Given that hip hop is largely an oral poetic expression, dependent on the flow of lyrics over the syncopated beat (rhythm from the Greek word *rheo*, meaning flow), and given that some of hip hop's best rappers have said they don't even write their lyrics down

(Jay-Z is known for his remarkable lyrical dexterity), rap lyrics are but one representation of rap's poetic quality. The other attribute is the realization of those lyrics in the performance of them, which is why rap conforms to a poetic standard and simultaneously rejects traditional hermeneutic analysis. Nevertheless, by focusing on the discrete elements of rap's poetic form, *The Anthology* offers insight into rap's poetic quality, displaying how complex rap lyrics can be seen in polysyllable rhymes and periodic sentences that rappers like Rakim, Nas, Eminem, and Talib Kweli use for dramatic and acrobatic effect.[♭]

> K'naan, "I Was Stabbed by Satan"

K'naan's lyrics are technically quite straightforward, but his intonation and his use of narrative add to the need for his music to be heard with the melody he writes it to. The melody is necessary for the full effect of his music to be felt: for how does one feel the words, "The pain in my song is crazy" without hearing K'naan's voice teeter between despair and self-determination? Listening to K'naan's lyrics is an invitation for the reader to liberate the song's inherent sound and resistive powers—the poetry in the song: "this song is a poem and the whole poem is a tear / dropped in your ear."[54] Lyrical analysis reminds us that words are always partly ambivalent and open to interpretation.

> K'naan, "My Old Home"

K'naan's self-referential role as witness, poet, and "lyricist before [he] even spoke a word of English" invites co-performative analysis of what it means to exist in a world that is ambivalent, that poetically manifests in his own mixed feelings about his old home.[55] In "My Old Home," which plays out in two long stanzas that build in intensity, K'naan provides a richly poetic portrait of his native Somalia and asks us to "Peep my poem." In viewing language as bell hooks suggests, as "a place of struggle," "My Old Home" presents K'naan's internal struggle as he starts off by fondly describing his old home:

[♭] An early instance of polysyllabic rhyme delivery is heard throughout Rakim's lyrics, for instance: "Write a rhyme in graffiti and, every show you see me in / Deep concentration, cause I'm no comedian / Jokers are wild, if you wanna be tamed / I treat you like a child, then you're gonna be named" ("I Ain't No Joke," emphasis added).

> My old home smelled of good birth
> Boiled beans, kernel oil, and hand me down poetry
> Its brick whitewashed walls widowed by first paint
> The tin rooftop humming songs of promise while time is

As the song progresses, K'naan's words become angrier and elegiac as the track builds to a mantra-like lament where every line ends with "in my old home," emphasizing K'naan's discomfort and self-exile and the ghost-like personification of evil that haunts his consciousness:

> Goodwill is looted (in my old home)
> Religion is burned down (in my old home)
> Kindness is shackled (in my old home)
> Justice has been raped (in my old home)
> Murderers hold post (in my old home)
> The land vomits ghosts (in my old home)

"My Old Home" opens with references to food and poetry. Then, in a volta moment in the song, K'naan complicates the very idea of home, which is made grotesque through the corruption of justice and the family unit, describing how murders and rapists are celebrated in his old home. Given the many instances of injustice—for example, a nineteen-year-old Somali woman was sentenced to a six-month jail term for reporting her rape, and two journalists were also sentenced for publishing her story—it is no surprise that K'naan is haunted by the "ghosts" of his past.[56] K'naan's fond memories of his childhood, synthesized with the corruption of the family space—the raping of his culture—are emphasized first by the euphony of thinking lovingly of the earlier sensations of his motherland. But those memories are then fractured through paradigms of injustice that precede the incantation phrase: "in my old home." In an act of poïesis—a making—K'naan constructs home as tradition and familial dwelling and then takes the listener directly into the quarters of those whose notions of home and nation are full of contradiction.

> K'naan, "What's Hardcore"

Tactical manoeuvring, from finding the good in the bad, his troubadourian moving from village to village (between Somalia, Canada, the United States, and the larger diasporic village), along with his ability to quickly adapt and survive in each environment, is part of K'naan's poetic drift. The horror of his experiences provides the framework for him to contest rappers who glamorize thug violence by pointing to the brutal violence and truncated opportunities he witnessed growing up in war-torn Mogadishu. "What's Hardcore?" is a lyrical barrage against thug posturing that again opens with K'naan using the image of the writer to evoke the craft of telling stories, however horrific: "I put a pen to the paper, this time as visual as possible / Guns blast at the hospital."[37] By being as "visual as possible," allowing the listener to picture his poetic tale of horror, depicting a scene he describes as "harder than Harlem and Compton intertwined," K'naan makes space for other narratives of struggling young people who exist outside the primary frameworks for those representations in hip hop.

> K'naan, "Smile"

Taking on the role of the outlaw, a role K'naan adopted as a disenfranchised Somalian man living in a poverty-stricken area of Toronto, he uses tactical manoeuvring to carefully reveal himself. In "Smile," K'naan embodies Baker's notion of the "mastery of form," which "conceals, disguises, floats like a trickster butterfly in order to sting like a bee," by asking his listeners (in a Gandhi, Mandela, and King, Jr. inspired tactic) to smile in the face of oppression and adversity: "(Smile) When you're strugglin' / (Smile) When you're in jail / (Smile) When you're dead broke / (Smile) And the rent's due / (Smile) You ain't got friends now / (Smile) And no one knows you / Never let 'em see you down, smile while you're bleedin'."[38] In "Smile," K'naan endures various hardships—he never thought he would "make it to fourteen"—and imparts the knowledge that despite the wars and violence he has witnessed, you need to find joy. K'naan calls sufferers together to resist their outlaw status by tactfully finding hope and unity in the power of self-determination and community.

> K'naan, "Strugglin'"

K'naan brings us directly into the struggle that he embodies, even in a supposedly safe space like Toronto (particularly, Rexdale), and unifies a community of post-sufferers in the anthemic track "Strugglin'," one of K'naan's first singles from *The Dusty Foot*

Philosopher. The music video opens with K'naan performing part of "Until the Lion Learns to Speak" with traditional Somali clothing, drumming, and women and children smiling and clapping along to the rhythm. Rather than perform with a DJ, K'naan prefers to draw from the oral poetic traditions of Somalia, and having seen him perform before, I know he often plays guitar or the traditional African *djembe*. After K'naan sings that his poetry "knows no boundaries," we are transported directly into the concrete jungle and local space of Toronto's Somali community, and "Strugglin'" begins, binding the traditional Somali rhythms of "Lion" to the North American folk-rap sound of "Strugglin'." Yet it is the lyrics and global politics that guide K'naan, as he raps that he is "Forced by the loop and the guitar, but I'm the boss of the groove." K'naan, as an ambassador for displaced people who are exiled from their Somalian—or elsewhere located—homes, guides us through the struggles he and others endure daily. "Strugglin'" addresses resilience in a new environment and culture (here, Canada), where gang violence presents its own challenge. The song is written from K'naan's perspective, using the lyrical pronoun "I" throughout: "I know struggle, and struggle knows me, / My life owes me, like an overdose / I'm slowly, drifting in the arms of trouble / Then trouble holds me." The enjambment and simile comparing trouble to an overdose underscores the constant groove of pain for K'naan, describing how "nothing else is close to me / More than pain unfortunately." Despite the personal nature of the song, the video for "Strugglin'" focuses closely on various disenfranchised people in K'naan's community, who struggle even while remaining resolved to maintain their cultural identity.

In the video, the struggle is shown through group affiliation: the local connotes communal identity, and those who march with K'naan in the video signify unification in numbers. Acts of rallying and protesting function as ways to denote meaning; identity is formed through communal struggle, and for K'naan that means drawing his audience in by depicting how ubiquitous oppression is, with pertinent cultural references, including then American President George W. Bush: "And ain't much changed / Bobby is still troubling Whitney / And Bush is still bombing poor people, yo he's deadly / And me I got a little recording gig, but evidently I'm / Strugglin'." Even though K'naan had a freshly signed record deal, he remains immersed in the struggle, largely because the fight for him is both personal and globally manifested in communal identification, which is much more of a threat to the oppressor than if K'naan simply detached himself from his people and played the role of solitary thug: a figure he disavows in his music. K'naan remains rooted through his various reroutings in the cyclical nature of community and tradition, which is why the video ends with a new baby that K'naan watches over, as if that child embodies the hope of a greater citizenship status, one where his people—Somalis and other oppressed peoples—struggle less. Through a poetry that knows no boundaries, "From Eritrea to the West Indies," K'naan shows how struggle is something we all endure and fight to overcome—from Africa to Canada.

This is AfriCa/nada

Captain Richard Phillips: There's got to be something other than being a fisherman or kidnapping people.
Muse: Maybe in America, Irish, maybe in America.

—Captain Phillips

"Dear Africa, you helped me write this by showin' me to give is priceless."

—K'NAAN, *Troubadour*, "Take a Minute"

In "Talking Back to the Empire," a piece written for *NOW Magazine*, K'naan tells us that when "watching events in Africa, it's so easy, surveying the hunger and the war, to forget how the dilemma faced by blacks today was all structured long ago at a conference table in Germany."[59] K'naan is alluding here to the Scramble for Africa—the invasion, colonization, and annexation of African territory by

European powers—that followed the Berlin Conference of 1884. K'naan describes how Europeans invaded Africa and imposed a map on the continent to suit their own needs, dividing tribes and communities and creating many of the problems that persist in modern Somalia. When asked at workshops whether there is a unified Black community in Toronto, he responds: "I was living in one, Jamestown (Rexdale), where we were dealing with weightier questions like 'Where are the guns coming from?'" K'naan negotiates the local problems he faces around identity, citizenship status, and gang violence with the issues of global injustice that his brethren and sistren face in a Somalia, Africa at large, and elsewhere. K'naan's choice to focus directly on life in Somalia more than on life in Toronto (although he does also touch on his immigrant experiences) is an effort to bring into greater focus those who exist outside the typical Canadian narrative—the immigrants, the plight of Somali people, essentially: the disposable—as fuller people and therefore more dynamic citizens. K'naan complicates the North American dream by depicting how people often speak on behalf of others who suffer outside that dream space.

The American summer blockbuster *Captain Phillips* (2013), starring Tom Hanks and Barkhad Abdi, was based on the true story of a 2009 hijacking in which a merchant mariner named Captain Phillips was taken hostage by Somali pirates in the Indian Ocean. The film does a poor job of rendering the Somali characters as fully human (for example, the central Somali lead doesn't get as much of a back story as Phillips). Even so, the glaring differences between opportunity in America and Somalia are emphasized when Phillips tells Muse (the pirate leader): "There's got to be something other than being a fisherman or kidnapping people." Muse replies: "Maybe in America, Irish, maybe in America." As K'naan asks in the chorus of his track "Somalia": "So what you know bout the pirates terrorize the ocean? To never know a simple day without a big commotion." K'naan has many times defended Somali pirates, telling the *Los Angeles Times*: "The west is completely ignoring the basis for piracy in Somalia. The pirates are in the water because there is a nationwide complaint about the illegal mass fishing going on in Somali waters. And nuclear toxic waste is illegally being dumped on our shores. People in Somalia

K'naan, "Somalia"

know about this."⁶⁰ By contrast, the film, mostly intent on feeding the theatrical marketplace, is not concerned about what those glaring inequalities might be, for if it was it would be obliged to examine the events that led to the civil war in Somali, as well as depict (even a little) how foreign fishing destroyed the Somali fishing industry and brought about a pirate insurgency. Never mind the fact that a film with a $55 million budget (and which grossed more than $100 million) paid the lead Somali American actor Barkhad Abdi only $65,000.[b]

K'naan, "I Come Prepared," "If Rap Gets Jealous" K'naan uses hip hop to paint a fuller picture of Somali culture and tribulations, as discussed earlier in "My Old Home." He undermines the superiority complex of "white" culture as the signifying category of Western society by providing examples of how in Canada he is still read under the racial construction of the Black/African outlaw. He then uses that image to empower others. In "I Come Prepared" K'naan depicts an occasion—there are hundreds in rap lyrics, including Jay-Z's well-known "99 Problems"—when he is pulled over because he looks foreign and therefore dangerous: "How many immigrants are in this here Sedan / And is anyone carryin' any contraband / Not really but I'm late for my concert man / And here's a card for my lawyer Mr. Sam Goldman."⁶¹ Despite being racially profiled, K'naan proudly announces his difference and Africanness, telling us straightforwardly in "If Rap Gets Jealous" that he was poor and is "a refugee been in prison and survived the war."⁶² K'naan assumes his prior refugee status to bring Africa into mainstream consciousness.

K'naan's debut album, *The Dusty Foot Philosopher*, was a critical success, winning the Juno Award for Rap Recording of the Year in 2006, and was shortlisted the same year for the Polaris Music Prize. The polished sound of the album—which he followed with *Troubadour*—and its unique vision come from K'naan's inclusions of traditional African rhythms and Somali lyrics, with carefully attuned

---

[b] It has been reported that even though Abdi was nominated for Best Supporting Actor at the Academy Awards, he showed up wearing a rented tux and stayed at the airport so he could be near a friend who could drive him to the awards ceremony.

production from well-known Canadian music icon Jarvis Church, who is best known for having propelled Portuguese Canadian singer Nelly Furtado to fame. The album's title reworks how Africans are typically displayed on television (most often in charity programs). K'naan here is reclaiming the stereotypes that plague African representations in Western society:

> The camera always kind of pans to the feet, and the feet are always dusty from these kids. What they're trying to portray is a certain bias connected to their own historical reasoning, and what I saw though instead, was that that child with the dusty feet himself is not a beggar, and he's not an undignified struggler, but he's the dusty foot philosopher. He articulates more than the cameraman can imagine, at that point in his life. But he has nothing; he has no way to dream, even. He just is who he is.[63]

In the track "For Mohamoud (Soviet)," from *Dusty Foot*, K'naan elaborates: "Dusty foot philosopher means the one that's poor, lives in poverty but lives in a dignified manner and philosophizes about the universe and they talk about things that well-read people talk about, but they've never read or been on a plane, but they can tell you what's beyond the clouds." Consequently, K'naan deconstructs what defines education (as more than reading books) and Africanness (as more than dirty feet), and uses the dusty foot philosopher, as Alastair Pennycook and Tony Mitchell suggest in "Hip Hop as Dusty Foot Philosophy," as a metaphor for how we can think about global politics and locality: "To have one's feet in the dust is an image of localization that goes beyond appropriation of sounds, or references to local contexts. It speaks to a particular groundedness, a relationship to the earth that is about both pleasure and politics. To walk barefoot is to be located in a particular way. In his adopted home, Canada, the impossibility of walking barefoot makes him 'feel like a foreigner.'"[64] As K'naan puts it, and I concur with Pennycook and Mitchell, the image of the dusty foot philosopher provides a potent metaphor to rethink what we mean when we use words like impoverished.

K'naan, "For Mohamoud (Soviet)"

> Bob Marley, Malatu Astatke, Alemayehu Eshete, Getatchew Mekurya, Tlahoun Gessesse

Many of K'naan's songs and videos are intended to take the listener and viewer directly inside an African space where language, hip hop, community, and identity coalesce. K'naan's music is part of a larger global hip hop movement, yet his concerted focus on the local experiences of his community in Somalia (Mogadishu) and Toronto (Rexdale) rejects the contemporary American imperialist form of hip hop that focuses on club music and gangster posturing. Hip hop remains a globally marketed phenomenon, adapting via a wide range of flowing circuits within the African griot tradition. Pennycook and Mitchell propose that K'naan uses "Hip Hop to revive oral traditions in Somalia. From this point of view, then, Hip Hop can be a tool not so much of cultural imperialism, nor even of cultural affiliation or appropriation, but rather of cultural revival."[65] While K'naan's music is usually composed with live musicians, the samples he does use are telling, since they often connect to Africa and the larger diaspora. The samples on *Troubadour* reflect K'naan's deliberate choice to use complex African sounds to carry ideas: Bob Marley and The Wailers' "Simmer Down" on "T.I.A. [This is Africa]"; Mulatu Astatke's "Kasalefkut Hulu" on "ABCs"; Alemayehu Eshete's "Tey Gedyeleshem" on "Dreamer"; Getatchew Mekurya's "Shellela" on "I Come Prepared," a track featuring Damien Marley; Tlahoun Gessesse's "Yene Mastawesha" on "Somalia"; Tlahoun Gessesse's "Lantchi" on "America"; and Tlahoun Gessesse's "Yene Felagote" on "15 Minutes Away." The strong African presence, particularly three renditions of songs from Ethiopian artist Tlahoun Gessesse (Ethiopia borders Somalia), indicates K'naan's desire to have his sound mix with Western and African music.

> K'naan, "The African Way," "Soobax"

In "The African Way" (*Dusty*) K'naan describes hip hop as a powerful tool for the poor, one that connects various African countries and cultures in a united front:

> I understood it [hip hop] as the new poor people's weapon . . .
> Dusty foot philosopher came to change things, trust me
> From Ethiopia, Tanzania, Somalia
> Heathrow airport and customs in LaGuardia

Uganda, Kenya, my people, up in Ghana
Kingston, Jamaica, big up, because you know it's time for
The African way

"The African Way" features Kenyan rapper Mwafrika, who raps an entire verse in Swahili and Sheng (a slang combination of English and Swahili), which matches K'naan's desire to display the reciprocal loop of hip hop, from, as K'naan raps, "Kenya to Canada." By blurring the lines of comprehension for his largely North American audience, K'naan preserves cultural context (and language), displaying cultural distinctiveness, challenging his listeners to situate themselves beyond a typical English hip hop framework. K'naan often raps in Somali, as in the chorus of "Soobax" (a word meaning "come with it"):

Nogala soobax, nogala soobax
Dadkii waa dhibtee, nagala soobax
Dhibkii waa batee, nagla soobax
Dhiigi waad qubtee, nagala soobax
Nagala soobax, nagala soobax ♭

"Soobax" calls out injustices in "Somalia;" K'naan relates that he works "for the struggle / I don't do it for dough / I mean what I say / I don't do it for show / Somalia needs all gunmen right out tha door." The song depicts the degradation of Mogadishu and explains K'naan's choice to remain a "refugee," describing a puppet Somali government with no cards left to show. From Canada, K'naan can celebrate Somalia and remain critical of the oppressive regime that forced him into exile: a negotiation very much like his conciliation of dual cultural identities, expressed in his blending of English and

---

♭ Which, according to a user on the website "Genius," roughly translates as "You have exasperated the people, so come out with it / The troubles have increased, so come out with it / You've spilled the blood so that it drains on the roads, so come out with it / You've burnt the root of the earth, so come out with it / Come out with it, come out with it."

Somali. Lamenting the paucity of English, K'naan tells Pennycook he prefers Somali for its poetic quality, but ultimately blends the two because English is a language that crosses borders: "I mean, even if I was to speak to you in Somali just in conversation, you'd hear rhythm, and you'd hear rhyme, and most of the words I would use would have to begin in the same letter. It's just because it is set up in poetry. So, when I compare it to Somali, English is very dry, and also very young sounding."[66] By using English, K'naan can reach a wider audience—not just in North American, but also African—about the desperation facing life in Mogadishu; by including Somali lyrics throughout *Dusty Foot* and *Troubadour*, he allows for a hip hop of synthesis between North America/Canada and cultural art practices in Africa.

K'naan, "ABCs," "15 Minutes," "T.I.A."

K'naan's use of Africa in his music is vast: his slumdog millionaire tale "ABCs" presents Africa as a land of conflicting priorities where survival is more essential than education; "15 Minutes" describes how receiving and then sending much-needed wire transfers can save lives in Africa; the opening track "T.I.A." from *Troubadour* offers a very direct depiction of Africa.[67] The choice of Bob Marley and the Wailers' first single, "Simmer Down," as the sample in "T.I.A." is illuminating, for that song directs the Rude Boys of the ghettos of Jamaica to simmer (calm) down; similarly, K'naan's track condemns American rappers' fabricated depictions of violence and hedonism, as well as Africa's own dark history of aggression and bloodshed. The video for "T.I.A." opens with a TV screen depicting typical gangster rap videos and the subjective fantasy of an Africa formulated vis-à-vis the phantasmagorical West. The viewer's own gaze is transported into the screen as K'naan guides us "on a field trip" to Africa, during in the course of which he blends mirage and reality to create the popular African space, stating at the opening that he "hopes [we] got our passports and vaccine shots." In the video for "Soobax," K'naan literally takes us to Africa, performing alongside Kenyan musicians and Somali exiles in Mombasa and Nairobi. The video for "Soobax"

k-os

led fellow Toronto hip hop artist k-os to call the video an act of colonialism, largely for what k-os saw as the manufacturing of cultural authenticity, rapping in "B-boy Stance": "Oh yes, the great pretenders / Religious entertainers who want to be life savers."[68] K'naan responded with "Revolutionary Avocado," which describes his own struggles to promote peace along with his impetus to fight injustice, calling k-os a "Suburban negro turned hip hop hero," asking: "Is there a reason he really hates me, though?" The feud has been squashed between k-os and K'naan, who have since performed together. Essentially, the dispute points to the challenge of representing or trying to speak about, or for, Africa—even for an exiled African—in a Canadian setting.

From the cultural milieu of Toronto, K'naan has created a brand of hip hop that mixes a variety of stylistic influences, from American hip hop to traditional African rhythms, to bring the struggle of Africa directly to Canada and beyond. K'naan told CBC that Toronto fit all the textbook expectations of Canada as a just society, with the qualification that in practice, justice is not necessarily the same for all people:

> Here was a place where you weren't in war. Great quality of life, good culture, good schools, but you have to understand that that is relative. Those checked boxes and dreams don't apply to people equally in Canada. When you are an immigrant and a black immigrant where your parents don't come with a certain education and you are running from war and you have nothing, you are at the mercy of society."[69]

By bringing Africa to Canada and by discussing immigrant and refugee experiences, K'naan opens up new psychological facets of Black marginality in Canada and shows that identity for the newly transported is complex. Identification with place is, as Stuart Hall contends, a progression never completed, always in process: "actual identities are about questions of using the resources of history, language, and culture in the process of becoming rather than being."[70] K'naan's transferring—his cross-continental shipping—of his African past into a Canadian space says not only T.I.A. (this is Africa), but also *this is me*—infinitely complex and mixed like the waters of the Atlantic crossing from Africa to Canada, freely flowing like music.

H2O Mix: "Music Is Water"

Mos Def

Water: H_2O. In nearly every religion and culture around the world, water is a purifier and also an act of creation. Lacking water, life withers, yet it was paradoxically through water that the transatlantic slave trade prospered; and it was due to a lack of water, as described in chapter 3, the result of a navigational error aboard the slave ship the *Zong*, that slavers felt justified in throwing African "cargo" into the sea to claim insurance for them. How many bodies have been lost to the sea? Or equally as frightening, how many die every year for want of clean water? People die every day fighting for water, or worse, they die by being denied access to clean drinking water, sometimes by multinational corporations.[71] The COVID-19 pandemic has made the situation worse and more tenuous for people living in aggrieved communities. Yet water washes and sustains all people just the same; as Mos Def puts it in "New World Water": "The rich and poor, black and white got need for it." Water within the so-called developed world remains a common element of little value.

K'naan, "Wash it Down"

Water is devalued in North America because it is so common. Diamonds are less ubiquitous, although due to the conflict diamond (blood diamond) trade during civil wars in countries like Angola and Sierra Leone, they are certainly *more* widespread than in the past. Capitalism is a system of exploitation, and rich countries continue to dig holes in poor countries around the world in order to extract resources like diamonds (often promising those countries economic prosperity or or a means to get out of debt). K'naan's "Wash It Down," the first track from *Dusty*, inverts the diamond/water paradox, describing water as tantamount to life itself. He uses water as a metaphor and manifesto that relates to music and ultimately to freedom. The only instrumentation in the track is the rhythmic splashing sound of water made by women washing clothes in a river. K'naan's voice—pitched higher than that of most rappers—flows smoothly over and within the rhythm of water as the rapper/poet reminds us of the vital importance of clean water for people in Africa (water-based diarrheal diseases kill some million children every year there), whereas in North America, people take it for granted. In the

North American framework of the track's opening, water is referred to as purifier to release stress:

> When you here in the water
> You feel like it's sorta
> Releasin' the tension, distress and disorder
> Is big in America
> Stephanie, Erica, both of them suffer from livin' in here
> Because
> Livin' is very competitive:
> Hasslin' creditors, hazardous accidents
> Drivin' with negligence
> Too many beverages
> People got too many things on they lettuces
> TV's deadliest professin': the ugliest war, war, war, WAR!
> What the hell you keep on killin' me for?

Being within the water of the track releases the daily stress and disorder of simply trying to live. People in America (and the Americas) are immersed in a life of stress from competition ("Livin' is very competitive"), credit debt ("hasslin' creditors"), reckless driving ("drivin' with negligence"), alcohol and soft drink consumption ("too many beverages"), obesity ("too many things on they lettuces"), and the constant bombardment of wars on their TV (Iran, Iraq, Afghanistan, poverty, drugs, etc.). The "distress and disorder" is killing people emotionally, K'naan included; the daily flood of media-based living devalues life and leaves many people emotionally anaesthetized.

The song's next stanza takes us across the ocean to K'naan's wartorn homeland of Somalia, where he describes how he was "born in a pot boilin' black and hot / Waitin' to be tasted and rappin' a lot / But justice would not come and eat my flesh / Instead, I had poverty to feed my stress . . . So, I thought I was just made to exist / Not to live or change and resist." K'naan's trauma of growing up during a civil war is juxtaposed with the disorder and anxiety that consume people in North America. It is through music (which flows like water) that K'naan finds the strength to change and resist, calling others into the purification mix: "This is the therapy needed, so use it / People need music like they need excuses / People need water like Kanye needs Jesus / So wash it down." The mention of Kanye—similar to a reference to "J-lo" in "My Old Home"[72]—uses a popular music source, here a simile referring to Kanye's "Jesus Walks," as a global identifier for people around the world. It also recalls, for me, the following line from Kanye's "Diamonds": "My father been said I need Jesus / So he took me to church and let the water wash over my Caesar." Water represents purification as the church water washes over Kanye's "Caesar" (a type of haircut) and inverts the diamond/water paradox. Water and music have healing properties, binding us together as people and citizens of the earth.

The chorus at the end of "Wash It Down," "So wash it down," is repeated like a mantra, and, as K'naan says in a spoken-word moment, provides a "meditation for you to relax." The onomatopoeic "wash it down" over the splashing rhythm of water allows K'naan's meditative poetics to wash over us and invites cleansing from absolute difference in favour of our shared creative and egalitarian social existence. K'naan then shifts the focus back to the importance of water to the Somali people as an instrument of music, life-substance, and even war and death: "My people drum on water / Drink on water / Live on water / Die for water." Water affirms life, and because of the lack of access to it, Somalia has had droughts that have left thousands of people dead; water also represents cultural struggle to attain value. By only using the sound of water to score "Wash It Down," K'naan shows how water itself is instrumental to all people—it is the starting point of life and music. Music like water carries information and serves as a border-crossing praxis. K'naan describes hip hop, sent to him across the ocean by his father in America, as one of the forces that sustained his life and gave him strength to overcome his struggles. We create borders and maps, and decide who merits clean drinking water, yet even things that appear stable, like continents, "are fluid and malleable assemblages whose boundaries have shifted over time."[73] With time the values of a diamond and of water can shift, especially if people find themselves suddenly without access to water.

Access to water is an entry to creative potential and freedom. For K'naan, music is fluid and malleable like water, and since no one owns water (or should), no one owns music (or should). When asked about the various remixes of his anthemic "Wavin' Flag," particularly the remix with fifty different Canadian musicians, K'naan relates how the song started off as part of something he began, but as in Somali tradition, once a song is released it no longer belongs to the artist who first performed it:

> It was an incredible experience, and I remember not even being able to register that it was a song that I wrote. The Somalis have a great tradition in music where when you write and release a great song, everyone in the Somali artist community makes a rendition of it and sings it back to you. No one ever owns publishing on any Somali song, because an artist knows it no longer belongs to him. So a part of me feels like a guest of this song, like it's this rare find, and I'm just fortunate to be the artist that first sang it.[74]

K'naan's humble approach to his most popular song is a reminder that the value of his music is hardly his alone—it belongs to all people in the same way that citizenship is an inalienable right to all those who belong to a nation even as those rights are often under threat, especially in times of crisis. We can see the horrific physical and psychological consequences in Clyde Woods' assessment of the Katrina hurricane in New Orleans as a blues moment: a blues moment because it stripped away all the veneer of acceptance and tolerance and showed contemporary racism in the United States.[75] The Katrina moment—that is, the response to Katrina, not the hurricane itself—compels us, and especially Americans, to consider what citizenship actually means for those who are dispossessed, who suffer in the waters we once again ignore, for the "thousands of people ain't got no place to go" (in Bessie Smith's "Backwater Blues"). We turn from muddy waters to another purification moment that works against and within a blues moment, using K'naan's song of global fraternity as another case study to explore the complicated notion of what it means

<aside>Bessie Smith</aside>

to be a citizen within multicultural Canada—more universally: what citizenship sounds like as voiced by disparate nations seeking to coexist within the larger global politics that connect us together—once again, like water.

"Wavin' Flag": Multicultural Planet

Pierre Trudeau's desire for a truly just society—one that is pluralistic and multicultural—is largely the same desire that K'naan articulates in his global smash hit, "Wavin' Flag," and certainly both require critique. I think we need to move beyond the tolerance of the other's difference, for there is also, as Trudeau states, "no such things as a model or ideal Canadian," since it is in difference, in the space of *whatever* (Agamben)—where it does not matter who we are so much as how we participate in celebrating diversity—that we can truly be free.[76] Of course, unless you want to practise hate or intolerance, or inflict harm on others, in which case you will not fit within a truly multicultural society. K'naan's "Wavin' Flag" (from *Troubadour*) and its various remixes articulate the desire for the individual to belong to the larger collective of the nation, along with the desire to fit within a concept of united nations, much like the United Nations model in place. In one possible reading, "Wavin' Flag" articulates multiculturalism as a tool for normalizing ethnic diversity and for creating tolerance rather than intercultural dialogue. In a more fruitful reading, "Wavin' Flag" expresses multiculturalism's desire to unite us despite our vast differences, that regardless of our own inter- and multi-nationhood we can come together as a holistic group to celebrate and imagine what a truly just society might sound like, particularly in a heterotopic space like Canada—the only officially multicultural country on the planet. Nevertheless, official multiculturalism remains fraught.

At best, as Foster attests, multiculturalism is "effectively a variant of a creolized, plural society, a noble and realizable goal"; in the middle, multiculturalism, as Smaro Kamboureli states, "recognizes the cultural diversity that constitutes Canada but it does so by practicing a sedative politics, a politics that attempts to recognize ethnic differences, but only in a contained fashion, in order to manage them"; at worst, Neil Bissoondath argues, multiculturalism creates "idealized Blackness that is chaos and fragmentation with no clear sense of common unity, history, or culture."[77] Robyn Maynard provides critique, particularly of the policy itself, which she sees as a self-congratulatory policy that does not change the lived reality of those whose citizenship remains vulnerable: "Multiculturalism has served a similar role to that of the Underground Railroad, allowing Canadian state officials and the general public to congratulate themselves on Canada's comparative benevolence, while rendering invisible the acute economic and material deprivation currently facing many Black communities."[78] In "Why Multiculturalism Can't End Racism," NourbeSe Philip disparages multicultural policy because it does not actually address the problem of racism. Furthermore, many critics argue that multicultural policies and practices concentrate on the preservation of the (static) heritage of the Other and on containment within a dominant society, which has given rise to discourses of recognition, which is often a kind of "tolerance," promoted by Charles Taylor in "The Politics of Recognition."

I tend to agree with these critiques of official multicultural policy (a policy Daniel McNeil has called "snake oil") and its often-failed attempts to promote cultural pluralism and diversity without enacting material change. Yet I also see how important multiculturalism is for understanding and negotiating difference and belonging to the larger sonic mix. As stated in the overture, my approach mixes political and theoretical critique. On the positive end, I envision what I call *sonic multiculturalism* as an open signifier that views difference and social belonging as part of a mix that is open to change, which canons well with K'naan's own desire for "Wavin' Flag" to enter the larger community, which then "makes a rendition of it and sings it back to you."[79] The various remixes of "Wavin' Flag" indicate that through the remix of the original song a new creation/individual/state is born. Like multiculturalism, which is itself always changing—or should be—"Wavin' Flag" is a call to resist (the original version), or to celebrate difference and diversity (the "Celebration Mix").

K'naan, "Wavin' Flag"

While *The Dusty Foot Philosopher* gained K'naan critical recognition as a gifted poet/MC, it was his song "Wavin' Flag" from his follow-up album, *Troubadour*, and its subsequent versions that propelled him to the heights of international fame. Besides the original version that appeared on the album, there have been three official English-language remixes, each with a music video (and each with millions of YouTube views), and dozens of bilingual mixes in multiple languages, including the particularly popular Spanish cover featuring David Bisbal, which received its own music video. K'naan even published a children's book, *When I Get Older: The Story Behind Wavin' Flag* (2012), which covers the meaning behind the lyrics and the song's history. In 2010, three English-language music videos of the song were released, each with a different audience in mind. The original version (audio only) focuses on the struggles of refugees displaced by war, with direct references to K'naan's native Somalia; later mixes, such as the World Cup version, focus on celebration and global unity, which Coca-Cola calculatedly used to represent its global brand. The first remix, the Young Artists for Haiti version, was made as a response to the 2010 Haiti earthquake and featured an ad hoc group of fifty Canadian artists performing a line or two of the lyrics. The song became a charity single in Canada and featured everyone from Nelly Furtado, Sam Roberts, and Broken Social Scene to Kardinal Offishall, Avril Lavigne, and a rap verse from Drake. The popularity of this version—which reached number one in Canada—was followed a few months later when Coca-Cola decided to use a new "Celebration Mix" as a promotional anthem for FIFA World Cup 2010, hosted by South Africa. This version remains the most popular rendering, reaching number one in Canada, Germany, Switzerland, and Austria, and number two in Italy, the UK, and Ireland.[80] Coca-Cola integrated the song with its own well-known jingle into its commercials, in an act I term corporate multiculturalism. Lastly, a remix of "Wavin' Flag," featuring French electronic music producer David Guetta and American rapper will.i.am was made for an international audience (mostly American) with parts of the lyrics once again amended.

The multiple versions of a straightforward song attest to how pop markets will get as much traction (money) as possible from a given single. A less skeptical reading, fitting within the various indices of *Soundin' Canaan*, sees the value of remix, particularly given that the song was catchy enough to allow for cultural transference many times over (there are Japanese, Chinese, Arab, and Nigerian mixes, among many others). As a hip hop and folk anthem, "Wavin' Flag" showcases how hip hop as a global phenomenon, not only with international audiences, but also for a host of other cross-cultural identifications, provides a global forum though which displaced subjects can negotiate multiple concepts of identity/citizenship. The manifold versions of "Wavin' Flag" display how easy it is to use hip hop to form allegiances—however sound or untenable—to fight injustice or claim cosmopolitan solidarity. The original captures the dissonance of being outside the dominant order and demands justice, describing the "violent prone, poor people zone" K'naan comes from, where Somalians are "struggling, fighting to eat / And we wondering, when we'll be free." The "Celebration Mix," despite being made with opulent organizations such as World Cup and Coca-Cola in mind, envisions a society where freedom is achieved and where difference and poverty are overcome. In an interview with *Maclean's*, K'naan seizes the opportunity to find celebration "from the melancholy nature of the original, which is about emerging from darkness, to one that considered what would happen if we actually acquired that freedom. Then it becomes a celebration." Both versions articulate the tragedy and comedy of living in a society, envisioning a world where nations are no longer at war with their people, or other nations.

Born to a throne, stronger than Rome
A violent prone, poor people zone
But it's my home, all I have known
Where I got grown, streets we would roam
Out of the darkness, I came the farthest
Among the hardest survivors
Learn from these streets, it can be bleak
Accept no defeat, surrender, retreat
(Original)

Give me freedom, give me fire
Give me reason, take me higher
See the champions take the field now
You define us, make us feel proud
In the streets our heads are liftin'
As we lose our inhibition
Celebration, it surrounds us
Every nation, all around us
(Celebration Mix)

As K'naan describes, the initial song was about struggle, while the "Celebration Mix" signifies "the world coming together [rather] than a land coming apart."[81] Read in juxtaposition, the original captures the feelings of displacement and dissonance that come with feelings of ambiguity towards belonging to the nation (Somalia/North America), along with K'naan's own shifting refugee status, while the celebratory version is idealistic and assumes a level of homogeneity to the global construction of an international sport like soccer.

The celebration mix feels somewhat disingenuous, particularly since it was used throughout Coca-Cola's entire campaign, from commercials to the FIFA World Cup Trophy Tour by Coca-Cola, yet when read beside the original, the remixes dually articulate what Cecil Foster in *Genuine Multiculturalism* calls the tragedy and comedy of multiculturalism. Essentially, the tragedy is in society's inability to bridge the differences of its diverse citizens (as in the original version), while the comedy is in imagining it is possible to organically progress towards fraternity and solidarity among disparate groups of people, which K'naan uses through the international game of soccer: "See the champions take the field now ... Celebration, it surrounds us." The music video for the "Haiti mix" maintains the original lyrics (with some amendments and a rap verse from Drake), using video footage of the devastation caused by the earthquake to elicit sympathy, encouraging audiences to donate and participate in the crucial comedy of rebuilding tragedy-stricken communities; by contrast, the "Celebration Mix" video uses the implied multicultural format of FIFA to assume unity. Gone is the minor tone of the original, which is replaced by kids of various ethnic backgrounds playing soccer.

Like state-sponsored multiculturalism, Coca-Cola's corporate multiculturalism is particularly limited in what it manifests in the real world. During the Trophy Tour, K'naan worked hard with the FBI, Coca-Cola, and the Somali government to find a safe place for the cup to land in Somalia, describing how when "Coke and FIFA decided they couldn't do it, I was so disappointed I actually considered not going on the trophy tour at all."[82] Once again, we see the tragedy of trying to promote unity through a corporate framework: a structure that is only marginally interested in the hopes of an artist whose own country remains on the borders of the very celebration K'naan promotes. K'naan tells *Maclean's* that he decided not to drop off the tour because he would "only be denying [himself]. What I was doing on the trophy tour was a great thing—exploring different parts of the world, getting to know my continent that I was born in. But, literally the day after the African portion of the trophy tour ended, I took the plane back home and I decided to go to Somalia myself." K'naan's adapting his lyrics for Coca-Cola and FIFA is certainly problematic, especially since Coca-Cola's corporate profile reads like a list of crimes against humanity: from the health effects of the pesticides in their products, to exploitative labour practices, environmental degradation, and monopolistic business practices, to building plants in Nazi Germany that employed slave labour, and much more that could be explored beyond the scope of this brief critique.[83] Coca-Cola asked K'naan to change his lyrics chiefly because the references to "a violent prone, poor people zone," and people "struggling, fighting to eat," did not fit the campaign's themes.[84] However, for K'naan Coca-Cola is a mechanism in a larger transnational framework that allows his mix to be more widely heard: a mix that puts conflict and poverty momentarily aside to celebrate diversity.

The same challenges arise in "Young Artists for Haiti," where a large group of mostly privileged Canadian musicians create a multicultural and bilingual mix to raise awareness and send relief aid to Haiti. In some ways, it falls silent as tangible action, much like the 2020 celebrity remix of John Lennon's "Imagine" during the first year of the COVID pandemic. That said, I think the "Young Artists for Haiti" version, especially since it maintains some of the original lyrics and feel, is more successful than the "Celebration Mix" in articulating the tragedy and comedy of multiculturalism. The song uses the flag—kids in the video hold the Haitian flag, rather than the Canadian one—as a unifying element that promotes the right to equal citizenship, recalling that the Canadian flag represents, for most Canadians, an inalienable right to citizenship status and equality, although this is becoming less and less the case; recall that white nationalists (especially during the so-called Freedom Convoy to protest mask and vaccine mandates) used the flag to assert an individualist understanding of freedom. More widely, Drake's rap verse places responsibility on Canadians to think of themselves as part of a larger global network (something Canadians imagine themselves being good at) to help those in need: "How come when the media stops covering / And there's a little help from the government / We forget about the people still struggling." The video displays a united front (a chorus) of Canadian musicians of all genres and ethnic backgrounds, incorporating clips from the Haiti disaster to facilitate a cross-neighbourhood and transnational dialogue that assumes joint responsibility for creating the world we want to imagine. Each video for "Wavin' Flag" reinterprets the universality of struggle and coalition politics, serving as an example of how the popular appropriates the margin to the centre. "Wavin' Flag" becomes even more unrecognizable in the international and up-tempo version featuring will.i.am and David Guetta, which uses a solid black flag to further abstract the concept of (inter)nationalism. This is partly how global multiculturalism works: by removing specificity it allows for more diversity and accommodation, but therefore greater abstraction of individualism and regionalism—although, as individuals, we can still resist and change. As K'naan suggests in the original, people are stronger than the attempts to control them by the leaders of conflict, and we are capable of "mov[ing] forward like Buffalo Soldiers."♭ To be truly multicultural is to be *in process* and to resist the old orders that K'naan believes "can't hold us." Like a flag moving back and forth in the wind, or like the mix moving back and

---

♭ The Buffalo Soldiers were an all-Black cavalry unit that was part of the 10th Cavalry Regiment of the United States Army, formed on 21 September 1866. at Fort Leavenworth, Kansas (Wikipedia, s.v. "Buffalo Soldier," https://en.wikipedia.org/wiki/Buffalo_Soldier). "Buffalo Soldiers" appear through popular music, notably in Bob Marley's well-known song "Buffalo Soldier" (added to the playlist), which recasts the image of the Buffalo Soldier as a symbol of Black resistance. It should be noted that these reggae lyrics of heroism overlook the historical context of these soldiers, who served as enablers in the attempted genocide of Plains Indians and later found themselves deployed as tools of empire in Cuba and the Philippines and in General Pershing's campaigns in Mexico as part of the 24th Regiment.

forth on the turntable platter, to be a citizen within the imaginative act of a country represented by its flag is a multicultural process—by which I mean, we are not fatally determined by our pasts, however "violence prone."

Sonic Multiculturalism: An Exercise in Blackness

So far, I have used "Wavin' Flag" as a global anthem that imagines that we are united by our individual connections to the nation within the larger cosmopolitan—perhaps cosmological, even—imagining of transnational unity between nations. This negotiation between the self, the nation, and the larger global sphere is represented by hip hop's own framework—a specific form of creolization and mix that recalls the process of multiculturalism. Thinking of multiculturalism as an unfixed variable locus of culture is useful in considering that wherever there is culture, acculturation, and contact zones, there is multiculturalism. Canada itself, the only officially multicultural country at the level of policy, provides a unique locus that allows acculturation to occur, providing space for a Liberal prime minister like Pierre Trudeau to imagine Canada as a just society comprised of many diverse peoples who are all immigrants to the larger project of constructing a Canada that is always changing. In 1971, Trudeau declared that Canada would have a multicultural policy, and in 1972 he formed the Multiculturalism Directorate, followed by the Race Relations Unit in 1982, although the Multiculturalism Act was not passed until 1988, when Brian Mulroney was prime minister.

At its most basic level, the act recognizes Canada's multicultural heritage, the need to preserve that heritage, Indigenous rights, English and French as the official languages, equality rights regardless of skin colour or religion, and the right of minorities to honour their cultures. The initial enunciation was also a strategy on Trudeau's part to ensure that the English and French languages remained central to Canada's heritage, thus directly confronting the schism in Quebec between the English and the French; more subversively, as a policy, the Multiculturalism Act provided support—even if largely in discourse—to immigrants and migrants in their efforts to overcome the job discrimination and language conflicts that were endemic to those experiences. Multiculturalism is often peddled to newcomers and immigrants as proof of Canada's utopian qualities, even though the country was founded on anti-Indigenous and anti-Black violence on occupied land. At best, as Mark V. Campbell has suggested, "Canadian Multiculturalism is a utopian governmental ideal, an unfinished project that is always in process."[85] Given Canada's history of exclusion, it is no surprise that many immigrants and Indigenous people do not see themselves as Canadian, preferring absolute difference, rather than something along the lines of K'naan's "Celebration Mix," which is founded (in part) on tolerance when what is needed is a more discordant sounding that acknowledges the improvisatory process of sounding citizenship together and not necessarily in unison.

Critiques of multiculturalism are many—I outlined some of them in the Overture—and are often framed by those who have lived through immigrant or refugee experiences in Canada and who find multiculturalism little more than a discursive strategy of tolerance that, as Mark V. Campbell warns, "positions social difference as deviant from the 'norm,' creating a hierarchy where the 'norm' must put up with people who are not deemed normal."[86] In *Making a Difference*, Smaro Kamboureli states that for "some Canadians, then, the tolerance they see multiculturalism advocating threatens their understanding of Canadian history and augurs against the development of a cohesive Canadian identity, which they think should be the goal of the nation."[87] Tolerance can promote sameness; conversely, it can represent the fear that the nation itself will not be cohesive, but rather will manifest a variety of dissonant soundings without harmony. Peter S. Li, in "The Multiculturalism Debate," views multiculturalism as a muddled policy that lacks lucidity since that policy seems to change with its political emphasis, without precise or substantial content. I argue, in accordance with Cecil Foster's radical imaginings of multiculturalism, that it is precisely this lack of definitive terms that allows multiculturalism in Canada to function idealistically as a hope that individuals can overcome the finite limits of geographical boundaries and social stratification to imagine a more inclusive version of the nation: the imagined holding place we belong to as Canadian citizens. K'naan's "Wavin' Flag" complicates the official Canadian multicultural model by asking us to consider what happens when you take that idealistic model and think it through on a global level.

Sabine Milz thinks through the connection between multiculturalism and global and national capitalism to provide a reading that views multiculturalism as the latest buzzword to sell neoliberal politics and identity to the masses: "Global capitalism has increasingly legitimized multicultural politics as a means to create economic progress and identity . . . Canadian multiculturalism has become a positive guise for Canadian neoliberal capitalism and English- and French-Canadian cultural hegemony."[88] Milz's argument is not without merit, as she presents a frightening prospect of multiculturalism as a sedative, especially when we comparatively examine how drastically hip hop has changed as capitalism has appropriated the music and culture closer to the norm and less as a productive voice of cultural agency belonging to the oppressed. In fact, the association of "Wavin' Flag" with Coca-Cola's own brand recognition suggests that the track has become part of the corporate multicultural machine. In an interview, K'naan was asked if he thought that Coca-Cola, "that great emblem of economic imperialism," compromises his message. Somewhat evasively, he replied: "No. I know how I got to where I am, and I've never had to adapt to become something else. I write my songs, I play them and I'm very honest about my stage presence."[89] While I hardly want to chastise an artist who has given so much of himself to his music, K'naan himself, in a confessional piece, after recording his latest record, *Country, God or the Girl* (2012), described in the *New York Times* how the pressure of the music industry altered the sociopolitical content of his latest music (so much so that it remains his last album to date):

> Right now, the pressures of the music industry encourage me to change the walk of my songs . . . So some songs became far more Top 40 friendly, but infinitely cheaper . . . I come with all the baggage of Somalia—of my grandfather's poetry, of pounding

rhythms, of the war, of being an immigrant, of being an artist, of needing to explain a few things . . . I may never find my old walk again, but I hope someday to see beauty in the graceless limp back toward it.[90]

It is in a charged confessional moment like the one that K'naan shares with the *New York Times* that the corporate machine's machinations become more visible, as a company like Coca-Cola, whether K'naan intends it or not, subsumes multiculturalism and Blackness as *authentic* signposts essentially to sell more soft drinks.

I've outlined some of the qualms around state multiculturalism and the appropriation of multicultural ideals by major corporations like Coca-Cola. Now I turn to the notion that *sonic multiculturalism* idealistically declares that people can live freely and sound together. Building on Vincent Andrisani's idea of a "sonic citizenship" developed from the bottom-up and enacted by citizens listening together against the forces of authority and the nation, I imagine the same concept applied to a group of people of all diverse backgrounds figuring out how to sound together against the oppressive forces of the nation-state. Multicultural Canada is a fragmented collective of many ethnic and racialized groups who are held together by a notion to believe in what is good and what is right. I think it is right to herald that the death of whiteness in Canada has already passed—even if it survives and pushes back, as I have argued in various places in *Soundin' Canaan*—for we now live in a multicultural reality. Multiculturalism is, as Foster suggests, "part of the consciousness of Blackness . . . at least ontologically, epistemologically, and ethically, multiculturalism is Black and an exercise in Blackness."[91] Consequently, multiculturalism presents an opportunity for creative and iconoclastic destruction of the old structures, hierarchies, and even some individual rights, in the creation of more non-authoritarian soundings that embrace difference and allow more citizens to sound with or against one another in a polyphonous mix. Thus, my imagining of the potential of multiculturalism participates in the comedy of multiculturalism that Cecil Foster foresees: "*genuine multiculturalism* is that it assumes that nations and states are constructed mechanically, indeed pragmatically, in the moment, by the people, for the people, and of the people—that is, *citizens*.[92] The only constant in life is change, which is why even the original darker version of "Wavin' Flag" is predicated on the hope that one day justice and universal citizenship rights can become a multicultural reality for all people: "But we struggling, fighting to eat / And we wondering, when we'll be free / So we patiently wait for that faithful day / It's not far away, but for now we say." K'naan's "Wavin' Flag," in its various manifestations, tells the story of a world that changes organically if the people are willing to fight for what they believe in.

Foster's notion of genuine multiculturalism is "about telling tales of a coming time when tragedy will end": it "is about clinging to humanity in the face of unimaginable alternatives."[93] The very notion of multiculturalism is subversive and chaotic since it implies that the modern nation and the self are always processes; they are exercises that involve improvising with others and cultures that appear foreign to our own ways of life—they involve a stepping outside of ourselves to allow for the greatest amount of freedom for all people in a society. Hence, there is a reason why more and more countries are declaring multiculturalism dead or dangerous. As an idea, multiculturalism is dangerous to whiteness. Given that Canada is so new—not as a land mass, or as a place to live (it's been inhabited by Indigenous peoples for thousands of years), but as a country called Canada—we are presented with a unique opportunity to model what a "sonic citizenship" might sound like, drawing inspiration from the diverse cultural composition of Canada. *Sonic multiculturalism* acknowledges that our identities are not fixed but are always changing and require in-the-moment engagement, the same way as musicians when they are playing together for the first time. Just to live is, as Foster articulates, inauthentic, so why not embrace the beautiful *in*authenticities? The chorus of "Wavin' Flag"—"When I get older / I will be stronger / They'll call me freedom just like a waving' flag"—is an act of faith that assumes not only that we can change as we dream what we can be, but that the larger society can continue to work towards the ideal that Martin Luther King Jr. imagined as the just society. At the end of "Wavin' Flag," K'naan sings about the ultimate goal of multiculturalism and imagines global fraternity between all people: "And everybody will be singing it / And you and I will be singing it / And we all will be singing it." While I have argued throughout *Soundin' Canaan* for the value of what Ajay Heble calls "things not in harmony," there is also value in imagining what harmony itself might sound like, for even dissonance can promote a kind of social concord.[94]

A *sonic multiculturalism* is more than tolerance, and it is certainly more than integration. *Sonic multiculturalism* (which functions outside policy) is about learning to improvise and build (and even deconstruct) the Canada we all want to imagine, which means reworking and revisiting what that might mean every couple of years: a good reason we have political elections in democratic countries, and a good reason why people should vote, and participate in the construction (and deconstruction) of the imagined nation. If Canada is to be a truly just country, then community rights need to exist in parallel with individual rights. The highest expression of our connection to others is our shared status that comes with equal citizenship, which is why Foster describes citizenship as that which "renders meaningless stratification and socialization according to such categories as ethnicity, gender, language, place of birth, sexuality—indeed of all social categorizations other than citizenship itself."[95] Canada represents a possible opportunity—put on the world stage through K'naan's own multicultural "Wavin' Flag"—to model what that citizenship might sound like, even though "Canada has played," as K'naan suggests for the immigrant, "both the saviour and the villain, especially at the beginning, during the time of integration and assimilation."[96] By embracing immigrants, refugees, Indigenous sovereignty, and Blackness more fully in the multicultural mix—by no longer racially stratifying people in relation to their citizenship—we can move beyond Canada as a closed homogenous national community, and into, as Heble suggests, "a recognition of the role that multiple other histories have played in the construction of Canadian identity, to move beyond nationalism into a consideration of the complex traffic between and within cultures and regions."[97] I'm not sure exactly what this might sound like in the context of Canada's multicultural future, but we will be stronger, "And we all will be singing it."

REMIX 4

> Who's speakin' Canada's truth?
> Who's standin' for peace?
> Live from the home of the slaves and the land that was thiefed
> Lot of broken and lost souls on this planet of freaks...
> We out of touch now.
>
> —SHAD, "Out of Touch," TAO

Hip hop remains an immigrant-inspired medium that resists the old hierarchies and promotes opportunities to negotiate dissonant communities that feel out of tune with the normalized production of the nation-state. *Sonic multiculturalism*, like hip hop, unfolds in an organic process much like that of a hip hop cypher: a charged circular space where different MCs extemporaneously exchange verses in the construction of the mix. I contend that neither hip hop nor multiculturalism is dead, certainly not in Canada, and that both are concerned with the hopes and struggles of existence in a modern world that is becoming increasingly digitized, fragmented, and insular in its politics. More than any other musical genre today, hip hop is embraced by youth cultures that are interested in the form for its storytelling potential, its resistance, and the entertaining reprieve it offers from the daily grind. Hip hop is a conduit for enhancing cultural competence, and the fact that youth have embraced the medium for over forty years is an indication that there is value in learning how to incorporate hip hop pedagogies into our teaching; yes, even in CanLit. Hip hop remains an effective tool for political mobilization, despite how major corporations often appropriate Black culture as a commodity to sell to white kids in the suburbs.

Hip hop music might just be the ideal starting place for the Cultural Revolution. As Mark Anthony Neal writes in "Jazz, Hip-Hop, and Black Social Improvisation," "hip-hop provides powerful evidence of the ability of black youth to use their improvisatory musical practice(s) to also create and improvise opportunities in their social, political, and cultural lives."[98] Black youth (although hardly exclusively) continue to use hip hop to improvise meaning from the unmeaning status they have been assigned. Moreover, hip hop remains a wake-up call to continue to adapt and stay in touch with the times, lest we, as Shad warns, become out of touch. We need to speak Canada's truth, warts and all, however difficult, while making more space in the larger Canadian remix project.

K'naan, "Voices In My Head" and "Fatima"

K'naan's music, the primary focus of this chapter, uses hip hop and Somali culture as an imperative mix for social change. K'naan sees himself as a cultural translator since he has lived in both worlds and truly understands them: "I understand the discontent that comes from not having. But I also understand the anxiety that comes from wealth and convenience."[99] Hip hop incites cultural translation, teaching people about the struggles of others they might otherwise never consider, bringing marginalized voices more strongly into the citizenship and sociocultural mix. Describing himself as "something like Gil Scott-Heron" with the "bitterness in the killer the poet," K'naan remains resolute in his desire to tell his story as an inspiration to others who suffer on a daily basis.[100] While many of K'naan's lyrics are politically charged—from his depictions of the challenges of home/homeland and war in "My Old Home," to his songs of personal crisis such as in "Fatima" (*Troubadour*), which describes the true story of a girl he was incredibly close to named Fatima who was left behind in Somalia, and who was shot and killed only a few days after he left the country—his songs, for the most part, are not particularly dissonant, or sonically challenging, in terms of how they are produced. His music as produced lacks much of the militancy heard in groups like Public Enemy or Dead Prez, or in a rapper like Immortal Technique; rather, it is the pop structure, mixed with traditional Somali elements, that allows K'naan—with his mastery of form—to bring his message to a large audience. K'naan uses hip hop to challenge social norms, to provide critical interventions around citizenship and refugee rights, and to enact social change. And now, just like a waving flag, "then it goes back," I move to Compton's active citizenship through his sonic mixing of the past. For Compton, that means turning his reinventing wheels to the history of the Vancouver community he grew up in, pulling out, discovering, and spinning truths recovered from the crates of history.

Chapter 5

RECOVERY AND REMIX: WAYDE COMPTON'S *TURNTABLE POETICS*

"The future is always here in the past."

—AMIRI BARAKA, "Jazzmen: Diz & Sun Ra," 255

Listening: Kid Koala, "Moon River"♭

Thinking through technology and tradition in relation to the work of Kid Koala, Wayde Compton told me, "Kid Koala, he's . . . still a vinyl guy, a vinyl and turntables guy. It's all still there. So, talking

Kid Koala, "Moon River"

Liner Notes

♭ I've added several Kid Koala songs as well as the other tracks (cued in the margins) from this chapter to the Spotify playlist (https://open.spotify.com/playlist/0BidCMJ3oBP2drCY4gB6Jz). Make sure you watch the live performance of "Moon River," which is even more fun because Kid Koala is decked out in a full koala suit (the result of having lost a bet to a friend). See "Kid Koala, Moon River (Studio Version)," posted by Periscope, 22 September 2011, YouTube video, https://www.youtube.com/watch?v=Pp0U7SkYl2E; and "Kid Koala Performs Moon River," 8 July 2011, posted by Ankur Malhotra, YouTube video, https://www.youtube.com/watch?v=fjFi4MHO_go.

about tradition, he is working with the traditional tools that are old."[1] Kid Koala, born Eric San in 1974 in Vancouver, British Columbia, is a Canadian DJ, turntablist, musician, and author/illustrator, among other things, who is known for his incredible tactile manipulations on the turntables. His enigmatic style of turntablism mixes disparate samples together: everything from Charlie Brown television specials, old comedy sketch routines (including those that mock turntablism), people sneezing, and people reading a menu in Cantonese. His shows often include vaudeville-style performances with high levels of audience participation. I've been fortunate enough to see Kid Koala several times, including at a reunion show of alternative hip hop supergroup Deltron 3030, although my favourite show was his *Space Cadet* concert, which involved relaxing in an inflatable space pod with a set of headphones.

Kid Koala popularized a method of playing the turntable like a melodic instrument. This effect can be heard on his mix of "Moon River," where he creates and inserts an extended violin solo by playing long violin notes from the song's instrumental section at different pitches on three turntables, all live. As the story goes, Kid Koala's mom didn't understand how and why he was making his music, and so he asked her what her favourite song was and remixed it. Henry Mancini initially composed "Moon River" with lyrics by Johnny Mercer. The song received an Academy Award for Best Original Song for Audrey Hepburn's performance of the piece in the 1961 movie *Breakfast at Tiffany's*. It's been covered thousands of times, although Kid Koala's version is the most adventurous. Compton was enraptured by Koala's performance: "There were certain points where I was looking at it, saying, 'You can't do that. You can't do the thing I'm watching you do. It just can't be done. And yet you're doing it.'"[2] It is precisely Kid Koala's version of a 1961 easy-listening song—far removed from the context of hip hop and remix culture—that highlights how the past is a network for DJs to rework.

In this chapter, I examine recording machines and DJ/remix culture, and apply this background to examine the turntable poetics of Wayde Compton. Through his turntable poetics, Compton provides a unique perspective on Vancouver's historical (and current) Black community (Hogan's Alley). Working with/against traditions perceived as inauthentic and culturally ersatz, Compton's work reminds us that one's identity and citizenship in relation to a larger community is a project always to be remixed. By engaging with Compton's historical resonances, mashups, and remixes of Hogan's Alley we can recover Hogan's Alley as (*living*) metaphor and even—idealistically—imagine more inclusive notions of citizenship, multiculturalism, and community.

I. Spinning Towards the Future: Mechanical Reproduction and the Rise of the DJ

Sonic Anecdotes: From an Ear to Here

"Every ear shall here. Every eye shall sea"

—WAYDE COMPTON, "The Reinventing Wheel," *Performance Bond*, 106

The rise of mechanical production and reproduction has engaged foundational scholars like Theodor Adorno, Walter Benjamin, and Marshall McLuhan, as well as more contemporary scholars like Jonathan Sterne, Lisa Gitelman, Alexander G. Weheliye, and Paul D. Miller (DJ Spooky), to consider how new "audiovisual technologies—the phonograph, film, radio, and eventually television—presented an opportunity to reconsider the relationship between technological and cultural production," and to explore how "the seemingly anti-human world of machines produces the modern political subject, extends the human body, and splits sounds from their sources, especially the human voice."[3] For instance, the telephone liberated the individual and allowed for the transmission of the human voice over long distances, changing the very nature of how we communicate. Put succinctly, our listening practices are informed by the very technologies that

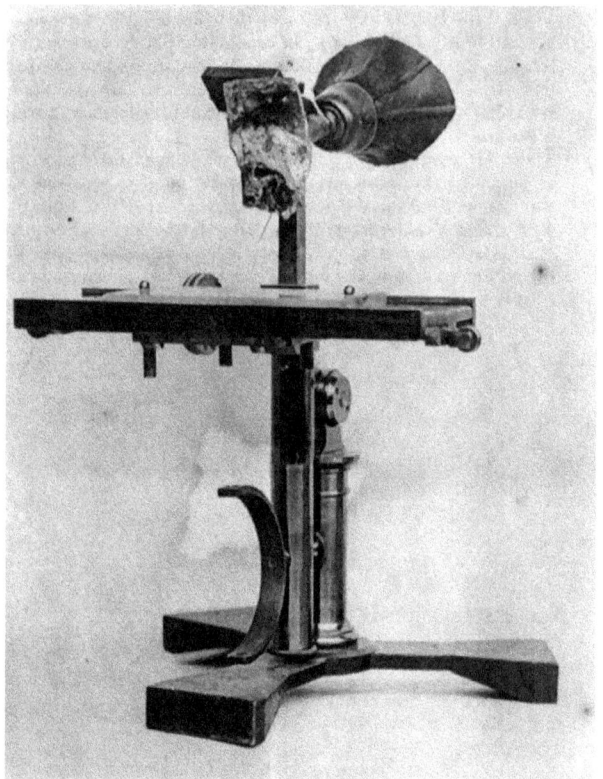

Figure 5.1 Bell and Blake's ear phonautograph. Source: Library of Congress, manuscript division, Alexander Graham Bell family papers at the Library of Congress.

frame them and make certain kinds of listening possible in the first place. There remains prescient truth in Marshall McLuhan's aphorism "the medium is the message" (or "massage" or "mass age"), particularly in the notion that today's virtual media can be an adequate substitute for actuality. Today's digital practices, including sampling and mashup, merge the past with the present, but these devices, even when digital, remain framed, as Lingold, Mueller, and Trettien state, "by the human body and the ways it listens."[4]

The turntable is itself a reinvention of an older incarnation. It could be argued that Alexander Graham Bell's 1874 ear phonautograph (see figure 5.1), or sound writer, which used an actual human ear and part of the skull of a dead man obtained by Bell's associate, Dr. Blake, was intentionally about repetition as simulacrum. The sound waves coming into the eardrum were traced on smoked glass by means of a bristle brush, as determined by the ossicles (a group of three small bones in the human ear). The machine was designed with the hope of educating the deaf to replicate the speech of others, which for Bell was, as sound and media theorist Jonathan Sterne states, "about the eradication of linguistic difference."[5] Perhaps ironically then, deafness marks the beginning of sound reproduction, yet sound reproduction has always been concerned with a reproduction, or a repetition, of the human, especially given that Bell's phonautograph used a human ear.[6]

In 1877, Thomas Edison invented the phonograph, which would become the model for the gramophone and ultimately the turntable. The phonograph played sound from wavy lines scratched, engraved, or grooved onto a rotating cylinder or disc. As the cylinder or disc rotated, a stylus or needle traced the wavy lines and vibrated to reproduce the recorded sound waves. In 1887 Emile Berliner patented the gramophone, a device that implied a blend between speech and writing. With the gramophone came sound recordings of music, and by 1900 there were some 5,000 advertised choices of records one could purchase; by 1930, 60 percent of homes had a radio. Just as book publishing changed the way people thought about and read books (certainly changing their accessibility), so too did the recording industry alter our approach to music and sound—from physical to digital, from iPods to AirPods to online streaming.

The rise of the DJ fits within the desire of contemporary masses to bring things closer. As Compton writes in "The Reinventing Wheel," "the author was born in 1972," a direct reference to the invention of the Technics 1200 turntable, the primary signifier of hip hop and remix culture.[7] Technology changes culture. The invention of the Technics SL-1200 series of turntables, manufactured from October 1972 until 2010 (and then relaunched in 2016) by Matsushita (then Panasonic), is what made DJ culture largely possible in the first place, even though the Technics 1200 was never intended to be repurposed as a musical instrument, for, as Charles Mudede writes,

"To replay a record with your hands is different from playing an instrument with your hands... The turntable is always wrenched out of sleep by the hand that wants to loop a break or to scratch a phrase."[8] The Technics SL-1200 (in hip hop, often referred to as the "Tec 12," the "Wheels of Steel," or the "Ones & Twos") had a direct-drive high-torque motor design, which initially made it suitable for cueing and starting tracks on the radio, although young DJs in New York would soon realize how much they could do with a turntable and some records.

For instance, listen to a landmark work like DJ Shadow's 1996 *Endtroducing*, which is renowned for being entirely composed of sampled content and was created with two turntables and a sampler.♭ In *Shades of Blue*, Madlib infuses old jazz records from the Blue Note catalogue with hip hop production, cuts, and new contexts, translating original pieces into new creations. Old music continues to create new music. This was happening long before hip hop, but it's certainly quite prevalent in hip hop music. For example, Melvin Bliss's 1973 45 rpm B-side "Synthetic Substitution" provided the backbone for hundreds of hip hop classics throughout the 1980s and 1990s.♯ For all the newness of hip hop, it only really exists because it adheres to the past. Over time, various technological innovations changed the listening experience to a digital one—a medium people could access and share right from their computers or mobile devices. For the most part, the digital format provides the most democratic possibilities for both remix and music sharing.

For Kid Koala or Wayde Compton, the past is a living network to recover and remix: new acoustic spaces emerge out of the complex synthesis/antithesis of the Black electronic tradition, recorded history, and a variety of cultural spaces. Often, but not always, criminality for sampling is censorship at its most fierce, problematic, classist, and often racist, given that sampling laws have historically marginalized

Margin note: DJ Shadow, The Avalanches, Madlib, and Melvin Bliss

---

♭ Also see The Avalanches, *Since I Left You*, which is reportedly comprised of some 3,500-vinyl samples (Pytlik, "The Avalanches"). "Frontier Psychologist" can be heard on the chapter 5 playlist.

♯ Check it out!: http://www.whosampled.com/Melvin-Bliss/Synthetic-Substitution

youth the most.[b] Hip hop music is a gestalt of samples and found elements. Perhaps the greatest misnomer about DJs is that they want to destroy traditions. Rather, the DJ is often one of the most studious students of musical history and tradition. A DJ's ear—like Bell's phonautograph—is glued to the past.

The Rise of the DJ

> "We used to play a lot of Fela Kuti in the early days of hip-hop. In my DJ sets I'll jump off into rock, salsa, African. I like to play some crazy stuff and see the vibrations of the people."
>
> —AFRIKA BAMBAATAA quoted in Richards, *The Guardian*

The DJ is a person who notices sounds and goes into the archive to recover them. Arguably, we are in the era of everything "re" (from readymade to remix) as Martha Buskirk, Amelia Jones, and Caroline A. Jones contend in their essay "The Year in 'Re-'" in *Slant* magazine. They define remix as "taking parts of existing musical tracks (or by extension, visual or performance material) and cutting them together to create new material."[9] In his essay "Performing Zora: Critical Ethnography, Digital Sound, and Not Forgetting," Myron M. Beasley looks at the work of Zora Neale Hurston as a pioneer of sound studies for her recordings of folk songs and traditions, many of which she sang herself. Hearing a DJ mix Hurston's voice—

---

[b] It's beyond the scope of this chapter to outline the various legal battles over sampling, but the reader might like to examine some well-known cases, such as *De La Soul vs. The Turtles* and *Vanilla Ice vs. Queen*. A more current example is Twin Sisters' "Meet the Frownies" being sampled in Kendrick Lamar's "The Recipe." A James Brown sample might become unrecognizable in the pastiche of a Public Enemy track containing some eighty different samples. ("Planet Rock" is too incredible to not add to the playlist, you dig!)

"Halimuhfack"♭—into a mix that included Nina Simone, Maya Angelou, Langston Hughes, among others, at the Red Rooster in Harlem gave Beasley pause: "Hurston's track halted the flow. The gritty, dusty, scratchy quality transported the listener to another time, to another place. The pastiche of sounds curated by the DJ was a 'remix' for sure. The audio palimpsest—layering a mix-match of music weaving literature, ethnography, biography, and history—the techno-digital moves of the DJ announced the confluence of digital sound and humanistic inquiry."[10] Hurston's digitized voice haunts the listener and shows us that a vast archive of recordings (many not yet digitized for accessibility) are ready to be recovered by DJs, students, and scholars.

<small>Grand Wizard Theodore</small>

Fundamentally, a DJ (a disc jockey) is a person who plays recorded music for an audience. This can be as basic as putting on records to create a musical mix, or it can involve much more complex forms of turntablism, as turntable artists (turntablists) play records, beat match, scratch, beat juggle, among other techniques, while using the needle like a plectrum to produce sounds that are unique, yet not reproduced, turning the turntable into a live instrument on which improvisation is possible.[11] The term "disc jockey" ("disc" referring to phonograph records, not CDs, and "jockey" to an operator of a machine) was coined by American radio commentator Walter Winchell back in 1935 to describe the first star DJ, radio announcer Martin Block. Since then, the term "DJ," along with its surrounding culture, has continued to evolve alongside musical innovations, many of which came at the hands of hip hop DJs. For example, in 1975, Grand Wizard Theodore invented scratching by accident. Playing his music loud in his room while his mother was trying to talk to him downstairs, Theodore placed his hand on the record so he could hear his mother speaking, and, as she spoke, he moved the record back and forth to the rhythm of his mother's words. Thus, the art of scratching

---

♭ If you have never heard Hurston sing, stop what you are doing and prepare to be amazed. "Zora Neale Hurston '28 Sings: 'Halihmuhfack,'" YouTube Video, 1:00, January 18, 2017 (1939), https://www.youtube.com/watch?v=Ut0xmfgcK3w.

was born. Innovation is often a result of chance, such as Louis Armstrong's impromptu scatting in "Heebie Jeebies" (the first scat caught on a recording), which was the result of a mistake. As the legend goes, Armstrong's lyric sheet fell while he was recording, so he began to scat/improvise. More important than whether either story is verifiable is how these apocryphal narratives attest to the creative spirit of young Black musicians who changed the template for how we understand creative music making.

Louis Armstrong

The most significant DJ is Jamaican-born American DJ Kool Herc, who developed the blueprint for hip hop music in the early 1970s in The Bronx. Herc focused on the short, heavily percussive part in a track, referred to as the "break," and isolated it, going back and forth between two turntables (cueing the same record on a second turntable while the first was playing) in order to sustain the music in a loop so that breakers could dance longer, which in turn led to more inventive dance moves. These early dance parties are the stuff of legend, and while the MC (master of ceremonies) is the central figure in popular hip hop music today, it was the DJ, at hip hop's inception, who was the prime signifier of the music, creating community with little more than two turntables and some records. Early DJs mixed disco with hard funk, rock, and Latin percussion, among other elements; pan-Africanist and Afrofuturist DJ Afrika Bambaataa describes how he likes "to play some crazy stuff and see the vibrations of the people." Additionally, Herc drew from his own Jamaican background of "toasting," punctuating his mixes by shouting out various phrases to keep the party going, such as "To the beat, y'all!" and "You don't stop!" Herc remains a cultural icon, having inspired everyone from DJs like Bambaataa and Grandmaster Flash to hip hop's first rappers, who drew on his style of toasting. Herc was instrumental to our conception of the DJ's role. It is said that he left the hip hop scene after being stabbed one night while trying to intervene in a fight. Playing the role of hip hop's tragic hero, by 1980 Herc had stopped DJing and was working in a record shop in The Bronx. For a while in the mid-eighties he was addicted to crack cocaine. Despite these struggles, Herc used his wheels to set history

Grandmaster Flash

in motion—DJ culture had taken its first steps towards becoming a respected art form.♭

Turntablism developed out of a long tradition of hip hop, reggae, disco, radio DJs, and recording innovations, as the possibilities of vinyl manipulation became gradually apparent. This is nothing new, although it is certainly the unintended outcome of the turntable. As Zora Neale Hurston writes in her "Characteristics of Negro Expression," "what we really mean by originality is the modification of ideas."[12] Alexander Weheliye contends that even repetition with difference may involve be more difference than repetition: "difference will, indeed, be different in each of its incarnations . . . not repetition with a difference so much as repetition of difference, wherein the original/copy vanishes" so that only the *sui generis* of the original remains.[13] Sampling, as we will see in Compton's poetry, helps provide the power of focus and recontextualization. Repetition as a cultural tactic, however, is often viewed negatively by cultural theorists as a by-product of capitalism, rather than perceived as part of Black diasporic tradition and innovation.

Social theorist Jacques Attali argues that repetition is primarily considered a manifestation of mass culture, characteristic of the age of sound reproduction.[14] Early in his career, Adorno described the pre-swing jazz "break" as nothing other than a disguised cadence: "The cult of the machine which is represented by unabating jazz beats involves a self-renunciation that cannot take root in the form of a fluctuating uneasiness somewhere in the personality of the obedient."[15] By contrast, Paul Anderson argues that Paul Gilroy's concept of repetition in *The Black Atlantic* provides a pointed countertype to Adorno's antipopulist modernism, with "its thin hope that the elite and oppositional 'autonomous work of art' might fuel the critical utopian imagination in the battle against the politically and aesthetically futile commodity pleasures of mass culture entertainments."[16]

♭ The turntables are often referred to as the wheels of steel. On the playlist you can listen to Grandmaster Flash's breakthrough "The Adventures of Grandmaster Flash on the Wheels of Steel," released in 1981, and which over the course of seven minutes displays Flash's virtuosic turntable skills.

Wayde Compton defends repetition as a Black ontological priority in the creation of newness: "Repetition whether in the form of ancestor worship or the poem-histories of the *griot*, informs black ontologies more than does the Europeanist drive for perpetual innovation, with its concomitant disavowals of the past."[17] Taking up these ontological priorities of repetition, Compton manipulates words to create a disruptive practice of interpretation.

Sampling is a new way of doing something that has been with us for a long time—creating meaning with found objects. Hip hop groups and DJs use samples as tactics that create space, as old-school rap group Stetsasonic states: "You see, you misunderstood / A sample is just a tactic, / A portion of my method, a tool." Sampling, like quotation, provides diacritical difference, *détournement*, carnival, wildstyle, and parade, and, as Paul D. Miller (DJ Spooky) suggests, it allows "people to replay their own memories of the sounds and situations of their lives ... sampling is dematerialized sculpture."[18] The DJ, much like the scholar, is a cultural archivist. DJs collect thousands of pieces of recorded material to construct a present from the vast archive of recorded material. As Sterne attests, "Countless hip hop producers, DJs, and audio collage artists have claimed that the use of prerecorded material to make new sound art is a self-consciously political and historiographic project."[19] I would say this is hardly a claim—it is a fact. Various DJs, producers, and archivists use recorded material in inventive ways that show they are highly aware of the improvised nature of history and cultural practice. DJ culture insinuates that nothing, especially music, is fixed: the whole world is manipulatable. Ralph Ellison, who was able to read T.S. Eliot's 1922 poem *The Waste Land* and hear jazz, understood how music is largely about modulation. This is a central tenet of this book: remix is an act of identity and citizenship, since both, like a sound recording, are mutable.

The mutability of a DJ performance provides a valid enactment against the notion of fixity. A Latin etymology of the word person is "being of sound." Those who claim that the DJ removes the human from the music-making process would have a hard time validating their claim if they were at a show where hundreds of people were dancing to a live mix. Of course, laptop DJs often leave something to

margin note: Stetsasonic

be desired, such as a more tactile approach to *musicking*. A valuable way to assess a DJ's performance would be to focus on how it engages with the human, since improvisation, from blues to DJing, remains a central component of how music is received. As creative artist and innovator Bob Ostertag writes,

> So one of the things that improvisation has come to mean in the context of highly technological performance is that improvisation is the last claim to the legitimate presence of a human in the performance of music. This is what I think: DJs are actually, the reason we have a DJ, why don't we just have iPod mixes at all these places where fundamentally what they're doing is playing back previously recorded music? The DJ's claim to a legitimate role in the whole ordeal is that he or she is improvising, so without the claim of improvising there'd be no reason to have a human involved in the process at all.[20]

Certainly, you can have programmed machines create music without a human presence, but Ostertag's point that improvisation in DJing maintains the human is germane. Glenn Gould quit performing live music in 1964 and the Beatles did the same thing in 1966, both feeling that the concert had become a place where people go to remember a performance (a recording) rather than experience a new sound event. Both Gould and the Beatles were interested in the possibilities that technology could provide for their music, which is why I contend that a well-crafted and improvised DJ performance is a place we go to listen to our memories become fractured, since life, identity, and our memories are unstable and changing. The new listener is a DJ, and there is much to be said about the democratic possibilities that configurable music affords a culture that is re-examining the past to conceive of a more participatory future.

II. "The Changing Same"

DJing Is Writing

> "DJ-ing is writing, writing is DJ-ing. Writing is music, I cannot explain this any other way. Take Nietzsche, for instance, whose brilliant texts are almost musical. Obviously, you feel the rhythm inside a great poet's stanzas, but it's there within the great philosopher's paragraphs as well."
>
> —DJ SPOOKY, *Rhythm Science*, 57

Listen to Thelonious Monk's *Underground*, and then flip the script and hear Dostoevsky's *Notes from Underground*. Then read Ellison, who was reading Dostoevsky, who likely was reading Dante, and read Amiri Baraka's *Systems of Dante's Hell*, as he was probably reading Richard Wright's *The Man Who Lived Underground*, along with the other three. The changing same, flipped again, as Brand's Yasmine in *Ossuaries* listens to Monk in an underground space. To reiterate, Black music and literature retain traditional practices while reflecting the shifting changes of a given era. Amiri Baraka called this "unmoved mover" of Black cultural practices and resistance, "The Changing Same." As DJ Spooky declares, "DJ-ing is writing, writing is DJ-ing." The word phonograph acknowledges this juncture in its very name: *phone*, in Greek, denotes sound and voice, and *graph* signifies writing. Thus, we can think of a phonograph and later machines like the turntable or a computer as sound writers—essentially: inscription is at the root of any kind of writing.

Wayde Compton remixes various traditions—oral and written, sonic and visual, African and European, Black and white, local and global, Canadian and American, and Indigenous—in order to provide more nuanced critiques of power, identity, and history. I don't think Compton rejects the notion of the author; for example, the only capitals in the opening poem of *Performance Bond*, "Declaration of the Halfrican Nation" are the author's "I." Nevertheless, given the constant mixing and hip hop structural metaphors in *Performance Bond*, we can think about how the work is intertextual, a postmodern function that Linda Hutcheon argues rejects the role of the author, which she then says functions a little differently in her *A Theory of Parody*, noting how parody always features an author actively encoding a text as an imitation with critical difference. I think Compton engages both author functions, using parody/pastiche as diacritical difference, while maintaining traditional voices and communities, but always through dialogic engagement. Hence, Compton continually contests how an image or sound signifies in his work, often through split or reappropriated representations, bonding as in one poem the word "Afro" to "Saxon," writing: "own rose-coloured lenses: black roses. / own a cat named Dialectic: mirror smoked grey."[21] Like a vessel/DJ, Compton challenges existing discourses and introduces neglected histories (such as the Black community of Hogan's Alley) and connects these various voices together. In an email conversation, he told me that he borrows "from the history of turntablism to create poetry in the way that early hip hop deejays began to create music out of a medium that was not meant to create music, but rather to merely be a vessel for it."[22] As a vessel for the many voices, across the diaspora, that appear in *Performance Bond*, he confronts the commodification of Black culture, improvising his own conception of Blackness.

Compton told me that improvising Blackness is about his "relationship to the tradition . . . to race, racism, racial law, black solidarity and diaspora, and the movements that come out of that . . . That's all improvisational. And I think it's why I've gravitated toward forms that are more experimental or forms that are probing possibilities."[23] Blackness for Compton is not an *a priori* meaning, but rather a valuable way to conceive of identity, as well as interrogate "black" as a politically and culturally constructed category. In his article "The Lost Tribe of a Lost Tribe: Black British Columbia and the Poetics of Space," Peter Hudson contends that Compton's "Afroperipheralism," along with his "sense of isolation and alienation" in British Columbia, allows his work to challenge "any sense of blackness as a known shape, an *a priori* entity, whose main goal is to police its own limits and the terms of its membership."[24] By challenging a narrow set of perceived traditions, but in thinking of traditions as circular, like historical waves washing over the past, present, and future, in relation to Kamau Brathwaite's *tidalectics,* Compton works to "find non-clichéd ways to describe what a lot of people call experimental, or avant-garde... work that doesn't just happily receive and then carry on."[25]

Kamau Brathwaite uses the term *tidalectics,* a theory counter to Hegel's dialectics, for an Africanist model for thinking about history. Discussing *tidalectics* in an interview with Nathaniel Mackey, Brathwaite describes how we can see history as cyclical: "In other words, instead of the notion of one-two-three Hegelian, I am now more interested in the movement of backwards and forwards as a kind of cyclic, I suppose, motion, rather than linear."[26] Hence, we are part of an ongoing continuum full of ruptures, repetitions, everyday vagaries, and (most productively) constant change that can potentially contribute to an increasingly freer society.

I first encountered the term *tidalectic* in reading Compton's engagement with Braithwaite's useful neologism. Compton told me that Braithwaite is the most important writer for him: "Braithwaite is just vitally important to me... His writing is the biggest influence on my writing, and my thinking. I'm attracted to formal innovation, and experimentation, and concept, and writing that tries to go to the root of what it's doing and, in a lot of ways, start all over again every time you're creating something."[27] Compton's formal innovations are inspired by techniques of the DJ. In the poem "DJ," from Compton's first poetry collection, *49th Parallel Psalm,* the short enjambed lines recall a DJ scratching: "conduit of the herd / shepherd of the unheard / hands on vinyl ... scratches 'bring that beat back' / catches / the loop on the off / beat matches / that per minute mix like magic."[28] The book, which is often a prosthesis for the various human senses, is replaced with the prosthesis of the phantom limb: the turntable. In fact, the turntable, or the vinyl record, is very much like the book in that it needs a reader or listener to make it sound and in that it distresses over time.

The poem "DJ" is itself a flip, a reverse, a mirror image of the earlier poem "JD" (also from *Psalm*), which looks at James Douglas, first governor of British Columbia, as mixed-race ("*father Scottish, mother from British Guyana*") and as passing as white. Compton asks: "O James Douglas, / did you ever see yourself / in us? / did you ever stop / in your war versus the wilderness / and think / *we*?"[29] The poem mixes Black and white identifications as the crossfader blends "shuffling passports," a balancing act too much for nineteenth-century Douglas, who encouraged Black folk to come to British Columbia from California but then withdrew his support when they arrived. A few poems later, Compton inverts the title "JD" as "DJ," inviting the reader into the mix as a co-performer of the poem. As DJ/archivist/griot/trickster, Compton digs into the crates of the past and finds that there are unlimited samples/stories to be played and remixed, writing/scratching: "more singles in the crates than scrolls in the ancient library / of Alexandria."[30] Dropping the stylus on the past—historical revision at the crossroads/crossfader—resonates in the present, as DJing is an apt metaphor for (re)writing.

While I've written about how Compton's use of repetition challenges Adorno's antipopulist rhetoric, I also think Compton participates in the aesthetic criteria by which Theodor Adorno judges a conception: "the soundness of a conception can be judged by whether it causes one quotation to summon another."[31] Loosely drawing divergent traditions together is the act of the DJ, as well as the reality of those who belong to multiple traditions and cultures and engage with numerous canons. Poetry itself can be thought of as a mix; certainly, this is how William Carlos Williams thought of poetry, suggesting that a poem "is a small (or large) machine made of words."[32] Like a well-made machine there is no part in a good poem that is redundant, as each sounding in Compton's work is an act of reverb/recall.

Compton's splitting of traditions, allowing multiple voices/samples to be heard, is an act, as it functions in Brathwaite's writing, of versifying, which Compton explains to Nigel Thomas is an intentionally disruptive force: "It forces a slower reading, and suggests multiple meanings, and asks for full reader participation."[33] Compton's turntable poetics, such as in his poem "The Commodore" (*49th Parallel Psalm*) about a paddle steamer that transported British Columbia's first Black settlers from San Francisco to Victoria during the Fraser

Canyon Gold Rush, are about transformation and intersection, as the poem provides many voices in short bursts, like quick samples, asking: "I wonder how / our blues will rhyme with Vancouver."[34] There is no simple transportation of culture: in this case African American histories moved onto Vancouver soil. Music (and the blues), like writing, crosses borders, as Compton reminds us that culture—and poetry—is always in process and open to remix. Since Compton's own "family history is fractured, impure" ("The Reinventing Wheel"), his consummate blurring of written, sonic, and oral traditions allows him to create new spaces and entry points into "A spiral lineage" that changes over time, yet remains the same.[35]

History as Remix

In his poem "The Reinventing Wheel," Wayde Compton samples Ziggy Marley's words from "Tomorrow People,"[♭] writing: "My family history is fractured, impure, / history imported with deft warp and weft. / You don't know your past, you don't know your future. / History imperative."[36] The alliterative "warp and weft" refers to weaving—the weft (yarn carried by the shuttle) is drawn through the warp (lengthwise yarn)—which is a salient metaphor for how Compton spins and weaves histories together. Compton's interwoven approach to history lends an immediacy to the past that makes it active, as Compton acknowledges that history, especially Black Canadian history, is often "fractured." Black Canadian history as remembering—even if that history is fractured and then run through samplers and turntables—is a creative act that urgently seeks innovative ways to remember and remix the past in a way that occasions new forms of knowledge production in Canada.

Ziggy Marley

Compton told me that white writers in Canada often infuriate him since they deem the past as an absolute, oppressive, or static event

---

♭ Or, perhaps he samples Public Enemy, since a vocal clip in the opening of *Fear of a Black Planet* (1990) contains the same phrase.

to be destroyed in order to conceive of the future, often ignoring that marginalized writers often need/want tradition:

> So you look at writers in this country, conceptual writers, and conceptual poets right now. To me white writers drive me mad because they can't see around themselves so often, and they don't recognize that they're an ethnic group. One of the issues of their ethnicity is that their people took over the world, so they tend to think that the stuff they're doing is the universal. So whatever they're doing which is their specific business they proclaim as universal movements. Conceptual poetry, they call it, and it's really just white folks' concerns when they become poets. And white folk's concerns are to kill their parents. They are punk rockers at heart. Counterculture is their core. And that doesn't work for us. That doesn't work for us at all. We don't want to kill our parents. Because our parents barely survived and they carry the means of our liberation in their everyday business. So that conceptual stuff doesn't work for us because it wants to destroy tradition.[37]

Hence, Compton "perpetually beat juggl[es] history and ethnicity" to respond to "the brokenness [of] the tradition."[38] He continues, "We have archived ourselves," as Black history becomes an act of echo/feedback/repetition that survives in the "intractable track / of the word."[39] Compton hears sonic Black traditions from the ancients to Jimi Hendrix as he plugs himself into his mixer: "I / am plugged into my mixer, lashed, with wax / stopping my ears. Tracking / into Tradition ... I am plugged into the tradition."[40] So, while conceptual poetry often uses appropriation to create a "new" work focused on the concept rather than the final product, Compton's appropriations (or, better, samplings) are invested in the creation/memory of histories that mesh to recover the past.[41] For Compton, liberation is largely directed towards the neglected and rooted/rerouted history of Black British Columbia.

In his work *Bluesprint: Black British Columbian Literature and Orature*, which was the first literary anthology of its kind to archive BC's Black communities, Compton describes how "black pioneers had come to Canada not only for economic relief, but to fulfill their dreams of full citizenship and equality under British law, which was—on paper, at least—non discriminatory."[42] The stories in *Bluesprint* document that in BC, Black people encountered segregation, racism, and political corruption "that accounted for such things as the spurious cancellation of black ballots in an election."[43] The notion of Canaan/Canada as a site of magical transformation that erased the trials of the past proved painfully untrue for those early settlers who arrived with the hopes of full citizenship. Thus, after the American Civil War, and as the United States relaxed some of its citizenship laws, and even later in the 1960s when Hogan's Alley was destroyed for an urban renewal project, what Compton refers to as "Negro removal," many of the original San Francisco Blacks returned to the United States, while others stayed or moved elsewhere in British Columbia, or spread among other regions of Canada.[44] As Compton describes, "B.C.'s black history has been one of continued exodus, immigration, settlement, exploration, miscegenation, communitarianism, integration, segregation, agitation, uprooting and re-rooting and re-routing."[45] Travel and exodus are essential parts of Canada's immigrant history, and we can think of Compton's scratching—his versifying—as lines of ruptured movement that inscribe over written histories that attempt to erase (white/out) Black histories.

Peter Hudson notes that the first baby born in BC was of mixed race, even though the papers documented the baby as white: "There is no memory of Vancouver before 1873. In that year, according to the late journalist Alan Morley, the city's first white baby was born ... In the Vancouver City Archives, a scratched microfiche preserving the typewritten notes of Major Matthews, the city's first archivist, hold this record. "FIRST WHITE CHILD WAS BLACK" ... The Child was born to a mixed couple and was light enough to pass ... History is a funny thing."[46] "The history of BC is the history of whiteness," as Compton writes in the poem "Performance Bond."[47] Like the first governor of British Columbia, James Douglas, who was of mixed-race ancestry but passed as white his entire life, and the "scratched" microfiche that screams out BC's own mixed history, Compton's "JD" sounds a potent reminder that history itself (like

JD's ancestry) is always mixed. Although Indigenous people were in BC tens of thousands of years before Europeans arrived, like Black history in BC, Indigenous history has been reduced to footnotes by some white scholars. The issues of citizenship, settler and Indigenous relations, identity, white/black/mixed-race, and Canadian and American borders are much more complex once you realize that BC is a site of diasporic, transnational, and Indigenous identifications. As the monoliths and institutions of Vancouver's Black history are glossed over, or demolished as in the case of Hogan's Alley, Indigenous and diasporic histories and spaces become increasingly important.

To ignore these histories is an act of condemnation to the hell of non-history and non-citizenship: "Those who have no history are doomed."[48] The issue of citizenship, identity, white/black/mixed-race, and Canadian and American borders is much more complex once you realize that BC's—and Canada's—"geo-heterodoxy" (Iton) was, and is, a site of diasporic and transnational identifications. As the monoliths and institutions of Vancouver's Black history are glossed over, or demolished, diasporic spaces become increasingly important, particularly in the mixed-race identities Compton circumspectly explores on the outer peripheries of Vancouver's cultural geography.

Jimi Hendrix

The cadences of jazz and hip hop in *Performance Bond* function as a type of historical revisionism and diasporic consciousness, as well as a soundtracking of historical record. Vancouver's own musical history has its share of cross-cultural musical mavericks who, for a period, made the Downtown Eastside (what would be classified as Hogan's Alley) in Vancouver their home. The closely knit Black community of Hogan's Alley was a result of the community's proximity to the train stations, since sleeping car porters were predominantly Black men.[49] All the major vaudeville acts passed through Vancouver as circuits moved by train. Furthermore, the musical scene in Hogan's Alley, which included many local acts, like the Crump Twins, prefigured what we now refer to as "Hollywood North," and featured some of the biggest names in music, who would pass through to perform in the bars there, including Sammy Davis Jr., Ella Fitzgerald, Count Basie, Louis Armstrong, and Duke Ellington.[50] For a time, a number of cross-cultural musical mavericks, such as Jelly

Roll Morton and Jimi Hendrix, even made Vancouver's Downtown Eastside their home. At the Patricia Hotel, jazz legend Jelly Roll Morton joined the house band and played there between 1919 and 1921. Nora Hendrix, a former vaudeville dancer and the paternal grandmother of Jimi Hendrix, immigrated to Vancouver in 1911 and helped found the church in Hogan's Alley. Jimi Hendrix would often visit Vancouver and even lived there during the winter of 1962–63, practising and often playing in nightclubs.[51] Today, in Vancouver's Downtown Eastside, there is a shrine dedicated to Jimi Hendrix. Jelly Roll Morton and Jimi Hendrix deserve honorary Canuck status, despite their American origins; vitally, both musicians defied the negative status of their mixed-race identities and often skillfully passed between white and Black worlds, but nevertheless remained semiotically Black. Morton was born to creole (mixed-race) parents in New Orleans in 1890, and Hendrix's ancestry included African American, Irish, and Cherokee. These mixed-race histories challenge the spurious notion of racial purity as a marker of citizenship since it is impossible to deny the musical prowess and humanity of Morton or Hendrix. Like British Columbia's own history of flux, both musicians represent a diasporic crossing of unbound possibility.

Jelly Roll Morton

Compton's "Declaration of the Halfrican Nation," the poem that opens *Performance Bond*, asks, "is a black / rose natural? is it indigenous to this / coast? my grammar teacher said a semi- / colon is just a gutless colon."[52] The enjambment recalls scratching, but most central to the form is that the split words animate a divided consciousness battling against a racist historical impetus that attempts to racially codify people, and expects, "one drop rules aside," mixed-race people to identify as Black, or, if they can, pass as white.[53] Compton complicates such reductive readings of race by asking his "fellow mixed sisters and brothers [to] mount / an offensive for our state."[54] Compton further interrogates race by inflating the heterogeneity of culture as a disease itself that often makes race appear as forged and culturally conflated, describing "black hippies," "black punk rockers," and "black goths with white masks *literally*" who obscure definitions of Blackness.[55] By describing mixed-race as "Halfrican," and by turning the poem into a nationalist manifesto of sorts, Compton resists, "Like a motherless child" (traditional spiritual), a history that feels like it "got [him] / by the throat."[56] In "Declaration," as elsewhere in *Performance Bond*, Compton takes cultural assumptions and remixes them to recall what is lost and what is excluded under such practices. I read Compton's work as multicultural, as culture always involves a previous acculturation, and his term "Halfrican" challenges racial epithets by using his own agency to self-identify. The term "Halfrican" is, as Compton describes in an essay written some years after his twenty-four-year-old self in "Halfrican," "facetious, a satirical tonic for the problem of a disunified identity."[57] The poem contests monoracial identity even while paradoxically desiring a stable identity. The poem powerfully ends by desiring its own declarative history of value for those who belong between categories, at least within language: "I know more than enough who've ex- / pressed an interest in dying on the wire just for the victory / of being an agreed upon noun."[58] In longing for an established racial identity (at least an identifier with which to refer to himself) while obscuring the fallacious languages of mixed-race nouns, Compton enacts a history—like Ellison's Invisible Man—from below.

While Compton's *Performance Bond* most explicitly concerns the history of BC, it does so within the *tidalectic* nexus that considers and welcomes the larger diaspora of geopolitical thinking across time and borders/continents. As Joanne Leow writes in her article, "Mis-Mappings and Mis-Duplications: Interdiscursivity and the Poetry of Wayde Compton," Compton's poetics enact "a radical re-appropriation of the intertext of the Black Atlantic, which also situates the experience of British Columbia in a greater historical context of global mixtures and movements, and challenges the imagined isolation of the province."[59] In effect, Compton's diasporic writing connects the past and present together to engage in a fluid transnational approach to both history and identity. "If the recent past," as Ashok Mathur writes, "is a palimpsest, partially erased but readable in its remnants, then we cannot help but view the identity movements of the nineties—full of bombast and righteousness as well as acute criticality and political awareness—as historically significant and omnipresent."[60] Compton's *Performance Bond*, written in 2004—certainly informed by the identity movements of the nineties, as well as the DJ culture of that period—confronts and challenges the globalization of culture through Black diasporic practices. By turning history into an unstable sonic frequency, Compton shows how it is vital to remember the past to build the foundations for a more sustainable future.

Schizophonophilia and Mixed-Race

> "in African music there are always two rhythms going on."
>
> —JOHN MILLER CHERNOFF, *African Rhythm and African Sensibility*, 42

> "James Brown never said, 'Say it loud, / I'm mixed-race in a satellite of the U.S. and proud.'"
>
> —WAYDE COMPTON, "The Reinventing Wheel," 106

James Brown

Chernoff's essential work on African drumming, *African Rhythm and African Sensibility*, outlines how African polymetric music employs multiple rhythms that compete for our attention. As soon as we seize one rhythm, we lose track and hear another. The goal of the listener is to grasp many rhythms working together while hearing each rhythm as individually distinct.♭ African drumming tells us something about the DJ mix, as well as the mix of mixed-race identity, since in both instances competing rhythms (or epistemologies) vie for authenticity. Authenticity—as an

---

♭ While there are several African artists I could include on the playlist for this chapter, I've chosen Nigerian percussion master Babatunde Olatunji, as he was a major influence on popular music and worked with artists like Carlos Santana and Mickey Hart of the Grateful Dead. He was particularly popular during the Black Arts Movement of the sixties and seventies.

abstract concept—exists in the fragmentation and plurality of things, and certainly it does so within Compton's own connection between turntable poetry and his mixed-race identity. In his essay "Turntable Poetry, Mixed-Race, and Schizophonophilia," Compton defines "schizophonophilia" as the "love of audio interplay, the pleasure of critical disruptions to natural audition, the counter-hegemonic affirmation that can be achieved through acoustic intervention."[61] Compton's audio disruption is particularly relevant in a context where race and mixed-race are explicitly addressed.

In 2010, in Vancouver, I saw Compton cast his poetry from *Performance Bond* in *tidalectical* relation to other works that deal with notions of hybridity, DJ culture, and Canadian citizenship, emulated via the music's own polyphonic and hybridized layering of sound and thematic. This performance involved a sampler and three turntables: the sampler played a vocal sample of Compton reading from his poem "The Reinventing Wheel," while the entire performance was cued to various electro and hip hop beats with the aid of co-performer and turntablist Jason de Couto. The performance included an out-of-print vinyl of *Alex Haley Tells the Story of His Search for Roots* on one turntable, which was followed directly on another turntable by an excerpt from Margaret Atwood's *The Journals of Susanna Moodie*, read by actress Mia Anderson. The excerpt focused on a moment where "Atwood's Moodie re-perceives her whiteness." Here, as Compton suggests, "sampling provides the power of focus and re-contextualization" and reminds us that identity is a remix project.[62]

Envisioning rupture as a creative act, Compton employs remix as a democratic principle that polymetrically sounds citizenship. Compton's useful neologism, "schizophonophilia," appropriates and contests what Canadian acoustic ecologist and composer R. Murray Schafer terms "schizophonia." Schafer defines "schizophonia" as a "dislocation of the voice from the body through recording technologies, and electronic amplification."[63] Schafer views such technological manipulations as negative; Compton argues that Schafer believes "schizophonia" "disrupts the natural flow of life and breaks our connection to an ecologically contiguous world."[64] However, through the unsettling nature of being mixed-race in North America, Compton embraces this rupture between the natural world and the decentralized body and author precisely "because it is unsettling."[65] Like a body split from its sources—neither belonging fully to European, Canadian, or African culture—mixed-race identity can challenge expectations and resist simple binaries around race and identity. As Compton writes in "The Reinventing Wheel":

> mulatto
> mestizo
> métis
> cabra
> eurasian
> creole,
> coloured,
> colored
> split.[66]

Even language subjugates as Compton separates the American English spelling of "colored" from the British/Canadian spelling, "coloured." Compton's mix doesn't merely receive, it also anachronistically troubles, like a cueing/back-cueing scratch, race, and nation. Schafer points out that the "Nazis were among the earliest adopters of the loudspeaker," and he suggests that imperialism is a "radiophonic ideology."[67] However, Compton for the most part finds that Schafer's concerns (he was writing in the mid-seventies) have been undercut by DJs who recombine sounds split from their sources: all the more relevant, since these sonic splits were largely articulated by a disenfranchised population trying to find a voice that articulated their experience of feeling disembodied. The phonograph/turntable is the perfect medium for this split/disembodied message of acoustic intervention, as Compton describes the phonograph as "a machine turned inside-out; a machine whose workings are always visible, whose interface is literally tangible, and whose production of sound is visceral. The body of the phonograph, like the body of a racialized object, can never close."[68] Through the medium of disembodied sound, yet always of the body (think of the human ear of Bell's phonautograph), the experience of mixed-race subjectivity is made sonically tangible by showing how race and identity formation never fully close. Schizophonophilia is an opening. The DJ-poet digs into the crates of the past to recover soundscapes and to assert the notion that neither sounds nor identities are stable.

Compton told me of an interview he did with writer George Bowering who told him that sounds are always going extinct, reflecting on his days using a typewriter: "He said at night—because there are so many writers in Kitsilano—you'd be coming from the bar and you'd walk down the street, and it was summer and people's windows were open, and you could just hear typewriters ... Walking down the street, *chk chk chk chk*, typewriters. And R. Murray Schafer talks about this specifically in *The Tuning of the World*, about how there are lost sounds. We won't remember that apart from the oral history because it doesn't get recorded anymore. And if you think further back, before recording, there are all sorts of sounds that are just lost."[69] In line with Schafer's concerns, we can think of DJing as creating an ecological soundscape that preserves forgotten recordings, even if they are mixed with concurrent rhythms. Hence, there is value in the DJ, poet, or scholar who archives, cues, and improvises over previously arranged sounds. Unsurprisingly, it's difficult for many mixed-raced individuals to feel a strong connection to place or tradition—to a natural acoustic environment—when their environment has been one of dissonance, rupture, and continually lost or forgotten sounds. Compton describes this rupture between tradition and the present as an identity crisis: "when I look back at some of my early writing, I realize that very early on I'd already accepted that the truth of it all was somewhere in the inauthenticity, the *in*authenticity, and that that was okay. I mean I look back on it and I remember being motivated by wanting something more stable, but when I look back again, when I reread myself early on, I realize I kind of knew."[70] The genuineness, as Compton puts it, is somewhere in the *in*authenticity, much like the sonic *in*authenticities found in turntablism. The DJ is the person, as Compton tells me, "who notices sounds, but electronic sounds, recorded sounds and the pastiche of all that. I love how

DJs are just these creatures of the crates."⁷¹ Compton's *Performance Bond* engages in renewal, resistance, and revival precisely because it mines the crates of the past, ultimately showing that music is finding patterns in random sounds, much like the random visual patterns by which we *race* others.

Winfried Siemerling suggests that hip hop in Compton's work functions as a "literary structural metaphor and practiced improvisational form."⁷² Through the improvisational form of hip hop and remix, Compton effectively deconstructs race. Race, like pure representation or exact repetition, is an imaginative act, something we perform on others. Compton describes race as pareidolia, "a trick of the eyes, an imposition of the imagination."⁷³ "Pareidolia" is the innate human susceptibility to finding patterns in naturally random stimulus. Trying to find homogeneity or sameness of repetition is an act of imagination, and often a very destructive one, fascism largely coming out of a desire to control and read bodies as ineluctably and ontologically raced and unchanging. Rather, by contrast, Compton's schizophonophilic poetics value the polyphonic nature of being mixed-race, sounding the differentiated self in a world that often promotes sameness, emphasized more so than ever by the digital copy. Race, like astrology, is a kind of a pseudoscience, and as critical thinkers we must continue to contest race as an absolute. As Compton suggests, "to speak against, perhaps, is the only way to speak at all of race—after, or not—and into lasting liberation."⁷⁴ In that they constantly remix race, Compton's poetics are markedly anti-racist, most directly confronting anti-Black racism in Vancouver.

Compton's poems challenge any reductive or "authentic" expression of Blackness. In the poem "Bluer Blues," from *49th Parallel Psalm*, Compton writes of his own uncertainly around his conception of his Blackness: "I'm still ambiv / alently coloured and liv / ing in Xanada, / trying to spell and accent *Santeria* and *Aime Cesaire*, / trying to pronounce *houngan*, trying to try, trying to care ... trying / to keep my / self smouldering, thinking, / 'Halfrican.'"⁷⁵ For Compton, Blackness is about mixedness and play, similarly found in an earlier section titled "Diamond," which puns on hip hop acts with names like N.W.N. (Niggas With Négritude), DJ Osiris, and Grand Master Narrative. Yet, throughout Compton's poetry there is a pervasive danger being articulated that Blackness risks becoming reified and disembodied sound, traded like stock sound bites without context, as in his poem, "49th Parallel Psalm" (*49th Parallel Psalm*), which depicts a white DJ manipulating the word "nigga," seemingly disconnected from the subject and historical positioning of the word:

> white b-boy
> at the turntables
> cutting up the track,
> cutting on the word (((nigga))) on the
> cross
>   cross
>   fader.[76]

The crossfader—moving back and forth like *tidalectical* waves—hints at a metaphorical border crossing, echoing sounds that carry meaning beyond the body cutting the sample on the turntable. Context is important, and race matters because the fiction of race and whiteness often dehumanizes people of colour, Indigenous people, and Black folk. Compton's schizophonophilic poetics embody personhood as *being* between sounds and borders like a DJ cutting up a record, directly addressing us—the listener—in a matrix of possibilities.

III. Word is Bond: Wayde Compton's *Performance Bond*

> "Word is bond I go on and on
> For you it's tragic, I got magic like wands."
>
> —GANG STARR, "Mass Appeal"

Gang Starr

Legba: Trickster Narratives

> "James Douglas, / you held the keys / like a lesser Legba—laughing, shuffling passports, passing"
>
> —WAYDE COMPTON, "JD," 18

> "[Eshu/Legba] knows that the power of ambiguity and the multiplicity of perspectives can change the fixed into the free. New connections always create a new world, and Eshu/Legba puts creative chaos in the heart of tradition and shows what advantages can be taken of it."
>
> —ERIK DAVIS, "Trickster at the Crossroads"

Many Black writers across the diaspora have incorporated (and practised) Vodou/Vodun (religion) and hoodoo (folk magic) into their texts.[b] As Zora Neale Hurston wrote back in 1935: "Hoodoo, or Voodoo, as pronounced by the whites, is burning with a flame in America, with all the intensity of a suppressed religion. It has its thousands of secret adherents. It adapts itself like Christianity to its

---

[b] One musical group, among many, that incorporates elements of vodou into their music is the Haitian *Mizik rasin* (roots) group Chouk Bwa Libète. Their music features hypnotic drums and percussion with call-and-response that is rooted in Haitian vodou practices.

locale."⁷⁷ Vodou's ability to adapt and change accords with its central figure—found, as Hurston describes, at the centre of the Black diasporic vodou/hoodoo tradition—who is the first and last spirit evoked in any ceremony: the multifaceted Papa Legba.⁷⁸ In Haitian Vodou, Papa Legba is the *loa* (spirit) of the crossroads. Guarding the spiritual crossroads, Legba permits or denies passage and is thus a messenger god—an opener and closer of gateways—whom we can think of as a West African/African American equivalent of Hermes/Mercury, or perhaps the Hindu lord Ganesh (a remover of obstacles). Furthermore, Papa Legba is a trickster figure who not only creates chaos but also escapes the codes of the world. Like Eshu (the Yoruba name of Legba), who, as Gates argues in *Signifying Monkey*, "serves as a figure for the nature and function of interpretation and double-voiced utterance," Papa Legba embodies a metaphysics of change and communication at the crossroads.⁷⁹

<small>Robert Johnson</small>

We find the very same Papa Legba represented, as the character of Papa La Bas, in Ishmael Reed's *Mumbo Jumbo* as we do in Hurston's anthropological work, or in Robert Johnson's "Cross Road Blues" when he sings about the crossroads in Mississippi: "I went to the crossroad, fell down on my knees." Papa Legba, in a poorly appropriated version, even appeared in TV's *American Horror Story: Coven*, dressed in a top hat and black tuxedo. Legba remains an adaptable spirit whose skillful ability to change and improvise contests stasis. As Houston A. Baker Jr. so eloquently writes on the value of change to contest fixity (power): "Fixity is a function of power. Those who maintain place, who decide what takes place and dictate what has taken place, are power brokers of the traditional. The 'placeless,' by contrast, are translators of the nontraditional . . . Their appropriate mark is a crossing sign at the junction."⁸⁰ Hence, Compton's usage of Legba throughout his work as a structural force resists the "function of power" and, from the space of the "placeless," asserts creative chaos, change, and transience, which Erik Davis says can even "change the fixed into the free."⁸¹ Compton/Legba are trickster turntablists providing passage at the crossroads.

Describing his role within a trickster tradition, Compton tells Nigel Thomas that his first encounter with Legba was through Reed's

Mumbo Jumbo and then later in works like Gates's *Signifying Monkey*, which uses Eshu/Legba to formulate critical theory. Compton, however, departs from Reed's politics and uses Legba to open his work up: "I don't share Reed's right wing politics. He seems to get in trouble with his fetishization of Voodoo, his praising of the Duvalier regime in Haiti . . . I like the way you can use Legba to undercut: he's a sort of satirical figure . . . The trickster gives you good and bad things . . . It's never how you intended it."[82] Compton goes on to describe how the "contrasting openness and materiality" of Vodou spirits provides a nice contrast to his own Christian background.[83] In another interview he attests that Legba "provides a cue to a literary method, a heuristic process" that allows for "indeterminacy, the crossroads, and chance," which he finds "useful in terms of politics and aesthetics . . . as a good basis for culture-producing praxis."[84] I agree with Siemerling: "Turntablism thus becomes the sign and the medium of the DJ-Legba and of tidalectics: two circles doubling, mixing time at the crossroads between past and present, turning horizontal progression and dialectics into vertical repetition and counterclockwiseness."[85] DJ-Compton-Legba's mixing provides both agency and chance, but it also suggests that border crossing is a process of disruption, dissonance, and displacement.

In Compton's poem "Legba Landed" (*49th Parallel Psalm*), Legba represents the various "liminal" crossings of migrant/immigrant/slave experiences, particularly crossing "the border / line in a northern corner" into "Canada, land," and the xenophobic encounters the newly arrived migrant faces as a non-citizen: "here eyes bear the white burden / of watchful wardens / dutiful citizens in / lower mainlands / patrol each shade of un / white."[86] "Legba Landed" exposes the rhetoric of tolerance associated with multiculturalism, which often falls flat in the eyes of the non-citizen and complicates the issue of belonging and citizenship for those who, like Legba, are liminal and exist, as a custom officer declares, "in the razor-thin space between my lines, / you may fit in."[87] Compton uses Legba— who provides passage between worlds—to expose the white gaze and the damaging effects of Canada's hostility toward immigrants and non-citizens.

The poem "Vévé" (*Performance Bond*) features a dialogue (like a play script) between Analogue and Digital beside the Georgia Viaduct, at the former site of Hogan's Alley, and once again concerns the liminal space between worlds and technology, mixing the past and present together in *tidalectical* fashion to explore how boundaries limit fruitful dialogue. Vévé is a Vodou religious symbol, and in the poem, using Digital's bag of trail mix, Analogue draws a version of Legba's symbol on the sidewalk. Within a few minutes, pigeons come by and eat the symbol, which causes Digital to inquire about more permanent types of writing, such as ink; they discuss Brathwaite's poem, also titled "Vévé," and the ritual power of writing and culture. As Brathwaite writes in his poem: "So on this ground, / write: / within the sound / of this white limestone *vévé*, talk / of the empty roads, vessels of your head, claypots, shards, ruins."[88] For Brathwaite, whose poem invokes earthy and ephemeral images, Vévé becomes a poetic rite and a figure of the act of writing. Digital states that the problem with that kind of writing is it "will eventually get mussed up," while Analogue states that it's not quite writing but, more specifically, what "Brathwaite means is that it's the *beginning* of writing, or the urge to make a new kind of language to the New World."[89] Compton's poem suggests that both analogue and digital offer creative potentials and that both are kinds of portals—that digital technology is, according to Analogue, "nothing new ... They just needed the tools to make you real."[90] "Vévé" thus opens a portal to the past. The poem appears in the section "Rune," which remixes Hogan's Alley narratives, and provides, as Siemerling states, "a conjuring that invokes a new language with transforming powers, crossing borders from a past that elides Black histories into new history and future mediated by acts of tidalectic writing."[91] Like a trickster, much like the coyote who is misrecognized as a dog by Digital and Analogue in the same poem, Compton's performance crafts new spaces and alternatives as a means to think about the past and space, and to envision how new and traditional methods are needed to create the future.

The various DJ technologies in Compton's writing and performances allow him to craft a sonic space characterized by an evocative blending of traditions such as hip hop and Haitian mythology, and he does so at the margins of Black Canadian identity, most specifically through the historically peripheral voice of Black Vancouverites. I agree with Leow's assessment that in *Performance Bond* Compton moves "beyond narratives of arrivals and cultural discoveries to longer, more complex mixings of history, historiography, street culture, voodoo, the Bible, intellectual theory, political slogans, and philosophy. Compton is concerned with recovering, remapping, and re-performing official histories in ways that question fixed ideas of nationhood, identity, and belonging."[92] And so Legba, and the larger DJ and hip hop structural metaphors that sound *Performance Bond*, allow Compton, and us, as readers, to explore the various tensions between the past and present, as well as the various received ideas of tradition and multiculturalism and the larger influence of Afro-diasporic narratives that punctuate the work. The multiple reference points and intertexts, the technologies within Compton's "Vévé" discussing Brathwaite's "Vévé," infer that tradition needs to be active, preserved, and (at times) remade. *Performance Bond* remains at the crossroad of meaning as Compton blurs where analogue stops and digital begins, or when they are in effect simultaneously sounding. Like the Three-Card Monte men before him, telling us how the trick works even as they pull it off, or like rappers rapping about rapping, Compton's narrative is fluid because his improvisatory schizophonophilic poetics allows for both concrete meaning and contradiction to emerge—his poetics are experimental, yet as old as magic.

Compton's schizophonophilic poetics remain improvisational, because they engage with the ancestors as present, much as NourbeSe Philip told me: "Within African cosmologies this is not at all unusual, since the Ancestors, albeit no longer alive, are a living force. When we engage with them they repay us by releasing their grip on us. The grip, I maintain, is because of the haunting, and when released we can be in a more playful relationship with them."[93] Like Philip's own visually challenging and playful text, *Zong!*, Compton's poetics allow new meanings to (e)merge as he engages multiple traditions. Hence, Winfried Siemerling reads Compton's work as improvisatory, writing in response to Compton's oeuvre: "Improvisation is one of the responses to transcultural liminality in the contact zones of diasporic and transnational cultures. Through adaptation, appropriation, and sampling materials, backgrounds, and techniques, earlier repositories and the local present are combined to produce new effects and performance."[94] By contrast, Joanne Leow directly contests the improvisational quality of Compton's work, preferring to qualify Compton's poetics as constructed and carefully considered: "I argue that Compton's more recent work presents a more carefully considered [rather than improvised], constructed, and performed approach to black identity, history, and memory in Canada."[95] The problem with Leow's assessment is that she reads improvisation under too rigid a definition, assuming that improvisation lacks nuance or consideration, as if it is happenstance. Leow falls into the falsehood that improvised music, as critiqued in *The Other Side of Nowhere*, "involves adherence to neither convention nor protocol, that it tolerates no system of constraint,"[96] which is patently false. Thinking of Compton's work as improvisational places participatory onus on the reader who is part of the process, which is precisely what I think Compton wants.

By changing up styles and incorporating trickster narratives, Compton challenges us, particularly through his use of music—*Performance Bond* even includes a performance CD—to do our own research and make decisions as listeners in the moment. Writing on improvisation in relation to listening, pianist and scholar Vijay Iyer writes, "Placing the skillful listener in such an active role explodes the category of experiences that we call listening to music, because it allows the listener the improvisatory freedom to frame any moment or any experience as a musical one. *The improviser is always listening; the listener is always improvising.*"[97] I understand Leow's concern that a term such as improvisation might evade the careful placement of history and words in Compton's poetry, but as Iyer and others have shown, improvisation, framed against more stagnant systems of knowledge production, provides an emancipatory source that embodies multiple perspectives and real-time decision-making.

Compton's schizophonophilic poetics remain active, both through the graphic representations (Compton writes in *49th Parallel Psalm*: "here we speak / in pictographs, glyphs") that appear in *49th Parallel Psalm* and *Performance Bond*, and in how the poetry welcomes embodied and engaged readings, largely through the various rhythmic effects Compton employs, from caesuras and enjambments to puns and other oral/aural qualities.⁹⁸ Compton's poetics engage in both rupture and flow, and like a DJ manipu-lating a sample, essentially by chopping them up the way a DJ cuts over a sample, he shows how a reference can be lifted to complicate our understanding of how we remember the past. Compton's poem "Performance Bond" opens with a reference to the song "As Time Goes By," made popular in the film *Casablanca*, by replacing the word "fundamental" with "multicultural": "The multicultural things apply / as time goes by."⁹⁹ This misduplication (Leow) of the chorus of "As Times Goes By," further recalls the song's well-known opening line, "You must remember this," which emphasizes that as time goes by, immigrant and migrant histories are often written over or forgotten.♭ Compton reminds us that in BC—and in Canada, with the exception of Indigenous people—"Everybody's a migrant. Every body gyrates / to the global bigbeat . . . and multiculturalism can't arrive / by forgetting, but remembering . . . because those who don't remember / repeat."¹⁰⁰ Disturbing the punctum of official state history and state-sponsored multiculturalism, Compton connects the migrant and multicultural experience to the diasporic em-bodiment of the "global bigbeat." Using the cut-up method (although more Flash than Burroughs), Compton emphasizes—through a synecdoche where "Everybody" embodies a physical "body" that gyrates, and even though Vancouver exists on the peripheries "of empire, and time has / gone by"—that

Dooley Wilson

♭ The song was originally written by Herman Hupfeld in 1931 and made famous by Dooley Wilson as Sam in *Casablanca*. I've also included the Billie Holiday version, as I enjoy her rendition of the song.

bodies and physical stories still inhabit the geography and need recovery/sounding.♭¹⁰¹

As Joanne Leow writes, "issues of geography are implied here, whether these are hectares taken from First Nations peoples or non-white communities in Vancouver who lost their neighbourhoods to urban redevelopment."¹⁰² Remembering becomes an act of recovery at the crossroads of erasure, and while Compton's poetics are cadenced with sonic repetitions, by contrast, forgetting signifies an illusory broadcasting of multiculturalism that dooms one to repeat the mistakes of the past. Like Legba, standing at the crossroads of the past and providing entry into the future, Compton backcues the historical record, spinning "the ready-made blues in the backwoods, backwards" to find a spiral "root through."¹⁰³ Compton finds innovative ways to cross borders to allow more space for the citizen. By confounding and circling within defined borders Compton's poetics asks, "What does Citizenship sound like in BC?"

Citizenship Sounded

"If we were not so wedded to the arcane notions of blood, we would be freer to celebrate our various, complex, and divergent identities relating to family and notions of talent and ability, citizenship, and race. We would be more whole, self-accepting people, and less judgmental of others."

—LAWRENCE HILL, *Blood: The Stuff of Life*, 194

♭ Beat generation writer William S. Burroughs used a cut-up technique to rearrange texts in innovative ways that challenge institutional discourse. Grandmaster Flash is one of the early innovators of DJing, hip hop, and scratch. Go to the playlist to hear Grandmaster Flash's breakthrough "The Adventures of Grandmaster Flash on the Wheels of Steel."

Lawrence Hill's 2013 Massey Lectures, titled *Blood: The Stuff of Life*, explore how blood discursively functions as a marker of identity, race, gender, belonging, nationhood, citizenship, and much more. Hill argues that the notion of authenticity of the blood is pseudoscience at best, and that race, like our identities, is constructed. Hill hopes that blood, like citizenship, will eventually unite us. In the way blood fills our imagination, as it does our veins, so too does citizenship: another imaginative marker that bonds us together as a larger group connected to a nation. The nation-state is a collective sampling, an imaginative act that bonds us together. Compton's *Performance Bond* riffs on the word "bond," from an "appearance bond" (to appear in court), to the various performative acts that bond us together, often across geographical and imaginative spaces. The collection opens with an excerpt on detention from Citizenship and Immigration Canada, referencing the Performance Bond form (which has changed a fair amount since the text was published), required when a guarantor is necessary to ensure compliance. The chapter (ENF 20: Detention) puts emphasis on establishing a detainee's identity, providing steps for how to do so, particularly for a foreign national. By opening a highly performative text with a document that suggests how citizenship is both performed and surveilled in Canada, Compton establishes citizenship as something that is conferred by official law; he then undermines the law and state by complicating what comprises a citizen, especially for those whose citizenship status is historically in flux. For those in the process of immigrating to Canada it remains a mystery whether they will be granted entry and passage to become a citizen, or will have their status deemed "illegal" (i.e., deportable).

In the summer of 1999, nearly six hundred Chinese migrants arrived on the BC coast in four dilapidated boats and one shipping container. The majority had paid at least $30,000 to smugglers for their passage, and many had not survived the trip. While every migrant was given due process (although certainly not fair process), 444 of the 577 refugee claims were rejected. Most were sent back home—a home they had fled in desperation in the first place. Larissa Lai, in her article "Asian Invasion vs. the Pristine Nation: Migrants Entering the Canadian Imaginary," outlines the grassroots efforts in Vancouver to contest the media backlash against the Fujianese migrants who arrived in Canada by ship in 1999.[104] Lai addresses the crisis as one around legitimacy, particularly asking, who has the right to say who comes and goes? Compton remixes this incident in a poem dedicated to the Chinese maroons, writing in "Illegalese: Floodgate Dub": "if you arrive in the belly of a rusting imagination, there are grounds to outlaw you."[105] Compton goes on to depict how both identity and status are imaginative acts and how democracy and inclusiveness in Canada can quickly become racism and exclusiveness when outsiders try to enter the nation, which is still very much like Frye's garrison. Compton writes,

> when jurisdiction cuts the earth to the bone,
> the proper diction is the unspoken issue, and the flesh
> of the people's colour in the boats in the hull in the belly
>   of a dream
> without papers or definition, in quotations, "refugee," a penstroke
> from relief. languishing in the languaged exile of illegalese.[106]

Compton points out the hypocrisy of Canada's supposed inclusivity, as Canada likes to heroically remember itself as a haven for runaway slaves. He asks, "why is it villifiable for Chinese migrants to hide in the belly of a dream / now?"[107] If, in the most literal and legal sense, one is only a citizen by virtue of *jus sanguinis* (citizenship by inheritance), or *jus soli* (citizenship by state territory), then where do the stateless fit? *Performance Bond* provides voice to those who are considered illegal and without citizenship status, interrogating Canada's history of exclusion.

Canada tends to congratulate itself as a country that did not practise slavery (even though it did), and former prime minister Stephen Harper once falsely claimed that Canada has no history of colonialism.[108] Given that colonialism basically involves one society seeking to conquer another and then rule over it, Harper might as well have said that Canada has no history of Indigenous peoples. Indigenous people only won the right to vote in federal elections without losing their status rights in 1960. Harper's distorted view of history is unfortunately one that remains embedded in the minds of many Canadians today. Many white Canadians view Canada as a place that grants citizenship status to refugees or those who want to take part in the nation, but historically the government has been tough on migrants, immigrants, racial others, and the foreign-born; in the 1920s it stripped hundreds of naturalized Canadians of their citizenship status simply because they were suspected of being Communists. In 1974 a law (since repealed) allowed the government to revoke the citizenship status of any foreign-born Canadian convicted of treason, potentially making them stateless. These are not just concerns of the past, as a recent citizenship law, Bill C-24, provided the Canadian government with unprecedented authority to revoke citizenship from Canadians—including those born in the country—if they have been convicted of treason, terrorism, or espionage.[109] Fortunately this was repealed by the Liberal government, but it was quite frightening that the cabinet could make these decisions rather than a court. *Performance Bond* contests official citizenship status, while seeking it for those who have historically been deemed as non- or second-class citizens. I take the stance that for citizenship to have real meaning it needs to be performed, although there are infinite representations of that performance. Standard citizenship needs to be challenged and defined from below—those subsonic bass notes—for those people whose presence is often felt but rarely heard.♭ For Compton, that relates specifically—although hardly exclusively—to the history of Black people in British Columbia.

The history of Black immigrants to British Columbia, mostly from California, dates back to 1858. Most of these Black settlers initially settled in Victoria and on Salt Spring Island, but eventually many moved to Vancouver as it became the economic epicentre of BC. In Vancouver, they made their homes on the East Side in the southern part of Strathcona—a working-class neighbourhood that would become known as Hogan's Alley.♯ Hogan's Alley (see figure 5.2)

♭ As Chuck D of Public Enemy said on "Bring the Noise," "Bass! How low can you go?"

♯ See the interactive website Black Strathcona (http://blackstrathcona.

Figure 5.2 Hogan's Alley, 1958. City of Vancouver Archives, #Bu P508.53. Photo by A.L. Yates.

was the local, unofficial name for Park Lane, a T-shaped alley that ran through the southwestern corner of Strathcona in Vancouver during the first six decades of the twentieth century. It went between Union and Prior Streets from around Main Street to Jackson Avenue. Hogan's Alley was not solely a Black neighbourhood: Italian immigrants also trace their history there, and it was right on the edge of Chinatown.[110] By the 1920s the Black community had built an African Methodist Episcopal Church and opened various businesses, and by 1940 the Black population had risen to some eight hundred people. In 1967 the City of Vancouver began to level the western half of the neighbourhood to build a freeway, which displaced the communities living there. While Vancouver provided a more hospitable environment to Black people than the United States, with some even achieving

com/) for pictures, a chronology, video links, and a detailed history of Vancouver's Black community.

a level of societal appreciation that rivalled that of whites, such as Joe Fortes,[b] as Compton and others have depicted in their work, Vancouver could be particularly hostile to racial others. Compton's first poetic collection, *49th Parallel Psalm*, depicts border crossing over the 49th Parallel North by San Francisco blacks into Canada. He presents it as an entropic act that symbolized freedom, as if *"literally setting foot / on its soil = citizenship, freedom."*[111] Compton then disrupts this reading by showing how anti-Black and anti-Asian BC can be, calling together the voices of a marginalized collective striving for greater citizenship in the context of Canadian cultural history.

As Compton depicts throughout *49th Parallel Psalm*, somatic identifiers, such as skin colour, often affect one's citizenship status: "your skin is your ID. You are what you wear"; "getting eyed. ID'ed."[112] Citizenship is more than skin colour, and certainly it is much more than a passport photo, as the speaker of Compton's "The Book" keeps his "passport-photo-wide smile / I's artfully averted" as he attempts to cross into Canada, only to be turned away by the gatekeeper who asserts, "you won't be coming into my country today."[113] The speaker must avert his own multiplicity (his various "I's" and eyes) from a gatekeeper who, despite the illusory reality of a border on a map, claims ownership over a space, referring to Canada as "my country." Ultimately, Compton imagines, much like those who left San Francisco for BC in 1858, "borders giving way just the same / as a read sea."[114] The red/read sea is an act of reading between malleable/*tidalectical* spaces—"we read be / tween . . . be be / tween / the lines"—in order to draw strength from the past to assert an active citizenship.[115] Achieving citizenship for the migrant is, as Compton shows in his work, notably in his graphic novel, *The Blue Road: A Fable of Migration*, a complicated process that leaves many in a liminal space.

---

[b] Joe Fortes (1863–1922), born in Bridgetown, Barbados, devoted much of his free time to teaching children to swim and to patrolling the beach at English Bay in Vancouver. In February 2013, Canada Post released a postage stamp to commemorate Joe Fortes during Black History Month. There is also a popular upscale restaurant named after him in Vancouver.

Compton draws strength from his ancestral connection to the history of Black communities in BC, and like Papa Legba he finds ways to cross and "read between the lines."[116] In "Inlet Holler," from *Performance Bond*, Compton further implicates his own unease as a settler—his ancestors did not arrive as enslaved people—viewing the Vancouver inlet as "no more mine than yours," a direct contrast to the possessive "my" of the border guard in "The Book," viewing geographical space as a conglomeration of peoples.[117] He writes that like others he just happens to be here: "I am a settler / I am uneasy / there is nowhere to go."[118] Compton's geographical and ethnic origins are split. In *Performance Bond* he describes himself as "Halfrican" and "Afro-Saxon," and it is his sense of splitness, of the in-between, that defines Canada's own mixed identity. Compton further complicates place by viewing citizenship under international identifications, identifying with figures such as Sidney Poitier and Charley Pride.

Performance Bond consists of four sections, and the first is aptly titled "Stations," recalling a tableau of locations, identifications, sounds, and geographical places/neighbourhoods where one arrives and departs at various stops. Like transit stations, radio stations, or even stations of the cross, Compton, the DJ-conductor of the mix/train, takes us from BC-specific poems in "Stations," such as "Declaration of the Halfrican Nation" and "Illegalese: Floodgate Dub," to poems a few pages later (such as "To Poitier" and "The Essential Charley Pride") that enact a "geo-heterodoxy" (Iton) that cadences citizenship as partly global, especially for those whose roots are scattered. By moving from the specific to the transnational, Compton's sounding displays how one's identity and citizenship is often mixed (despite a single country of origin or birthplace).

In "To Poitier," Compton writes a polemical ode to actor Sidney Poitier and intimately calls the actor by his first name, proclaiming: "Sidney: I am a creation of the *Guess Who's Coming to Dinner?*-generation, / of the post-first-on-screen-interracial-kiss baby boom. In age and features, I am the offspring of those flickering images. / And the disembodied voice of me." Like a Legba figure, Poitier fearlessly crossed borders—he was the first Black actor to win the Academy Award for Best Actor in *Lilies of the Field* in 1963—and represents, for Compton, a global "ambassador of Integration for the Black Diaspora, the representative / of every black on the planet." As a global ambassador, Poitier quells white "fear / of a black planet" and does so as "the exception / to every stereotype," even getting to "get with Katharine Houghton." Tactically, Compton displays Poitier as more than a passive representative of Black and white solidarity or interracial relations, as one who "colonized English in reverse, teaching / a classroom full of Cockney racists / how to speak *BBC* English," a reference to the film *To Sir with Love*. Such intertextual references (or samplings) appear throughout the poem, such as "and we got to move to the suburbs," referring to Poitier's role in *A Raisin in the Sun*, and provide examples of how Poitier was able to undercut—via "a mastery of form" (Baker)—racist values by remaining stoic and challenging previous stereotypes of Black characters in cinema. The lack of ambivalence or critique of Poitier in Compton's poem sets Poitier up as an ideal entropic force for how borders are often crossed. Strides in citizenship status are often made through calculated subversions and "flickering images," which Compton feels thankful to be the offspring of, figuratively and in his own parents' interracial marriage.[19]

Poitier expanded the visual range of Black representation by not adhering to white expectations of how a Black man should act on film, even though it could be argued that the roles he played were safe portrayals, rather than more fraught characters (more a product of Hollywood than of Poitier's own making). Similarly, "The Essential Charley Pride," a poem about the African American (of mixed race) country singer, confronts Black ethos by not adhering to Black expectations. Given how white country music was in the 1960s (and still is today), for the first few years of Pride's career no pictures of him were distributed, to avoid Jim Crow backlashes. Hence, Compton's poem opens with the following lines:

Charley Pride

> There is a Church of John Coltrane;
> Charley Pride is a heretic.
>
> There is a Funkadelic Parliament;
> Charley Pride is Guy Fawkes.

By calling Pride a heretic and comparing him to Guy Fawkes (a man who tried to kill the king and was hanged for treason), Compton sets up how radical the concept of a Black country singer was in the 1960s, even though country is the music of Black and white people playing together in the rural south. Compton calls Pride "the Jackie Robinson of country and western" and claims him as part of the Black canon, even "though the Afrocentrists won't even have him." Compton goes on to write that the "first black person in the Country / Music Hall of Fame ranks somewhere lower / than the seventh black astronaut in space." Pride's crossing over into a predominately white genre, and Compton's assertion of the value of that crossing, defies the specious notion that skin colour determines identity, or citizenship for that matter. "The Essential Charley Pride" references (samples) essential Charley Pride recordings throughout, much in the way that "To Poitier" samples various Poitier films, in order to represent the diaspora and Blackness as boundless. "The Essential Charley Pride" contests racial profiling and highlights the pervasive nature of music, showing how citizenship and identity—which are often entwined—can never be any one thing, as both essentially function, exist really, only by reference to a larger collective. Essential figures like Poitier and Pride animate the possibilities of "sonic citizenship," discordant notions of democracy, and the reality of multicultural exchange and reciprocity.[120]

Such boundless conceptions of Black identity (and lack of a singular or cohesive linear narrative) is what leads many of the detractors of multicultural policies, such as Neil Bissoondath, to argue that multiculturalism idealizes Blackness and creates chaos and fragmentation.[121] Bissoondath's concern is a desire for an organized cultural narrative, as citizenship and multiculturalism inherently affirm perennial alterations that deny simple reconciliations in favour of discordant possibilities. Such cacophonous possibilities are what Sheldon S. Wolin describes as a discordant democracy embodied in one's civic responsibility to embrace and negotiate dissonance: "The central challenge at this moment is not about reconciliation but about dissonance, not about democracy's supplying legitimacy to totality but about nurturing a discordant democracy—discordant not in the flashy but empty ways of latter-day Nietzscheans but discordant because, in being rooted in the ordinary, it affirms the value of limits."[122] In fact, citizenship itself, as Wolin argues, lives in the "ebb-and-flow of everyday activities, responsibilities and relationships."[123] The efficacy of Wolin's "discordant democracy" is really what many DJs and citizens attempt when negotiating differences through creative and resistive improvisations upon the standards set before them. Poitier and Pride improvise their citizenship—that is, they sound it from below—and reject the second-class status that was handed to them, as well as the borders they are expected to remain confined within.

Poitier and Pride, who often symbolize accommodation rather than resistance, are indeed, as Compton shows, effective oppositional forces that open Black identity and challenge the notion of a closed concept of citizenship. Through oppositional forces, Compton's own schizophonophilic poetics—his discordant democratic collages—recall Edward Said's challenge for intellectuals to remain productively inspired and engaged by disadvantaged groups. Said's words are particularly redolent with my own hopes: "It is a spirit in opposition, rather than accommodation, that grips me, because the romance, the interest, the challenge of intellectual life is to be found in dissent against the status quo at a time when the struggle on behalf of underrepresented and disadvantaged groups seems so unfairly weighted against them."[124] All the more reason that Compton finds value in oppositional figures outside of Canada to think through the very specific and regional issues that Black folk face in British Columbia.

Citizenship must consider multiple allegiances and cross-border/continent pollinations while remaining simultaneously engaged with individual and group rights alongside the larger rights that protect all Canadians under equal citizenship. If Canada and Canadians can manage this, then citizenship will hold real value, particularly for migrants, immigrants, and refugees who still actively seek such status; otherwise, citizenship remains closer to stasis and provides room in the nation only for those who adhere to stringent guidelines. Hence, by making history more dissonant we can challenge homogenous constructions of Canadian identity and citizenship that are based on old models that privilege white history and identity as normative. As

Ajay Heble usefully suggests in his essay "Sounds of Change," "What dissonance offers, then, is the chance to hear the world anew, the opportunity for encounters with radically different orders of historical experience." Reframed, Rinaldo Walcott usefully asks, "Can CanLit read me? That is, Black faggot, dual citizen, sociologist, cultural critic? How would CanLit read me if it could? As exceptional? Who wants to be that? I take everything 'trans' seriously, and therefore I understand that much is at stake when trans is invoked—the very foundation of the human becomes at stake, in my view."[125] Walcott's transformative thinking makes space for new conceptual frameworks and discordant democracies, even if we are using new tools to think through the past as Compton often does. People, like language, are heterogeneous, and citizenship in relation to a truly or genuinely multicultural country must reflect that, even if the wheel must be reinvented in the process.

Backspin: "The Reinventing Wheel"

You can blame / all ignorance on the failure to feed / the ghosts in these Technics

—WAYDE COMPTON, "The Reinventing Wheel," 103

In Susanna Moodie's *Roughing It in the Bush*, Mr. D— notoriously states, "There are no ghosts in Canada" because "the country is too new for ghosts!" Moodie then attributes Canada's shortage of ghosts to what she believes Canada lacks: "a foundation in the consciousness of guilt."[126] Of course, Canada, as a country populated by a wide spectrum of people, should feel some connection, at least empathy (however far removed) regarding Canada's colonial past. Case in point, as Moodie wrote her words the genocide of Indigenous people was taking place, and it continues to haunt the present.[127] If you listen closely, you will realize that Canada is "hauntological." Compton's most fully realized single poem in *Performance Bond*, "The Reinventing Wheel," is populated by ghosts of the past, even as it uses new technologies to reinvent the wheel: a larger symbolic metaphor for the turntable, or "the wheels of steel." Ghosts haunt Compton's Technics (turntables) and the "drum / has gotten ghost," as he works through the "brokenness the tradition" to make the past immediate, palpable, dissonant, and repeated.[128]

Compton's inspirational home/community/hood of Hogan's Alley exists in the ghosting of history and the portals of retold stories: "It's a thin lane / between Hogan's Alley and self-hatred. / My ghosthood, those old standards." Compton's own disembodied voice—he often performs "The Reinventing Wheel" by manipulating a recording of himself reading sections of the poem—speaks to the loss of a community that was put under erasure; through a resampling/ghosting process, he demonstrates that community can never be erased. Compton isn't preserving so much as he is celebrating repetition and misduplications of the past as an achievable version of history and self-awareness, spinning together a wide range of ghost-like voices that make the poetic mix immediate and polyphonous. Compton draws inspiration as "The descendant's [sic] speak / unsheathing the record," invoking Damballah (the Vodou Sky God and creator of life), Jimi Hendrix, Chuck D, Shango (the Yoruba god of fire, lightning, and thunder), Osiris (Egyptian god of the afterlife), James Brown, Raiju (a thunder animal of Japanese mythology), Thoth (the Egyptian god of knowledge), Kurtis Blow, Legba ("Legba's rood cock-rockism, / forever coming"), Prometheus, and others. From a genealogy that stretches across borders and centuries, melding biblical and Vodou stories with hip hop aesthetics, Compton stereophonically represents his sphere of influence as a Black Canadian poet situated in Vancouver. Compton performs with *tidalectical* reverence for the past: "The ancestors we have honoured / will be born as our descendants / to remember us." His strategy is hip hop inspired.[129]

In his article "The Reinventing Wheel: On Blending the Poetry of Cultures through Hip Hop Turntablism," Compton writes how hip hop has changed the world, describing how "hip hop is the conduit of a new kind of black American voice, and therefore a new globally-known black voice. I believe that hip hop's forms are reflective of (to name a few important things) the failure of the American civil rights movement, and the near totalization of electronic media in black expressive life in the first world." For Compton, such conditions constitute a new relationship to orality and collective memory, and hip hop functions concomitantly to the blues and jazz, as it too is an expression of lived experience. However, Compton remains particularly skeptical about the emancipatory potential of hip hop music, even as he applies hip hop aesthetics to his writing, largely because he finds that the influence of hip hop on small, culturally isolated communities, such as those in BC, is not only overly pervasive, but might, at times, be a form of American imperialism. As he told Nigel Thomas, his poem "The Reinventing Wheel" (which he hadn't published yet) is actually, "anti-hip-hop in certain ways, and most of what has come out of it are my criticisms of hip-hop and of the passive reception of hip-hop in Canada. It has forced me to think more and more about American culture."[130] Compton embraces some of the aspects of hip hop, notably turntablism as a possible metaphor "in and of itself, for a reflective *mise-en-abyme* of influences," but critiques the tone of much of hip hop as emotionally limited, citing anger as the primary expression.[131] The hip hop lingo in the poem intentionally falls a little flat when situated in the geographical and psychological experience of Vancouver: "Take us home. Keep it real. Word is bond."[132]

Compton again affirmed to me that he is disturbed by the childish tone of hip hop:

> I don't understand the origins of it, the childishness of hip-hop, which has turned me away from it in recent years. I don't understand why it's such a childish culture . . . action movies and nostalgia. If you compare hip hop to jazz, and look at it, black men of this generation compared to black men of the sixties, and you look at those guys, they seem so mature by comparison, in their subject matter, and how they were on the world stage. They were also underground. They were all underground artists.[133]

In my opinion, Compton is a little too hard on hip hop, and I pushed him to think about how artists like Miles Davis and Charles Mingus, as written in their biographies, could express the same gruffness and anger that fuels much of hip hop music, to which Compton responded that the hip hop aesthetic is at times itself unambitious in terms of content, but very ambitious in terms of sound.

Compton's concerns reflect both his anxiety around the influence of hip hop and his own self-reflexive critique and desire to use contemporary media to bring the masses and the past closer to the present. In another interview he describes hip hop music as foreign to his own

> sensibilities; it's not about here. It's all created by conditions that are very different from the conditions of Western Canada. So I'm kind of ambivalent about it that way. Okay, you're going to seek out black culture if you're a black kid growing up in Vancouver, and if that's the first one you find, then that's cool, use it. But there has to be some intervention with your whole experience at some point.[134]

While hip hop might be more endemic to Vancouver than Compton allows (he critically describes "Hip hop [a]s black Canada's CNN [sic]"), his point about hip hop overshadowing the local experiences of Black Vancouverites is taken, and is, like Clarke's own autochthon approach to Blackness in Nova Scotia, rather conservative.♭ Compton's critique of a medium he applies throughout *Performance Bond*, especially in "The Reinventing Wheel," highlights his desire to confront the globalization of Black culture while finding the value in that very same globalization along with "the literary potential for hip hop."[135] His use, love, and uncertainty of hip hop, speaks to his multilayered approach toward contemporary Black politics. "The

---

♭ For instance, the American group The Incredible Bongo Band recorded the song "Apache" in Vancouver in 1973, arguably the most influential sample in all of hip hop music. As good as the song is, we must also call it out, as the name and sounds are built on caricaturing Indigenous identity. Furthermore, in the 1990s, Vancouver hip hop group The Rascalz provide an example of how important hip hop was to marginalized youth looking for a creative outlet. The Rascalz are anthologized in Compton's *Bluesprint*. "Apache" can be heard on the playlist, and The Rascalz feature in the prior chapter. The "[sic]" appears in the original poem and the "sic" might refer to Canada's National Railway, which is abbreviated as CN.

Reinventing Wheel" opens with some very hip hop-esque lines that read the Red Sea and place the reader in a border crossing: "The reading of the Red Sea bleeds into me / as parable. The parabola / of the word crossing water, / *Kamby Bolongo*. / The perambulation / of call and response, / the word made vinyl."[136] "Parable" transforms into "parabola," a mathematical concept that engages with numerous possibilities since a "parabola can open up in any geometrical direction."[137] Furthermore, in this instance, the rhetoric of a parable (the parting of the Red Sea) and aesthetics of its visual representation in the poem as parabola (symmetrically shaped like a parted sea) are cognate, nearly part and parcel. The term "Bolongo" in Mandinka (a West African language), which represents a flowing of water such as a river, is likely a reference to Alex Haley's *Roots*, one of the vinyl records that Compton often plays in his performances.

Junior Wells and Arrested Development

Sampling, a key component of hip hop production, is used throughout "The Reinventing Wheel," often at times as a self-reflexive *mise en abyme* for how culture repeats itself. The second stanza of the poem connects blues to hip hop and states: "'Snatch it Back and Hold / It,' Junior Wells told us, / and Arrested Development sampled / it." The line is directly followed by a reference to the biblical Moses and passing/passage that shows the *tidalectical* trajectory of Compton's reinventions, as Moses is implicated in "The groove / moving the text," as he "Snatched back and held" and took the people to the bridge.[138] Literature sampling music is hardly new, nor is hip hop sampling literature, but Compton's turntable poetics, mixing elements of vestigial African culture with contemporary hip hop, is unique in Can Lit.[♭] Compton describes the poetic power of the

---

[♭] For example, the line "Young man, yo' arm's too short to box wid God!" (1194) from James Weldon Johnson's *Autobiography*, appears in numerous hip hop songs with some minor repurposings: Black Star's "Thieves in the Night": "Your firearms are too short to box with God"; the line appears in "Mortal Combat" by Big Daddy Kane; Nas uses the line in his song "You're Da Man" from *Stillmatic* (2001); and GZA of the Wu-Tang Clan also used a variation of the line on his song "Paper Plates": "Rhymes too short to box with God." In fact, Black Star's entire concept for their fantastic song, "Thieves in the Night," was inspired by Toni Morrison's novel *The Bluest* "ones and twos" of the turntables: "the cornerstones of hip hop, the DJ's materials—the left and the right turntable, two halves of a dichotomy. The poetry would arise through the cultural 'feedback' these loops would spark." Compton then describes that the agency in the poem is perhaps found in the doubling, describing how he enjoys the idea of transforming his voice into a static disc to be manipulated by himself later: "remix is a way of—in one moment and one performance—re-enacting the manipulation of history and source culture. In *The Reinventing Wheel*, this happens in the body of one man made into two voices by the turntables."[139] Taking his "cue out of crates and boxes," the speaker in the poem, amplified in Compton's real-time mixes of the poem, intentionally misduplicates the text. These misduplications and palimpsestic soundings highlight the improvisational and embodied nature of interpretation.[140]

Compton embodies his turntable poetics by continuing to reinvent the poems in *Performance Bond*, particularly "The Reinventing Wheel," which has gone through numerous incarnations, including the first digital/CD version (which remixes and further fractures the poem), included as an audio companion with the book. The recording of the poem, "The Reinventing Wheel"—originally mixed with beats and breaks by Trevor Thompson—is about "call and response" and antiphonic counterpoint, with the doubling of Compton's own voice in recorded form, different in each incarnation. Compton told me in an email that his spoken-word vinyl recording of "The Reinventing Wheel" is "close to unplayable now, but I sort of like the scratched-up effect. They [the records] are about 13 years old now, and have travelled with me to Montreal, Toronto, Calgary, etc. Just the two. In the

Eye. In the album's liner notes, Talib Kweli explains that the paragraph "struck me as one of the truest critiques of our society, and I read that in high school when I was 15 years old. I think it is especially true in the world of hip hop, because we get blinded by these illusions." The chorus on the track is a clear homage: "Not strong, only aggressive / Not free, we only licensed / Not compassionate, only polite (now who the nicest?) / Not good but well-behaved / Chasin' after death so we could call ourselves brave, still livin' like mental slaves / Hiding like thieves in the night from life / Illusions of oasis making you look twice."

age of increasing digitization, I love the fact that these two objects are so fragile and rare in their tenuous physicality."[141] With every "live" performance the record changes as perhaps does its aura, if we dare to call it that. Compton's poetry, using the cadences of repetition in jazz and hip hop, are reminders that repetition—like Compton's desire to hold on to the tangible form of a dub plate—can never escape its ascension or atrophy into difference. The rupturing effect of using creative performance and music—via rewriting, bricolage, repetition, and difference—in settings that typically nullify such approaches to page-bound poetry, compels us to think about how disruption can function as a model for critical innovative practice.

Since the performance is always changing, which includes our reading of the poem, the wheel is an apt metaphor for wider interventions, considerations, and discussions around Canada's own socially, sonically, and culturally remixed character. Compton's conscious choice to include the CD (a kind of wheel) opens the *text* as a hyperreal space that attests that Black creativity can also repurpose textual and poetic media supposedly reserved for a certain kind of poetry. Compton's decision to include a recording of "The Reinventing Wheel" is a resistive act that claims sonic and visual confluence not merely as part of Black Canadian experiences, but also as a literary reclamation for inclusion within the larger CanLit sphere that often disavows performance in favour of silent page-bound contemplation. Sonic and visual confluences appear throughout the poem, with numerous repetitions between hearing, seeing, and spatial embodiment: "every ear here"; "Every ear shall here. / The words of the prophets are written in graf"; "Every ear shall here. Every eye shall sea." Both the sea and seeing recall the Middle Passage and remain like the static of a heavily scratched and distressed vinyl record. Compton, like DJ Osiris ("The word is the body / of Osiris, it's spliced"), gives words new afterlife: by splicing visual and sonic properties together in an audio synesthesia, Compton shows the mutability of words and history—further complicated since the homophone between "here" and "hear" appears clearly on the page, but not in a recording or a performance. In blurring the division between text, orality, aurality, recorded, and performed, "The Reinventing Wheel" interdiscursively presents Blackness as something that cannot be fully commoditized as citizenship rights continue to resist a unitary understanding.[142]

Meaning and Blackness within Compton's own mixed-race experience is perpetually remixed, which is why wheels, discs, records, ghosts, samples, and various historical anachronisms are plugged into the speaker: the person who is transmitting sound. The DJ (Compton) drifts between meaning and ambiguity and spins the wheel by quick turns, changing, yet staying the same ("the changing same"), drifting in and out of time like a shaman: "Virtuosos / of the used record. In the out there, somewhere, / drifting, / dreaming, / backcueing." The drift and the flow are key components of Compton's schizophonophilic poetics, which operate through repetition as difference. Compton's call to the collective finds valuable feedback in the cadences of jazz and hip hop, apt tools as Compton mashes together language, history, and the politics of race to create a sonic and literary mix. It is "miscellany culture," yet the DJ approach allows Compton to be hyperspecific to Black British Columbian history in his proclamations. He is, after all, essentially telling stories, which Compton nicely connects with a quotation from George Bowering, a literary influence of his: "Stories are open like doors, and no one can shut them ever." The methods for how we tell stories might change, but the messages, particularly ones around cultural survival and ancestral rooting/routing, remain the same, as Compton effectively shows by drifting sonically between scores of diasporic connections and mis-duplications. Like a modern-day Prometheus with his hands touching down on the turntable platters, Compton calls other remixers, lost at the sea of fractured history, to join him: "All my fellow postsufferers / at sea in the new lingua franca, the stutter: we are a cargo cult / of reception." It is fitting that his most Afrofuturist poem (in the section immediately following "The Reinventing Wheel") sets up the framework for us to time travel with him back through the archives of Hogan's Alley. With plenty of ghosts and anachronistic riffings, the wheel spins again.[143]

From Analogue to Digital: "Rune"

> "A revolution is first and foremost a movement from the old to the new, and needs above all new words, new verse, new passwords—all the symbols in which ideas and feelings are made tangible."
>
> —C.L.R. JAMES quoted in Ransby, 374

Compton's recovery of Hogan's Alley through his turntable poetics is a political act, particularly via his resolute desire to tell the stories that do not get told. We cannot escape politics because we live in systems built within political structures; histories within those systems are innately political, and every day we choose whether to remember, forget, interrogate, or re-envision the past. We are agents of change and citizens who can choose either to remain silent about injustices—for whatever reason—or to speak up against dominant or dormant inequalities. Using the tools of the new, moving between analogue and digital as emphasized in Compton's "Véve," what C.L.R. James calls "new verse, new passwords," Compton's recovery of Hogan's Alley is an act, much like the formation of hip hop communities that Tricia Rose describes as "black urban renewal." Hip hop as "black urban renewal" is a style that Rose says "cannot be easily understood or erased, a style that has the reflexivity to create counterdominant narratives against a mobile and shifting enemy . . . to fortify communities of resistance and *simultaneously* reserve the right to communal pleasure."[144] Compton's imaginative and schizophonophilic engagement with Vancouver's Black history (specifically in "Rune," the final section of *Performance Bond*) contests the historical and physical erasure of Hogan's Alley (an act of "Negro removal") by providing counter-narratives that refortify that community.

Compton writes in his essay "Seven Routes to Hogan's Alley and Vancouver's Black Community" that "Vancouver's black community suffered what their American cousins, punning on the term 'urban renewal,' called 'Negro removal'—the destruction of the politically weakest community of a city for large modernist planning schemes." Compton's renewal is the antithesis to the forced removal of Vancouver's historic Black community. Hogan's Alley was likely named after Richard Outcault's cartoon entitled *Hogan's Alley*, published between 1894 and 1896, which featured a fictional New York ghetto with crowded streets and urban squalor. This depiction fits the public perception of Hogan's Alley, described by journalist Jack Stepler as standing for three things: "squalor, immorality and crime." And while Hogan's Alley was hardly perfect—Compton reminds readers we must be careful not to romanticize it, and had been told he was lucky to have not grown up there—Hogan's Alley was full of honest labourers, Black businesses, a newspaper press, and a church. The removal of the community under the guise of "urban renewal"— the proposed building of an overpass—was, as Compton describes, "old-fashioned racism: freeways were invariably run through black neighbourhoods or Chinatowns, poor districts whose populations were least able to lobby civic governments." Hence, citizenship afforded different rights to those living in the prosperous (predominantly white) West End of downtown Vancouver than it did to those in Vancouver's East Side.[145]

In a 2013 interview with Compton, I probed him to think about the trajectory of his work around Hogan's Alley and Black British Columbian history, particularly in relation to a larger national or transnational project. He told me that his initial need to work on the recovery of Black British Columbian history came out of a raw necessity "to understand Black history in the province, in Western Canada . . . We were at first focused on a memorial, a public memorial, and then as we got rolling we quickly realized we didn't know much. So then it became more about information, consciousness raising, and information gathering." Compton goes on to describe that the project was always intended to be a multicultural one that would not be merely for "black folks"; rather, it would be "a history of the city, and we got a lot of help from non-black people, and I thought that was right, that was how it should be."[146] Compton's performance of making Hogan's Alley come to life again is hardly a passive approach or merely a Black Nationalist one; rather, as he describes, it is a historical—even though he uses anachronistic tools like collage and sampling—imperative to present a fuller picture of Vancouver's history, which is much more multicultural than history books or newspaper records depict.

"Rune," the title of the final section of *Performance Bond*, is a word with multiple meanings that appropriately animate Compton's magical, cryptic, and performative lament for Hogan's Alley: it can mean "onward movement"; any "of the letters or characters of the earliest Germanic alphabet"; "a similar character or mark believed to have mysterious or magical powers"; or, as a verb, "to compose or perform poetry or songs; to lament" (OED). "Rune" also sounds apocalyptically close to *ruin*, recalling the ruins and visual remains of Hogan's Alley. "Rune," as Jonathan Dale Sherman contends in "The Hip-Hop Aesthetics and Visual Poetry of Wayde Compton's *Performance Bond*," "creates a union of hip-hop aesthetics and visual poetry to create a space for Vancouver's historical and present black community."[147] Essentially, Compton enacts what theorist Christina Sharpe calls "Black visualsonic resistance" (mixing sound and the visual) by including graffiti signs, Vodou symbols, pictures, a simulated newspaper facsimile of a *Vancouver Daily Province* article, and various typographic characters that don't necessarily come from written words. As Christine Sharpe writes, referring to the seminal film *Daughters of the Dust*, "it was Dash and cinematographer Arthur Jafa's aim to unmake colonial optics," as the film engaged in a "Black visualsonic resistance" to "the imposition of non/being."[148] Engaging in his own "Black visualsonic resistance," Compton's mixing of word, image, and performance push against the colonial optics that have put Hogan's Alley under erasure.

In the book's acknowledgments, Compton writes that while much of "Rune" riffs on historical record, the section contains some "fictitious elements: a newspaper article, four landmarks, and two transcribed interviews."[149] Compton elaborates that "Rune" is "about the memory of Hogan's Alley, and specifically the problem of how to remember Hogan's Alley . . . The poem deals with the ambivalences of looking back, and the enduring curiosity of those times and conditions." Compton opts for an elliptical remembering ("semi-hoaxes" based on "actual corollary"), rather than a realistic representation, since a realistic representation is itself a kind of imaginative impossibility.[150] By staging and misduplicating various historical works (articles, oral histories, and so on) concerning Hogan's Alley, Compton's "Rune" provides, as Leow suggests, "dense layers of historical, literary, and theoretical intertexts" that allow Compton "to have them interact and create new ways of understanding his contemporary contexts."[151] Hence, it makes sense that the first poem in "Rune" concerns the various historical and spatial blank spaces of Hogan's Alley. Through creative interplay, Compton imaginatively fills those lacunae.

The poem "Blight" opens with an invitation to the reader to fill in the empty and abandoned spaces of the poem, much like the missing landmarks of Hogan's Alley: "When _____ take _____ pictures of _____, there are no people there; the decay will speak for itself."[152] Compton cleverly uses blank spaces—silence—to show how Hogan's Alley has been historically blighted. Blank spaces in the poem represent missing details, abandonment, and erasure, as well as a historical whitewashing as words in black ink have been replaced by white spaces that Compton then rebuilds into new structures and sites of performance: "There are whole languages built out of how _____ aren't. / Absences chopped down, hewn into beams, and raised."[153] The blank spaces in the poem also function like a "cloze test," a psychological exercise "in which a person is required to supply words which have been deliberately omitted from a passage."[154] Given that cloze tests are often used in learning language and facts, Compton's poem suggests it is important to remember and recall the blighted history of Hogan's Alley. Building inspectors and the city described Hogan's Alley as a blighted neighbourhood that was essentially diseased and that needed to be cut out of the city for fear the squalor would spread. Historians might deliberately omit important passages of a people's history, but those deliberate omissions can, at times, be creatively recovered, providing an opening or a closing: "instead of a shutter / it could have been an opener. / A closer. A closure. A cloze test. / A flutter."[155] Compton's playful literary consonance, arriving at a cloze test that then erupts into a flutter—a taking off—recalls how easily portals, like a shutter (a screen, or a camera device allowing light to pass) are closed and opened. And while Compton sings an "occlusion blues," a closure in the vocal tract, "Blight" is ultimately about reinscription and remix "in / _____ ever-lovin way."[156] Like the DJ improvising a mix, inviting listeners to put their own interpretive mix together—each person will, after all, fill the blank spaces differently—Compton's recovery poetics, his audio-interplay, has more meaning when we participate in the imaginative performance of Hogan's Alley.

The same creative act of filling in blanks is displayed in Compton's visual poems/re-creations of "Lost-Found Landmarks of Black Vancouver." By including visual images within "Rune"—such as, in "Lost-Found Landmarks of Black Vancouver," the mirror images of "Forme and Chase," a photograph titled "Vividuct," and the graffiti tag of "Rev. Oz" taking up an entire white page in "Ghetto Fabulous Ozymandias"—and the various runes throughout *Performance Bond*, Compton creates a visual poetry that resists typical poetic inscription. Visual poetry, according to painter Lázló Moholy-Nagy, seeks to "liberate literature from the disparateness of eye and ear, from the monotony connected with the dullness of regular typography."[157] Compton's photographic staging of Black Vancouver is not intended, as he explains, "to hoax readers, but rather to at once allegorize the ontological feelings emanating from the social and historical conditions . . . and to experiment formally with cultural memorialization as a representational act." Understandably, he feels anxious creating manufactured images "of a community in the midst of a difficult 'real' memorialization," but the process, much like the "cloze test," is intended to engage and implicate readers in the process of fiction, which imitates history, and a lack of action by official city councillors around what they have come to believe is an ambiguous Black populace.[158] Given the apparent invisibility of the experience of Black people in Vancouver—past and present—photography represents one way to remember that actual people made Hogan's Alley home.

The physical rupture and displacement of the inhabitants of Hogan's Alley for an overpass (the Georgia Viaduct) remains in the ruins of the failed "urban renewal"/"negro removal" project. The construction of the Georgia Viaduct (see figure 5.3) was part of the first phase of a planned interurban freeway that would run through

Recovery and Remix 353

Figure 5.3 Georgia Viaduct construction on the old Hogan's Alley site, 1971. City of Vancouver Archives, CVA 447 – 374. Photo by Walter E. Frost.

Hogan's Alley and much of Chinatown and Gastown. The freeway was stopped by an alliance of Strathcona community activists and Chinatown business people. While the construction of the freeway (which would have involved demolishing buildings throughout the Downtown Eastside and Chinatown) was blocked, the Georgia Viaduct overpass was ultimately completed, causing most of Hogan's Alley to be demolished and the most vulnerable people there to be displaced. While the work of activists should be rightly celebrated, the damage to Hogan's Alley was done, and Vancouver would never again have such a concentrated Black community. Compton's concrete poem (informed by the form of concrete) "Forme and Chase" mirrors the image of two viaducts in a piece titled "Vividuct" on the page beside the poem and, like a viaduct, provides a crossing, a ghosting, between the past and present.[159] The poem also uses a typewritten font to emphasize the loss of an entire analogue community, as if the history of Hogan's Alley was buried under the bridge.

Consisting of two stanzas that parallel two viaducts on the photo on the next page, Compton's poem employs "Black visualsonic resistance" to depict that while structures degenerate and cities change, memories and the histories of people continue to phantom the present, like the spectre haunting his font and dictation, much like "the ghosts in these Technics" embodying his turntable poetics.[160] Compton's choice to use the archaic spelling of form, "Forme," with the word "Chase," a printing term referring to the arrangement of text, emphasizes that while he is concerned with finding new ways to speak to the past, his "bastard grapholect" shows that written words are but a bridge to what can only be partly recovered. The viaducts recall where a vibrant community once lived, whose imprints remain, like the graffiti written on the viaducts—erased, then rewritten—since Compton's neologistic spelling of viaduct, as "Vividuct," comes from the Latin *vivi*—to live, to be alive, to survive.

Compton's tidalectical spinning of the past with the present is, as he describes in "The New Station," "alchemical work, spinning / meaning out of meandering... I go over / the remains; I transform, / I translate." Compton's translation is very much an analogue one into a digital present; that is, he takes the absences of a faded past and transforms the remains/ruins/runes into a digital mix that speaks to the very mixedness of his own arrival. The poem "The New Station" is dedicated to "*Clarence Clemons, a black longshoreman beaten to death by Vancouver police in the alley behind New Station Café in 1952,*" "*Kary Taylor, a black dentist beaten by Burnaby RCMP in 1999,*" and "*my high school buddies... who became Lower Mainland police officers, all of them Asian.*" In the poem Compton takes us through various stations, describing a near collision in a car at age seventeen, recalling the experience "every time I cross this overpass. I'm keying / on my PC now towards this terminus... between the old train station rising / at Terminal Ave. and the vanished / New Station Café." Stations vanish and new ones crop up, recalling the passage of runaway slaves on the Underground Railroad towards their terminus in Canada. Time changes the stations and, given that Kary Taylor was beaten because the officer responsible (in his words) "'*saw a black man in a nice car with an Oriental female, and, given the area, he wasn't sure if it was possibly a prostitute-pimp situation,*'" it is poetic justice (or co-optation, depending on how you read it) that Compton's Asian Canadian friends are now police officers. Racism in Vancouver still exists (and persists); Compton's "Illegalese: Floodgate Dub" and other poems announce this much, but we have also entered a multicultural era: many of the stations are liminal spaces between worlds, spaces of possibility, hope—digital spaces of remix.[161]

"Ghetto Fabulous Ozymandias," the final poem in "Rune," riffs on Percy Shelley's sonnet "Ozymandias," reading the poem within the poem. Shelley's poem contrasts the inevitable decline of leaders and empires with the lasting power of art and contains the often-quoted lines engraved on the statue of Ozymandias: "My name is Ozymandias, king of kings: / Look on my works, ye Mighty, and despair!" Around the colossal wreck of Ozymandias nothing remains, as the poem speaks to the arrogance of empire, except that the site of ruin for Compton is Hogan's Alley. In Compton's poem, the speaker, who is in dialogue with Rev. Oz, a homeless preacher, explains that "Shelley's poem was about arrogance'" while "this place—the community that was here—they were driven / out. Their neighbourhood was flattened by the City. There's nothing / left here because of an injustice. It doesn't make sense / to call the targets of this unfairness 'arrogant.'" Rev. Oz replies, in a telling moment in *Performance Bond*, that it does make sense, since "It is arrogant to disappear."[162] We can try to forget the past, but as Compton poignantly puts it, such a gesture would be an act of extreme arrogance.

Marianne Faithfull

Today Vancouver has over 20,000 Black residents.[163] Compton points out that the "perceived absence of blacks in Vancouver is an optical illusion: black people today represent a higher percentage of the total population than they did fifty or a hundred years ago."[164] Yet most of Vancouver's population understands very little of the history—or existence, even—of Hogan's Alley. Compton, as "a person who has more white than black biological ancestry" and few direct familial ties to the area itself, has devoted so much time to the Hogan's Alley memorial project because he sees himself as "an afterimage of our history."[165] The work of Compton and others has not gone unnoticed: a plaque was put up in 2013 to commemorate the community, which Compton described as a substantial success: "knowing that generations that are coming up now are going to have this as part of the regular landscape is very satisfying. [It] speaks loudly about a community that people too often seem surprised exists at all."[166] Canada Post, as part of Black History Month in 2014, commemorated Hogan's Alley on a stamp, which featured Fielding William Spotts Jr., the first Baptist in western Canada, and Nora Hendrix, grandmother to Jimi Hendrix and a cook at Vie's Chicken and Steak House in Hogan's Alley.[167] In 2014, visual artist Stan Douglas created an app for iOS devices with which you can walk through Hogan's Alley circa 1948. In 2016, Telus released a short and highly informative documentary about Hogan's Alley called *Secret Vancouver: Return to Hogan's Alley*.[b] In 2021, a mural honouring Hogan's Alley won a heritage award.[168] And, perhaps most fruitfully, depending on how the project plays out, there are plans for an actual space that will revive the community of Hogan's Alley. Currently, there are plans to remove the Georgia Viaducts (although much is in flux).[169] The City of Vancouver has hired American architect Zena Howard to help with the revitalization project, although at the time of writing this project is stalled, in part due to COVID-19.[170] In June 2020, the viaducts were blocked by protesters (seven of whom were arrested) to highlight anti-Black racism and injustices towards Black Canadians in Vancouver. The viaducts remain a source of pain and possibility as the Hogan's Alley Society works to turn the land into a "land trust to be stewarded by the Black community."[171]

These efforts by activists and artists, and recent commitments by the city, are a gift to future generations, who will have these works and memorials and possibly an actual area to gather and remember Hogan's Alley as part of their cultural landscape. The past matters because Compton, and all of us, remember in the present tense. To think that a historically Black community (however small) in British Columbia that was forcibly removed doesn't matter to everyone is arrogant. We can only build a more multicultural future by understanding what has come to pass but is never fully past. Collectively,

---

[b] While it is hard to find, it is also worth checking out the 1994 documentary *Hogan's Alley*, by Cornelia Wyngaarden and Andrea Fatona.

when we work together to remember and reinvigorate the past—as Compton and others have done with Hogan's Alley—we work against the politics of division and look for ways to heal the ruins of the past, ultimately providing avenues forward. Read, listen, and act: Hogan's Alley *lives*.

REMIX 5

> "The key questions come when we try to discern the consequences of cultural collusion and collision: which kinds of cross-cultural identification advance emancipatory ends and which ones reinforce existing structures of power and domination."
>
> —GEORGE LIPSITZ, *Dangerous Crossroads*, 56

I want to echo George Lipsitz, as one of the hopes for this book is to challenge existing power structures through acts of cultural collusion and collision to show how Canadian citizenship, when looked at from below, can (and should) be more inclusive. Such cross-cultural practice is also at the heart of Wayde Compton's schizophonophilic poetics, as Compton remixes the past and combines various historical, theoretical, and literary intertexts (from the Bible to Vodou) to sound a more inclusive version of Canadian citizenship that opens space for those—like the historical Black community of Hogan's Alley—whom official history has elided. If the past is represented as "analogue" and the present as "digital," then we must consider both as part of the *tidalectical* process of creating the future, especially since, as Baraka, drawing on the wisdom of the ancients, puts it, "The future is always here in the past." The ubiquity of digital culture colliding with the past continues to alter how we interact with others, but it also dramatically changes our approach to reading, as evidenced throughout Compton's work. In both analogue and digital spaces there are always connections to be made—we can never get away from embodied experience (like Bell's phonautograph).

Compton's own mixed-race identity informs his turntable poetics and makes the discordant collision of multiple epistemologies essential to his desire to eradicate spurious notions of race that divide people; Compton uses technology to map, blur, spread ideas freely, and cross racial borders. Compton's use of multimodal and turntable poetics allows him to explore the form's literary potential and provides a challenge to the very monocultural model (and garrison mentality) that has dominated CanLit for so long. Through his turntable poetics, Compton challenges national myths while making space for Black history, ideas, and literary forms. The past remains a vast network for DJs, poets, and citizens to draw from, allowing new acoustic spaces to emerge out of the complex synthesis/antithesis of colliding cultural spaces. For Compton, the past is immediate because we always think through the past in the present tense. The practice of DJing is the appropriate metaphor for the modern griot finding new ways to tell the old stories to bring the past closer to contemporary audiences.

The music often takes us outside the text only to take us back into it, just as Compton's use of visual images intends to get us thinking outside the context of words on the page. The bonds in *Performance Bond* are multiple, and once we cross over the borders of a fixed book, we go out into the living world and engage with the heterogeneous sounding of ourselves, always changing like the reinventing wheel. The past helps sound who we are now, but as Compton's experimental turntable poetics show, sometimes the old metaphors and institutions need to be challenged as we shift to new modes of cultural production. More useful and productive than the illusion of an authentic cultural narrative is imagining how the DJ metaphor provides a sonic representation of multiple narratives all sounding together, not necessarily in unison, but polymetrically in the sonic remix that is Canada. We have come full circle—or better yet, I've played all the records I intended—in my version of a Black Canadian poetic and sonic mix. In the final remix I offer a few sonic echoes with the larger ideas of this book as I imagine the community still to come.

OUTRO

THE NEW BLACK CAN(AAN)LIT AND THE COMMUNITY TO COME

Listening: Sam Cooke,
"A Change Is Gonna Come"

Sam Cooke's "A Change Is Gonna Come" is one of the most emblematic songs of the civil rights movement, so it is appropriate that it is the final listening of this book, as I look forward with hope.♭ The song was inspired by various events in Cooke's life, particularly the time he and his group were turned away at a whites-only motel in Louisiana. Building on the energy of the civil rights movement, as well as his own shame for not having written something earlier (he was moved by Bob Dylan's "Blowin' in the Wind"), he decided to write and record the song. Later that year, change did come in the United States with the *Civil Rights Act* of 1964, followed a year later by the *Voting Rights Act* of 1965. The last segregated schools did not close until 1983 in Canada (see the 1977 *Canadian Human Rights Act*), and the last residential school didn't close until 1996. Despite

Sam Cooke, "A Change Is Gonna Come"

Bob Dylan

Liner Notes

♭ You've made it to the end, unless you've skipped ahead, which is totally fine too! Please enjoy the last few songs on offer: https://open.spotify.com/playlist/1eiuTIOvnXc7pKTXCaTNEs.

these changes throughout the latter half of the twentieth century, the United States and Canada are still very much anti-Black and anti-Indigenous spaces, and there are massive inequities in both countries. We remain haunted by the ghosts of Canada's past, whether we acknowledge them or not. We need to continue to grapple with the past to make it more visible, and for any of us who work on anti-racism and believe in a truly just society, we must hold hope that a change is still gonna come. I am reminded of one of my favourite quotations from Dr. Martin Luther King, Jr.: "We are now faced with the fact that tomorrow is today. We are confronted with the fierce urgency of *now*. In this unfolding conundrum of life and history, there is such a thing as being too late."[1] There is no time for apathy; rather, we must work to make positive change.

In music, the final section of a composition is referred to as the coda (the tail), or, in slang, as the outro. I prefer the slang term given that it takes the reverse of the "in" in "intro" and provides an "out"—a circular closing in relation to the beginning intro/overture, like bookends. The closure in an outro concerns thematic repetitions, as in the exposition in the tonic key in classical music, or repetition of the chorus or a gradually fading out in pop music. I have mixed many records and theorists together with a desire to play them, like Ellison's unnamed narrator, "all at the same time."[2] I'm aware that this level of eclecticism produces some abstraction, but my remixed approach reflects the various poets' desires to create—as poetry is always a making—texts that echo (canon) a vast sonic world of other soundings. This outro brings the primary themes back into the mix, examining how citizenship, identity, and resistance are articulated in Black Canadian/Afrosporic poetry. By making more space for Black voices (as well as Indigenous and other non-white voices)—whose histories have often been seen as discordant and disposable to the Canadian remix project—we can envision a more just community to come.

Outro 361

Side A: Remixing CanLit

"The journey is the destination"

—DIONNE BRAND, *A Map to the Door of No Return*, 203

Historically, Black Canadians have struggled for equal citizenship and the right to control their cultural depictions; one need only look at French Canadian artist François Malépart de Beaucourt's 1786 painting *Portrait of a Negro Slave or Negress*, now known as *Portrait of a Haitian Woman*, to see how Black people have historically had their representations depicted for them.[3] Thus, there is particular value to disturbing limited historical representations and creating representations that are more expansive and inclusive.

It is a kind of sanguine utopianism to assume that the old xenophobic myths of Canada as a white androcentric settler nation are gone from CanLit (David Gilmour and others of his ilk uphold such views).[4] However, we must also keep in mind that being born in CanLit are texts that interrogate Canada's past to dream of a more just society. Texts by Black Canadians (and Afrosporic people) such as M. NourbeSe Philip, George Elliott Clarke, Lawrence Hill, André Alexis, Austin Clarke, Dionne Brand, d'bi.young anitafrika, David Chariandy, Dany Laferrière, Suzette Mayr, Canisia Lubrin, Kaie Kellough, Nalo Hopkinson, Chelene Knight, Afua Cooper, Sonnet L'Abbé, Shane Book, Claire Harris, K'naan, Wayde Compton, and countless others teach us to be better listeners (citizens even), and they do so by taking us more into Canada's margins to expand and challenge the boundaries and where we historically place value. We must never forget that Canada is founded on colonization and genocide.

We need to engage with what Smaro Kamboureli describes as a collaborative rethinking of "the disciplinary and institutional frameworks within which Canadian literature is produced, disseminated, studied, and taught."[5] It would be myopic to assume that white people do not have an advantage in society, and the same goes for white writers in CanLit. White privilege needs to be understood within settler colonialism: it is not some artifact of history but rather a process that continues to unfold in society. A similar case could be made about Black and Indigenous writers being studied and taught in Canadian universities as well as the few Black- and Indigenous-owned publishers in Canada.[6] Haudenosaunee writer Alicia Elliott describes the current state of CanLit as a dumpster fire that perpetuates Canadian national myths, leaves little space for marginalized writers, and needs to do more to combat systemic discrimination.[7] Rinaldo Walcott has stated that he is quitting CanLit since it "fails to transform because it refuses to take seriously that Black literary expression and thus Black life is foundational to it. CanLit still appears surprised every single time by the appearance of Black literary expression and Black life."[8] This sentiment is echoed by Oji-Cree poet Joshua Whitehead, who states, "I am not CanLit, I am Indigenous Lit," and goes on to question "if CanLit will ever recognize it is part of the ecosystem of this literary nation-state and it too maintains a responsibility and accountability to its land base."[9] The New Canadian Library, which compiles classic works of CanLit, contains but one work by a Black author: Austin Clarke's *Amongst Thistles and Thorns*.[10] Returning to the neglect of Austin Clarke, Darcy Ballantyne, Paul Barrett, Camille Isaacs, and Kris Singh write—reflecting on the fact that zero people showed up for their 2017 ACCUTE panel on Austin Clarke, ironically titled "Austin Clarke's Critical Neglect"—"CanLit is still very much an anti-black space."[11] Yet how can you study and understand the shape of Canadian literature and history without engaging closely with the work of CanLit trailblazer Austin Clarke or with that of more contemporary writers like Wayde Compton?

Much of the innovative, engaging, and brilliant writing in this country is happening in Black writing and in Indigenous writing: few texts are as layered and complex as Afrosporic Caribbean poet M. NourbeSe Philip's *Zong!* (2008) or Nisga'a poet Jordan Abel's *Injun* (2016). "Canada is," as Compton writes in "Illegalese: Floodgate Dub," "a remix B-side chorus in the globalization loop."[12] Compton's words depict the negative ethos of globalization, as well as the possibility for continued remix in the musical loop of a Canada that is always changing as new people and ideas enter the mix. The poets explored in this book do precisely this with their poetry—they open new possibilities for change and remix. Poetry, then—and I extend this analogy to music—is a form of citizenship that is active, like labour, where ideas are wrangled with, shaped, dreamed up, and brought into the world. Therefore, while K'naan's rap poetry is customary to most rap songs, yet blended with unique Somali elements, and while M. NourbeSe Philip's poetry is fragmented and improvisationally dissonant, both approaches succeed in using music to sound a past that haunts the present. K'naan might have a larger audience than the other poets explored in this book, but his desire to provide new ways of seeing the world and to create more space for marginalized voices through hip hop is virtually the same longing Philip expresses through her dub chant; Clarke through his blackening of the sonnet and infrapoetic blues; Brand via her disruptive jazz poetics; and Compton vis-à-vis his schizophonophilic soundings. Black traditions of the poetic and sonic are interrelated and independent, and I've borrowed from many of them for my DJ mix: "the blues matrix" (Baker, Jr.); the signifyin(g) tradition (Gates, Jr.), "Black visualsonic resistance" (Sharpe); "the changing same" (Baraka), and others, including remix and sampling. It is through music and poetry that new ideas come into the world. Destinations are important, but, as Brand writes, "The journey is the destination," and we must keep finding new places to go.

 I hope this book serves as an important conceptual intervention in CanLit. It is an educational blight that many students go through entire English programs in Canada—even specializing in CanLit—and never encounter a Black Canadian text. I have only scratched the surface of one group of talented poets and songwriters. Some of the songs are rightfully angry, some confront anti-Black racism (as we all should), and others offer medicine and healing. The entire world benefits from the excellence and power of Black words, art, protest, and song. I do believe that poetry and music model ways of being in the world. That is, they show the ways we are ineluctably connected to one another.

 In his "Christmas Sermon on Peace" speech, King intoned, "all life is interrelated. We are all caught up in an inescapable network of mutuality, tied into a single garment of destiny. Whatever affects one directly, affects all indirectly."[13] We see this reality in war, climate change, and the economy; moreover, the coronavirus pandemic has shown just how connected we are. We depend on one another. King hit the nail on the head with the lightning of prophecy. He optimistically argued that solving these ever-growing problems was perfectly achievable, since the wealth of the United States alone had made the elimination of poverty perfectly practicable. Hence, multiculturalism in Canada (beyond policy) is an idealistic act of Blackness and goodwill—love even, what King calls *Agápē*[b]—because it promotes "the understanding and creativity that arise from the interaction between individuals and communities of different origins."[14] Borrowing from Cecil Foster and others, I've maintained that "sonic citizenship" and multiculturalism are exercises in Blackness. Blackness is the antithesis of the homogeneity that many white settlers sought out when they came to Turtle Island. Blackness offers a malleable metaphor that, as Robin Kelley argues, addresses "anyone bold enough to dream" and challenges us to "visualize a more expansive, fluid, 'cosmos-politan' definition of blackness."[15] Blackness is a universal feature common to all humans who embrace their creativity, disruptiveness, and spontaneity, for, as Cecil Foster puts it, "humanity is black when viewed from this perspective of full self-determination and a holistic humanity that is essentially equal."[16] Blackness is not ethnicity any more than whiteness is; rather, Blackness is resistance, freedom, creativity, hope, and fraternity. Blackness is dynamic in its ongoing process of formation and dismantling of white finality.

My use of *sonic multiculturalism* acknowledges that Canada is composed of many diverse people and soundings that sometimes clash, for the process of social belonging is complex, especially for those who are excluded. For instance, Indigenous people were here long before the colonists' ships arrived, and many Black folks were forcibly settled here by those same ships. It would take an entire

---

[b] *Agápē* (Greek) basically translates as "unconditional love." King describes *Agápē* as "understanding, creative, redemptive goodwill towards all men. *Agápē* is an overflowing love which seeks nothing in return." King, *Trumpet of Conscience*, 75.

book to adequately deal with the need for Indigenous sovereignty in Canada, but the reader might like to check out excellent work by writers such as Leanne Betasamosake Simpson, Arthur Manuel, and Tiffany Lethabo King, to name a few writers who unsettle Canada. Tiffany Lethabo King writes, "I also trust Black freedom dreams when they consider Native freedom."[17] Indeed, as King's work makes clear, the endeavours of Black abolition and Indigenous decolonization, which challenge liberal and other forms of humanism, provide nascent avenues for the development of new social structures and future possibilities. If the poetry discussed here does anything, it teaches us to be more attentive listeners and to make space for such future possibilities. Thus, community—one that is non-hierarchical and egalitarian—is still to come.

Side B: Community to Come

Listen: "There Are Other Worlds"

> "you realize *nobody's* listening. So *you've* got to listen. You got to find a way to listen."
>
> —JAMES BALDWIN, *Sonny's Blues*, 72

Listening is active: we constantly improvise with others. And it can provide an opening towards alternative forms of community—to other worlds, as one of Sun Ra's song's from *Lanquidity* insinuates: "There Are Other Worlds (They Have Not Told You Of)." Under these alternative models, I envision engaged listening not just as a physiological function, but also as a social responsibility with an impetus toward social change. It is from these lower "bass notes"— the bottoming of the work from which the various poet-musicians perform—that engaged listening (in French, *entendre* means both "to hear" and "to understand") can take shape and gesture toward more inclusive communities. As Sun Ra so articulated in his music, the entire universe is listening. Ultimately, listening involves the

Sun Ra

precarious act of yielding to others' voices, which is at the crux of *sonic multiculturalism* and, often, interesting music. The challenge is to deeply listen (Oliveros), as the narrator of James Baldwin's short story "Sonny's Blues" does: "you got to find a way to listen."

The various poets in *Soundin' Canaan*, like the call and response of instruments and players conversing back and forth in a jazz combo, constantly call on us to pay attention, inviting us to improvise a text's attendant dialogues and histories with each listening. Often the invocations in Black CanLit are particularly direct, invoking the reader as an interlocutor, much in the way that jazz-poet Frederick Ward cries out: "*'o listen to me / listen!*"[18] Listen—in a few instances, relisten—to some of the many listenings of the primary poets in the book: in M. NourbeSe Philip's *She Tries Her Tongue*, the speaker acutely listens throughout history, "the listening / breadth of my walk"; Clarke, in "Bio: Black Baptist/Bastard," etches the plea, "Listen closely: I am trying to cry / That's my condemned blood on the page"; despite the "many languages" and discordant moments of Brand's *Ossuaries*, we gather and "we listen"; or, as Compton asks us in "Berth Prayer" (*Psalm*), "listen. my song / is an answer, an imperative am / putation. Listen"; and lastly, K'naan opens his track "Voices in My Head" by stating, "Eh yo, welcome to my world, please listen."[19] These pleas draw the reader into direct relation with the work. Through the poet's invocations, we are called to listen to the echoes of the past in the present. These invitations to listen closely, to step into the book, reveal the complexity of identity, community, and citizenship.

The music that opens each chapter is another invitation to listen. For example, jazz performances provide formal models for numerous writers to approach the complex interweaving textures and soundings of Canadian culture and community. I have included the various listenings throughout (including playlists) to encourage readers to listen to the selected musical material, which comprises key intertextual soundings in the texts themselves. The musical digressions—a strategy of the larger DJ methodology—provide the underlying bass track for the poets to solo over. And while I have placed a certain value on this approach, as outlined in the introductory chapters, I can't stress enough that music and listening are not the only strategies for reading Black writers in Canada. We need to be careful to avoid subsuming all Black writers as musicians, for as d'bi.young writes in her poem "young black": "because I play ball like a ballah ... does not mean / my own dream / is to becomes a *basketball star* / a *track-and-field negro* / or *soul-singing sambo* / I can be an athlete or storyteller if I choose / knowing these are NOT my only options."[20] While I think the music and poetry animate the varied soundings of citizenship from the selected poets, I have tried to focus on other areas, such as Clarke's proficiency with the sonnet, or Brand's use of the long poem, to offer nuanced readings. Perhaps other "white" critics of Black Canadian literature have stayed away from the clear connection of these writers to Black music to avoid sounding like Jan and Mary Dalton when they ask Bigger Thomas in Richard Wright's *Native Son* to sing "Swing Low, Sweet Chariot" so that they can get the real feel of the song; or worse, sounding like the pack of vigilante racists who humiliate Bennett Bradshaw in William Melvin Kelley's *A Different Drummer* by making him sing "Curly-Headed Pickaninny Boy" before they kill him. In these instances, music becomes a form of oppression, but I would also point out that in these examples, the self-determination is taken away from the Black characters, who are made to fit into the white racist registers of the Black entertainer. As is often the case, many people want to enjoy the music of Black artists but fail to appreciate how these forms come from the beauty of Black life and culture.

Music is thus a discursive practice that views the poet as a musician whose identity is "a process never completed—always 'in process.'"[21] It is through difference that our identities are constructed, and it is through deep listening that we can hear and *feel* the many voices that combine to sound Canada. Just as there is no such thing as a pure sound, or pure music—any combination of sounds can become music—identity is never fixed; rather, it is improvised, negotiated, and performed. Improvising the self is like creating a piece of music: no musical work is an autonomous creation of one-way interaction between creator and audience; rather, music is a social undertaking where musical works ultimately exist to give performers something to perform. There is no singular way to play music just as there is no single way to define the self in relation to the citizenship status that comes with belonging to a larger nation/community. We need to find ways to create communities that allow for anti-racist, non-hierarchical, non-patriarchal organization. Such a community is possible.

Community Still to Come

> "I can imagine a community with as loose a form as you will—even formless: the only condition is that an experience of moral freedom be shared in common, and not reduced to the flat, self-cancelling, self-denying meaning of a particular freedom."
>
> —GEORGES BATAILLE quoted in Nancy, *The Inoperative Community*, 21

Community is a process that is never static; like the self, it is always *to come*. As Jean-Luc Nancy states, community "is always *coming*, endlessly, at the heart of every collectivity (because it never stops coming, it ceaselessly rejects collectivity itself as it rejects the individual)."[22] Building on the work of philosopher Georges Bataille, Nancy works to describe a community that welcomes dissonance—the unworking of itself—for it is our unsharable finitude that creates the very condition for our commonality. Value comes not from what we have in common with one another, but—as Alphonso Lingis suggests in *The Community of Those Who Have Nothing in Common*—from what makes us different. Any community that aims towards singularity (a fatherland, a body) loses the "being-with" and "being-in" that allows community to continually and improvisationally form (in its formlessness) with only the principle of shared moral freedoms (in Canada, for example, the *Canadian Charter of Rights and Freedoms*). The various poets in *Soundin' Canaan* envision a diversity of regional and globally aligned communities: George Elliott Clarke's cultural— yet cosmopolitan—African Canadian nationalism; M. NourbeSe Philip's Afrosporic community, which finds transnational identification in and across time via the *ebora* (spirits) who drowned during the

Zong massacre; Dionne Brand's improvised and coming community within a globalized framework; K'naan's global multicultural community that moves across waters from Somalia to Canada; and Wayde Compton's schizophonophilic community that moves between historic analogue (the past) and digital (the present) communities to recover (Hogan's Alley) and imagine new communal identifications. The poets in this book gift us sonic maps and pathways to imagine communities not yet born.

There is no singular, unitary community, nor should there be. There is, however, a larger national and federal framework at work in Canada. It is this framework that connects us together—despite how atypical our imaginings of community are—and it is precisely our differences that lead to a more musical and poetic society, teaching us to be attentive listeners—musicians and poets, even. As Cecil Foster puts it, we die in one moment only "to be reborn as states and new individuals in the next."[23] Idealistically, Canada is like one large potluck, where each person brings a different food to the cultural feast, recalling the line from Toni Cade Bambara's *The Salt Eaters*: "You never really know a person until you've eaten salt together."[24] We need to make additional room in the enormous jazz parade for those who continue to undo community, particularly Indigenous Nations, new immigrants, and refugees, because they put the modern fiction of settler sovereignty into crisis and challenge us to rebuild more inclusive communities. Moreover, I agree we still need to, as King said over forty-five years ago, "work passionately and unrelentingly for first-class citizenship."[25] Community continues to come—that is, to undo itself—when, as Lingis insists, "one exposes oneself to the naked one, the destitute one, the outcast, the dying one."[26] There is no essence to community, because if there were it would close; rather, community is something that, as Nancy suggests, has not taken place, it simply is: "*what happens to us*—question, waiting, event, imperative—*in the wake of* society."[27] By unworking community, by realizing that Canada presents a real opportunity for a model of first-class citizenship —and I realize I am being rather principled here—we can build on the dreams of the "freedom seekers" who crossed over into Canaan land.

Many enactments of citizenship and community are performed on the local level, even as those enactments dream up models for *sonic multiculturalism* beyond those regional specificities. For example, when I lived in Guelph and then Toronto, I attended, sat on the board of directors of, and participated in the Guelph Jazz Festival, which is a significant improvised and creative music festival where thousands of creative music listeners congregate. In Guelph, community's meaning is always *to come*, as people gather over a five-day period for a variety of activities and free community offerings, including the random and nomadic performances in seemingly accidental places such as the streets and parks of the city. A centrepiece of the Guelph Jazz Festival for many years has been the popular open-air jazz tent: the festival closes one of the city's most vibrant streets for a day, to offer hours of free music in a central public location. The Guelph Jazz Festival has come a long way since its humble beginning in 1994, when a small group of friends who shared a love of jazz made a commitment to the community of Guelph. Their ardour for the music and their love for the community have allowed the Guelph Jazz Festival to grow into one of the premiere avant-garde music festivals in North America. Every year artists come to Guelph from as far away as South Africa, Norway, Switzerland, Germany, Israel, India, and Brazil, as well as from the United States and Canada, and, of course, many are featured who hail from the home community of Guelph. One year the festival commissioned the jazz opera *Québécité* (2003) by George Elliott Clarke; another year, it featured a rare North American appearance by the legendary South African pianist Abdullah Ibrahim (2012). Ajay Heble, founder and former artistic director of the Guelph Jazz Festival, describes the acts of programming, organizing, and putting on a jazz festival as engaging in acts of "meaning-making: in constructing narratives, histories, identities, and epistemologies that—sometimes modestly, sometimes profoundly—shape the way in which the music gets understood, listened to, and talked about." The music at the Guelph Jazz Festival functions as "a vehicle for facilitating other social formations."[28]

Soundin' Canaan's poets use Black music, from blues, jazz, reggae, dub, hip hop, DJ culture, remix, and other styles, so ubiquitously because these musics at their roots are tenaciously democratic. Black musics have been used since the time of slavery in North America to celebrate the human spirit and show its resilience. That is why Frederick Douglass declared the slave song the final realm of resistance to slavery, and it is more generally why I use Blackness throughout as a prefiguring and sonic counterpoint for identity formation, modes of belonging, and citizenship. One need only get lost in the *riddim* at Caribana in Toronto, attend a poetry slam at Café Deux Soleils in Vancouver, or fall into the fold of multiple, often discordant sounds at the Guelph Jazz Festival to realize that it is only when you let go that community—and poetry—is possible. That is, we can only move towards a just society when we learn to sound within a multiplicity of shared and intersecting cultural spaces. If we get over the idea that we can all speak to one another in an "authentic" universal way (and in this book, I've trumpeted the specific soundings of a group of influential Black poets), I think it will begin to be possible, as it always has been, for us to listen to one another, one at a time, and in the various clusters that present themselves.

FINAL REMIX

> I have, like all of you, on a thousand occasions seen indescribable displays of man's very real inhumanity to man . . . I say all of this to say that one cannot live with sighted eyes and feeling heart and not know and react to the miseries which afflict this world . . . I think that the human race does command its own destiny, and that that destiny can eventually embrace the stars.
>
> —LORRAINE HANSBERRY, "The Negro Writer and His Roots: Towards a New Romanticism," 11–12

The epigraph from Lorraine Hansberry describes the tragedy we live with every day knowing that there are wars, hate crimes, sexism, poverty, ecological destruction, intolerances, bigotry, racism, and other perversions of the human spirit, yet Hansberry moves past those inhumanities to imagine that we can one day arrive at a more just society and "embrace the stars." Similarly, Gwendolyn Brooks, at the end of *Maud Martha*, finds realist hope, despite "the latest of the Georgia and Mississippi lynchings," by contemplating that "the sun was shining, and some of the people in the world had been left alive, and it was doubtful whether the ridiculousness of man would ever completely succeed in destroying the world . . . was not this something to be thankful for? And, in the meantime, while people did live they would be grand, would be glorious and brave, would have nimble hearts that would beat and beat."[29] Both Hansberry and Brooks managed to remain optimistic about the perseverance of the human spirit, manifested in the goodwill and creativity of Blackness, even though—and remarkably—they were writing in pre–civil rights 1950s Chicago, facing all sorts of inequalities, being not only Black women but Black women writers. Their message is a simple yet important and universal one: despite the struggle of human existence, beauty, and the capacity to overcome tyranny, exists in all of us. It is important to remember Black joy and to learn from it rather than to focus solely on Black pain and exploit it.

The poet's role, as Clarke, Brand, Philip, K'naan, and Compton show, is to translate both the beauty and the ugliness of humanity and craft poems that move us, change our perceptions about the world, and even occasionally persuade us—if that be the intent—that we are not doing as much as we should to create a better world. Works by Clarke, Brand, Philip, K'naan, and Compton ask us to think critically about the function of poetry and to consider the implications of our soundings. Such an engagement is a collective calling to imagine different futures. As DJs, listeners, and improvisers on the edge, it is also a call to orient oneself to the music and poetry of the everyday realities of oppressed peoples and to help bend the moral arc of the universe a little closer towards justice (to paraphrase MLK).

All the poets in this book provide textual (and sonic) spaces that allow us to dream that we may one day achieve a more equitable society for all people. Believing in a pedagogy of hope affirms love, especially when we stand on the side of justice. Rethinking and reshaping Canada (even being open to unsettling it and remaking it into something else) requires us to envision our presence on this land without relying on the privileges inherited from conquest and empire. This entails acknowledging the significant historical Indigenous presence and actively supporting ongoing struggles for social and economic justice, particularly for Indigenous and Black communities. It involves advocating for substantial changes in government policies and recognizing the impact of our actions not only within Canada but also in places like Sudan, Syria, and Palestine. Ultimately, it signifies the pursuit of freedom for all. I do not have all the answers, not even close, but I hope *Soundin' Canaan* provides a few worthwhile interventions, fruitfully participates in the vast conversations already taking place about Black Canadian literature, and bestows a few new tracks to make the journey along the chosen literature a little more rewarding. Poetry remains an essential medium in which to articulate engaged soundings of citizenship that are always negotiated in relation to others. Indeed, we can get the news from poems/songs. We need to continue to define the role of the citizen—an exact definition would cancel itself out—by remaining engaged listeners, since citizenship is an ad hoc performance always happening, like listening, moment to moment.

Canada is a remix project. When "freedom seekers" travelled the Underground Railroad and entered Canada (Canaan land) they encountered anti-Black racism and faced new hardships that compelled them to rethink what Canada could be for them, and formed diverse communities such as Africville and Hogan's Alley. It is only through fraternity and collective understanding, allowing for ruptures, that we will arrive at that place the African American spirituals coded as heaven. As King stated in 1967, "we still have a long way to go before we reach the promised land of freedom . . . indeed, we need some North Star to guide us into a future shrouded with impenetrable uncertainties."[30] We have crossed many borders, yet we might still ask, where is here, or more importantly, where might we want here to be? What might that future sound like? We must continue to dream community to come, like those following the North Star, like Coltrane playing "Song of the Underground Railroad," like the various poets of *Soundin' Canaan* making the impossible possible for a moment, stepping out of the tragedy we so casually inflict on others, and into the light to hear the echo of the ancestors along with Douglass, reaching for that imaginary, but necessary heaven on earth—that just society—singing, with sadness and hope: "'O Canaan, sweet Canaan, I am bound for the land of Canaan.'"[31]

SHOUT OUTS!

My name may appear on the cover of this book, but the work is an intricate DJ mix comprised of many speaking voices. The ideas herein are the result of hundreds of conversations and self-reflections, thousands of pieces of spun vinyl, various and varied readings, and too many cups of tea to possibly count. Some of these early interlocutors include Cecil Foster, Christine Bold, Mark Kaethler, Smaro Kamboureli, Daniel Fischlin, Kevin McNeilly, Paul Barrett, and Jade Ferguson. Cecil's own writing about multiculturalism is, in many ways, the catalyst for my own conception about how we sound together to form meaningful (even if at times dissonant) communities comprised of citizens. And my old PhD supervisor, mentor, and dear friend Ajay Heble has done far more than guide my writing; he has shown me countless times that academic work is an opportunity to enact social change, particularly when rooted in the community. I am also thankful to all the poets in this book who made time and shared their ideas with me: George Elliott Clarke, Dionne Brand, M. NourbeSe Philip, Lillian Allen, d'bi.young, and Wayde Compton. Much appreciation for all the support, dialogue, and creative kinship from my all my colleagues at VIU, especially to Sonnet and Melissa for their conversations and modeling of activism. Thanks to Alison Jacques for her early copyediting work to convert an early manuscript from MLA to Chicago. And while reader reports are always a slightly terrifying thing to receive, both A1 and A2 offered fruitful suggestions to improve the book, and I am incredibly thankful for their interventions when I missed a key point or over-sounded an idea. Of course, any mistakes or oversimplifications remain my own.

Juliana Caicedo created the cover image based on my suggestions and created something better than I could dream up! A big shout out to my talented editors, Siobhan McMenemy and Murray Tong, and all the fine folks at WLU Press. Thanks for helping me to get my ideas out into the world. A special shout-out to my partner, Meg, for her invaluable eye and ear, and for her continued support. Her energy and love help to hold these words and myself together and sound beauty. Lastly, I also acknowledge that some parts of this research were supported by the Social Sciences and Humanities Research Council and Vancouver Island University's Publish Grant. Word!

Notes

Prelude

1 Gilroy, *The Black Atlantic*, 96.
2 Blanchard, "Black Protest Is Music."
3 "Oscar Peterson: The Life & Times of a Jazz Legend."
4 The idea of the "long civil rights movement" comes from historian Jacquelyn Dowd Hall, and many would argue that the movement continues in Black Lives Matter and the ongoing fight for freedom and equality.
5 Foster, *Where Race Does Not Matter*, 154.

Overture

1 Cooper, *The Hanging of Angélique*, 68.
2 Brown quoted in in Compton, *Blueprint*, 155. For a detailed account of how prevalent, rampant, and manifest, yet subversively subdued, slavery was and is in the canals of early Canadian history, see also the first two chapters of Robin Winks's seminal *The Blacks in Canada*.
3 Winks, *Blacks in Canada*, 235. While there is much to admire about Winks's text, as scholar David Austin describes, "Winks leaves little room for self-activity or self-organization of Blacks – that is, their own efforts to organize themselves in order to humanize their existence or confront Canadian racial oppression." Austin, *Fear of a Black Nation*, 139. Winks makes the point that investigations of Southern slave songs show that Canaan, the promised land, was equated most often with Africa and seldom with Canada. Winks, *Blacks in Canada*, 237. However, theologian and scholar James H. Cone argues that Canaan had multiple associations: "Heaven referred to Africa, Canada, and the northern United States." Cone, *The Spirituals and the Blues*, 80. Whether the slave songs—the spirituals—were directly associated with Canada or not, the use of Canaan to refer to Canada as heaven continues to this day and carries important mythic value for Black writers in Canada.
4 Douglass, *Narrative*, 51.

5 Mary Ann Shadd quoted in Silverman, *Unwelcomed Guests*, 158. Also see Shadd, *A Plea for Emigration*. While settlers' guides like Susanna Moodie's *Roughing It in the Bush* (1852) have been studied as paradigmatically Canadian, Shadd's *Plea for Emigration*, published roughly around the same time (1853), sheds new light on lived African Canadian realities in the nineteenth century. Often Shadd does suggest, given the dangers of the Fugitive Slave Law (which made life dangerous for American Blacks), that Canada West was an ideal place to start a new life—a just society and a good place to earn a decent living: "If a coloured man understands his business, he receives the public patronage the same as a white man ... There is no degraded class to identify him with, therefore every man's work stands or falls according to merit, not as is his colour ... [Canada is] a country in which slavery is not tolerated, and prejudice of *colour* has no existence whatsoever" (59–60). Shadd's rhetoric is largely about the possibilities for Canada as other to the United States, and often the realities of Canadian racism very clearly manifest themselves in her straightforward prose. For example, she describes how white residents moved away from Black residents as they formed the settlement of Elgin, about ten miles from Chatham, Ontario: "When purchase was made of these lands many white families were residents ... At first, a few sold out, fearing that such neighbours might not be agreeable" (68). And so, white Canadian racism remains subtly, and yet very clearly, couched within Shadd's text.
6 Hartman, *Lose Your Mother*, 6.
7 Hudson, "Building Community, Building Resistance."
8 Winks, *Blacks in Canada*, 24.
9 Douglass, *The Life and Times*, 110.
10 Maynard, *Policing Black Lives*, 11.
11 Hall, "Cultural Identity and Diaspora," 222.
12 Sylvia Wynter's definition of the human challenges traditional Western ideas and calls for a more inclusive and culturally diverse understanding of humanity, emphasizing the importance of narratives and recognizing the impact of colonialism and race on our perceptions of the human. Her work invites us to reconsider and expand our concept of humanity to be more inclusive and sensitive to different cultural perspectives. While much more could be said on this topic, the reader might want to check out her numerous essays, or the 2015 edited collection of essays about her work. See McKittrick, ed., *Sylvia Wynter*.
13 For example, see the 1951 Massey Report, which asks, "Is there a national literature?"
14 Brand and De Shield, eds., *No Burden to Carry*, 29; Mensah, *Black Canadians*, 45; Walker, *A History of Blacks in Canada*, 3.
15 Sanders, "White Teacher, Black Literature," 169, 172, 173.
16 Lipsitz, *The Possessive Investment in Whiteness*, 3, 22.
17 Lipsitz, *The Possessive Investment in Whiteness*, 2. Lipsitz describes the devastating effects of racism: "Environmental racism makes the possessive investment in whiteness literally a matter of life and death; if African Americans had access to

the nutrition, health care, and protection against environmental hazards offered routinely to whites, seventy-five thousand fewer of them would die each year" (10).
18 Shadd quoted in Chancy, *Searching for Safe Spaces*, 80.
19 Cools, "Womanhood," 8.
20 Fern Shadd Shreve quoted in Brand and De Shield, eds., *No Burden*, 279.
21 Fanon, *Wretched of the Earth*, 232; Walcott, *Queer Returns*, 236.
22 It is worth noting that the Ohio River as Jordan figures in various novels concerning slavery, from Harriet Beecher Stowe's *Uncle Tom's Cabin* to Toni Morrison's *Beloved*, both of which contain scenes of enslaved mothers making incredible escapes across the river with children in tow. Also worth referencing is the title of Cecil Foster's *A Place Called Heaven*, since heaven was how many freedom seekers thought of Canada until fiercely racist encounters proved them unfortunately wrong.
23 The ongoing struggle for justice by the people of Palestine is crucial to acknowledge and encompasses settler violence in the West Bank and the military occupation of Gaza by Israel. Subsequently, there have been indiscriminate bombings of citizens—mostly women and children—in Gaza, most recently and severely in response to Hamas's violent attack on October 7, 2023. While the abuses faced by Palestinians, dating back over 100 years, fall outside the focus of this book, it is essential to recognize the connection and kinship between the struggles of Indigenous Peoples in Canada, freedom seekers worldwide, Jewish people seeking safety and homeland, and Palestinians in the Middle East. This recognition is particularly pertinent as the book explores theoretical approaches to citizenship and community. In the context of Palestine, and in my understanding, this does not mean expelling Israelis from Israel any more than Land Back means expelling Canadians from Canada/Turtle Island through a reinscribed violence, but it does mean a mutual recognition and anticolonial approach to sustainable and reconciliatory existence. As Palestinian-American historian Rashid Khalidi writes in the conclusion of his book, *The Hundred Years' War on Palestine*, "While the fundamentally colonial nature of the Palestinian-Israel encounter must be acknowledged, there are now two peoples in Palestine, irrespective of how they came into being, and the conflict between them cannot be resolved as long as the national existence of each is denied by the other. Their mutual acceptance can only be based on complete equality of rights, including national rights, notwithstanding the crucial historical differences between the two." Rashid Khalidi, 460. Black, Jewish, and Palestinian liberation are all interconnected, and we can identify lines of affinity with Jewish thinkers (including Noam Chomsky, Ilan Pappé, Gabor Maté, and Naomi Klein) and organizations (initially in Bundism and later in Jewish Voice of Peace), as well as with Black thinkers (such as Nelson Mandela, Malcolm X, James Baldwin, and June Jordan) and organizations like Black Lives Matter.
24 Said, "Michael Walzer's 'Exodus and Revolution,'" 91.
25 West, "Minority Discourse," 197.

26 Spivak, *Outside in the Teaching Machine*, 304, 305. I also concur with African American feminist Deborah E. McDowell that canons in literary studies can function usefully as a "unit of disciplinary organization and understanding." McDowell, *"The Changing Same,"* 22.
27 I find value in the literatures I study while trying to leave any singular aesthetic taste out of my analysis. As Marcel Duchamp said, "I consider taste—good or bad—the great enemy of art." Duchamp quoted in Kuh, *The Artist's Voice*, 94.
28 Mackey, *Discrepant Engagement*, 3.
29 While I occasionally apply quotations when possible from the living authors whose work is examined in this book, opinions in interviews are hardly the sole focus; rather, they provide another layer of polyphonic dialogue or antiphonic response to "the mix" of *Soundin' Canaan*. Also, see Nigel Thomas's conversations with various Black Canadian writers in *Why We Write*.
30 I try to be as specific as possible, although I often use "Black Canadian" as the default even though it might not always be perfect. I realize that no label can or should unequivocally speak to all people of African descent in Canada, and both "Black Canadian" and "African Canadian" acknowledge the hyphenated/split nature of the Black and African Canadian experience (although I've chosen to leave African Canadian unhyphenated to avoid any association with the word as a hyphenated epithet, such as was common in the early twentieth century for those of foreign birth) emphasized in many of the texts I explore. I keep the "Canadian" in both terms largely for the three reasons Nigel Thomas does: (1) on a literal level, people in Canada choose to hold a Canadian passport, or at least remain here; (2) it indicates the embracing of Canadian values, particularly the right of children to grow up in a safe environment free from a fear of violence; and (3) it indicates a strong belief and value in community.
31 *Listening for Something*.
32 Marlene NourbeSe Philip, personal communication [email], 5 May 2014. In *Blank*, Philip gives a definition of Afrosporic: "a neologism I have coined to describe the scattering of Africans around the world. It contains the roots of the place, Afro, and the idea of spore which is scattered" (37).
33 Walcott, ed., *Black Like Who?*, 27.
34 Maynard, *Policing Black Lives*, 5.
35 Clarke, *Odysseys Home*, 48. Clarke deliberately hyphenates "African-Canadian" to emphasize the split nature of the term. I personally think the term could be used either way but have chosen "African Canadian" for the reasons stated in an earlier note and to remain stylistically consistent.
36 Clarke, *Odysseys Home*, 188. It is also important to remember—and these tensions get fleshed out more in the chapter on (and in my interview with) George Elliott Clarke—that Clarke's ideas expressed in "Treason of the Black Intellectuals?" have changed over the years and that the essay itself is intended to spark debate and open up new conversations regarding scholarship from Black intellectuals.
37 Walcott, *Black Like Who?*, 13.

38 Walcott, *Black Like Who?*, 22.
39 Philip, *Blank*, 75.
40 Agamben, *The Coming Community*.
41 Agamben, *Homo Sacer*, 131.
42 Sharpe, *In the Wake*, 9.
43 Joseph, "Recollections: A Seventees [sic] Black RAP," 20.
44 Clarke, *Directions Home*, 4. To not investigate the history and legacy (over 350 years) of African Canadian people—including the various social and cultural vicissitudes—is, in the words of George Elliott Clarke, to opt for a "veritable intellectual treason." Clarke, *Odysseys Home*, 198.
45 There were many other Black communities in Canada beyond Africville and Hogan's Alley. For another, see Vernon, ed., *The Black Prairie Archives*.
46 Brand, *Bread out of Stone*, 37.
47 King, *The Inconvenient Indian*, 2–3.
48 Winks's *The Blacks in Canada* was originally published in 1971, with a second edition containing a new introduction by Winks and his thoughts on the impact of his work published in 1997. His work details the diverse experiences of slavery and Black immigration in Canada, focusing on both the French and English periods of slavery, the abolitionist movement in Canada (including the cross-border continental anti-slavery crusade), the experiences of enslaved people brought to Nova Scotia and throughout the rest of Canada by Loyalists after the American Revolution, Black refugees who fled to Nova Scotia following the War of 1812, the experiences of the Jamaican Maroons (as well as the fugitives who fled to various regions of British North America), and the formation of the Canadian Canaans.
49 See Cooper, *The Hanging of Angélique*; her "Confessions of a Woman Who Burnt Down a Town," in *Copper Woman and Other Poems*, 73–76; and Gale, *Angélique*.
50 McKittrick, *Demonic Grounds*, 118.
51 McKittrick, *Demonic Grounds*, 18.
52 *The Provincial Freeman* was published from 24 March 1853 to 20 September 1857, first in Windsor, then in Toronto and Chatham. Published weekly, it advocated equality, integration, and self-education for Black people in Canada and the United States. The tone of the paper towards *Uncle Tom's Cabin* (and white North America generally) was more critically fervent than most African Americans and African Canadians living at the time, including Frederick Douglass, allowed themselves to be.
53 King, *The Trumpet of Conscience*, 3.
54 Clarke, *The Survivors of the Crossing*, 31, 57, 104.
55 Freire quoted in Macedo, Introduction to *Pedagogy of the Oppressed*, 13.
56 Davis and Troupe, *Miles: The Autobiography*, 406.
57 Philip, *A Genealogy of Resistance*, 116. Philip's position towards non-linearity is in clear opposition to George Elliott Clarke's desire to record a specific African Canadian history that informs his nationalist stance towards Black writing in

Canada. Philip's general approach to history—informed by African conceptions of time—speaks to why she took issue with people interpreting *12 Years a Slave* as historical vérité. As she told me, "It is, for instance, one of the reasons I find *12 Years a Slave* a profoundly problematic film. A throw back and I was amused to read in a *Guardian* interview with the filmmaker that he didn't look at any pre-existing films on slavery. I am surprised that he wouldn't have seen a film such a *Sankofa*, for instance. A film which flew under the radar. I understand this urge and even the need to 'tell the story'—as if in telling the story as realistically as possible will accomplish something—make it more real, perhaps? *12 Years a Slave* remains trapped in that belief, locked in the hold of a sort of historical vérité approach—a belief that you can tell the story. This is what gives it the Slavery 101 feel—every trope of slavery must be hit, and then we all go off believing that all is well with the world. We understand how horrible slavery was and, therefore, are all the better for it. I say there must be more and less to the process than that." Philip quoted in "We Can Never Tell the Entire Story of Slavery."

58 Heble, "Sounds of Change," 27.
59 Clarke, *Trudeau: Long March, Shining Path*, 110; Spillers, "Cross Currents, Discontinuities," 250.
60 Compton, "Declaration of the Halfrican Nation," 15. Compton is riffing upon Countee Cullen's poem "Heritage" [1925], which asks, "What is Africa to me?"
61 Clarke, *Odysseys Home*, 6.
62 Clarke, *Odysseys Home*, 7.
63 See, for example, Richardson and Green, eds., *T-Dot Griots*; Siemerling, *The Black Atlantic Reconsidered*; and Vernon, ed., *Black Prairie Archives*.
64 In the preface to the 2004 edition of *Survival*, Margaret Atwood argues in regard to Canadian literature that "still today, we have to start with the same axioms: i) it exists, and ii) it's distinct." Atwood, *Survival*, 7.
65 Atwood, *Survival*, 19.
66 It is worth noting that Camille Haynes's *Black Chat: An Anthology of Black Poets* (1973) is the first anthology of Black poets in Canada.
67 Frye, "Conclusion," 338. Black Canadians have had to ask themselves both "Where is Here?" and "Who am I?"
68 Brand, *Bread Out of Stone*, 137.
69 Sadly, many of these texts are difficult to find or have not been reissued except for Laferrière's popular text, which was made into a feature film and has been translated into several languages.
70 Nielsen, *Black Chant*, 13.
71 Baraka, "Black Dada Nihilismus," in *The Dead Lecturer*, 63.
72 Richardson and Green, *T-Dot Griots*, viii–ix.
73 Kelley, *Race Rebels*, 4, 5, 8. *Race Rebels* further provides an interesting reassessment of what we traditionally consider viable political action, moving from the struggles waged by factory workers to the insurgent politics of Malcolm X (while he was still Malcolm Little) to the modern gangster lyricism of present-day rappers.

74 Lisa Coulthard, "Great Artists Steal," in Augaitis, Grenville, and Rebick, eds., *MashUp*, 238.
75 Compton, "Turntable Poetry," 199.
76 Taylor, *The Archive and the Repertoire*. While the archive is certainly important to scholarly work, Taylor usefully argues that performance (from plays to grassroots movements) must be taken as critical forms of knowledge transmission, a transmission that is conveyed in the "embodied memory" of spoken word, movement, dance, song, and various gestures. Performance provides alternative perspectives to those of the written archive, which I've conflated via the DJ metaphor to highlight the active nature of how an archive can be sounded in a variety of media in the liminality of transnational contact zones.
77 Small, *Musicking*, 2.
78 Head, ed., *Canada in Us Now*, 9.
79 Mackey, *Discrepant Engagement*, 122.
80 Clarke quoted in Thomas, *Why We Write*, 16.
81 Douglass, *Narrative*, 57. African American liberation scholar James H. Cone echoes Douglass when he states that "through music black slaves ritualized their existence and gave to their lives a dimension of promise and new reality that could not be contained in human theologies and philosophies." Cone, *The Spirituals and the Blues*, 90.
82 Ellison, "Richard Wright's Blues," 8.
83 Parker, *Who Owns Music?*, 58.
84 Philip, *Zong!*, 207.
85 Philip, *Blank*, 24.
86 Baker, *Black Studies, Rap, and the Academy*, 81.
87 Baker, *Blues, Ideology*, 3.
88 Lewis, "Improvised Music after 1950."
89 Thomas, ed., *Why We Write*, 3.
90 Thomas, ed., *Why We Write*, 76.
91 Walcott, *Black Like Who?*, 28, 22.
92 Weheliye, *Phonographies*, 6, 45, 8.
93 For scholarly examples that explore such literary confluences, see, among others, Baker, *Blues, Ideology*; Gates, *The Signifying Monkey*; and Weheliye, *Phonographies*.
94 Stewart, "Call and Recall," 240.
95 Baraka, *Digging*, 102.
96 Although published in 1952, *Invisible Man* remains as pertinent as ever, particularly when set against the 2014–15 backdrop of social unrest and uprising in Ferguson and all too frequent incidents of racial profiling, often with dire consequences, as in the cases of Oscar Grant III and Trayvon Martin; within a Canadian framework, the novel's theme of invisibility relates heartbreakingly to the general invisibility of Indigenous people, specifically the disappearance and murder of Indigenous women.
97 Ellison, *Invisible Man*, 7–8.

98　Weheliye, *Phonographies*, 47.
99　Du Bois, *The Souls of Black Folk*, 157.
100　Birney, *The Cow Jumped Over the Moon*, 2.
101　Okri, *A Way of Being Free*, 46.
102　Barrett, *Blackening Canada*, 4.
103　Lyotard, "The Other's Rights," 184.
104　The 2016 census indicates that 46.9 percent of Toronto's population is foreign-born.
105　Cole, *The Skin We're In*, 8.
106　Mackey, *Discrepant Engagement*, 34. Cornel West also articulates that in jazz collectives "individuality is promoted in order to sustain and increase the *creative* tension within the group—a tension that yields higher levels of performance to achieve the aim of the collective." West, *Race Matters*, 105. Jazz critic Ekkehard Jost emphasizes a similar sentiment: "One of the emancipatory effects of free jazz throughout its evolution, is that each and every member of a group is theoretically equal to all the others." Jost, *Free Jazz*, 195. We also find an emphasis upon the notion of jazz collectivity in Ralph Ellison's collection of essays, *Shadow and Act*, where he states that "the delicate balance struck between strong individual personality and the group during those early jam sessions was a marvel of social organization." Ellison, *Shadow and Act*, 189.
107　Brand quoted in Chancy, *Searching for Safe Spaces*, 117. The public's conception of the margin is semiotically codified by what the "centre" considers outside the norm. M. NourbeSe Philip writes that the "margin . . . has another meaning . . . That meaning is 'frontier.' Surely this meaning is encapsulated in Stuart Hall's phrase, 'emergent energies and experiences which stubbornly resist' the dominant culture." Philip, *Blank*, 84.
108　Again, I am identifying with Blackness as a theoretical position that is anti-colonial, anti-racist, and the antithesis of whiteness as the default for the human.
109　Thompson, *Aesthetic of the Cool*, 29, 145.
110　Butler, *Precarious Life*, 49.
111　Small, *Musicking*, 203.
112　Thompson, dir., *Summer of Soul*.
113　Bailey, *Improvisation*, ix.
114　Roy, "The Pandemic Is a Portal."
115　Scahill, "Scholar Robin D.G. Kelley."
116　Giovanni, *Racism 101*, 154–55.
117　Fischlin and Heble, eds., *The Other Side of Nowhere*, 7.
118　Douglass, *Narrative*, 57.
119　This claim fits with arguments advanced by an evolving body of research and scholarship, loosely defined as critical studies in improvisation, which sees in improvisational artistic practices a vital model for social practice and social change. Most recently, this research culminated in the release of pivotal books in critical improvisation studies through the Improvisation, Community, and

Social Practice Series, a series of six co-authored and co-edited volumes with Duke University Press. Readers might also want to familiarize themselves with new and exciting research in critical improvisation studies by looking at the free online journal *Critical Studies in Improvisation/Études critique en improvisation*. Lastly, see the International Institute for Critical Studies in Improvisation (IICSI), a research institute (fifty-nine scholars from twenty institutions) whose mandate is to create positive social change through the confluence of improvisational arts, innovative scholarship, and collaborative action (http://improvisationinstitute.ca).

120 One example of such an approach is Wallace, *Improvisation and the Making of American Literary Modernism*, which analyzes how modernist writing was influenced by or engaged with improvisation—perhaps the central feature of twentieth-century American music—by looking at four modernist poets: Ezra Pound, Langston Hughes, Gertrude Stein, and Wallace Stevens. Another example is Philip James Pastras's unpublished dissertation, "A Clear Field: The Idea of Improvisation in Modern Poetry," which, although written in 1981, rings true in literary studies to this day: "scholarship has been silent on the subject of improvisation." Pastras, "A Clear Field," v.
121 Richardson and Green, eds., *T-Dot Griots*, ix.
122 Rubin Museum, "Pauline Oliveros."
123 Sterne, "Sonic Imaginations," 11.
124 Bernstein, *Close Listening*, 9, 21.
125 Iton, *In Search of the Black Fantastic*, 136.
126 Hill quoted in Thomas, *Why We Write*, 145.
127 Andrisani, "The Sweet Sounds of Havana."
128 Brubaker, *Citizenship and Nationhood*, x.
129 Brubaker, *Citizenship and Nationhood*, 23.
130 "Brad Wall: Syrian Refugee Plan Should Be Suspended," https://www.nationalnewswatch.com/2015/11/16/saskatchewan-premier-wall-wants-trudeau-to-suspend-plan-for-25000-refugees.
131 It is relevant to mention that this was not as much an issue of Canadian citizenship as one of British Empire citizenships. There was no Canadian citizenship until 1946, when Parliament passed the *Canadian Citizenship Act*, which established the basis of Canadian citizenship.
132 King, *The Inconvenient Indian*, 137.
133 Justice, *Why Indigenous Literatures Matter*, 10.
134 Beckford, *Naturally Woman*, 36.
135 There have been a variety of racist immigration policies and acts that emphasize Canada's desire to remain a white settler nation, including the following: *Canada West's Common Schools Act of 1850*, which reinforced segregated education; *Immigration Act of 1906*, which prohibited the landing of the "feeble-minded," "beggars," etc.; *Immigration Act of 1910*, which empowered the government to prohibit the entry of "any race deemed unsuited to the climate or requirements

of Canada"; and *Immigration Act of 1952*, which allowed the minister to prohibit the entry of any immigrant because of nationality, ethnic group, citizenship, occupation, class, climatic criterion, and so on. It wasn't until the 1940s that Canada began to undo some of the damage of its early racist policies through acts such as the *Racial Discrimination Act of 1944*, which in Ontario prohibited any sign or publication that expressed racial or religious discrimination. The West Indian Domestic Scheme of 1955 to 1967 allowed Caribbean women to come to Canada, many of whom would go on to pursue other professions. The *Immigration Act of 1976* placed emphasis on family unification and the settlement of refugees, leading to an influx of Black people in Canada.

136 Maynard, *Policing Black Lives*, 182.
137 See Ontario Human Rights Commission, *A Collective Impact*.
138 Walcott, *On Property*, 34.
139 Foster, *They Call Me George*, 89.
140 Heater, *What Is Citizenship?*, 114.
141 *Dred Scott v. Sandford* (1857), also known as the Dred Scott Decision, was a landmark decision by the US Supreme Court that made two primary rulings: first, that African Americans were not citizens and therefore had no standing to sue in federal court, and second, that the federal government did not have the power to regulate slavery in any territory of the United States. Wikipedia, s.v., "Dred Scott v. Sandford," last modified 15 March 2022, 19:24, https://en.wikipedia.org/wiki/Dred_Scott_v._Sandford.
142 While rights are fundamentally about principles of freedom and entitlement, I raise the question about animal and environmental rights, even if these issues are too far outside the scope of the book to meaningfully engage, given that once we start thinking about global citizenship we must consider not only how our actions on the environment affect animals but also how pollution, or the dumping of waste in the sea surrounding poor countries, directly affects the delicate ecosystem that binds us all together.
143 Iton, *In Search of the Black Fantastic*, 202.
144 Siemerling, "Bi-culturalism, Multiculturalism," 150.
145 Compton, *49th Parallel*, 92–93.
146 Foster, *Blackness and Modernity*, 503.
147 Pierre Elliott Trudeau argued that the modern state is pluralistic, and one in which citizens must come together as individuals with equal rights and mutual tolerance, irrespective of their ethnic background, class, or religion. Trudeau, *The Essential Trudeau*, 100.
148 Watkins, "Writing Jazz" [interview transcript], 6.
149 In my interview with Foster, he articulates: "Trudeau was the only candidate to mention Martin Luther King, to mention the importance of what was happening, and the fact that there were weapons in the street. And he would then go on to argue in much of his speeches, especially when he was facing down the nationalists in Quebec, that the kind of violence that they were suggesting—he said, 'there is

a right way or wrong way,' and I'm not passing judgment on that—he said that kind of violence was the same kind of violence that had resulted in the death of Kennedy, the second Kennedy, Robert, and Martin Luther King. So he always had those frames of reference." Watkins, "Writing Jazz," 7.
150 It was John Stuart Mill who first asked the question "What is a just society?" The Just Society was a rhetorical device used by Trudeau to depict his vision for the nation. It was part and parcel of his governmental ideology and was used in all his policies from multiculturalism to the *Charter of Rights and Freedoms* (1982). Although the Just Society was intended to provide more freedom to all Canadians—as Trudeau argued, "The Just Society will be one in which our Indian and Inuit population will be encouraged to assume the full rights of citizenship"—many Indigenous people saw the policy as yet another governmental policy for assimilating Indigenous people into Canadian society. Trudeau, *The Essential Trudeau*, 19. Cree leader Harold Cardinal turned the phrase around in his book *The Unjust Society* (Vancouver: Douglas & McIntyre, 1969) to argue against the assimilation of First Nations into white Canadian society.
151 Davis, *Horizon, Sea, Sound*, xvii.
152 Walcott, *Black Like Who?*, 35, 119, 139.
153 Walcott, *Queer Returns*, 85.
154 Nancy, *Being Singular Plural*, 152.
155 Robert Kroetsch contends that Canadians cannot agree on what their meta-narrative is and suggests that "this very falling-apart of our story is what holds our story together." Kroetsch, "Disunity as Unity," 61.
156 Walcott, *Black Like Who?*, 22.
157 Nancy, *The Inoperative Community*, 71.
158 Ramsey, *Race Music*, 187.
159 Philip, *A Genealogy of Resistance*, 127.
160 Small, *Musicking*, 208.
161 Lingold, Mueller, and Trettien, eds., "Introduction," in *Digital Sound Studies*, ed. Lingold, Mueller, and Trettien, 5
162 Dionne Brand, "Imagination, Representation and Culture," in *Bread Out of Stone*, 133–46; Fiske, "Surveilling the City."
163 Leland, *Hip: The History*, 36.
164 Hip hop scholar M.K. Asante Jr. defines an "artivist" as the artist who uses his or her "artistic talents to fight and struggle against injustice and oppression—by any medium necessary." Asante, *It's Bigger Than Hip Hop*, 203.
165 Freire, *Pedagogy of the Oppressed*, 54.

Coda

1 Grove Music Online, s.v. "Coda," by Roger Bullivant, rev. by James Webster, https://doi.org/10.1093/gmo/9781561592630.article.06033.
2 Hughes, *The Collected Works*, vol. 7, 228.

3 Brand, *A Kind of Perfect Speech*, 17.
4 Hughes, *The Collected Poems*, 5.
5 Frye, *Northrop Frye on Canada*, 288. Frye's view of poetry was a modernist view about form: "the poet's quest is for form." See Frye, *The Bush Garden*, 179.
6 Fischlin, Heble, and Lipsitz, *The Fierce Urgency of Now*, 233.
7 Singer and Dunn, eds., *Literary Aesthetics*, 3.
8 Du Bois, "Criteria of Negro Art."
9 Amiri Baraka, "'People Get Ready' / The Future of Jazz: Amiri Baraka and William Parker in Conversation," ed. Paul Watkins, 1 August 2014, http://www.improvcommunity.ca/sites/improvcommunity.ca/files/research_collection/96/Future_of_Jazz_transcript.pdf. Note that Baraka was interested in socialist causes throughout his life, as was Du Bois before him, and that both put what they wrote into practice. I certainly hear an echo with Mao Zedong, who wrote, "[our purpose is] to ensure that literature and art fit well into the whole revolutionary machine as a component part, that they operate as powerful weapons for uniting and educating the people and for attacking and destroying the enemy, and that they help the people fight the enemy with one heart and one mind." Mao, *Selected Works*, vol. 3, 70. While I advocate for group rights and revolutionary thought, some of Mao's militaristic language infringes on individual rights. Furthermore, while I am encouraging a mixture of art and aesthetics, there remains a danger that political rhetoric might impose a limited standard upon beauty, turning what is interpreted as beautiful into a civilizing project to create desired citizens, as communist (and fascist; Hitler loved art) revolutions, for instance, often ban certain artworks or art forms in the name of ideology. Still, it is my intention that the mixing of beauty and propaganda can open up more inclusive notions of citizenship and belonging. Once again, this is where poetics and hermeneutics come back into the mix and where I remind my reader that this book is both an interpretation of a body of textual work and a theoretical manifesto of hope.

Chapter 1: Blues Vernacular and "Harmonious Dissonance" in George Elliott Clarke's Colouring Pentateuch

1 Miles Davis, *Kind of Blue* (Columbia, 1959).
2 Clarke, *Black*, 94.
3 The notes to Bill Evans's *The Complete Riverside Recordings* (1984) give credit to both Evans and Davis. In the Fall 1993 issue of *Letter from Evans*, Earl Zindars claims that the piece is 100 percent Bill Evans's "because he wrote it over at my pad where I was staying in East Harlem, 5th floor walkup, and he stayed until 3 o'clock in the morning playing these six bars over and over." Zindars quoted in Hinkle, "Interview with Earl Zindars," 20.
4 Clarke, *Blue*, "L'Asassinat," 77.
5 Davis and Troupe, *Miles: The Autobiography*, 231.
6 Clarke, *Black*, 95.

7 Thomas, "Some Aspects of Blues Use," 42.
8 Johnson, "Autobiography of an Ex Colored Man," 1197.
9 Du Bois, *The Souls of Black Folk*, 2.
10 Weheliye, *Phonographies*, 82.
11 Kelley, "Notes on Deconstructing the Folk," 1402.
12 Gioia, *Delta Blues*, 38.
13 Davis, *Blues Legacies and Black Feminism*, 42, 55.
14 Cone, *The Spirituals and the Blues*, 1, 5.
15 Malcolm X and Haley, *The Autobiography of Malcolm X*, 129.
16 Cone, *The Spirituals and the Blues*, Spirituals, 111.
17 Baker, *Blues, Ideology*, 8.
18 Wilson, *Ma Rainey's Black Bottom*, 82.
19 Baker, *Blues, Ideology*, 3.
20 Clarke, *Blue*, 11.
21 Baker, *Blues, Ideology*, 5.
22 Baraka quoted in Wallace, *Improvisation*, 68.
23 It is important to remember that Black writers did not unequivocally appreciate Hughes's contributions, as James Baldwin criticized "The Weary Blues," saying that it "copies, rather than exploits, the cadences of the blues." Baldwin quoted in Wallace, *Improvisation*, 96. Hughes's performances were perceived more often as those of a musician reading a score rather than as improvising. Harold Bloom also had a distaste for Hughes, but Bloom's cantankerous disposition regarding change (as mentioned, he also dislikes slam poetry) renders his opinion rather conservative and institutional.
24 Clarke, *Odysseys Home*, 188.
25 Gates, *The Signifying Monkey*, 81, 105.
26 Ellison, *Invisible Man*, 388.
27 Semiotics, defined as the interpretation of signs, has moved through both structural and post-structural applications. The application of the term as a science of signs relating to human language was introduced by Ferdinand de Saussure in his *Course in General Linguistics* (1916). What is foundational in Saussure is that the sign is both arbitrary and differential, and thus we can distinguish between signs. As Gates points out, in standard English signification denotes meaning and in the Black tradition it denotes ways of meaning, thus allowing the sign/signified more malleability.
28 Gates, *The Signifying Monkey*, 51.
29 Clarke, ed., *Eyeing the North Star*, xxiv.
30 Clarke, *Lush Dreams*, 16.
31 Clarke, "Invocation of the Prophet" and "Campbell Road Church," in *Lush Dreams*, 57, 73.
32 Compton, "'Even the stars are temporal,'" 18.
33 Clarke, *Saltwater Spirituals and Deeper Blues*, 41; Anne Compton, "Standing Your Ground: George Elliott Clarke in Conversation," *Studies in Canadian Literature* 23, no. 2 (1998): 142–43.

34 Compton, "Standing Your Ground," 146.
35 Watkins, ed., "'Your bass sounds like a typewriter.'"
36 Clarke, *Eyeing the North Star*, xii.
37 Ayanna Black quoted in Clarke, *Eyeing the North Star*, xix.
38 Clarke, "George & Rue," in *Execution Poems*, 12.
39 Gilroy, *The Black Atlantic*, 15.
40 Davey, *From There to Here*, 16.
41 Clarke, *Trudeau: Long March*, 72.
42 Clarke, *Directions Home*, 6.
43 Clarke, *Odysseys Home*, 45.
44 Clarke, *Directions Home*, 5.
45 Clarke, *Directions Home*, 6.
46 Clarke, *Directions Home*, 5.
47 Philip quoted in Thomas, *Why We Write*, 207.
48 Clarke quoted in A. Compton, "Standing Your Ground," 160.
49 We find some echo of this approach in Theophus Smith's *Conjuring Culture*. In that book, Smith delves into the utilization of the Christian Bible within the Black community as a gateway to Black nationalism that goes beyond the confines of specific nations. This perspective emphasizes a dedication to a global perspective that extends beyond one's affiliation with temporal nation-states, bypassing the need for citizenship in such entities.
50 Quill, "Toronto's Fourth Poet Laureate."
51 Clarke, *Odysseys Home*, 16.
52 Baker, *Modernism and the Harlem Renaissance*, 93.
53 Baker, *Modernism and the Harlem Renaissance*, 50.
54 McKay and Clarke might use the sonnet just as Shakespeare does (examining the passage of time, beauty, love, and mortality), the form being a perfect battlefield for warring ideas, yet they explore issues of race, gender, and regionalism, which—although also concerns of Shakespeare—are presented in wholly new ways influenced by the experience of being raced in a modern/postmodern context far outside Shakespeare's universalism.
55 Clarke quoted in Compton, "Standing Your Ground," 141.
56 Clarke, "George Elliott Clarke to Derek Walcott," 16–17.
57 Gates, *Signifying Monkey*, 92.
58 Clarke, "Antiphony," in *Blue*, 21.
59 Clarke, *Odysseys Home*, 9.
60 Clarke, "The Crime of Poetry," 62.
61 Clarke, "The Crime of Poetry," 57.
62 Clarke, "Towards a Geography of Three Miles Plains, N.S.," in *Black*, 56.
63 Clarke, "Afterword," in *Blues and Bliss*, 60; Clarke, *Where Beauty Survived*, 247.
64 Watkins, "Your bass," 3.
65 Clarke, *Where Beauty Survived*, 86.
66 Clarke, *Where Beauty Survived*, 113.

67 *Whylah Falls*, like his poetic colouring books, uses a language closely aligned with the lyricism of blues music: "*Whylah Falls* was born in the blues." Clarke, *Whylah Falls*, xxiii. Clarke does not seem to care too much about being described as a formalist, so long as he is read or, as he describes, sung: "Say I scribe 'vernacular formalism' [McNeilly] I don't care—so long as I be sounded, recited, sung." Clarke, "Afterword," 63.
68 Clarke, *Whylah Falls*, 171; Clarke, *Trudeau*, 53.
69 Clarke, *Illuminated Verses*, 32; Clarke, *Québécité*, 36, 77.
70 Compton, "Standing Your Ground," 146.
71 Watkins, "Your bass," 3.
72 Clarke often mentions his indebtedness to Bob Dylan. In reformulating T.S. Eliot's self-identification he describes himself as a tyro bard, "Poundian in poetics, Dylanesque in politics, and African American in faith." Clarke, "Afterword," 60.
73 Watkins, "Your bass," 10.
74 Clarke, *Where Beauty Survived*, 249.
75 Watkins, "Harmonious Dissonance."
76 Watkins, "Your bass," 10.
77 Clarke, "Cool Politics: Styles of Honour in Malcolm X and Miles Davis." *Jouvert: A Journal of Postcolonial Studies* 2, no. 1 (1998), https://legacy.chass.ncsu.edu/jouvert/v2i1/CLARKE.HTM.
78 Gilroy, *The Black Atlantic*, 110.
79 Clarke, "Africadian Experience," in *Black*, 60. And from *Whylah Falls*: "The end of this world is beauty"; "How can any poem / picture my beauty?"; "Is our fate / to become beautiful / only after tremendous pain"; "Every act must reveal Beauty. / Hence, under the orange moon/ of Whylah Falls, / I am plucking this poem." Clarke, *Whylah Falls*, 21, 70, 109, 180.
80 Clarke quoted in Watkins, "Your bass," 5.
81 Clarke, "Secret History," in *Blue*, 83.
82 Fiorentino, "Blackening English." Some of the ideas for my reading of *Blue* are adapted from Fiorentino's reading of Clarke's work.
83 C.L.R. James refers to himself, and by extension to West Indians, as Caliban in the preface to his *Beyond a Boundary*. James argues, "To establish his own identity, Caliban, after three centuries, must himself pioneer into regions Caesar never knew." James, *Beyond a Boundary*, 9. Caesar is a metaphor for the British colonialists.
84 Clarke, *Blue*, 21.
85 Thanks to my former student Kent Smith for helping to flesh out some of these connections. In an interview with René Despestre in 1967, Césaire defines Negritude "as an awareness of the solidarity among blacks . . . I have a feeling that it was somewhat of a collective creation. I used the term first, that's true. But it's possible we talked about it in our group. It was really a resistance . . . adopt[ing] the word nègre as a term of defiance . . . found[ing] a violent affirmation in the words nègre and Negritude . . . above all it is a concrete rather than abstract coming to consciousness." Césaire, "Interview with René Depestre."

86. In "III. i" Clarke self-reflexively confronts assumptions of appropriateness for poetic voice, highlighting xenophobic hegemonies towards Black Talk: "Your black mouth ought to be elegant with snow— / So words emerge icy, paralyzed: Britannic / They say, 'Put away all that alliteration. It's too much jazz, or other Negro musics.'" Clarke, *Blue*, 137.
87. Clarke, "Afterword," 60.
88. Clarke, *Odysseys Home*, 16.
89. Clarke, *Odysseys Home*, 288.
90. Fraile-Marcos, "The Transcultural Intertextuality," 115.
91. Colley, "After 200 Years."
92. Jennifer Harris, "Black Life in a Nineteenth-Century New Brunswick Town," 141.
93. Clarke, *Blue*, 22.
94. Clarke, *Blue*, 23. The event recalls Fanon's being called the "n" word by a young white boy with his mother, and Richard Wright's Bigger Thomas, who "in the end," writes Fanon, "acts. To put an end to his tension, he acts, he responds to the world's anticipation." Fanon, *Black Skin, White Masks*, 113, 139.
95. Clarke, "Bio: Black Baptist/Bastard," in *Blue*, 25, 26.
96. Thompson, "Clarke: Linguistically Brilliant and Sensual."
97. Clarke, *Blue*, 28.
98. Clarke, "Miles Davis: An Autobiography," in *Blue*, 77.
99. Clarke, *Blue*, 77.
100. Clarke, "II. I," in *Blue*, 126.
101. Clarke, "Onerous Canon," in *Blue*, 71, 72.
102. M.L. Rosenthal quoted in William J. Harris, introduction to Baraka, *The LeRoi Jones/Amiri Baraka Reader*, xxi.
103. While I only point to it, it is worth mentioning that there are a lot of racist images in the poem, which we should rightfully condemn. An entire chapter of this book could be devoted to Baraka's poem, but I focus on the kinship between the poems.
104. Baraka, *Transbluesency*, 142.
105. Gates, *Loose Canons*, 31.
106. Baraka, *Transbluesency*, 143.
107. Clarke, "Calculated Offensive" and "Au Tombeau de Pound," in *Blue*, 28, 56.
108. Compton, "Standing Your Ground," 148
109. Clarke, "The Crime of Poetry," 53.
110. Clarke quoted in Watkins, "Your bass," 6.
111. Clarke quoted in Watkins, "Your bass," 6.
112. Anderson, "Ellington," 179.
113. Pound, "Canto LIII," in *Selected Cantos*, 65.
114. Watkins, "Harmonious Dissonance."
115. Clarke, *Blue*, 42.
116. Fiorentino, "Blackening English."
117. Clarke does not include T.S. Eliot on this list, but by virtue of mentioning canonical poets he invokes the entire spectrum. Perhaps Pound and Eliot need not be

mentioned because they participate in the dialogue by virtue of their own recuperative approaches to resurrecting dead poets. Eliot writes, "We shall often find that not only the best, but the most individual parts of [a poet's] work, may be those in which the dead poets, his ancestors, assert their immortality most vigorously." Eliot, "Tradition and the Individual Talent," 40.

118 Clarke, *Blue*, 27.
119 Clarke, *Whylah Falls*, 23.
120 Clarke, *Blue*, 71, 72, 68.
121 Morrison quoted in Gilroy, *The Black Atlantic*, 79.
122 Clarke, *Blue*, 27.
123 Clarke, "Antiphony," 12.
124 Clarke, "Afterword," 61.
125 Clarke, *Blue*, 33, 89.
126 Nancy, *Listening*, 7.
127 Clarke, "Burning Poems," in *Blue*, 160.
128 Clarke, *Black*, 16. The murder is described as "Rufus slammed the hammer ... into Burgundy's head"; this is riffed on in the larger coda of the collection, "Black Mail," where Clarke relates the Hamiltons' killing of a taxi driver with a hammer to the killing of a Black boy, "slain by a blow from a hammer wielded by his master" in Nova Scotia during slavery. Clarke, *Black*, 13, 143. Interestingly, *Execution Poems* opens with a reduced version of "Negation" (*Blue*), playing once again with race construction and trespassing (George and Rue were after all, "Negro, and semi-Micmac"), tragedy, and redemption. Clarke, *Execution Poems*, 12.
129 Clarke, "George Elliott Clarke on the Many Poetic Meanings of Red."
130 Clarke, *Black*, 7.
131 Clarke, "Language," in *Black*, 18.
132 Clarke, *Black*, 20.
133 Clarke, "Language," "Of Black English," and "Spoken Word," in *Black*, 20, 21, 22.
134 Clarke, *Black*, 17.
135 Clarke, *Black*, 38.
136 Clarke, "I. ii.," in *Black*, 15.
137 Clarke, "IV. Iii," in *Black*, 28.
138 Sontag, "Fascinating Fascism," 90.
139 Clarke, *Black*, 28.
140 Clarke, *Blue*, 108; Clarke, "IV. Iii," in *Black*, 29.
141 Clarke, "Poetry: 1/7/75–1/7/05," in *Black*, 38, 37.
142 Clarke, *Black*, 34.
143 Clarke, *Black*, 34, 38.
144 Clarke, "VI. I," in *Black*, 59.
145 Clarke, *Black*, 59.
146 Eliot, "Tradition," 104.
147 Clarke, "Gynography," in *Black*, 86; Clarke, "A Discourse on My Name," in *Black*, 125.
148 Clarke, "Canadian Biraciality," 203.

149 Clarke, *Illuminated Verses*, viii.
150 Davis and Troupe, *Miles*, 38, 338, 127, 126.
151 Watkins, "Harmonious Dissonance."
152 Clarke, *Black*, 104.
153 Austin Clarke quoted in Clarke, "Canadian Biraciality," 209. It is worth noting that Malcolm X eventually conceded that interracial marriage is a spurious term and should be a personal choice and right: "I believe in recognizing every human being as a human being—neither white, black, brown, or red; and when you are dealing with humanity as a family there's no question of integration or intermarriage." Haley, epilogue in Malcolm X and Haley, *Autobiography*, 424.
154 Malcolm X and Haley, *Autobiography*, 226; Clarke, "Assassination of Malcolm X (II)," in *Black*, 107.
155 Malcolm X and Haley, *Autobiography*, 371, 382.
156 Clarke, *Black*, 106, 106, 111, 112.
157 Haley, epilogue in Malcolm X and Haley, *Autobiography*, 400.
158 Clarke, *Black*, 129.
159 Clarke, *Black*, 141.
160 Clarke, *Red*, 9; Clarke, "Veil'd Devil" and "17, 34, 51," in *Red*, 30, 157.
161 Clarke, *Red*, 68, 67, 68.
162 Clarke, *Red*, 19–20.
163 Davis and Troupe, *Miles,* 205.
164 Clarke, *Red*, 71.
165 Clarke, "Red Tape," in *Red*, 149
166 Clarke, *Red*, 127.
167 Clarke, *Red*, 143.
168 Clarke, *Red*, 144, 140, 141.
169 Mingus, *Beneath the Underdog*, 350–51.
170 Watkins, "Your bass," 7.
171 Clarke, *Red*, 157.
172 Clarke, "Pushkin," in *Red*, 105.
173 Clarke, *Red*, 77.
174 Clarke, "Looking at Alma Duncan's Young Black Girl (1940)," in *Red*, 97–102.
175 Clarke, "The Most Lamentable Roman Tragedy of Titus Andronicus," in *Red*, 122.
176 Williams, "Amiri Baraka."
177 Watkins, "Harmonious Dissonance."
178 Clarke, *Gold*, 11.
179 Clarke, *Gold*, 18–19.
180 Clarke, *Gold*, 52.
181 Clarke, *Gold*, 126–27.
182 Clarke, "Living History," in *White*, 142.
183 Clarke, *White*, 63.
184 Clarke, *White*, 51.
185 Clarke, *White*, 51.

186 Clarke, *Where Beauty Survived*, 81.
187 Clarke, "Hymn for Portia White (II)," in *White*, 195.
188 Clarke, *White*, 119.
189 Clarke, *White*, 110.
190 Clarke, *White*, 160.
191 Williams, excerpt from "Asphodel, That Greeny Flower."
192 Thomas, "Some Aspects," 50; Clarke, *White*, 156.
193 "George Elliott Clarke Says Poetry, 'the Soul of the Arts,' Can't Die," CBC Radio, 28 January 2016, https://www.cbc.ca/radio/q/schedule-for-thursday-january-28-2016-1.3423368/george-elliott-clarke-says-poetry-the-soul-of-the-arts-can-t-die-1.3423381.
194 Watkins, "Harmonious Dissonance."
195 Clarke, "III. Iii," in *Blue*, 140; Clarke, "V. I," in *Black*, 48; Clarke, "Autumnal," in *Red*, 28.
196 McLeod, "'Oui, Let's Scat,'" 99.
197 Clarke, *Eyeing the North Star*, xv.
198 Clarke, "Charles Mingus," in *Red*, 145.
199 Lorde, *The Selected Works*, 4.

Chapter 2: Listening to a Listening

1 Washington, "'Don't Let the Devil,'" 150.
2 Stanbridge, "Jazz," 286.
3 Achebe, "Colonialist Criticism," 76.
4 Ellison, *Shadow and Act*, 208.
5 Fischlin, Heble, and Lipsitz, *The Fierce Urgency of Now*, 4.
6 Olson, *Muthologos*, 72.
7 Clarke, *Directions Home*, 193.
8 Hale, "Jazz in Canada."
9 While Miller is hardly the only scholar writing on this topic, he is the most prolific. See his works *Jazz in Canada: Fourteen Lives* (Toronto: University of Toronto Press, 1982); *Boogie, Pete & The Senator: Canadian Musicians in Jazz: The Eighties* (Toronto: Nightwood Editions, 1987); *Cool Blues: Charlie Parker in Canada, 1953* (Toronto: Nightwood Editions, 1989); *Such Melodious Racket: The Lost History of Jazz in Canada, 1914–1949* (Toronto: Mercury Press, 1997); and *The Miller Companion to Jazz in Canada and Canadians in Jazz* (Toronto: Mercury Press, 2001).
10 Rockhead's Paradise—along with other jazz clubs in Montreal, such as the Nemderoloc Club ("colored men" spelled backward), the Boston Café, and the Terminal Club—helped establish Montreal's reputation as "Harlem of the North." See Gilmore, *Swinging in Paradise*; Winks, *The Blacks in Canada*, 332–35; Williams, *The Road to Now*, 44. The club was in Little Burgundy, an area known for producing talented jazz musicians, most notably Oscar Peterson and Oliver Jones. The three-storey club was founded in 1928 by Rufus Rockhead, a Jamaican-born

railway porter who was able to draw some of the biggest names in blues and jazz during Montreal's Sin City heyday from the 1930s to the 1950s. Rockhead opened the club with the income he earned on the rails as a porter, and then later as a bootlegger, allegedly running booze for Al Capone (Mathieu, *North of the Color Line*, 71, 201, 240). Of all the jazz clubs in Montreal throughout the twentieth century, Rockhead's Paradise, located at 1254 St. Antoine Street, was the most popular until it closed its doors permanently in 1980, at which point it was sold and soon after demolished; the building of the Ville Marie Expressway overhead solidified the club's demise. During its fifty-year tenure, numerous renowned jazz players were drawn to Rockhead's Paradise: Duke Ellington, Louis Armstrong, Fats Waller, Cab Calloway, Billie Holiday, Ella Fitzgerald, Lead Belly, Nina Simone, Dizzy Gillespie, and Sammy Davis Jr., and countless others. See Wikipedia, s.v. "Rockhead's Paradise," last edited 30 March 2022, https://en.wikipedia.org/wiki/Rockhead%27s_Paradise.
11 Mathieu, *North of the Color Line*, 6.
12 "Musical Impurity."
13 Edugyan, *Half-Blood Blues*, 76–77.
14 Callaghan, *The Loved and the Lost*, 68, 55.
15 Morrison, *Jazz*, 58.
16 Brooks, *Selected Poems*, 73.
17 Parker, *Who Owns Music?*, 61.
18 Wah, "Strang(l)ed Poetics," 25.
19 Brand, *A Map to the Door of No Return*, 5.
20 Brand, *Ossuaries*, 53; Brand, *A Map*, 18.
21 Brand, *Ossuaries*, 11.83. Olaudah Equiano (1745–97) was one of the most prominent Africans involved in the British movement to abolish the slave trade. His *Interesting Narrative* is also one of the staples of slave narratives, popularly read, much like Frederick Douglass's *Narrative* and *Life and Times*.
22 Equiano, *The Interesting Narrative*, 63.
23 Brand, *Ossuaries*, 12.102.
24 Beckford, *Naturally Woman*, 88.
25 Parks, "Possession," 4.
26 Goldman, "Spirit Possession," 145.
27 Brand, *A Map*, 35.
28 Sharpe, *In the Wake*, 99.
29 Brand, *Ossuaries*, 3.31, 3.35, 11.81.
30 Brand, *Ossuaries*, 63.
31 Mullins, "'My Body Is History,'" 14, 20.
32 Brand, *Ossuaries*, 82.
33 Sanders, "Introduction," in *Fierce Departures*, ix, x.
34 Brand, *Ossuaries*, 80, 81, 83.
35 Brand, *No Language Is Neutral*, 23.
36 Bernstein, *A Poetics*, 1.

37 Brand, *Bread Out of Stone*, 155, 158.
38 Brand, *Bread Out of Stone*, 153.
39 Fischlin, Heble, and Lipsitz, *The Fierce Urgency*, xi.
40 Walcott, *Black Like Who?*, 50.
41 Jones [Amiri Baraka], *Blues People*, 181–82.
42 hooks, "Performance Practice," 220.
43 Brand, *Ossuaries*, 2.27.
44 Brand, *Ossuaries*, 3.38.
45 The first deviation occurs on page 42 with a description of Yasmine's lover's "motionless face," the two lines (less the third) perhaps denying him of agency. The second deviation occurs on page 111 with a quartet and during a poetic tirade that presents a catalogue of disembodied parts, the extra line perhaps balancing out the former line lost, paradoxically through the embodiment of destroyed form: in this case, the description of dismembered body parts.
46 Brand, *Ossuaries*, 3.33.
47 Brand, *The Blue Clerk*, 76.
48 Brand, *Ossuaries*, 1.20.
49 Morrison, *Jazz*, 120.
50 Brand, *What We All Long For*, 149.
51 Hunter, "After Modernism," 269. To be fair, Hunter was writing in the early 1990s, but these kinds of critiques persist in terms of what poetry gets classified as innovative.
52 Yu, "Introduction," in *Race and the Avant-Garde*, 2.
53 Brand, *Ossuaries*, 8.63, 8.63, 2.22.
54 Ellington quoted in Ulanov, *Duke Ellington*, 276.
55 Yu, "Introduction," 1.
56 Brand, *Ossuaries*, 9.
57 Brand, *Ossuaries*, 5.50, 5.54, 8.64, 5.50.
58 Kamboureli, *On the Edge of Genre*, 45–46.
59 In many ways the poem participates in and deviates from the epic form. While epics often open *in media res*, *Ossuaries* opens in a liminal space of recollection, in an unfixed time frame. The setting is vast, also like the epic, moving across countries and motioning towards uncharted territories, such as outer space. While there is no invocation to a muse, the jazz invocations throughout can be read as inspiration for the text's melodic sounding. In working somewhat against the epic, the text does not announce its theme from an onset, but rather continually takes part in numerous thematic undercurrents. Perhaps one of the poem's strongest deviations from the epic genre is its avoidance of divine intervention; nevertheless, the divine is still a powerfully symbolic system of destruction in the text: "the sharp instruments for butchering, / to appease which rain god, / which government god, which engine god." Brand, *Ossuaries*, 123. Similar to many epics, *Ossuaries* makes much use of repetition and epithets, one example being the colour blue and its repetitions throughout the text: see pages 20, 35, 36, 46, 53, and 86 for examples. The text also contains the epic's use of cataloguing, "Ossuary XIII" containing a long list of body parts. Another

characteristic of the epic is its use of long or formal speeches; while *Ossuaries* avoids many of the formalisms of address, it does contain many long stream-of-consciousness speeches that can go on for pages. Lastly, *Ossuaries* doesn't contain any simple representation of a hero, as Yasmine is more of an outcast or an antihero, incredulous of absolutes, and always in process.

60 Brand, *Ossuaries*, 33.
61 Brand, *Ossuaries*, 6.52–53.
62 Coleman, *Science Fiction* (liner notes).
63 Nielsen, *Black Chant*, 236.
64 Amiri Baraka argues that Pound's poetic dictum to "make it new" is fundamentally African: "Make it New attributed to Ezra Pound is Eastern. It is the African (and Sufi) explanation of why life, even though contained by an endless cycle, or not contained, is an endless cycle." Baraka, "Notes," 46.
65 Brand, *Ossuaries*, 5.44.
66 Brand, *Ossuaries*, 11.84.
67 Harris, *The Poetry and Poetics*, 26.
68 Philip, *A Genealogy of Resistance*, 51.
69 Brand, *Ossuaries*, 66.
70 Brand, *Ossuaries*, 66. Sean B. Carroll's *Endless Forms Most Beautiful*, a text Brand references in her acknowledgments, contains the hypothesis that "it is through changes in embryos that changes in form arise." Carroll, *Endless Forms*, x.
71 Brand, *Ossuaries*, 2.21.
72 Brand, *Ossuaries*, 7.61, 12.94.
73 Gates, *The Signifying Monkey*, 104.
74 Nealon, "Refraining, Becoming-Black," 83.
75 Brand, *Ossuaries*, 8.65, 65, 1.13, 15.124. The showcasing of Africans as spectacle recalls the captivity of Saartjie Baartman (1789–1815), the most famous of Khoekhoe women who were exhibited as sideshow attractions in nineteenth-century Europe under the name "Hottentot Venus." Wikipedia, s.v. "Sarah Baartman," last modified 9 May 2022, https://en.wikipedia.org/wiki/Sarah_Baartman.
76 Lai, "*Ossuaries*: Life Underground."
77 Brand, *Ossuaries*, 4.41, 42.
78 Sanders, "Introduction," in *Fierce Departures*, xii.
79 Brand, *Ossuaries*, 10.77, 10.72.
80 Morrison, *Sula*, 142.
81 Brand, *Ossuaries*, 6.53.
82 Brand, *Ossuaries*, 11.86, 3.31.
83 Fischlin and Heble, "The Other Side," 4.
84 Brand, *Ossuaries*, 7.60, 60, 13.111.
85 Brand, *Ossuaries*, 15.124, 4.43.
86 Agamben, *The Coming Community*, 43, 1, 86.
87 Agamben, *The Coming Community*, 1.
88 Brand, *Ossuaries*, 12.107.

89 Sanders, "Introduction," in *Fierce Departures*, xi.
90 Brand, *Ossuaries*, 2.28.
91 DeVito, ed., *Coltrane on Coltrane*, 270.
92 John Szwed, *Space Is the Place*, 141.
93 Brand, *Ossuaries*, 2.22, 11.81.
94 Brand, *What We All Long For*, 184.
95 Fischlin and Heble, "The Other Side," 17.
96 Mackey, *Discrepant Engagement*, 34.
97 Brand, *Ossuaries*, 14.115, 120, 119, 119.
98 Brand, *A Map*, 190.
99 Brand, *Ossuaries*, 149, 3, 11.84, 15.123.
100 Brand, *Ossuaries*, 123. The speaker of Brand's *Thirsty* takes a similar humbling approach to her citizenship at the end of the text: "Look it's like this, I'm just like the rest, / limping across the city, flying where I can." Brand, *Thirsty*, 30. Her commonness calls the reader into the implicit construction of meaning: if the poet is ordinary, and can attempt change, then why not us?
101 Brand, *Ossuaries*, 14.120.
102 Saul, *Freedom Is, Freedom Ain't*, 210.
103 Brand, *The Blue Clerk*, 101.
104 Brand, *The Blue Clerk*, 75–78.
105 Kellough, "Abstract Propulsion."
106 Brand, *The Blue Clerk*, 201.
107 Brand, *The Blue Clerk*, 51.
108 Brand, "The Shape of Language."
109 Oliveros, *Deep Listening*, xxiii.
110 Brand, *Ossuaries*, 2.26, 2.30.
111 Bernstein, *A Poetics*, 2.
112 Brand, A *Map*, 63.
113 Like Brand and Achebe, Claire Harris describes music as a gift that connects various cultures together: "Some years ago our consul in Switzerland told me there were twenty-five steelbands in Switzerland. I asked if there were Trinidadians in Switzerland. She said no; moreover, the pans are imported from Japan. Black Trinidad and Tobago has given the world a great deal." Harris quoted in Thomas, *Why We Write*, 123.
114 Brand, "Jazz," *Bread Out of Stone*, 149, 161.
115 Harney and Moten, *The Undercommons*, 140.

Chapter 3: Dub Poetics and Improvised Chant in M. NourbeSe Philip's *Zong!*

1 Allen, "De Dub Poets," 19.
2 Philip, *A Genealogy of Resistance*, 127.
3 Dawes, *Natural Mysticism*, 14, 16, 32.

4   Dick Hebdige, *Cut 'n' Mix* (New York: Routledge, 2005), xv.
5   Dawes, *Natural Mysticism*, 110.
6   Carr, "'Come Mek Wi Work Together,'" 10.
7   The Niyabinghi Order is the oldest of all the Rastafari mansions, and the term translates as "black victory" (*niya* = black, *binghi* = victory). The Niyabinghi resistance inspired several Jamaican Rastafarians, who incorporated Niyabinghi chants into their celebrations. The rhythms of these chants—full of improvised syncopation—greatly influenced popular ska, rocksteady, and reggae music. Wikipedia, s.v. "Mansions of Rastafari," accessed 10 August 2013, https://en.wikipedia.org/wiki/Mansions_of_Rastafari.
8   Johnson, "Jamaican Rebel Music," 398.
9   Cooper, ed., *Utterance and Incantations*, 2.
10 Habekost, *Verbal Riddim*, 4.
11 Wong [Onoura Oku], *Echo*.
12 Brathwaite, *History of the Voice*, 32.
13 Cooper, *Utterance*, 1, 2.
14 d'bi.young, "r/evolution begins within," 27.
15 d'bi.young uses all eight principles to form the acronym s.o.r.p.l.u.s.i.: "representing self-knowledge, orality, rhythm, political content and context, language, urgency, sacredness, and integrity." "r/evolution begins within," 27.
16 d'bi.young, "r/evolution begins within," 27.
17 d'bi.young, interview by Paul Watkins, "'we tellin' stories yo,'" 8 August 2013, transcript, 3, http://www.improvcommunity.ca/content/dbiyoung-anitafrika.
18 Dawes, *Midland*, 18.
19 Mutabaruka quoted in Habekost, *Verbal Riddim* 3; Breeze quotes on 47.
20 Chan, review of *Dub Poetry*, 50.
21 Rohlehr, "Introduction," in *Voiceprint*, 18.
22 Dawes, *Natural Mysticism*, 83.
23 Carr, "'Come Mek Wi Work Together,'" 11, 12.
24 Philip, *She Tries Her Tongue*, 56.
25 Cooper, *Utterances*, 6.
26 Austin, *Fear of a Black Nation*, 126.
27 Cooper, *Utterances*, 2.
28 Cooper, *Utterances*, 10.
29 Knopf, "'Oh Canada,'" 85.
30 d'bi.young told me that Mandiela "has been a very important part of my growth as an artist and has mentored me . . . Ahdri coined the term 'dub theatre' and my mom coined the term 'dubbin theatre,' and so I'm somewhere in the middle." d'bi, "'we tellin' stories,'" 5. d'bi.young has performed twelve different dub theatre pieces at the time of my writing.
31 The additional slashes (/) touching the words duplicate the original text.
32 Mandiel, *dark diaspora*, 465, 466, 467, 470.

33 Cooper, *Utterances*, 9.
34 Dawes, "Midland," in *Midland*, 86.
35 Thomas, *Why We Write*, 198.
36 Brown quoted in Compton, *Bluesprint*, 157.
37 Watkins, "Disruptive Dialogics," 4.
38 Fred Booker, "Can You Dig It?," in Compton, *Bluesprint*, 143.
39 Joseph, *Metropolitan Blues*, 42–43.
40 Heble, *Landing on the Wrong Note*, 20.
41 Philip, *A Genealogy*, 46. In addition, Frantz Fanon argues that to "speak a language is to take on a world, a culture." Fanon, *Black Skin, White Masks*, 38.
42 Harris, *Drawing Down a Daughter*, 14, 25.
43 Baldwin quoted in Standley and Pratt, eds., *Conversations with James Baldwin*, 4.
44 Philip, *A Genealogy*, 55, 51. Philip derives *kinopeia* from what she describes as Ezra Pound's omission in his discussion of *logopoeia* (the logical), *phanopoeia* (the visual), and *melopoeia* (the auditory): the three qualities of language best exhibited in English, Chinese, and Greek.
45 Duppy is a Jamaican patois word that means ghost, human vampire, or spirit and has been used in many musical works of Caribbean origin. I occasionally use the word, as it has been used at times, to refer to dub, for dub uses improvisation and adaptation as well as echo and reverb as a kind of ghosting, as Timothy White puts it, "to enhance the 'haunted house' effect." *Catch a Fire*, 230.
46 Philip, *Blank*, 57, 68.
47 James Scott quoted in Dawson, *Mongrel Nation*, 18.
48 Wong [Oku], *Echo*, 44.
49 Knopf, "'Oh Canada,'" 96; Cooper, *Memories Have Tongue*, 85.
50 Philip, *She Tries Her Tongue*, 54.
51 The idea of a "pure" gender would be inert and lifeless. There is no such thing as "pure" race or gender. Like community and the self, gender is a process to be reclaimed, reworked, adapted, and, for the poet, expressed in a sounding text, all the more complex in its textualization and subsequent interpretation by readers. d'bi.young told me, "being able to think outside of gender, that that's a part I feel of what our responsibility is that we recognize that *ALL* of this is a construction, right?" d'bi.young, "'we tellin' stories yo,'" 2.
52 Beckford, *Naturally Woman*, 2.
53 Philip, *A Genealogy*, 115.
54 Harris, "Why Do I Write?," 31.
55 Philip quoted in Thomas, *Why We Write*, 202.
56 Carr, "'Come Mek Wi Work Together,'" 22.
57 Allen, "A Writing of Resistance," 67.
58 Carr, "'Come Mek Wi Work Together,'" 29.
59 Philip, "Adoption Bureau" and "Sightings," in *She Tries Her Tongue*, 27, 33.
60 Philip, "Introduction: Echoes in a Stranger Land," in *Frontiers*, 23–24.
61 Philip, *She Tries Her Tongue*, 54.

62 Philip, *She Tries Her Tongue*, 56.
63 Philip, "Who's Listening?," 9; Casas, *Multimodality*, xxv.
64 d'bi.young, "Rivers," in *rivers...and other blackness*, 15.
65 "Notanda," afterword to *Zong!*, 205.
66 Hurston, *Mules and Men*, 183, 202. Hurston remains an important figure in both anthropology and literature, particularly for Black women writers. As Henry Louis Gates Jr. emphasizes in "Zora Neale Hurston: A Negro Way of Saying" (the afterword to *Mules and Men*), "several black women writers, among whom are some of the most accomplished writers in America today, have openly turned to her works as sources of narrative strategies, to be repeated, imitated, and revised, in acts of textual bonding" (292).
67 Nielsen, *Black Chant*, 19.
68 Brathwaite, "English in the Caribbean," 21.
69 Philip, *She Tries Her Tongue*, 50–51.
70 Philip, *A Genealogy*, 83.
71 Philip, *Looking for Livingstone*, 35.
72 Philip quoted in Thomas, *Why We Write*, 198.
73 Baldwin quoted in Asante, *It's Bigger Than Hip Hop*, 146.
74 Philip, "Notanda," 191.
75 Saunders, "Defending the Dead," 71.
76 d'bi.young, "r/evolution," 29.
77 Philip, *Looking for Livingstone*, 75.
78 Barrett, "The Poetic Disturbances."
79 Philip, *Blank*, 13.
80 Philip, *A Genealogy*, 130–31. The Language poets (often referred to as the L=A=N=G=U=A=G=E poets, after the magazine of that name) are an avant-garde group of poets who emerged in the late 1960s and 1970s in the United States and then elsewhere. Language poetry emphasizes the reader's role in bringing meaning out of a work, viewing the poem as an inherent construction in and of language itself. The L=A=N=G=U=A=G=E movement built upon the modernist poetics of Gertrude Stein and its precursors, including the New American poets, the Black Mountain school, the Beat poets, and others, with later affiliations in Canada with the Kootenay School of Writing (in Vancouver).
81 Moïse, "Grasping the Ungraspable," 23.
82 Iton, *In Search of the Black Fantastic*, 135. As Cecil Foster informatively pointed out to me, not all duppies are evil or haunt the living. In fact, many duppies are considered good, and are part of a West African cosmology that views the world as comprised of eternal spirits and temporal corporeal beings. It is a world where eternal spirits can manifest themselves in bodies that die. In death, one's spirit is released, but they maintain their presence in society, occasionally taking shape so that they can manifest to the still embodied. They might even take the form of a sound, or silence, or even the smells of perfume or flowers. Often duppies can be quite happy, which is why death—the flying "back home" theme we encounter in

Toni Morrison, Dionne Brand, and others—is often a return to the spirit world of ancestors. Furthermore, while I acknowledge that Richard Iton's definition of duppy is an unusual definition, it does fit with the authoritative *Dictionary of Caribbean English Usage*, which in one definition describes a duppy as "[a] malevolent spirit that may be kept in a bottle, to be released to do harm to [somebody]; a malevolent spirit that may take some frightening animal form or other form." Allsopp, ed., *Dictionary of English Caribbean Usage*, 2008. Furthermore, as Foster pointed out in an email, "in this cosmology, a truly free person is one who is totally freed of memories and impressions of the current embodied generations, so that there is no real interaction between those of a current embodied status and those without." My use of haunting, borrowed from Iton, is largely to emphasize the nature of the underwater spirits in *Zong!* who continue to embody (and even haunt) our memories.

83 Philip, "Notanda," 201.
84 Chamberlain, "Diasporic Memories," 186, 179.
85 Scott, "Introduction," vi.
86 Philip, *A Genealogy*, 229.
87 Philip, *She Tries Her Tongue*, 82.
88 Philip, "Notanda," 209.
89 Philip, "Notanda," 201.
90 While known primarily as a writer, Philip studied law at the University of Western Ontario and practised law for a number of years in Toronto before becoming a full-time writer in the mid-1980s.
91 The exact number of drowned Africans aboard the *Zong* is a slippery number: the legal case mentions 150 killed, Walvin in *Black Ivory* mentions 131, and others 130 and 132. Philip decides on the number 150 but concludes that the number of the "murdered remains a slippery signifier of what was undoubtedly a massacre." Philip, "Notanda," 208. Nevertheless, the legal document cites the number as 150. Philip, *Zong!*, 210. It is noted in some accounts that one survived and crawled back onto the ship.
92 Fehskens, "Accounts Unpaid," 407.
93 Rupprecht, "'A Limited Sort of Property,'" 266.
94 Sharpe, *In the Wake*, 19.
95 Austen, "*Zong!*'s 'Should We?,'" 64.
96 Philip, "Notanda," 197.
97 Philip, "Notanda," 197.
98 Philip, "Notanda," 203.
99 Philip, "Gregson v. Gilbert," in *Zong!*, 211. For ease of following along with the source text in this paragraph and in a few other places, subsequent references to *Zong!* will be cited in parentheses in the text.
100 Where possible I've tried to represent the original's typographic appearance, although *Zong!* often makes such reproduction, without the aid of fascmille, virtually impossible.

101 An Italian translation (Benway Series) missed this important detail and then refused to fix the issue at the request of NourbeSe Philip, which led to a petition to destroy this version of the text; see "A public call for the immediate destruction of the unauthorized translation of 'Zong!'," change.org, accessed 23 March 2022, https://chng.it/bXV997gmt5.
102 Kate Siklosi, "'the absolute / of water'," 116.
103 Dowling, "Persons and Voices," 55.
104 Avantgarden is a Toronto-based performance series that seeks to provide a space for innovative and experimental poetry. To listen to Philip read from her work, including *Zong!*, see the video from North of Invention: A Festival of Canadian Poetry (20 January 2011), at *PennSound*: http://writing.upenn.edu/pennsound/x/North-Of-Invention.php.
105 I also had the chance to take part in a book-length reading/performance/version of *Zong!* with live musicians. It was a profound experience, although I wish I had lasted until the end. The event appropriately took place on 29 November 2013, which is the anniversary date of the 1781 massacre that was perpetrated somewhere on the Atlantic Ocean between West Africa and the island of Jamaica.
106 Thomas, *Why We Write*, 199.
107 Philip, "Zong! #14," in *Zong!*, 24.
108 Fehskens, "Accounts Unpaid," 408.
109 Philip, "Gregson v. Gilbert," 210.
110 Philip, "Notanda," 193
111 Barrett quoted in Philip, "Notanda," 196.
112 Moïse, "Grasping the Ungraspable," 24.
113 Baldwin, "A Letter to My Nephew."
114 Brathwaite, "English in the Caribbean," 24.
115 Hall, "Continent of Silence," 1.
116 Philip, "Notanda," 204, 205.
117 Philip, "We Can Never Tell."
118 Austen, "*Zong!*'s 'Should We?,'" 66.
119 Philip, "The Ga(s)p," 39–40.
120 The epigraph by Thomas More to the section "Ventus" (Latin for "wind") is telling: "*The poet is the detective and the detective a poet.*" Philip, *Zong!*, 78.
121 Philip, "Notanda," 193.
122 Philip, "Notanda," 207.
123 Philip, "Notanda," 68, 75, 79, 84, 98.
124 Philip, "Notanda," 69, 70, 80, 100.
125 Queyras, "On Encountering *Zong!*," n.p.
126 Philip, *Zong!*, 107–8, 127.
127 Philip, *Zong!*, 63, 68.
128 Moten, *In the Break*, 197–209.
129 Philip, "Notanda," 205.
130 Philip, "Notanda," 206.

131 Jenkins, *Poetic Obligation*, xiii.
132 Philip, Notanda," 199.
133 Philip, *A Genealogy*, 113.
134 Philip, *Zong!*, 64, 65.
135 Philip, *Blank,* 60.
136 Philip, "Notanda," 201, 206.
137 Philip, "Notanda," 199, 200.
138 Fehskens, "Accounts Unpaid," 422.
139 Philip, "Notanda," 207.
140 Philip, *Zong!*, 160.
141 Philip, *Zong!*, 17.
142 Philip, "Notanda," 204; Philip, *Zong!*, 64, 186.
143 Philip, "Notanda," 205.
144 Demotic English and Demotic Caribbean English are terms that Philip uses to describe her language experience. She writes, "*King's English is in my head, demotic english of the Caribbean in my body*" (italics in original). Philip, *A Genealogy*, 50.
145 Philip, *Zong!*, 66. In an interview between Philip and Myriam Moïse, Philip explains, "the slave ship was a globalised world, a multilingual globalised prison on the sea that was a part of the first globalisation—the globalisation grounded on black skin and bills of exchange that fuelled and initiated speculative financing." Moïse, "Grasping the Ungraspable," 26. Similarly, rethinking the crammed multicultural slave ship in terms of a subway propelled by the economics of slavery, political rapper Immortal Technique asserts: "The subway stays packed like a multicultural slave ship / It's rush hour, 2:30 to 8, non stoppin' / And people comin' home after corporate share croppin.'" Immortal Technique, "Harlem Streets."
146 Dowling, "Persons and Voices," 44.
147 Butler, *Precarious Life*, 20, xviii–xix.
148 Warner, "Indigo," 12.
149 Philip, "We Can Never Tell."
150 Dawes, *Midland*, 15.
151 Philip, "Notanda," 196.
152 Philip, "We Can Never Tell."
153 Philip, *She Tries Her Tongue*, 94, 96.
154 Carr, "'Come Mek Wi Work Together,'" 7.
155 Philip, *Blank,* 67–68.
156 Philip, "Introduction: Echoes," 20.

Chapter 4: Wavin' the Multicultural Flag

1 Shad, "Fam Jam (Fe Sum Immigrins)."
2 Asante, *It's Bigger Than Hip Hop*, 250, 255.
3 Shepp, "A Dialogue."
4 hooks, *Outlaw Culture*, 135.

5   Gilroy, *The Black Atlantic*, 103.
6   Rose, *Black Noise*, 95.
7   Rose, *Black Noise*, 86.
8   Kittler, *Gramophone, Film, Typewriter*, 36.
9   Weheliye, *Phonographies*, 146.
10 Williams, *The Dead Emcee Scrolls*, xi.
11 Chuck D, "Afterword," Bradley and DuBois, eds., *Anthology of Rap*, 794.
12 Baker, *Black Studies, Rap, and the Academy*, 89.
13 Common, "Afterword," in Bradley and DuBois, eds., *Anthology of Rap*, 799.
14 Wallace and Costello, *Signifying Rappers*, 57–58.
15 Kool Herc quoted in Asante, *Bigger Than Hip Hop*, 79.
16 Baraka, *Digging*, 115.
17 Kelley, *Yo' Mama's Dysfunktional!*, 39.
18 Asante, *Bigger Than Hip Hop*, 71.
19 Nielsen, *Black Chant*, 235. Nielsen's argument consists of six essentialist critiques of rap, using the music as a straw man to assert his preference for jazz-infused poetry: (1) he contends that the current academic fetishization of rap has served to obscure further the continuing experimentation with text by jazz composers (174), which seems like a strange statement given that music departments encourage these types of cross-pollinations with poetry and jazz more readily than they do with hip-hop and jazz; (2) he seems disturbed that critics have devoted entire volumes to the examination of rap and its cultural contexts (176), but I'm not quite sure why; (3) he unconvincingly outlines the difference between "black rapping" and "black poetry" (176); (4) he insists that jazz-rap fusion often trivializes rap, citing early examples such as Miles Davis's *Doo-Bop*, instead of focusing on any contemporary moments or more successful earlier ones (184); (5) he insists critics (especially cultural studies critics) have little interest in jazz-poetry because it is unpopular (235), which is somewhat ridiculous since a quick search on Google Scholar retrieves more than three times the results for "jazz poetry" than it does for "hip hop poetry"; and finally, in perhaps the most sweeping generalization in an otherwise *tour de force* work on experimental poetics, (6) he describes rap as conservative, which he leaves unqualified and without real engagement (235).
20 *The Anthology of Rap* somewhat loosely (since movements are never so neatly divisible by dates) groups hip hop lyrics based on four time periods: 1978–84 (The Old School); 1985–92 (The Golden Age); 1993–99 (Rap Goes Mainstream); and 2000–10 (New Millennium Rap).
21 Chuck D, "Afterword," in Bradley and DuBois, eds., *Anthology of Rap*, 789.
22 See Fogel and Engerman, *Time on the Cross*.
23 Chuck D, "Interview." In 2010, ten years after the original statement, Chuck D's vehemence towards corporate hip hop remains largely the same: "Major-owned hip hop is now about as packaged as Kraft Cheese with some suited asshole waiting for the results from the registers." Chuck D, "Death of a Nation," 268.

24 Ornette Coleman quoted in Spellman, *Four Lives*, 129–31.
25 Rose, *Black Noise*, 21, xiii, 38, 39.
26 hooks, *Teaching to Transgress*, 168.
27 Talib Kweli, "Going Hard," *The Beautiful Struggle* (Rawkus Records, 2004).
28 Shad, "Brothering Watching," *The Old Prince* (Black Box Canada, 2007).
29 Douglass, *Narrative*, 57.
30 Lewis, *A Power Stronger Than Itself*, 44, ix.
31 Fischlin, Heble, and Lipsitz, *The Fierce Urgency of Now*, 24.
32 Lyte quoted in "Introduction," Bradley and DuBois, eds., *Anthology of Rap*, xxxviii.
33 Mayfield quoted in Gonzales, "Gangster Boogie," 88.
34 Maynard, *Policing Black Lives*, 3.
35 Walcott, "Towards a Methodology," 239.
36 To get a larger sense of the complex ways communities engage with hip hop within Canada's borders, see Marsh and Campbell, eds., *We Still Here*. See also the Northside Hip Hop Archive, https://www.nshharchive.ca.
37 Michie Mee and L.A. Luv, *Jamaican Funk: Canadian Style* (First Priority, 1991).
38 Rakim, "I Know You Got Soul," *Paid in Full* (4th & Broadway, 1987).
39 Neal, *What the Music Said*, 136.
40 Walcott, "Towards a Methodology," 239.
41 Walcott, "Towards a Methodology," 248–49.
42 LeBlanc, "Rascalz Refuse Award."
43 Walcott, "Towards a Methodology," 250.
44 Regarding her gender and mixed-race heritage, rapper Eternia told *SixShot* that "in Canada it was never really that much of a big deal because it's a very multi-cultural place, so everyone hung together and it was just a case of if you're dope, you're dope. But since moving to New York it's definitely been made very apparent to me that my gender and race can be an issue for some people and others are just shocked to learn that someone like me even exists, a half-white, half-middle-eastern female who loves hip-hop and is good at it." "Eternia—Where I'm At—The Setup," *SixShot*, 13 November 2007.
45 K'naan, "Coming to America," *Country, God, or the Girl* (A&M/Octone, 2012).
46 K'naan, "The Dusty Foot Philosopher," *The Dusty Foot Philosopher* (Phantom Records, 2006).
47 K'naan, "Better," *Country*.
48 Bradley and DuBois, eds., *Anthology of Rap*, 656.
49 K'naan, *Troubadour* (Universal, 2009).
50 K'naan, "Take a Minute," *Troubadour*.
51 hooks, *Talking Back*, 28.
52 K'naan, "My Old Home," *Dusty Foot Philosopher*.
53 Gates, foreword, *Anthology of Rap*, xxiv, xxii, xxxiv.
54 K'naan, "Strugglin'" and "I Was Stabbed by Satan," *Dusty Foot Philosopher*.
55 K'naan, "The African Way," *Troubadour*.

56 Scherker, "Somali Woman, 2 Journalists."
57 K'naan, *Dusty Foot Philosopher*.
58 K'naan, *Dusty Foot Philosopher*.
59 K'naan, "Talking Back to the Empire," *NOW Magazine*, 1 February 2007.
60 "SXSW Thursday Preview: K'naan," *Los Angeles Times*, 18 March 2009. Similarly, in a radio interview K'naan stated: "Massive western companies would come to Somalia and dump nuclear toxic waste containers on the shore because there was no government controlling the shorelines. So these pirates initially went into the ocean to make them pay for that sort of thing. So they just take everything for ransom. That actually helped us clear our environment." K'naan quoted in "SWSX Thursday Preview: K'naan."
61 K'naan, *Troubadour*.
62 K'naan, "If Rap Gets Jealous," *Dusty Foot Philosopher*.
63 K'naan quoted in Pennycook and Mitchell, "Hip Hop," 25.
64 Pennycook and Mitchell, "Hip Hop," 25–26.
65 Pennycook and Mitchell, "Hip Hop," 33.
66 K'naan quoted in Pennycook and Mitchell, "Hip Hop," 37.
67 K'naan, *Troubadour*.
68 k-os, "B-Boy Stance," *Joyful Rebellion* (Astralworks, 2004).
69 Arsenault, "Soccer and Song."
70 Hall, "Introduction," in *Questions of Cultural Identity*, 4.
71 771 million people (1 in 10) lack access to clean water, and a staggering—frightening, incomprehensible, reprehensible—"1 million people die each year from water, sanitation and hygiene-related diseases which could be reduced with access to safe water or sanitation." "The Water Crisis," water.org, accessed 4 July 2022, https://water.org/our-impact/water-crisis.
72 K'naan often uses pop star references in his music to draw the audience into his story. In "What's Hardcore," he raps that if he rhymed "about home and got descriptive / I'd make 50 Cent look like Limp Bizkit."
73 Adams, *Continental Divides*, 7.
74 Gillis, "Maclean's Interview: K'naan."
75 See Woods, "Do You Know What It Means."
76 Trudeau, *The Essential Trudeau*, 146.
77 Cecil Foster, *They Call Me George*, 33; Kamboureli, *Scandalous Bodies*, 82; Bissoondath quoted in Foster, *Blackness*, 373.
78 Maynard, *Policing Black Lives*, 82.
79 Gillis, "Maclean's Interview."
80 Wikipedia, s.v. "Wavin' Flag," last modified 20 March 2022, 18:85, https://en.wikipedia.org/wiki/Wavin%27_Flag.
81 Zerbisias, "How K'naan's 'Wavin' Flag' Became Anthem."
82 Gillis, "Maclean's Interview."
83 On the history of Coca-Cola, see Pendergrast, *For God, Country, and Coca-Cola*.
84 Price, "How K'naan's Song."

85 Campbell, "Connect the T.Dots," 265.
86 Campbell, "Connect the T.Dots," 256.
87 Kamboureli, ed., *Making a Difference*, xxix.
88 Milz, "Multicultural Canadian World Literature," 153.
89 Gillis, "Maclean's Interview."
90 K'naan, "Censoring Myself for Success" [opinion], *New York Times*, 8 December 2012, https://www.nytimes.com/2012/12/09/opinion/sunday/knaan-on-censoring-himself-for-success.html.
91 Foster, *Blackness and Modernity*, xiv.
92 Foster, *Genuine Multiculturalism*, 3.
93 Foster, *Genuine Multiculturalism*, 15, 22.
94 Heble, "Sounds of Change," 26.
95 Foster, *Genuine Multiculturalism*, 5
96 Gillis, "Maclean's Interview."
97 Heble, "Sounds of Change," 27.
98 Neal, "A Way Out of No Way," 220.
99 Gillis, "Maclean's Interview."
100 K'naan, "Voices in My Head," *Dusty Foot Philosopher*.

Chapter 5: Recovery and Remix

1 Compton quoted in Watkins, "'Schizophonophilia.'"
2 Compton quoted in Watkins, "'Schizophonophilia,'" 8.
3 Lingold, Mueller, and Trettien, "Introduction," in *Digital Sound Studies*, 6.
4 Lingold, Mueller, and Trettien, "Introduction," 6.
5 Sterne, *The Audible Past*, 39.
6 Part of Bell's approach surrounds his view of sign language as pernicious. See Bell's controversial paper, "Memoir: Upon the Formation of a Deaf Variety of the Human Race," National Academy of Sciences, 1884, Internet Archive, https://archive.org/details/cihm_08831.
7 Compton, *Performance Bond*, 106.
8 Mudede, "The Turntable."
9 Buskirk, Jones, and Jones, "The Year in 'Re-.'"
10 Beasley, "Performing Zora," 48.
11 Oswald, "Bettered by the Borrower," 132.
12 Hurston, "The Characteristics of Negro Expression," 267.
13 Weheliye, *Phonographies*, 32.
14 Attali, *Noise*, 21.
15 Adorno, "On Popular Music," 265.
16 Anderson, "Ellington," 196.
17 Compton, *Bluesprint*, 17.
18 Miller, *Rhythm Science*, 28–29.
19 Sterne, *Audible Past*, 350–51.

20 Ostertag, interview by Mauricio Martinez.
21 Compton, "Afro-Saxon," in *Performance Bond*, 17.
22 Compton, personal communication, October 2009. I also asked Compton about his use of hip hop as a medium, and he responded, "I can say that I place my audio art within the long tradition of black diasporic orality more so than the more limited and recent innovation of hip hop. *Performance Bond* is largely about the anxiety of the globalization of hip hop. Is it a form of American sub-imperialism? Or does the diaspora cut across borders in a way that makes hip hop identification political resistance?" However, given that hip hop has more than forty-five years of history, and shows no signs of slowing down, I would have to say that the larger cultural practice of hip hop is not limited in its approach as a diasporic orality.
23 Compton, "Schizophonophilia," 1.
24 Hudson, "The Lost Tribe of a Lost Tribe," 156.
25 Compton, "Schizophonophilia," 3.
26 Brathwaite quoted in Mackey, "An Interview with Kamau Brathwaite," 44. As Christian Habekost argues in *Verbal Riddim*, "the black tradition emphasizes [time] as crucial means of distinct improvisation and extemporization ... circulation and cyclical development, as opposed to the European principle of progression." Habekost, *Verbal Riddim*, 94.
27 Compton, "Schizophonophilia," 3.
28 Compton, *49th Parallel Psalm*, 24.
29 Compton, *49th Parallel Psalm*, 18–19.
30 Compton, *49th Parallel Psalm*, 25.
31 Adorno, *Minima Moralia*, 87. While I find Adorno to be an elusive and captivating theorist (hence my use of his ideas a number of times in this book), it must be acknowledged that Adorno, himself a purveyor of avant-garde atonal music, was quite averse to jazz and viewed the music as populist, repetitious, and ultimately a product of capitalism. However, later in his career it seemed that he avoided responding to free jazz, perhaps being somewhat haunted by his older critiques of jazz.
32 William Carlos Williams, "Introduction (*The Wedge*)," 54.
33 Thomas, *Why We Write*, 62.
34 Compton, *49th Parallel Psalm*, 47.
35 Compton, *Performance Bond*, 106, 110.
36 Compton, *Performance Bond*, 106–7.
37 Compton, "Schizophonophilia," 3.
38 Compton, "The Reinventing Wheel," in *Performance Bond*, 102, 103.
39 Compton, "The Reinventing Wheel," 104, 105.
40 Compton, "The Reinventing Wheel," 104, 105.
41 For example, see the controversial Kenneth Goldsmith reading that used Mike Brown's autopsy report as poetry. Goldsmith's performance lacked self-reflexivity, ultimately redissecting Brown's body under the guise of conceptualism.
42 Compton, *Bluesprint*, 18. See also Compton's poem "Claiming," in *49th Parallel Psalm*, which details the Black experience during the gold rush.

43 Compton, *Bluesprint*, 18.
44 Compton, "Seven Routes to Hogan's Alley," 84.
45 Compton, *Bluesprint*, 20.
46 Compton, *Bluesprint*, 269.
47 Compton, *Performance Bond*, 43.
48 Compton, "The Reinventing Wheel," 105.
49 See Mathieu, *North of the Color Line*; and Foster, *They Call Me George*.
50 See Friedman's insightful documentary *Secret Vancouver: Return to Hogan's Alley*, which includes an interview with the Vancouver entertainers the Crump Twins and background regarding their musical importance.
51 See Taraneh Jerven, "Vancouver's Legendary Jimi Hendrix Shrine Now Open for Summer," *Inside Vancouver*, 11 June 2013, http://www.insidevancouver.ca/2013/06/11/legendary-vancouver-jimi-hendrix-shrine-now-open-for-summer.
52 Compton, *Performance Bond*, 15.
53 Compton, *Performance Bond*, 15.
54 Compton, *Performance Bond*, 16.
55 Compton, *Performance Bond*, 16.
56 Compton, *Performance Bond*, 16. By focusing on the language politics of being mixed-race, Compton embraces difference so that he may name the oppression being named upon him. He self-reflexively writes, in relation to the word "mulatto," "Without it, it's very difficult to identify my lived racialized experience ... Like when someone looks at me and sees this sentence: 'A black person slept with a white person.' Those are mulatto moments, and without that word, it's hard to even articulate that they're happening to you. Naming an oppression, or a response to it, is important. I'll keep the word, thanks." Compton, "Self-Interview," 83.
57 Compton, *After Canaan*, 216.
58 Compton, "Declaration," in *Performance Bond*, 16.
59 Leow, "Mis-mappings and Mis-duplications."
60 Mathur, "Transubracination," 149.
61 Compton, "Turntable Poetry," 199.
62 Compton, "Turntable Poetry," 197.
63 Compton, "Turntable Poetry," 194.
64 Compton, "Turntable Poetry," 194.
65 Compton, "Turntable Poetry," 195.
66 Compton, *Performance Bond*, 105.
67 Compton, "Turntable Poetry," 198.
68 Compton, "Turntable Poetry," 199.
69 Compton, "Schizophonophilia," 6.
70 Compton, "Schizophonophilia," 1.
71 Compton, "Schizophonophilia," 7.
72 Siemerling, "Transcultural Improvisation," 32.
73 Compton, "Turntable Poetry," 184.
74 Compton, *After Canaan*, 218.

75 Compton, *49th Parallel Psalm*, 166.
76 Compton, *49th Parallel Psalm*, 169.
77 Hurston, *Mules and Men*, 183.
78 I avoid the use of the term "voodoo" since many find it offensive, especially the way the word has been used in Western society to mock and disparage a religion and lifestyle many hardly bother to understand. Even the *Oxford English Dictionary* uses words like "superstitious" and "serpent worship" to describe the term. In *Flash of the Spirit* (New York: Vintage, 1984), Robert Farris Thompson challenges the superficial understanding of voodoo (*vodun*) "as abominable primitivism" and describes it as sophisticated synthesis of traditional African religions with an infusion of Roman Catholicism (163). Is Jesus in Christianity, like a zombie risen from the dead, that different from the zombies in vodou? It's also worth mentioning that the word "voodoo" is still used in association with Louisiana Voodoo/ New Orleans Voodoo.
79 Gates, *The Signifying Monkey*, xxi.
80 Baker, *Blues, Ideology*, 202.
81 Davis, "Trickster at the Crossroads."
82 Thomas, *Why We Write*, 69.
83 Thomas, *Why We Write*, 70.
84 Compton, "The Epic Moment," 138.
85 Siemerling, "Transcultural," 36.
86 Compton, *49th Parallel Psalm*, 105–6.
87 Compton, *49th Parallel Psalm*, 106. This line likely refers to the lines Compton is writing, creating a space for the migrant in the poetry.
88 Brathwaite, *The Arrivants*, 265.
89 Compton, "Vévé," in *Performance Bond*, 119.
90 Compton, "Vévé," 121.
91 Siemerling, "Transcultural," 37.
92 Leow, "Mis-mappings."
93 Philip, "We Can Never Tell."
94 Siemerling, "Transcultural," 37.
95 Leow, "Mis-mappings."
96 Fischlin and Heble, "The Other Side of Nowhere," 23.
97 Iyer, "On Improvisation," 285.
98 Compton, "Red Light Blues," in *49th Parallel Psalm* 146.
99 Compton, *Performance Bond*, 42.
100 Compton, *Performance Bond*, 42.
101 Compton, *Performance Bond*, 42.
102 Leow, "Mis-mappings."
103 Compton, *49th Parallel Psalm*, 110.
104 Lai, "Asian Invasion," 30–40.
105 Compton, *Performance Bond*, 31.
106 Compton, *Performance Bond*, 31.

107 Compton, *Performance Bond*, 31.
108 Harsha Walia, in her response to Harper's blatant falsity, noted that "unsurprisingly, no world leaders walked out as he said this, nor was he subsequently denounced, for Indigenous Holocaust denial." Walia, "Really Harper, Canada Has No History of Colonialism?" Harper did issue an apology (delivered on 11 June 2008) to Indigenous people, acknowledging them as one of the founding peoples of Canada, but that was prior to his statement at the G20, showing that while it was perhaps heartfelt, and a very significant step towards reconciliation, his "We're sorry" was, as Native scholar and writer Thomas King expresses, an empty apology. King, *The Inconvenient Indian*.
109 In 2017, the Liberal government enacted Bill C-6 to repeal Conservative changes, including the controversial revoking of citizenship.
110 Compton paraphrased in Friedman, *Secret Vancouver*.
111 Compton, "The Chief Factor," in *49th Parallel Psalm*, 43.
112 Compton, "Jamb" and "The Book," in *49th Parallel Psalm*, 123, 109.
113 Compton, "The Book," in *49th Parallel Psalm*, 109, 110.
114 Compton, "49th Parallel Psalm," in *49th Parallel Psalm*, 175.
115 Compton, "The Mirror of the Times," in *49th Parallel Psalm*, 34.
116 Compton, "Afro-Saxon," in *Performance Bond*, 18.
117 Compton, "Inlet Holler," in *Performance Bond*, 21.
118 Compton, "Inlet Holler," 21.
119 Compton, "To Poitier," in *Performance Bond*, 35–36.
120 Compton, "The Essential Charley Pride," in *Performance Bond*, 37–38.
121 Neil Bissoondath in Foster, *Blackness and Modernity*, 373.
122 Wolin, *Politics and Vision*, 605–6.
123 Wolin, *Politics and Vision*, 604.
124 Said, *Representations of the Intellectual*, xvii.
125 Walcott, "Against Institution Established Law," 23.
126 Moodie, *Roughing It in the Bush*, 286, 287.
127 For example, there is a massive reckoning taking place as many Canadians are only now learning about the extent of the horrors of the residential school system, prompted in part by the discovery of a mass grave site at Kamloops Residential School in BC, where the remains of 215 children of the Tk'emlúps te Secwépemc First Nation were found. For all settlers, reading and knowing this shameful history is an important first step. There is so much more work to do, and I know, even as I often teach this material, that I haven't done nearly enough. There is no easy absolution from the past because it is still here. There needs to be much more truth and action before we can have hope for genuine reconciliation.
128 Compton, *Performance Bond*, 103.
129 Compton, "The Reinventing Wheel," in *Performance Bond*, 101–10.
130 Thomas, *Why We Write*, 71.
131 Compton, "The Reinventing Wheel."
132 Compton, "The Reinventing Wheel," 102.

133 Compton, "Schizophonophilia," 8–9.
134 Compton, "Epic Moment," 142–43.
135 Compton, *After Canaan*, 14.
136 Compton, "The Reinventing Wheel," in *Performance Bond*, 101.
137 Leow, "Mis-mappings."
138 Compton, "The Reinventing Wheel," in *Performance Bond*, 101, 103, 101.
139 Compton, "The Reinventing Wheel."
140 Compton, "The Reinventing Wheel," 108.
141 Compton, personal communication, 24 August 2012.
142 Compton, "The Reinventing Wheel."
143 Compton, "The Reinventing Wheel."
144 Rose, *Black Noise*, 61.
145 Compton, "Seven Routes," in *After Canaan*, 84, 92, 91, 109, 93.
146 Compton, "Schizophonophilia," 5.
147 Sherman, "The Hip-Hop Aesthetics," ii.
148 Sharpe, *In the Wake*, 124, 21.
149 Compton, *Performance Bond*, 10.
150 Compton, "Seven Routes," in *After Canaan*, 112, 113.
151 Leow, "Mis-mappings."
152 Compton, *Performance Bond*, 113. "Blight" refers to any "baleful influence of atmospheric or invisible origin, that suddenly blasts, nips, or destroys plants," as well as any "malignant influence of obscure or mysterious origin" that causes destruction. *Oxford English Dictionary Online*, s.v. "blight," 28 May 2021.
153 Compton, *Performance Bond*, 113.
154 *Oxford English Dictionary Online*, s.v. "cloze," 28 May 2021.
155 Compton, *Performance Bond*, 113.
156 Compton, *Performance Bond*, 114.
157 Quoted in Bohn, *Modern Visual Poetry*, 20.
158 Compton, "Seven Routes," 117.
159 As defined by the Poetry Foundation, concrete poetry is verse "that emphasizes nonlinguistic elements in its meaning, such as a typeface that creates a visual image of the topic." *Glossary of Poetic Terms*, s.v. "concrete poetry," Poetry Foundation, 11 May 2022.
160 Compton, *Performance Bond*, 103.
161 Compton, "The New Station," in *Performance Bond*, 150–52.
162 Compton, *Performance Bond*, 156.
163 It might surprise some to learn that there are more Black people in British Columbia than in Nova Scotia. See data from Statistics Canada, "Canada [Country] and Canada [Country]" (table), *Census Profile*, 2016 Census, Cat. no. 98-316-X2016001, released 29 November 2017.
164 Compton, "Seven Routes," 105.
165 Compton, "Seven Routes," 108, 112.
166 Compton, "Black History in Vancouver."

167 Wayde Compton, quoted in "Black History Month Stamp Celebrates Vancouver's Hogan's Alley," CBC News, 20 January 2014, http://www.cbc.ca/news/canada/british-columbia/black-history-month-stamp-celebrates-vancouver-s-hogan-s-alley-1.2516741.

168 "Mural Honouring Vancouver's Lost Black Neighbourhood Wins Heritage Award," *Daily Hive*, 23 April 2021, https://dailyhive.com/vancouver/vmf-bc-heritage-award-anthony-joseph.

169 The Northeast False Creek Plan (NEFC) "provides an opportunity to reconnect through reconciliation, replacing the Georgia and Dunsmuir viaducts with strong cultural, social and physical linkages." City of Vancouver, *Northeast False Creek Plan* (Vancouver, February 2018), 2, https://vancouver.ca/files/cov/northeast-false-creek-plan.pdf. The plan from the city includes a brief historical section on Hogan's Alley and Vancouver's Black community and, among other things, states the intention to "establish a Cultural Centre on the 898 Main Street block (Hogan's Alley block). The Cultural Centre will be a focal point for the Black Community, and will be welcoming and inclusive to all—a place 'from the community, for the community'" (23). In a Facebook conversation I had with Wayde Compton (12 January 2019), he informed me that "one political slate, Coalition Vancouver, was actually campaigning on killing the Northeast False Creek Plan." There continues to be a frustrating amount of ignorance in Vancouver about the historical Black community at the viaducts. As Compton went on to explain, "there was a lot of silence from the other parties, left and right, about the plan and the city's commitments in it to the Hogan's Alley Working Group [which included Anthonia Ogundele as a general city planning consultant and some thirty or so other people, including some former Hogan's Alley residents] and its successor, the Hogan's Alley Society. (The notable exceptions were Vision, whose plan it was to begin with, and One City, who explicitly supported Hogan's Alley restitution at the viaduct site.) We worked for two years in consultation with the City of Vancouver, but during the election, Vision Vancouver collapsed, and so it is not clear what the current council will do with the NEFC plan, or the Hogan's Alley portion of it." Compton then informed me that there is some promise, as one member of the Hogan's Alley Working Group is now on city council—Pete Fry, who is Trinidadian—and that there are a number of other important supporters, including Jean Swanson, a Vancouver city councillor and anti-poverty activist. More promising, as Compton pointed out, was that the Black community is now organized in a way it has not been since the 1990s and there is more understanding and support from the larger community for an official centre and a land trust. The Hogan's Alley Working Group, which has morphed into the Hogan's Alley Society, continues to pressure the city to complete the promised plan. As Compton says, "the Hogan's Alley Society is functional and active and will be pushing for the completion of our part of the plan." The society is being run by dedicated people like June Francis, Stephanie Alley, Adam Rudder, and Randy Clarke (a former resident of Hogan's Alley).

170 Anna Dimoff, "Vancouver to Revive Hogan's Alley Community with Help of American Architect," CBC News, 21 May 2017, http://www.cbc.ca/news/canada/british-columbia/hogans-alley-community-plan-1.4124018.

171 "Viaducts Are a Symbolically Important Place," CBC News, June 15, 2020, https://www.cbc.ca/news/canada/british-columbia/viaduct-hogan-s-alley-significance-1.5612399.

Outro: The New Black Can(aan)Lit and the Community to Come

1 King, *The Radical King*, 96.
2 Ellison, *Invisible Man*, 8.
3 See Nelson, *Representing the Black Female Subject*.
4 Canadian novelist David Gilmour incited incendiary debate in Canadian literature when he made the statement that he does not teach works by women, gay individuals, or those of Chinese ethnicity. In an interview with *Hazlitt* magazine (owned by Random House), Gilmour stated, "What I teach is guys. Serious heterosexual guys." Keeler, "David Gilmour on Building Strong Stomachs." Gilmour's comments led to several editorial pieces, with some, including conservative thinker Margaret Wente, defending his comments.
5 Kamboureli and Miki, eds., *Trans.Can.Lit*, xv.
6 As Philip writes in *Blank*, "Today, in 2017, there exist no Black-owned publishers here in Toronto or even in Canada, as far as my research has revealed." Philip, *Blank*, 89. This is not entirely true. Commodore books is the first Black Canadian literary press in western Canada (founded in 2006 by Wayde Compton, Karina Vernon, and David Chariandy), and Sister Vision Press, established by writer Makeda Silvera and visual artist Stephanie Martin, was a Canadian small press publisher in operation from 1985 to 2001. For Indigenous-owned presses see Theytus, Kegedonce, Pemmican, and Strong Nations. There are likely some that I am missing, and hopefully more will arise by the time this book is published.
7 Alicia Elliott, "CanLit Is a Raging Dumpster Fire," *Open Book*, 7 September 2017, http://open-book.ca/Columnists/CanLit-is-a-Raging-Dumpster-Fire.
8 Walcott quoted in Darcy Ballantyne et al., "The Unbearable Whiteness."
9 Whitehead, "Writing as Rupture," 197.
10 Ballantyne et al., "The Unbearable Whiteness." It is worth noting that Austin Clarke is one of the few Black writers included in any of the major overviews of CanLit, including Margaret Atwood's *Survival* (Toronto: House of Anansi, 1972) and Nick Mount's *Arrival* (Toronto: House of Anansi, 2017); both books depict a literary Canada that is largely anglophone and almost entirely white.
11 Ballantyne et al., "The Unbearable Whiteness."
12 Compton, *Performance Bond*, 31.
13 King, *The Trumpet of Conscience*, 71.
14 *Canadian Multiculturalism Act*, RSC 1985, c 24 (4th Supp), s 3(g).

15 Kelley, *Freedom Dreams*, 7, 2.
16 Foster, *Where Race Does Not Matter*, 36. Furthermore, in an interview with Nigel Thomas, Foster argues, "I discredit the notion of ethnicity ... I don't consider Blackness to be ethnicity." Foster quoted in Thomas, *Why We Write?*, 109.
17 King, *The Black Shoals*, xiii.
18 Ward, *Riverslip*, 68.
19 M. NourbeSe Philip, "Adoption Bureau," in *She Tries Her Tongue*, 27; Clarke, *Blue*, 77; Brand, *Ossuaries*, 20; Compton, *Performance Bond*, 53.
20 d'bi.young, "Rivers," in *rivers...and other blackness*, 3–4.
21 Hall, "Introduction: Who Needs 'Identity'?," 4.
22 Nancy, *The Inoperative Community*, 71.
23 Foster, *Blackness and Modernity*, 331.
24 Toni Cade Bambara, *The Salt Eaters* (New York: Vintage Books, 1980), 147.
25 King, *The Trumpet of Conscience*, 3.
26 Lingis, *The Community of Those)*, 12.
27 Nancy, *Inoperative Community*, 11.
28 Heble, *Landing on the Wrong Note*, 231, 233.
29 Hansberry, "The Negro Writer and His Roots," 12; Brooks, *Maud Martha*, 179.
30 King, *The Radical King*, 169.
31 Douglass, *My Bondage and My Freedom*.

Selected Discography

See the Spotify playlists in each chapter.

Allen, Lillian. *Revolutionary Tea Party*. Verse to Vinyl, 1986.
Armstrong, Louis. "Heebie Jeebies." Okeh, 1926.
———. "What Did I Do to Be So Black and Blue?" Vocalion, 1937.
Bacharach, Burt. "What the World Needs Now Is Love, Sweet Love." *Reach Out*. A&M, 1967.
Black Star. "Astronomy (8th Light)." *Black Star*. Perf. Mos Def and Talib Kweli. Rawkus, 1998.
———. "Liner Notes." *Black Star*. Rawkus, 1998.
Brown, James. "Say it Loud (I'm Black and I'm Proud)." *Say it Loud—I'm Black and I'm Proud*. King, 1968.
Coleman, Ornette. *Science Fiction* (liner notes). Columbia, 1967.
Coltrane, John. "Alabama." *Live at Birdland*. Impulse!, 1964.
———. *Ascension*. Rec. 28 June 1965. Impulse!, 1966.
———. *Interstellar Space*. Rec. 22 February 1967. Impulse!, 1974.
———. *My Favorite Things*. Rec. 21, 24, 26 October 1960. Atlantic, 1961.
———. "Naima." *Giant Steps*. Rec. 4–5 May 1959. Atlantic, 1960.
———. "Violets for Your Furs." *Coltrane*. Prestige, 1957.
Cook, Sam. "A Change Is Gonna Come." *Ain't That Good News*. RCA, 1964.
Davis, Miles. *Bitches Brew*. Columbia, 1970.
———. *Kind of Blue*. Columbia, 1959.
Dead Prez. "Hip-Hop." Per. by stic-man and M-1. *Let's Get Free*. Relativity, 2000.
"Eternia—Where I'm At—The Setup." *SixShot*, 13 November 2007.
Gang Starr. "Mass Appeal." Perf. by Guru and DJ Premier. *Hard to Earn*. Chyrsalis/EMI Records, 1994.
Gaye, Marvin. *What's Going On*. Tamla, 1971.
Grandmaster Flash and the Furious Five. *The Message*. Sugar Hill, 1982.
Ibrahim, Abdullah [as Dollar Brand]. *African Marketplace*. Elektra/Asylum Records, 1980.
———. *African Sketchbook*. Enja Records, 1969.

———— [Dollar Brand Duo]. *Good News from Africa*. Enja Records, 1974.
Immortal Technique. "Harlem Streets." Track 4 on *Revolutionary Vol. 2*. Viper, 2003. LP.
Johnson, Linton Kwesi. "Reggae Sounds." *Bass Culture*. Island, 1980.
Johnson, Robert. "Cross Road Blues." Rec. November 1936. *King of the Delta Blues Singers*. Columbia, 1961.
Joseph, Clifton. *Oral/Trans/Missions*. Blue Moon, 1990.
Kardinal Offishall. *Country, God, or the Girl*. A&M/Octone, 2012.
K'naan. *The Dusty Foot Philosopher*. Phantom Records, 2006.
————. *More Beautiful Than Silence*. A&M/Octone. 2012.
————. *Quest for Fire: Firestarter, Vol. 1*. MCA, 2001.
————. "Revolutionary Avocado." Mixtape. Unofficial, 2005.
————. *Troubadour*. Universal, 2009.
————. "Wavin' Flag: Coca-Cola Celebration Mix." Universal, 2010.
————. "Wavin' Flag featuring will.i.am and David Guetta. Universal, 2010.
————. "Wavin' Flag: Young Artists for Haiti." Universal Music Canada, 2010.
Kid Koala. *12 Bit Blues*. Ninja Tune, 2012.
————. "Kid Koala Performs Moon River." 8 July 2011, posted by Ankur Malhotra, YouTube video, https://www.youtube.com/watch?v=fjFi4MHO_go.
————. "Moon River" (Studio Version)," posted by Periscope, 22 September 2011, YouTube video, https://www.youtube.com/watch?v=PpoU7SkYl2E.
k-os. *Joyful Rebellion*. Astralworks, 2004.
KRS-One. "Hip-Hop vs. Rap." *Sound of the Police*. B-Side. Jive, 1993.
Kweli, Talib. "Going Hard." *The Beautiful Struggle*. Rawkus Records. 2004.
Lee "Scratch" Perry. "African Hitchhiker." *From the Secret Laboratory*. Mango, 1990.
Marley, Bob, and The Wailers. *Rastaman Vibration*. Island, 1976.
Marley, Ziggy and The Melody Makers. "Tomorrow People." *Conscious Party*. Virgin Records, 1988.
M.I.A. "Borders." *AIM*. Interscope, 2016.
Michie Mee and L.A. Luv. *Jamaican Funk—Canadian Style*. First Priority, 1991.
Mingus, Charles. *Pithecanthropus Erectus*. Atlantic, 1956.
Monk, Thelonious. "Epistrophy." *Genius of Modern Music*: Volume 1. Blue Note, 1952.
————. Pannaonica." *Brilliant Corners*. Riverside, 1957.
Morrison, Van. *Avalon Sunset*. Mercury, 1989.
Mos Def. *Black on Both Sides*. Rawkus. 1999.
Mutabaruka. "Dub Poem." *The Mystery Unfolds*. Shanachie,1986.
Nas. "Bridging the Gap." *Street's Disciple*. BMG/Sonny, 2004.
N.W.A. *Straight Outta Compton*. Priority Records, 1998.
Parker, Charlie. "Embraceable You." *Boss Bird,* disc 2. Proper Records, 1947.
————. "KOKO [sic]." *Boss Bird!* Official Record Company, 1988.
————. "Ornithology." *One Night at Birdland*. TriStar, 1950.
Peterson, Oscar. "Hymn to Freedom." *Night Train*. Verve, 1963.
Public Enemy. "Can't Truss It." *Apocalypse 91 . . . The Enemy Strikes Black*. Def Jam, 1991.
————. *It Takes a Nation of Millions to Hold Us Back*. Def Jam, 1988.

Rakim. "I Know You Got Soul." *Paid in Full*. 4th & Broadway. 1987.
Rascalz. *Cash Crop*. ViK/Figure 5, 1998.
Shad. *Flying Colours*. Black Box Canada, 2013.
———. *The Old Prince*. Black Box Canada, 2007.
———. TAO. Secret City Records, 2021.
———. *TSOL*. Black Box Canada, 2010.
Shepp, Archie. *Phat Jam in Milano*. Dawn of Freedom, 2009.
Simone, Nina. "Mississippi Goddam." Philips Records, 1964.
Smith, Bessie. "Backwater Blues." Columbia, 1927.
Snotty Nose Rez Kids. *Trapline*. Universal, 2020.
Stetsasonic. "Taking All that Jazz." *In Full Gear*. Tommy Boy, 1988.
Sun Ra. ""There Are Other Worlds (They Have Not Told You Of)." *Lanquidity*. Philly Jazz, 1978.
Touré, Ali Farka, and Toumani Diabaté. "Hawa Dolo." *In the Heart of the Moon*. World Circuit Limited, 2005.
War Party. *The Reign*. Styles Music Canada, 2000.
Wayne, Lil. "Lollipop." *The Carter III*. Cash Money, 2008.
West, Kanye. *Late Registration*. Roc-A-Fella, 2005.

Bibliography

Achebe, Chinua. "Colonialist Criticism." In *The Post-Colonial Studies Reader*, 2nd ed., edited by Bill Ashcroft, Gareth Griffiths, and Helen Tiffin, 73–76. New York: Routledge, 2006.

Adams. Rachel. *Continental Divides: Remapping the Cultures of North America*. Chicago: University of Chicago Press, 2009.

Adorno, Theodor. *Aesthetic Theory*. Minneapolis: University of Minnesota Press, 1997.

———. *Minima Moralia: Reflections on a Damaged Life*. Translated by E.F.N. Jephcott. London: Verso, 2005.

———. "On Popular Music." In *On Record: Rock, Pop, and the Written Word*, edited by Simon Frith and Andrew Goodwin, 256–67. New York: Routledge, 2005.

Agamben, Giorgio. *The Coming Community*. Translated by Michael Hardt. Minneapolis: University of Minnesota Press, 1993.

———. *Homo Sacer: Sovereign Power and Bare Life*. Translated by Daniel Heller-Roazen. Stanford: Stanford University Press, 1998.

Allen, Lillian. "De Dub Poets: Renegades in a One Poem Town." *This Magazine* 21, no. 7 (December 1987–January 1988): 14–21.

———. *Psychic Unrest*. Toronto: Insomniac Press, 1999.

———. "A Writing of Resistance: Black Women's Writing in Canada." In *In the Feminine: Women and Words Conference Proceedings*. Edmonton: Longspoon, 1985.

Allsopp, Richard, ed. *Dictionary of English Caribbean Usage*. Kingston: University of the West Indies Press, 2003.

Anderson, Benedict. *Imagined Communities: Reflections on the Origin and Spread of Nationalism*. New York: Verso, 2006.

Anderson, Paul A. "Ellington, Rap Music, and Cultural Difference." *Musical Quarterly* 79, no. 1 (Spring 1995): 172–206.

Andrisani, Vincent. "The Sweet Sounds of Havana: Space, Listening, and the Making of Sonic Citizenship." *Sounding Out!*, 17 September 2015. https://soundstudiesblog.com/2015/09/17/the-sweet-sounds-of-havana-space-listening-and-the-making-of-sonic-citizenship.

Angelou, Maya. *I Know Why the Caged Bird Sings*. New York: Random House, 1969.

anitafrika, d'bi.young. "r/evolution begins within." *Canadian Theatre Review* 150 (Spring 2012): 26–29.

———. *Rivers . . . and other blackness . . . between us: (dub) poems of love.* Toronto: Women's Press, 2007.

———. "'we tellin' stories yo.'" Interview with Paul Watkins. improvcommunity.ca, April 2014.

Arsenault, Adrienne. "Soccer and Song: K'naan's Passport to Global Exposure." CBC News, 18 March 2010. https://www.cbc.ca/news/canada/soccer-and-song-k-naan-s-passport-to-global-exposure-1.915498.

Asante, M.K. *It's Bigger Than Hip Hop: The Rise of the Post-Hip-Hop Generation.* New York: St. Martin's Griffin, 2008.

Attali, Jacques. *Noise: The Political Economy of Music.* Translated by Brian Massumi. Minneapolis: University of Minnesota Press, 1985.

Atwood, Margaret. *Survival: A Thematic Guide to Canadian Criticism.* Toronto: House of Anansi Press, 1972.

Augaitis, Daina, Bruce Grenville, and Stephen Rebick, eds. *MashUp: The Birth of Modern Culture.* Vancouver: Vancouver Art Gallery/Black Dog Publishing, 2016.

Austen, Veronica J. "*Zong!*'s 'Should We?': Questioning the Ethical Representation of Trauma." *English Studies in Canada* 37, nos. 3–4 (September–December 2011): 61–81.

Austin, David. *Fear of a Black Nation: Race, Sex, and Security in Sixties Montreal.* Toronto: Between the Lines, 2013.

Bailey, Derek. *Improvisation: Its Nature and Practice in Music.* New York: Da Capo Press, 1993.

Baker, Houston A., Jr. *Afro-American Poetics.* Madison: University of Wisconsin Press, 1988.

———. *Black Studies, Rap, and the Academy.* Chicago: University of Chicago Press, 1993.

———. *Blues, Ideology, and Afro-American Literature: A Vernacular Theory.* Chicago: University of Chicago Press, 1984.

———. *Modernism and the Harlem Renaissance.* Chicago: University of Chicago Press, 1987.

Baldwin, James. "A Letter to My Nephew." *The Progressive*, 1 December 1962. https://progressive.org/magazine/letter-nephew.

———. *Sonny's Blues*, edited by George Kirby. Stuttgart: Ernst Klett, 1970.

Ballantyne, Darcy, Paul Barrett, Camille Isaacs, and Kris Singh. "The Unbearable Whiteness of CanLit." *The Walrus*, 26 July 2017. https://thewalrus.ca/the-unbearable-whiteness-of-canlit.

Bambara, Toni Cade. *The Salt Eaters.* New York: Vintage Books, 1980.

Baraka, Amiri. *The Dead Lecturer.* New York: Grove Press, 1964.

———. *Digging: The Afro-American Soul of American Classical Music.* Berkeley: University of California Press, 2009.

———. "Jazzmen: Diz & Sun Ra." *African American Review* 29, no. 2 (Summer 1995): 249–55.

———. *The LeRoi Jones/Amiri Baraka Reader*, edited by William J. Harris. New York: Thunder's Mouth Press, 1991.
———. "Notes on Lou Donaldson and Andrew Hill." *The Cricket* 4 (1969): 46.
———. *Transbluesency: The Selected Poems of Amiri Baraka/LeRoi Jones (1961–1995)*, edited by Paul Vangelisti. New York: Marsilio, 1995.
Baraka, Amiri, and William Parker. "'People Get Ready' / The Future of Jazz: Amiri Baraka and William Parker in Conversation," edited by Paul Watkins. improvcommunity.ca, 3 August 2014.
Barrett, Paul. *Blackening Canada: Diaspora, Race, Multiculturalism*. Toronto: University of Toronto Press, 2015.
———. "The Poetic Disturbances of M. NourbeSe Philip," *The Walrus*, 21 September 2018. https://thewalrus.ca/the-poetic-disturbances-of-m-nourbese-philip.
Beasley, Myron M. "Performing Zora: Critical Ethnography, Digital Sound, and Not Forgetting." In *Digital Sound Studies*, edited by Mary Caton Lingold, Darren Mueller, and Whitney Trettien. Durham: Duke University Press, 2018.
Beckford, Sharon Morgan. *Naturally Woman: The Search for Self in Black Canadian Women's Literature*. Toronto: Inanna, 2011.
Bernstein, Charles. *Close Listening: Poetry and the Printed Word*. Oxford: Oxford University Press, 1988.
———. *A Poetics*. Cambridge, MA: Harvard University Press, 1992.
Birney, Earle. *The Cow Jumped Over the Moon: The Writing and Reading of Poetry*. Toronto: Holt, Rinehart and Winston of Canada, 1972.
Bivens, Ollie. "Archie Shepp: The Cries of My People." *All about Jazz*, 24 February 2005.
"Black History Month Stamp Celebrates Vancouver's Hogan's Alley." CBC News, 20 January 2014. https://www.cbc.ca/news/canada/british-columbia/black-history-month-stamp-celebrates-vancouver-s-hogan-s-alley-1.2516741.
Blanchard, Terence. "Black Protest Is Music. Learning the Melody Isn't Enough," *NPR*, 18 June 2020. https://www.npr.org/2020/06/18/879663904/opinion-terence-blanchard-black-protest-marvin-gaye-melody.
Bohn, Willard. *Modern Visual Poetry*. Newark: University of Delaware Press, 2001.
Borden, George A. *Canaan Odyssey: A Poetic Account of the Black Experience in North America*. Dartmouth: Black Cultural Centre for Nova Scotia, 1988.
Bradley, Adam, and Andrew DuBois, eds. *The Anthology of Rap*. New Haven: Yale University Press, 2010.
Brand, Dionne. *The Blue Clerk*. Toronto: McClelland & Stewart, 2018.
———. *Bread Out of Stone*. Toronto: Vintage, 1998.
———. "I Am Not That Strong Woman." In *Eyeing the North Star: Directions in African-Canadian Literature*, edited by George Elliott Clarke, 123. Toronto: McClelland and Stewart, 1999.
———. *A Kind of Perfect Speech*. Nanaimo: Institute for Coastal Research, 2008.
———. *A Map to the Door of No Return: Notes on Belonging*. Toronto: Vintage, 2001.
———. *No Language Is Neutral*. Toronto: McClelland and Stewart, 1998.
———. *Ossuaries*. New York: McClelland and Stewart, 2010.

———. "The Shape of Language." Lecture delivered on 16 June 2018. YouTube, 1:01:17. https://www.youtube.com/watch?v=r_HdOZIFElo.
———. *Thirsty*. New York: McClelland and Stewart, 2002.
———. *What We All Long For*. Toronto: Vintage Canada, 2005.
Brand, Dionne, and Lois De Shield, eds. *No Burden to Carry: Narratives of Black Working Women in Ontario, 1920s–1950s*. Toronto: Women's Press, 1991.
Brathwaite, Edward Kamau. *The Arrivants: A New World Trilogy*. Oxford: Oxford University Press, 1973.
———. "English in the Caribbean: Notes on Nation Language and Poetry." In *English Literature, Opening Up the Canon*, edited by Leslie A. Fiedler and Houston Baker Jr., 15–33. Baltimore: Johns Hopkins University Press, 1981.
———. *History of the Voice: The Development of Nation Language in Anglophone Caribbean Poetry*. London: New Beacon Books, 1984.
Brooks, Gwendolyn. *Maud Martha*. Chicago: Third World Press, 1993.
———. *Selected Poems*. New York: Harper Perennial, 2006.
Brubaker, Rogers. *Citizenship and Nationhood in France and Germany*. Cambridge, MA: Harvard University Press, 2002.
Buskirk, Martha, Amelia Jones, and Caroline A. Jones. "The Year in 'Re-.'" *Artforum* 52, no. 4 (2013). https://www.artforum.com/print/201310/the-year-in-re-44068.
Butler, Judith. *Precarious Life: The Powers of Mourning and Violence*. London: Verso, 2006.
Butling, Pauline. "Redefining Radical Poetics." In *Writing in Our Time: Canada's Radical Poetries in English (1957–2003)*, edited by Pauline Butling and Susan Rudy, 17–28. Waterloo: Wilfrid Laurier University Press, 2005.
Callaghan, Morley. *The Loved and the Lost* [1951]. Toronto: Exile, 2010.
Campbell, Mark V. "Connect the T.Dots—Remix Multiculturalism: After Caribbean-Canadian, Social Possibilities for Living with Difference." In *Ebony Roots, Northern Soil: Perspectives on Blackness in Canada*, edited by Charmaine A. Nelson, 254–76. Newcastle: Cambridge Scholars, 2010.
Captain Philips. Dir. Paul Greengrass. Sony Pictures, 2013. Film.
Cardinal, Harold. *The Unjust Society*. Vancouver: Douglas and McIntyre, 1969.
Carr, Brenda. "'Come Mek Wi Work Together': Community Witness and Social Agency in Lillian Allen's Dub Poetry." *Ariel: A Review of International English Literature* 29, no. 3 (July 1998): 7–40.
Carroll, Sean B. *Endless Forms Most Beautiful: The New Science of Evo Devo and the Making of the Animal Kingdom*. New York: W.W. Norton, 2005.
Casas, Maria Caridad. *Multimodality in Canadian Black Feminist Writing: Orality and the Body in the Work of Harris, Philip, Allen, and Brand*. Amsterdam: Rodopi, 2009.
Cassidy, F.G., and R.B. Le Page, eds. *Dictionary of Jamaican English*, 2nd ed. Cambridge: Cambridge University Press, 2009.
Césaire, Aimé. Interview with René Depestre from *Discourse on Colonialism*. *Monthly Review Press* (1972): 20, 23–25.

Chamberlain, Mary. "Diasporic Memories: Community, Individuality, and Creativity—a Life Stories Perspective." *Oral History Review* 36. no. 2 (Summer–Fall 2009): 186.
Chan, Victor. Review of *Dub Poetry: 19 Poets from England and Jamaica*, by Christian Habekost. *Jamaica Journal* 21, no. 3 (1988): 49–53.
Chancy, Myriam. *Searching for Safe Spaces: Afro-Caribbean Women Writers in Exile*. Philadelphia: Temple University Press, 1997.
Chernoff, John Miller. *African Rhythm and African Sensibility*. Chicago: University of Chicago Press, 1979.
Chuck D, "Death of a Nation—Where Ignorance Is Rewarded for a New Race Creation: The Niggro." In *Rhythm and Blues: The Political Economy of Black Music*, edited by Norman Kelley, 267–9. New York: Akashic Books, 2002.
———. "Interview." *Melody Maker*, 12 October 1991.
Clarke, Austin. *The Survivors of the Crossing*. Toronto: McClelland and Stewart, 1964.
Clarke, George Elliott. "Afterword: Let Us Now Attain Polyphonous Epiphanies." In *Blues and Bliss: The Poetry of George Elliott Clarke*, edited by John Paul Fiorentino, 59–63. Waterloo: Wilfrid Laurier University Press, 2008.
———. "Antiphony." *Canadian Literature* 157 (Summer 1998): 12. https://canlit.ca/article/antiphony.
———. *Black*, rev. 2nd ed. Kentville: Gaspereau Press, 2012.
———. *Blue*. Kentville: Gaspeareau Press, 2011.
———. "Canadian Biraciality and Its 'Zebra' Poetics." *Intertexts* 6, no. 2 (Fall 2002): 203–31.
———. "Cool Politics: Styles of Honour in Malcolm X and Miles Davis." *Jouvert: A Journal of Postcolonial Studies* 2, no. 1 (1998). https://legacy.chass.ncsu.edu/jouvert/v2i1/CLARKE.HTM.
———. "The Crime of Poetry: George Elliott Clarke in Conversation with Wayde Compton and Kevin McNeilly." *Canadian Literature* 182 (Autumn 2004): 53–64.
———. *Directions Home*. Toronto: University of Toronto Press, 2012.
———. *Execution Poems: The Black Acadian Tragedy of "George and Rue."* Kentville: Gaspereau Press, 2001.
———. "George Elliott Clarke on the Many Poetic Meanings of Red." CBC Books, 16 December 2013.
———. "George Elliott Clarke to Derek Walcott." *Open Letter* 11, no. 3 (Fall 2001): 15–17.
———. *Gold*. Kentville: Gaspereau Press, 2016.
———. *I&I*. Fredericton: Goose Lane Editions, 2009.
———. *Illuminated Verses*. Toronto: Kellom, 2005.
———. *Lush Dreams, Blue Exile*. Lawrencetown Beach: Pottersfield Press, 1994.
———. *Odysseys Home: Mapping African-Canadian Literature*. Toronto: University of Toronto Press, 2002.
———. *Québécité*. Kentville: Gaspereau Press, 2003.
———. *Red*. Kentville: Gaspereau Press, 2011.
———. *Saltwater Spirituals and Deeper Blues*. Porters Lake: Pottersfield Press, 1983.

———. *Trudeau: Long March, Shining Path*. Kentville: Gaspereau Press, 2007.
———. *Where Beauty Survived: An Africadian Memoir*. Toronto: Alfred A. Knopf, 2021.
———. *White*. Kentville: Gaspereau Press, 2021.
———. *Whylah Falls*. Winlaw: Polestar Press, 1990.
Clarke, George Elliott, ed. *Eyeing the North Star: Directions in African-Canadian Literature*. Toronto: McClelland and Stewart, 1999.
Cleage, Pearl. *Mad at Miles: A Blackwoman's Guide to Truth*. Southfield: Cleage Group, 1990.
Cole, Desmond. *The Skin We're In: A Year of Black Resistance and Power*. Toronto: Doubleday, 2020.
Coleman, Ornette. "Prime Time for Harmolodics." *Down Beat* (July 1983): 54–5.
Colley, Sherri Borden. "After 200 Years without Land Title, Nova Scotia Black Communities Offered Hope." CBC News, 28 September 2017. https://www.cbc.ca/news/canada/nova-scotia/legal-title-black-loyalists-north-preston-1.4309505.
Compton, Anne. "Standing Your Ground: George Elliott Clarke in Conversation." *Studies in Canadian Literature* 23, no. 2 (1998). https://journals.lib.unb.ca/index.php/SCL/article/view/12866.
Compton, Wayde. *49th Parallel Psalm*. Vancouver: Arsenal Pulp Press, 1999.
———. *After Canaan: Essays on Race, Writing, and Region*. Vancouver: Arsenal Pulp Press, 2010.
———. "Black History in Vancouver Recognized at Last: Hogan's Alley Memorial Project." Rabble.ca, 25 February 2013. http://rabble.ca/news/2013/02/black-history-vancouver-recognized-last-hogans-alley-memorial-project.
———. *Bluesprint: Black British Columbian Literature and Orature*. Vancouver: Arsenal Pulp Press, 2001.
———. "Declaration of the Halfrican Nation." In *Performance Bond*. Vancouver: Arsenal Pulp Press, 2004.
———. "The Epic Moment: An Interview with Wayde Compton." Interview by Myler Wilkinson and David Stouck. *West Coast Line* 36, no. 2 (2002): 131–45.
———. "'Even the Stars Are Temporal': The Historical Motion of George Elliott Clarke's *Saltwater Spirituals and Deeper Blues*." In *Africadian Atlantic: Essays on George Elliott Clarke*, edited by Joseph Pivato, 13–18. Toronto: Guernica Editions, 2012.
———. *Performance Bond*. Vancouver: Arsenal Pulp Press, 2004.
———. "The Reinventing Wheel: On Blending the Poetry of Cultures through Hip Hop Turntablism." *Horizon Zero* 8 (June 2003).
———. "Self-Interview." In *Side/Lines: A New Canadian Poetics*, edited by Rob McLennan, 80–85. London, ON: Insomniac Press, 2002.
———. "Seven Routes to Hogan's Alley and Vancouver's Black Community." In *After Canaan: Essays on Race, Writing, and Region*, 83–144. Vancouver: Arsenal Pulp Press, 2010.
———. "Turntable Poetry, Mixed-Race, and Schizophonophilia." In *After Canaan: Essays on Race, Writing, and Region*, 183–201. Vancouver: Arsenal Pulp Press, 2010.

Cone, James H. *The Spirituals and the Blues*. Maryknoll: Orbis Books, 2009.
Cools, Anne. "Womanhood." Black Spark ed., *McGill Free Press*, February 1971.
Cooper, Afua. *Copper Woman and Other Poems*. Toronto: Natural Heritage Books, 2007.
———. *The Hanging of Angélique: The Untold Story of Canadian Slavery and the Burning of Old Montreal*. Toronto: Harper Perennial, 2006.
———. *Memories Have Tongue*. Toronto: Sister Vision Press, 1992.
Cooper, Afua, ed. *Utterance and Incantations: Women, Poetry and Dub*. Toronto: Sister Vision, 1999.
Cullen, Countee. "Heritage." Poetry Foundation. https://www.poetryfoundation.org/poems/42619/heritage-56d2213a97c6c.
D'Aguiar, Fred. *Feeding the Ghosts*. New York: Ecco Press, 1997.
Davey, Frank. *From There to Here: A Guide to English-Canadian Literature since 1960*. Erin: Press Porcépic, 1974.
Davis, Andrea A. *Horizon, Sea, Sound: Caribbean and African Women's Cultural Critiques of Nation*. Evanston: Northwestern University Press, 2022.
Davis, Angela. "Black History Month Presentation." War Memorial Hall, 90 Gordon Street, University of Guelph, 2 February 2012.
———. *Blues Legacies and Black Feminism: Gertrude "Ma" Rainey, Bessie Smith, and Billie Holiday*. New York: Vintage Books, 1998.
Davis, Erik. "Trickster at the Crossroads." *Levity*. http://www.levity.com/figment/trickster.html. Originally published in *Gnosis: A Journal of the Western Inner Traditions* 19 (Spring 1991).
Davis, Miles, and Quincy Troupe. *Miles: The Autobiography*. New York: Simon and Schuster, 2011.
Dawes, Kwame. *Midland*. Fredericton: Goose Lane Editions, 2001.
———. *Natural Mysticism: Towards a New Reggae Aesthetic in Caribbean Writing*. Leeds: Peepal Tree, 1999.
Dawson, Ashley. *Mongrel Nation: Diasporic Culture and the Making of Postcolonial Britain*. Ann Arbor: University of Michigan Press, 2010.
Derrida, Jacques. *Specters of Marx: The State of the Debt, the Work of Mourning and the New International*. Translated by Peggy Kamuf. London: Routledge, 1997.
DeVito, Chris, ed. *Coltrane on Coltrane: The John Coltrane Interviews*. Chicago: Chicago Review Press, 2010.
Dimoff, Anna. "Vancouver to Revive Hogan's Alley Community with Help of American Architect." CBC News, 21 May 2017. http://www.cbc.ca/news/canada/british-columbia/hogans-alley-community-plan-1.4124018.
Douglass, Frederick. *The Life and Times of Frederick Douglass*. New York: Dover, 2003.
———. *My Bondage and My Freedom*. 1855. Project Gutenberg, 2008. https://www.gutenberg.org/files/202/202-h/202-h.htm.
———. *Narrative of the Life of Frederick Douglass, an American Slave*. New York: Penguin, 1986.

Dowling, Sarah. "Persons and Voices: Sounding Impossible Bodies in M. NourbeSe Philip's *Zong!*" *Canadian Literature* 210–11 (Autumn–Winter 2011). https://canlit.ca/article/persons-and-voices.
Du Bois, W.E.B. "Criteria of Negro Art." *Crisis* (October 1926): 295–6.
———. *The Souls of Black Folk*. Mineola: Dover Thrift, 1994.
Dunbar, Paul Laurence. *Selected Poems*. New York: Dover Thrift Editions, 1997.
Edugyan, Esi. *Half-Blood Blues*. Toronto: Thomas Allen, 2011.
Eliot, T.S. "Tradition and the Individual Talent." In *The Sacred Wood: Essays on Poetry and Criticism*, 39–49. London: Faber and Faber, 1997.
Elliott, Alicia. "CanLit Is a Raging Dumpster Fire." *Open Book*, 7 September 2017. http://open-book.ca/Columnists/CanLit-is-a-Raging-Dumpster-Fire.
Ellison, Ralph. *Invisible Man*. New York: Vintage International Edition, 1995.
———. "Richard Wright's Blues." In *Interpretations: Richard Wright's Black Boy*, edited by Harold Bloom, 7–20. New York: Chelsea House, 2006.
———. *Shadow and Act*. New York: Random House, 1964.
Equiano, Olaudah. *The Interesting Narrative and Other Writings*. New York: Penguin, 2003.
Fanon, Frantz. *Black Skin, White Masks*. Translated by Charles Lam Markmann. New York: Grove Press, 1967.
———. *Wretched of the Earth*. New York: Grove Press, 1963.
Fehskens, Erin M. "Accounts Unpaid, Accounts Untold: M. NourbeSe Philip's *Zong!* and the Catalogue." *Callaloo* 35, no. 2 (Spring 2012): 407–24.
Fiorentino, Jon Paul. "Blackening English: The Polyphonic Poetics of George Elliott Clarke." *Poetics.ca* 2 (June 2003). http://www.poetics.ca/issue2.
Fischlin, Daniel, and Ajay Heble. "The Other Side of Nowhere: Jazz, Improvisation, and Communities in Dialogue." In *The Other Side of Nowhere: Jazz, Improvisation, and Communities in Dialogue*, edited by Daniel Fischlin and Ajay Heble, 1–42. Middletown: Wesleyan University Press, 2004.
Fischlin, Daniel, Ajay Heble, and George Lipsitz. *The Fierce Urgency of Now: Improvisation, Rights, and the Ethics of Cocreation*. Durham: Duke University Press, 2013.
Fiske, John. "Surveilling the City: Whiteness, the Black Man, and Democratic Totalitarianism," *Theory, Culture, and Society* 15(2): 67–88.
Fogel, William Robert, and Stanley L. Engerman. *Time on the Cross: The Economics of American Slavery*. New York: W.W. Norton, 1995.
Foster, Cecil. *Blackness and Modernity: The Colour of Humanity and the Quest for Freedom*. Montreal and Kingston: McGill–Queen's University Press, 2007.
———. *Genuine Multiculturalism: The Tragedy and Comedy of Diversity*. Montreal and Kingston: McGill–Queen's University Press, 2014.
———. *A Place Called Heaven: The Meaning of Being Black in Canada*. Toronto: HarperCollins, 1996.
———. *They Call Me George: The Untold Story of Black Train Porters and the Birth of Modern Canada*. Windsor: Biblioasis, 2019.

———. *Where Race Does Not Matter: The New Spirit of Modernity*. Toronto: Penguin, 2005.
Foucault, Michel. *Discipline and Punish: The Birth of the Prison*. New York: Pantheon Books, 1977.
Fraile-Marcos, Ana Maria. "The Transcultural Intertextuality of George Elliot Clarke's African Canadianité: American Models Shaping George & Rue." *African American Review* 47, no. 1 (2014): 113–28.
Friedman, Melinda, prod. *Secret Vancouver: A Return to Hogan's Alley*. Calgary: Spotlight Productions, 2016. https://www.youtube.com/watch?v=B-8lgpvjoHg.
Freire, Paulo. *Pedagogy of the Oppressed*. Translated by Myra Bergman Ramos. New York: Bloomsbury, 2012.
Frye, Northrop. *The Bush Garden: Essays on the Canadian Imagination*, 2nd ed. Toronto: House of Anansi, 1995.
———. "Conclusion." In *Literary History of Canada: Canadian Literature in English*, 2nd ed., vol. 2, edited by Carl F. Klinck, 318–32. Toronto: University of Toronto Press, 1976.
———. *Northrop Frye on Canada*. Toronto: University of Toronto Press, 2003.
Gale, Lorena. *Angélique*. Toronto: Playwrights Canada Press, 2000.
Gates, Henry Louis, Jr. *Loose Canons: Notes on the Culture Wars*. New York: Oxford University Press, 1992.
———. *The Signifying Monkey: A Theory of Afro-American Literary Criticism*. New York: Oxford University Press, 1988.
———. "Zora Neale Hurston: 'A Negro Way of Saying.'" Afterword to *Their Eyes Were Watching God*, by Zora Neale Hurston, 195–206. New York: Harper Perennial, 2006.
Gillis, Charlie. "Maclean's Interview: K'naan." *Maclean's*, 6 April 2010. https://www.macleans.ca/general/macleans-interview-rapper-knaan.
Gilmore, John. *Swinging in Paradise: The Story of Jazz in Montreal*. Montreal: Véhicule Press, 1988.
Gilroy, Paul. *The Black Atlantic*. London: Verso, 1993.
Gioia, Ted. *Delta Blues*. New York: W.W. Norton, 2008.
Giovanni, Nikki. *Racism 101*. New York: William Morrow, 1994.
Goldman, Marlene. "Spirit Possession and the Transformation of Space in the Fiction of Dionne Brand." In *No Language Is Neutral: Writings on Dionne Brand*, edited by Dina Georgis, Katherine McKittrick, and Rinaldo Walcott, special issue, *Topia: Canadian Journal of Cultural Studies* 34 (Fall 2015): 141–56.
Gonzales, Michael A. "Gangster Boogie." *Wax Poetics* 38 (November–December 2009): 85–96.
Grizzle, Stanley G. *My Name's Not George: The Story of the Brotherhood of Sleeping Car Porters in Canada*. Toronto: Umbrella Press, 1998.
Habekost, Christian. *Verbal Riddim: The Politics and Aesthetics of African-Caribbean Dub Poetry*. Amsterdam: Rodopi, 1993.

Hale, James. "Jazz in Canada" [2006]. In *Canadian Encyclopedia*. Last modified June 2015. https://www.thecanadianencyclopedia.ca/en/article/jazz.

Hall, Phil. "Continent of Silence: Marlene NourbeSe Philip Is One of a Small Group of Writers Who Are Creating the First Modern Black Women's Written Culture in Canada." *Books in Canada* 18, no. 1 (1989): 1–2.

Hall, Stuart. "Cultural Identity and Diaspora." In *Identity: Community, Culture, Difference*, edited by Jonathan Rutherford, 222–37. London: HarperCollins, 1998.

——. "Introduction: Who Needs 'Identity'?" In *Questions of Cultural Identity*, edited by Stuart Hall and Paul du Gay, 1–17. London: Sage, 1998.

Hansberry, Lorraine. "The Negro Writer and His Roots: Towards a New Romanticism." *The Black Scholar* 12, no. 2 (March–April 1981): 2–12.

Harney, Stefano and Fred Moten. *The Undercommons: Fugitive Planning and Black Study*. New York: Minor Compositions, 2013.

Harris, Claire. *Drawing Down a Daughter*. Fredericton: Goose Lane Editions, 2011.

——. "Why Do I Write?" In *Grammar of Dissent: Poetry and Prose by Claire Harris, M. Nourbese Philip, and Dionne Brand*, edited by Carol Morrell, 26–33. Fredericton: Goose Lane, 1994.

Harris, Jennifer. "Black Life in a Nineteenth-Century New Brunswick Town." *Journal of Canadian Studies/Revue d'études Canadiennes* 46, no. 1 (2012): 138–66.

Harris, William. *The Poetry and Poetics of Amiri Baraka: The Jazz Aesthetic*. Columbia: University of Missouri Press, 1985.

Hartman, Carl O. *Jazz Text: Voice and Improvisation in Poetry, Jazz, and Song*. Princeton: Princeton University Press, 1991.

Hartman, Saidiya. *Lose Your Mother: A Journey along the Atlantic Slave Route*. New York: Farrar, Straus and Giroux, 2007.

Head, Harold, ed. *Canada in Us Now*. Toronto: NC Press, 1976.

Heater, Derek. *What Is Citizenship?* Cambridge: Polity Press, 1999.

Hebdige, Dick. *Cut 'n' Mix*. New York: Routledge, 2005.

——. *Subculture: The Meaning of Style*. New York: Routledge, 2002.

Heble, Ajay. "Destinations Out: Towards a Jazz-Inflected Model for Community-Based Learning." Keynote talk at "Key Changes: Transitions in Our Students, Our Classrooms, Ourselves." Association of Atlantic Universities Teaching Showcase Conference, University of Prince Edward Island, 24–25 September 2010. http://www.improvcommunity.ca/sites/improvcommunity.ca/files/research_collection/644/Destinations_Out_Jazz_Inflected_Learning.pdf.

——. *Landing on the Wrong Note: Jazz, Dissonance, and Critical Practice*. New York: Routledge, 2000.

——. "Sounds of Change: Dissonance, History, and Cultural Listening." *Essays on Canadian Writing* 71 (Fall 2000): 26–36.

Henson, Josiah. *The Life of Josiah Henson: Formerly a Slave*. Dresden: Uncle Tom's Cabin Museum, 1984.

Hill, Daniel G. *The Freedom Seekers: Blacks in Early Canada*. Agincourt: Book Society of Canada, 1981.

Hill, Lawrence. *Any Known Blood*. Toronto: HarperCollins, 2008.
Hinkle, Win. "Interview with Earl Zindars." *Letter from Evans* (Fall 1993): 18–22.
hooks, bell. *All About Love*. New York: William Morrow, 2001.
———. *Outlaw Culture: Resisting Representations*. New York: Routledge, 1994.
———. "Performance Practice as a Site of Opposition." In *Let's Get It On: The Politics of Black Performance*, edited by Catherine Ugwu, 210–21. Seattle: Bay Press, 1995.
———. *Talking Back: Thinking Feminist, Thinking Black*. Boston: South End Press, 1989.
———. *Teaching to Transgress: Education as the Practice of Freedom*. New York: Routledge, 1994.
Hudson, Peter James. "The Lost Tribe of a Lost Tribe: Black British Columbia and the Poetics of Space." In *Black Geographies and the Politics of Place*, edited by Katherine McKittrick and Clyde Woods, 154–76. Toronto: Between the Lines, 2007.
Hudson, Sandy. "Building Community, Building Resistance: Black Lives Matter–Toronto." Interview by Salmaan Khan. *Upping the Anti* 18 (28 June 2016), https://uppingtheanti.org/journal/article/18-black-lives-matter-toronto.
Hughes, Langston. "Introduction." In *The Collected Poems*, edited by Arnold Rampersad and David Roessel. New York: Vintage Classics, 1995.
———. *The Collected Works*, vol. 7: *The Early Simple Stories*. Columbia: University of Missouri Press, 2002.
Hunter, Lynette. "After Modernism: Alternative Voices in the Writing of Dionne Brand, Claire Harris, and Marlene Philip." *University of Toronto Quarterly* 62, no. 2 (1992–93): 256–91.
Hurston, Zora Neale. "The Characteristics of Negro Expression." In *Sweat*, edited by Cheryl Wall, 55–71. New Brunswick: Rutgers University Press, 1997.
———. *Mules and Men*. New York: HarperCollins, 1990.
Hutcheon, Linda. *A Theory of Parody: The Teachings of Twentieth-Century Art Forms*. Champaign: University of Illinois Press, 2000.
Iton, Richard. *In Search of the Black Fantastic: Politics and Popular Culture in the Post–Civil Rights Era*. New York: Oxford University Press, 2008.
Iyer, Vijay. "On Improvisation, Temporality, and Embodied Experience." *Journal of Consciousness Studies* 11, nos. 3–4 (2004): 159–73.
James, C.L.R. *Beyond a Boundary*. New York: Pantheon, 1983.
Jenkins, Matthew G. *Poetic Obligation: Ethics in Experimental American Poetry after 1945*. Iowa City: University of Iowa Press, 2008.
Johnson, James Weldon. "Autobiography of an Ex Colored Man." In *The Heath Anthology of American Literature*, edited by Paul Lauter, vol. D: *Modern Period (1910–1945)*, 6th ed., 1185–200. Belmont: Wadsworth, 2009.
Johnson, Linton Kwesi. "Jamaican Rebel Music." *Race and Class* 17, no. 4 (1976): 398.
Johnson, Lyndon B. "Special Message to Congress: The American Promise," 15 March 1965. LBJ Presidential Library. https://www.whitehousehistory.org/we-shall-overcome-lbj-voting-rights

Jones, LeRoi [Amiri Baraka]. *Blues People: Negro Music in White America*. New York: William Morrow, 1963.
Joseph, Clifton. *Metropolitan Blues*. Toronto: Domestic Bliss, 1983.
———. "Recollections: A Seventees Black RAP." In *Being Black*. Edited by Althea Prince, 13–21. Toronto: Insomniac Press, 2001.
Jost, Ekkehard. *Free Jazz*. New York: Da Capo Press, 1994.
Justice, Daniel Heath. *Why Indigenous Literatures Matter*. Waterloo: Wilfrid Laurier University Press, 2018.
Kamboureli, Smaro. *On the Edge of Genre: The Contemporary Canadian Long Poem*. Toronto: University of Toronto Press, 1991.
———. *Scandalous Bodies: Diasporic Literature in English Canada*. Waterloo: Wilfrid Laurier University Press, 2009.
Kamboureli, Smaro, ed. *Making a Difference: Canadian Multicultural Literature*. Toronto: Oxford University Press, 2006.
Keeler, Emily M. "David Gilmour on Building Strong Stomachs." Shelf Esteem. *Hazlitt*, 25 September 2013. https://hazlitt.net/blog/david-gilmour-building-strong-stomachs.
Kelley, Robin D.G. *Freedom Dreams: The Black Radical Imagination*. Boston: Beacon Press, 2002.
———. "Notes on Deconstructing the Folk." *American Historical Review* 97, no. 5 (December 1992): 1400–1408.
———. *Race Rebels: Culture, Politics, and the Black Working Class*. New York: Free Press, 1996.
———. *Thelonious Monk: The Life and Times of an American Original*. New York: Free Press, 2009.
———. *Yo' Mama's Dysfunktional! Fighting the Culture Wars in Urban America*. Boston: Beacon Press, 1997.
Kelley, William Melvin. *A Different Drummer*. New York: Anchor, 1990.
Kellough, Kaie. "Abstract Propulsion: 14 Reflections on 'Verso 14.'" *sx salon* 38–39 (February 2022). http://smallaxe.net/sxsalon/discussions/abstract-propulsion.
King, Boston. "Memoirs of the Life of Boston King, a Black Preacher, Written by Himself during His Residence at Kingswood School." *Methodist Magazine* 21 (1798): 105–10, 157–61, 209–13, 261–65.
Khalidi, Rashid. *The Hundred Years' War on Palestine. A History of Settler Colonial Conquest and Resistance*, 1917-2017. Metropolitan Books, 2020.
King, Martin Luther, Jr. "I've Been to the Mountaintop." 3 April. 1968. *American Rhetoric*. https://www.americanrhetoric.com/speeches/mlkivebeentothemountaintop.htm Web. February 2010.
———. *The Radical King*, edited by Cornel West. Boston: Beacon Press, 2015.
———. *Strength to Love* [1963]. Minneapolis: Fortress Press, 2010.
———. *The Trumpet of Conscience*. Boston: Beacon Press, 2010.
King, Thomas. *The Inconvenient Indian: A Curious Account of Native People in North America*. Toronto: Anchor Canada, 2012.

King, Tiffany Lethabo. *The Black Shoals: Offshore Formations of Black and Native Studies*. Durham: Duke University Press, 2019.

Kittler, Friedrich. *Gramophone, Film, Typewriter*. Translated by Geoffrey Winthrop Young. Stanford: Stanford University Press, 1999.

K'naan. "Censoring Myself for Success" [Opinion]. *New York Times*, 8 December 2012. https://www.nytimes.com/2012/12/09/opinion/sunday/knaan-on-censoring-himself-for-success.html.

Knopf, Kristen. "'Oh Canada': Reflections of Multiculturalism in the Poetry of Canadian Women Dub Artists." *Revue LISA/ LISA e-journal* 3, no. 2 (2005): 78–111.

Kroestch, Robert. "Disunity as Unity: A Canadian Strategy." In *UnHomely States: Theorizing English Canadian Postcolonialism*, edited by Cynthia Sugars, 61–70. Peterborough: Broadview Press, 2004.

Kuh, Katharine. *The Artist's Voice: Talks with Seventeen Modern Artists*. New York: Da Capo Press, 2000.

Lacey, Kate. *Listening Publics: The Politics and Experience of Listening in the Media Age*. New York: Wiley, 2013.

Lai, Larissa. "Asian Invasion vs. the Pristine Nation: Migrants Entering the Canadian Imaginary." *Fuse* 23, no. 2 (2000): 30–40.

———. "*Ossuaries:* Life Underground." *The Mark*, 13 May 2010.

Laferrière, Dany. *How to Make Love to a Negro without Getting Tired*. Translated by David Homel. Toronto: Coach House, 1987.

Layton, Irving. *A Red Carpet for the Sun*. Toronto: McClelland and Stewart, 1960.

LeBlanc, Larry. "Rascalz Refuse Award to Protest Junos: Rap Act Wants R&B Portion of Ceremony Televised." *Billboard*, 4 April 1998.

Leland, John. *Hip: The History*. New York: HarperCollins, 2004.

Leow, Joanne. "Mis-mappings and Mis-duplications: Interdiscursivity and the Poetry of Wayde Compton." *Canadian Literature* 214 (2012): n.p., 21 January 2014. https://doi.org/10.14288/cl.voi214.192764

Lewis, George E. "Improvised Music after 1950: Afrological and Eurological Perspectives." *Black Music Research Journal* 16, no. 1 (Spring 1996): 91–122.

———. *A Power Stronger Than Itself: The AACM and American Experimental Music*. Chicago: University of Chicago Press, 2008.

Lingis, Alphonso. *The Community of Those Who Have Nothing in Common*. Indianapolis: Indiana University Press, 1994.

Lingold, Mary Caton, Darren Mueller, and Whitney Trettien, eds. *Digital Sound Studies*. Durham: Duke University Press, 2018.

Lipsitz, George. *Dangerous Crossroads: Popular Music, Postmodernism, and the Poetics of Place*. New York: Verso, 1997.

———. *Footsteps in the Dark: The Hidden Histories of Popular Music*. Minneapolis: University of Minnesota Press, 2007.

———. *The Possessive Investment in Whiteness: How White People Profit from Identity Politics*. Philadelphia: Temple University Press, 2006.

Listening for Something: Adrienne Rich and Dionne Brand in Conversation. National Film Board of Canada, Studio D, 1996. Film. https://www.nfb.ca/film/listening-for-something-adrienne-rich.

Lorde, Audre. *The Selected Works of Audre Lorde*, edited by Roxane Gay. New York: W.W. Norton, 2020.

Lyotard, Jean-François. "The Other's Rights." In *The Politics of Human Rights*, edited by Belgrade Circle, 181–88. London: Verso, 1999.

Macedo, Donaldo. "Introduction." In *Pedagogy of the Oppressed*, by Paulo Freire. Translated by Myra Bergman Ramos, 11–28. New York: Bloomsbury, 2012.

Mackey, Nathaniel. *Discrepant Engagement: Dissonance, Cross-Culturality, and Experimental Writing*. New York: Cambridge University Press, 2009.

———. "An Interview with Kamau Brathwaite." *Hambone* 9 (1991): 42–59.

Malcolm X and Alex Haley. *The Autobiography of Malcolm X*. New York: Ballantine Books, 1992.

Mandela, Nelson. *Long Walk to Freedom: The Autobiography of Nelson Mandela*. Boston: Back Bay Books, 1995.

Mandiela, Ahdri Zhina. *dark diaspora*. In *Testifyin': Contemporary African Canadian Drama*, vol. 1, edited by Djanet Sears, 445–70. Toronto: Playwrights Canada Press.

Mao Tse-Tung. *Selected Works*, vol. 3. China: Peking Foreign Languages Press, 1965.

Marsh, Charity, and Mark V. Campbell, eds. *We Still Here: Hip Hop North of the 49th Parallel*. Montreal and Kingston: McGill–Queen's University Press, 2020.

Marx, Karl, and Frederick Engels. *The Communist Manifesto* [1848] *with Related Documents*, edited by John E. Toews. New York: Bedford/St. Martin's, 1999.

———. *The Eighteenth Brumaire of Louis Bonaparte* [1852] (excerpt from *The Communist Manifesto with Related Documents*), edited by John E. Toews, 147–50. New York: Bedford/St. Martin's, 1999.

Massey Report. Royal Commission on National Development in the Arts, Letters and Sciences (1949–1951). https://www.collectionscanada.gc.ca/massey/h5-430-e.html.

Mathieu, Sarah-Jane. *North of the Color Line: Migration and Black Resistance in Canada, 1870–1955*. Chapel Hill: University of North Carolina Press, 2010.

Mathur, Ashok. "Transubracination: How Writers of Colour Became CanLit." In *Trans.Can.Lit: Resituating the Study of Canadian Literature*, edited by Smaro Kamboureli and Roy Miki, 141–52. Waterloo: Wilfrid Laurier University Press, 2007.

Maynard, Robyn. *Policing Black Lives: State Violence in Canada from Slavery to Present*. Black Point: Fernwood, 2017.

McDowell, Deborah E. *"The Changing Same": Black Women's Literature, Criticism, and Theory*. Indianapolis: Indiana University Press, 1995.

McKay, Claude. "If We Must Die." https://www.poetryfoundation.org/poems/44694/if-we-must-die.

McKittrick, Katherine. *Demonic Grounds: Black Women and the Cartographies of Struggle*. Minneapolis: University of Minnesota Press, 2006.

McKittrick, Katherine, ed. *Sylvia Wynter: On Being Human as Praxis*. Durham: Duke University Press, 2015.

McLeod, Katherine. "'Oui, Let's Scat': Listening to Multi-vocality in George Elliott Clarke's Jazz Opera *Québécité*." In *Africadian Atlantic: Essays on George Elliott Clarke*, edited by Joseph Pivato. Toronto: Guernica, 2012.

Mensah, Joseph. *Black Canadians: History, Experience, Social Conditions*. Halifax: Fernwood, 2002.

Miller, Paul D. (DJ Spooky). *Rhythm Science*. Cambridge, MA: MIT Press, 2004.

Milz, Sabine. "Multicultural Canadian World Literature, or, the Cultural Logic of English-Canadian Economic and Political Power." *Zeitschrift für Kanada-Studien* 25, no. 1 (2005): 147–61.

Mingus, Charles. *Beneath the Underdog*, edited by Nel King. New York: Vintage Books, 1991.

Moïse, Myriam. "Grasping the Ungraspable in M. Nourbese Philip's Poetry." *Commonwealth Essays and Studies* 33, no. 1 (2010): 23–33.

Moodie, Susanna. *Roughing It in the Bush*. Toronto: McClelland and Stewart, 2007.

Morrison, Toni. *The Bluest Eye*. New York: Plume, 1994.

———. *Jazz*. New York: Plume, 1993.

———. *Sula*. New York: Alfred A. Knopf, 1986.

Moten, Fred. *In the Break: The Aesthetics of the Black Radical Tradition*. Minneapolis: University of Minnesota Press, 2003.

Moure, Erín. *My Beloved Wager: Essays from a Writing Practice*, edited by Smaro Kamboureli. Edmonton: NeWest, 2009.

Mudede, Charles. "The Turntable." *CTheory* (2003). https://journals.uvic.ca/index.php/ctheory/article/view/14561.

Mullins, Katie L. "'My Body Is History': Embodying the Past, Present, and Future in Dionne Brand's *San Souci and Other Stories*." *Ariel* 42, no. 2 (2012): 5–22.

Mulvey, Laura. "Visual Pleasure and Narrative Cinema." *Screen* 16, no. 3 (Autumn 1975): 6–18.

"Musical Impurity." *The Etude* 18 (January 1900): 16.

Mutabaruka. "Dis Poem." In *The Routledge Reader in Caribbean Literature*, edited by A. Donnell and S.L. Welsh, 462–63. London: Routledge, 1996.

Mural Honouring Vancouver's Lost Black Neighbourhood Wins Heritage Award," *Daily Hive*, 23 April 2021, https://dailyhive.com/vancouver/vmf-bc-heritage-award-anthony-joseph.

Nancy, Jean-Luc. *Being Singular Plural*. Translated by Robert Richardson and Anne O'Byrne. Stanford: Stanford University Press, 2001.

———. *The Inoperative Community*, edited by Peter Connor. Translated by Peter Connor, Lisa Garbas, et al. Minneapolis: University of Minnesota Press, 1991.

———. *Listening*. Translated by Charlotte Mandell. New York: Fordham University Press, 2007.

Neal, Mark Anthony. "A Way Out of No Way: Jazz, Hip Hop, and Black Social Improvisation." In *The Other Side of Nowhere: Jazz, Improvisation, and*

Communities in Dialogue, edited by Daniel Fischlin and Ajay Heble, 1–42. Middletown: Wesleyan University Press, 2004.

———. *What the Music Said: Black Popular Music and Black Public Culture*. New York: Routledge, 1999.

Nealon, Jeffery T. "Refraining, Becoming-Black: Repetition and Difference in Amiri Baraka's *Blues People*." *Symplokē* 6, no. 1–2 (1998): 83–95.

Nelson, Charmaine A. *Representing the Black Female Subject in Western Art*. New York: Routledge, 2010.

Nielsen, Aldon Lynn. *Black Chant: Languages of African-American Postmodernism*. New York: Cambridge University Press, 1997.

Okri, Ben. *A Way of Being Free*. London: Phoenix House, 1997.

Oliveros, Pauline. *Deep Listening: A Composer's Sound Practice*. Self-published, 2005.

———. "Quantum Improvisation: The Cybernetic Presence." In *Sound Unbound: Sampling Digital Music and Culture*, edited by Paul D. Miller [DJ Spooky], 119–30. Cambridge, MA: MIT Press, 2008.

Olson, Charles. *Muthologos: The Collected Lectures and Interviews*, vol. 2. San Francisco: Four Seasons Foundation, 1978.

Ontario Human Rights Commission. *A Collective Impact: Interim Report on the Inquiry into Racial Profiling and Discrimination by Black Persons by the Toronto Police Service*. Toronto: Government of Ontario, 2018. http://www.ohrc.on.ca/en/public-interest-inquiry-racial-profiling-and-discrimination-toronto-police-service/collective-impact-interim-report-inquiry-racial-profiling-and-racial-discrimination-black.

"Oscar Peterson: The Life and Times of a Jazz Legend," *International Musician*, 23 February 2002. https://internationalmusician.org/oscar-peterson.

Ostertag, Bob. Interview by Mauricio Martinez. *Improvisation, Community, and Social Practice*. 6 Jul. 2011. http://www.improvcommunity.ca/projects/oral-histories/bob-ostertag, 5 November 2013.

Oswald, John. "Bettered by the Borrower: The Ethics of Musical Debt." In *Audio Culture: Readings in Modern Music*, edited by Christopher Cox and Daniel Warner, 131–37. New York: Continuum, 2006.

Parker, William. *Who Owns Music?* Cologne: Buddy's Knife, 2008.

Parks, Suzan-Lori. "Possession." In *The America Play and Other Works*, 3–5. Toronto: Theatre Communication Group, 1995.

Pastras, Philip James. "A Clear Field: The Idea of Improvisation in Modern Poetry." PhD diss., Rutgers University, 1981.

Pendergrast, Mark. *For God, Country, and Coca-Cola: The Definitive History of the Great American Soft Drink and the Company That Makes It*, 2nd ed. New York: Basic Books, 2000.

Pennycook, Alastair, and Tony Mitchell. "Hip Hop as Dusty Foot Philosophy: Engaging Locality." In *Global Linguistic Flows: Hip Hop Cultures, Youth Identities, and the Politics of Language*, edited by Samy H. Alim, Awad Ibrahim, and Alastair Pennycook, 25–42. New York: Routledge, 2009.

Philip, Marlene NourbeSe. *Blank: Essays and Interviews*. Toronto: Book*hug, 2017.
———. "The Ga(s)p." In *Poetics and Precarity*, edited by Myung Mi Kim and Cristanne Miller. Albany: Buffalo: SUNY Press, 2018.
———. *A Genealogy of Resistance and Other Essays*. Toronto: Mercury Press, 1997.
———. "Introduction: Echoes in a Stranger Land." In *Frontiers: Essays and Writings on Racism and Culture*, 9–25. Stratford: Mercury Press, 1992.
———. *Looking for Livingstone: An Odyssey of Silence*. Stratford: Mercury Press, 1991.
———. Message to the Author [email], 5 May 2014.
———. "Notanda." Afterword. In *Zong*, 189–209. Middletown: Wesleyan University Press, 2008.
———. *She Tries Her Tongue, Her Silence Softly Breaks*. Toronto: University of Toronto Press, 1989.
———. "North of Invention: A Festival of Canadian Poetry" [presentation]. Kelly Writers House, Philadelphia, 20 January 2011. *PennSound*, 15 August 2013.
———. "We Can Never Tell the Entire Story of Slavery: In Conversation with M. NourbeSe Philip." Interview by Paul Watkins. *Toronto Review of Books*, 30 April 2014. https://torontoreviewofbooks.com/2014/04/in-conversation-with-m-nourbese-philip.
———. "Who's Listening? Artists, Audiences and Language." In *New Contexts of Canadian Criticism*, edited by Ajay Heble, Donna Palmateer Pennee, and J.R. (Tim) Struthers, 1–14. Peterborough: Broadview Press, 1997.
———. *Zong!* Middletown: Wesleyan University Press, 2008.
Pivato, Joseph, ed. *Africadian Atlantic: Essays on George Elliott Clarke*. Toronto: Guernica, 2012.
Plato. *Republic*. Translated by Robin Waterfield. New York: Oxford University Press, 1993.
Pound, Ezra. *Selected Cantos*. New York: New Directions, 1968.
Price, David J. "How K'Naan's Song Became Coca-Cola's World Cup Soundtrack." *Billboard*, 9 June 2010.
Pytlik, Mark. "The Avalanches." *Sound on Sound*, November 2002. https://www.soundonsound.com/people/the-avalanches. 12 December 2014.
Queyras, Sina. "On Encountering *Zong!*" *Influency Salon* 1 (2010): n.p. Web. 27 August 2013.
Quill, Greg. "Toronto's Fourth Poet Laureate Aims to Speak to the Heart of the City." *Toronto Star*, 16 December 2012. https://www.thestar.com/entertainment/books/2012/12/16/torontos_fourth_poet_laureate_aims_to_speak_to_the_heart_of_the_city.html.
Ramsey, Guthrie P. *Race Music: Black Cultures from Bebop to Hip-Hop*. Berkeley: University of California Press, 2003.
Retallack, Joan. *The Poethical Wager*. Berkeley: University of California Press, 2003.
Richards, Sam. "Afrika Bambaataa Q&A." *The Guardian*, 14 April 2012.
Richardson, Karen, and Steven Green, eds. *T-Dot Griots: An Anthology of Toronto's Black Storytellers*. Victoria: Trafford, 2004.

Roberts, Donald F., Ulla G. Foehr, and Victoria Rideout. *Generation M: Media in the Lives of 8–18 Year-Olds*. KFF Publication No. 7251. Menlo Park: Kaiser Family Foundation, 2005.

Rodgers, Carolyn M. "What Color Is Lonely." In *The Black Poets*, edited by Dudley Randall, 265–66. New York: Bantam Books, 1971.

Rodgers, Tara. *Pink Noises: Women on Electronic Music and Sound*. Durham: Duke University Press, 2010.

Rohlehr, Gordon. "Introduction." In *Voiceprint: An Anthology of Oral and Related Poetry*, edited by Stewart Brown, Mervyn Morris, and Gordon Rohlehr, 1–23. Harlow: Longman, 1989.

Rose, Tricia. *Black Noise: Rap Music and Black Culture in Contemporary America*. Middletown: Wesleyan University Press, 2004.

Roy, Arundhati. "The Pandemic Is a Portal." *Financial Times*, 3 April 2020. https://www.ft.com/content/10d8f5e8-74eb-11ea-95fe-fcd274e920ca.

Rubin Museum, "Pauline Oliveros: Listening and Consciousness." YouTube, posted 30 November 2016. 1:00. https://www.youtube.com/watch?v=u355U29bOto.

Rupprecht, Anita. "'A Limited Sort of Property': History, Memory, and the Slave Ship *Zong*." *Slavery and Abolition* 29, no. 2 (2008): 265–77.

Said, Edward W. "Michael Walzer's 'Exodus and Revolution': A Canaanite Reading." *Grand Street* 5, no. 2 (Winter 1986): 91.

———. *Representations of the Intellectual*. New York: Vintage Books, 1996.

Sanders, Leslie. "Introduction." In *Fierce Departures: The Poetry of Dionne Brand*, edited by Leslie Sanders, ix–xv. Waterloo: Wilfrid Laurier University Press, 2009.

———. "White Teacher, Black Literature." In *Talking about Identity: Encounters in Culture, Language, and Identity*, edited by Adrienne Lynn Shadd and Carl E. James, 168–76. Toronto: Between the Lines, 2001.

Saul, Scott. *Freedom Is, Freedom Ain't: Jazz and the Making of the Sixties*. Cambridge, MA: Harvard University Press, 2003.

Saunders, Patricia. "Defending the Dead, Confronting the Archive: A Conversation with M. NourbeSe Philip." *Small Axe* 26 (2008): 63–79.

Scahill, Jeremy. "Scholar Robin D.G. Kelley on How Today's Abolitionist Movement Can Fundamentally Change the Country." *The Intercept*, 27 June 2020. https://theintercept.com/2020/06/27/robin-dg-kelley-intercepted.

Scherker, Amanda. "Somali Woman, 2 Journalists Sentenced for Reporting Rape." *Huffington Post*, 10 December 2013.

Scott, David. "Introduction: On the Archaeologies of Black Memory." *Small Axe* 12, no. 2 (2008): v–xvi.

Shad, "Fam Jam (Fe Sum Immigrins)." Blog, 2013 (note removed). Archived on *Genius*, https://genius.com/Shad-fam-jam-fe-sum-immigrins-lyrics.

Shadd, Mary A. *A Plea for Emigration*, edited by Richard Almonte. Toronto: Mercury Press, 1998.

Sharpe, Christina. *In the Wake: On Blackness and Being*. Durham: Duke University Press, 2016.

Shepp, Archie. "A Dialogue with Archie Shepp." Interview by Scott Cashman. *SPIT: A Journal of the Arts*, 10 December 1990. Interview reproduced at https://www.detroitartistsworkshop.com/dialogue-with-archie-shepp.

Sherman, Jonathan Dale. "The Hip-Hop Aesthetics and Visual Poetry of Wayde Compton's *Performance Bond*: Claiming Black Space in Contemporary Canada." MA project, University of Saskatchewan, 2009.

Siemerling, Winfried. "Bi-culturalism, Multiculturalism, Transculturalism: Canada and Quebec." Special issue on "Culturalism." *New Literature Review* 45–46 (2009): 133–56.

———. *The Black Atlantic Reconsidered: Black Canadian Writing, Cultural History, and the Presence of the Past*. Montreal and Kingston: McGill–Queen's University Press, 2015.

———. "Transcultural Improvisation, Transnational Time, and Diasporic Chance in Wayde Compton's Textual Performance." *West Coast Line* 63 (March 2010): 30–37.

Siklosi, Kate. "'the absolute / of water': The Submarine Poetic of M. NourbeSe Philip's *Zong!*" *Canadian Literature* 228–29 (Spring–Summer 2016): 111–30.

Silverman, Jason H. *Unwelcomed Guests: Canada West's Response to the American Fugitive Slaves, 1800–1865*. Millwood: Associated Faculty Press, 1985.

Singer, Alan, and Allen Dunn, eds. *Literary Aesthetics: A Reader*. Malden, MA: Blackwell, 2000.

Small, Christopher. *Musicking: The Meanings of Performing and Listening*. Middletown: Wesleyan University Press, 1998.

Smith, Theophus. *Conjuring Culture: Biblical Formations of Black America*. New York: Oxford University Press, 1999.

Sontag, Susan. "Fascinating Fascism." In *Under the Sign of Saturn*, 73–108. New York: Picador, 2002.

Spellman, A.B. *Four Lives in the Bebop Business*. New York: Limelight Editions, 1990.

Spillers, Hortense J. "Cross Currents, Discontinuities: Black Women's Fiction." In *Conjuring: Black Women, Fiction, and Literary Tradition*, edited by Marjorie Pryse and Hortense J. Spillers, 249–61. Bloomington: Indiana University Press, 1985.

———. *Outside in the Teaching Machine*. London: Routledge, 1993.

Stanbridge, Alan. "Jazz." In *Continuum Encyclopedia of Popular Music of the World*, edited by David Horn and John Shepherd, vol. 8: *Genres: North America*, edited by David Horn, 286–307. New York: Continuum, 2012.

Standley, Fred L., and Louis H. Pratt, eds. *Conversations with James Baldwin*. Jackson: University Press of Mississippi, 1989.

Sterne, Jonathan. *The Audible Past: Cultural Origins of Sound Reproduction*. Durham: Duke University Press, 2003.

———. "Sonic Imaginations," in *The Sound Studies Reader*, ed. Jonathan Sterne, 1–17. New York: Routledge, 2012.

Stewart, Jesse L. "Call and Recall: Hybridity, Mobility, and Dialogue between Jazz and Hip Hop Cultures." PhD diss., University of Guelph, 2008.

Still, William. "Letter." *Provincial Freeman* (Toronto), 6 May 1854.

Szwed, John. *Space Is the Place: The Lives and Times of Sun Ra*. New York: Pantheon, 1997.
"SXSW Thursday Preview: K'naan." *Los Angeles Times*, 18 March 2009.
Taylor, Diana. *The Archive and the Repertoire: Performing Cultural Memory in the Americas*. Durham: Duke University Press, 2003.
Thomas, Nigel H. "Some Aspects of Blues Use in George Elliott Clarke's *Whylah Falls*." In *Africadian Atlantic: Essays on George Elliott Clarke*, edited by Joseph Pivato. Toronto: Guernica, 2012.
Thomas, Nigel H., ed. *Why We Write: Conversations with African Canadian Poets and Novelists*. Interviews. Toronto: TSAR, 2006.
Thompson, Ahmir "Questlove." Dir., *Summer of Soul (. . . Or, When the Revolution Could Not Be Televised*. Century City: Searchlight Pictures, 2021.
Thompson, Philip K. "Clarke: Linguistically Brilliant and Sensual." *Halifax Chronicle Herald*, 22 April 2012.
Thompson, Robert Farris. *Aesthetic of the Cool: Afro-Atlantic Art and Music*. Reading: Periscope, 2011.
———. *Flash of the Spirit*. New York: Vintage, 1984.
Toomer, Jean. *Cane*. New York: Liveright, 1993.
Trudeau, Pierre Elliott. *The Essential Trudeau*, edited by Ron Graham. Toronto: McClelland and Stewart, 1993.
Tucker, Mark, ed. *The Duke Ellington Reader*. Oxford: Oxford University Press, 1993.
Ulanov, Barry. *Duke Ellington*. New York: Da Capo, 1972.
Vernon, Karina, ed. *The Black Prairie Archives: An Anthology*. Waterloo: Wilfrid Laurier University Press, 2020.
"Viaducts Are a Symbolically Important Place." CBC News, 15 June 2020. https://www.cbc.ca/news/canada/british-columbia/viaduct-hogan-s-alley-significance-1.5612399.
Wah, Fred. "Strang(l)ed Poetics." In *Faking It: Poetics and Hybridity*, edited by Smaro Kamboureli, 21–44. Edmonton: NeWest, 2000.
Walcott, Rinaldo. "Against Institution Established Law, Custom, or Purpose." In *Trans.Can.Lit: Resituating the Study of Canadian Literature*, edited by Smaro Kamboureli and Roy Miki, 17–24. Waterloo: Wilfrid Laurier University Press, 2007.
———. *On Property*. Windsor: Biblioasis, 2021.
———. *Queer Returns: Essays on Multiculturalism, Diaspora, and Black Studies*. London: Insomniac Press, 2016.
———. "Towards a Methodology for Reading Hip Hop in Canada." In *Ebony Roots, Northern Soil: Perspectives on Blackness in Canada*, edited by Charmaine A. Nelson, 238–53. Newcastle, UK: Cambridge Scholars Publishing, 2010.
Walcott, Rinaldo, ed. *Black Like Who? Writing Black Canada*. Toronto: Insomniac Press, 2003.
Walia, Harsha. "Really Harper, Canada Has No History of Colonialism?" *The Dominion*, 28 September 2009. http://www.dominionpaper.ca/articles/2943.
Walker, James W. St. G. *A History of Blacks in Canada: A Study Guide for Teachers and Students*. Ottawa: Minister of State Multiculturalism, 1980.

Wallace, David Foster, and Mark Costello. *Signifying Rappers*. New York: Little, Brown, 2013.
Wallace, Rob. *Improvisation and the Making of Literary Modernism*. New York: Continuum, 2010.
Ward, Frederick. *Riverslip*. New York: Tundra Books, 1974.
Ward, Geoffrey C., and Ken Burns. *Jazz: A History of America's Music*. New York: Knopf, 2000.
Warner, Marina. "Indigo: Mapping the Waters." *Etudes britanniques contemporaines*, no. 5 (1994).
Washington, Salim. "'Don't Let the Devil (Make You) Lose Your Joy': A Look at Late Coltrane." In *John Coltrane and Black America's Quest for Freedom: Spirituality and the Music*, edited by Leonard L. Brown, 123–52. New York: Oxford University Press, 2010.
Watkins, Paul db. "Disruptive Dialogics: Improvised Dissonance in Thelonious Monk and Wu-Tang Clan's *36 Chambers*." *Critical Studies in Improvisation / Étude critiques en improvisation* 7, no. 2 (2011). https://www.criticalimprov.com/index.php/csieci/article/view/1346/2308.
Watkins, Paul db, ed. "Harmonious Dissonance: Paul Watkins in Conversation with George Elliott Clarke." *Malahat Review* (2016). http://malahatreview.ca/interviews/clarke_interview.html.
———. "'Schizophonophilia': An Audio-Interplay between Wayde Compton and Paul Watkins." improvcommunity.ca, August 2013. http://www.improvcommunity.ca/sites/improvcommunity.ca/files/research_collection/1049/Wayde_Compton_transcription.pdf.
———. "Writing Jazz: Gesturing towards the Possible." An interview between Paul Watkins and Cecil Foster. improvcommunity.ca, 2012.
———. "'Your bass sounds like a typewriter': A Reading and Interview with George Elliott Clarke." An interview between Paul Watkins, Katherine McLeod, and George Elliott Clarke. improvcommunity.ca, 1–13.
Weheliye, Alexander. *Phonographies: Grooves in Sonic Afro-Modernity*. Durham: Duke University Press, 2005.
West, Cornel. *Hope on a Tightrope: Words and Wisdom*. Carlsbad: Smiley Books, 2008.
———. "Minority Discourse and the Pitfalls of Canon-Formation." *Yale Journal of Criticism* (Fall 1988): 193–201.
———. *Race Matters*. Boston: Beacon Press, 2001.
White, Timothy. *Catch a Fire: The Life of Bob Marley*. New York: Holt, Rinehart and Winston, 1983.
Whitehead, Joshua. "Writing as Rupture: A Break-Up Note to CanLit." In *Refuse: CanLit in Ruins*, edited by Hannah McGregor, Julie Rak, and Erin Wunker, 191–98. Toronto: Book*hug, 2018.
"Why Women Musicians Are Inferior." *DownBeat*, February 1938.
Williams, Dorothy. *The Road to Now: A History of Blacks in Montreal*. Dossier Quebec Series. Montreal: Véhicule, 1997.

Williams, Saul. "Amiri Baraka: Poet Laureate." *Fader*, 9 January 2014. https://www.thefader.com/2014/01/09/amiri-baraka-poet-laureate.

———. *The Dead Emcee Scrolls: The Lost Teachings of Hip-Hop*. New York: MTV Books, 2006.

Williams, William Carlos. "Introduction" (*The Wedge*). *The Collected Poems of William Carlos Williams*, vol. 2: *1939–1962*, edited by Christopher MacGowan, 53–55. New York: New Directions, 2001.

———. Excerpt from "Asphodel, That Greeny Flower." poets.org, n.d. https://poets.org/poem/asphodel-greeny-flower-excerpt.

Wilson, August. *Ma Rainey's Black Bottom*. New York: Plume, 1985.

Winks, Robin. *The Blacks in Canada: A History*, 2nd ed. Montreal and Kingston: McGill–Queen's University Press, 2008.

Wolin, Sheldon S. *Politics and Vision*. Princeton: Princeton University Press, 2004.

Wong, Orlando [Onoura Oku]. *Echo*. Kingston: Sangster's, 1977.

Woods, Clyde Adrian. "Do You Know What It Means to Miss New Orleans? Katrina, Trap Economics, and the Rebirth of the Blues." *American Quarterly* 57, no. 4 (2005): 1005–18.

Young, Cate. "Solidarity Is for Miley Cyrus: The Racial Implications of her VMA Performance." 26 August 2013. https://www.cate-young.com/battymamzelle/2013/08/Solidarity-Is-For-Miley-Cyrus.html.

Yu, Timothy. "Introduction: Toward a Sociology of the Contemporary Avant-Garde." In *Race and the Avant-Garde: Experimental and Asian American Poetry since 1965*, 1–18. Stanford: Stanford University Press, 2009.

Zerbisias, Antonia. "How K'naan's 'Wavin' Flag' Became Anthem for the World." *Toronto Star*, 23 April 2010.

Copyright Acknowledgements

Excerpts from "I Fight Back," "The Subversives" from *Revolutionary Tea Party*, on Verse to Vinyl. Copyright © 1986, 2022 Lillian Allen. Reprinted by permission of Lillian Allen.

Excerpts from "In These Canadian Bones" from *Psychic Unrest* and *Make the World New*, published by Insomniac Press and Wilfrid Laurier University Press. Copyright © 1999, 2022 Lillian Allen. Reprinted by permission of Lillian Allen.

Excerpts from: *Thirsty* Copyright © 2022 by Dionne Brand, published by McClelland & Stewart; *The Blue Clerk: Ars Poetica in 59 Versos* Copyright © 2018 by Dionne Brand, published by Duke University Press, and *No Language Is Neutral* Copyright © 1990 by Dionne Brand, published by McClelland & Stewart, used by permission of The Wylie Agency LLC.

Excerpts from *A Map to the Door of No Return* by Dionne Brand, Copyright © 2001 Dionne Brand. Reprinted by permission of Doubleday Canada, a division of Penguin Random House Canada Limited. All rights reserved.

Excerpts from *Ossuaries* by Dionne Brand, Copyright © 2010 Dionne Brand. Reprinted by permission of McClelland & Stewart, a division of Penguin Random House Canada Limited. All rights reserved.

Excerpts from *What We All Long For* by Dionne Brand, Copyright © 2005 Dionne Brand. Reprinted by permission of Vintage Canada/Alfred A. Knopf Canada, a division of Penguin Random House Canada Limited. All rights reserved.

Excerpts from *Bread out of Stone: Recollections, Sex, Recognitions, Race, Dreaming, Politics* by Dionne Brand, Copyright © 1994 Dionne Brand. Reprinted by permission of Vintage Canada, a division of Penguin Random House Canada Limited. All rights reserved.

Excerpts from *49th Parallel Psalm*, *After Canaan: Essays on Race, Writing, and Region*, *Bluesprint*, and *Performance Bond* by Wayde Compton, Copyright © 2010, 1999, 2002, 2004 Arsenal Pulp Press. Reprinted by permission of Arsenal Pulp Press.

"What's Going On," Words and Music by Renaldo Benson, Alfred Cleveland and Marvin Gaye. Copyright © 1970 Stone Agate Music, Jobete Music Co., Inc., MGIII Music, NMG Music and FCG Music. Copyright Renewed. All Rights Administered by Sony Music Publishing (US) LLC, 424 Church Street, Suite 1200, Nashville, TN 37219. International Copyright Secured. All Rights Reserved. Reprinted by permission of Hal Leonard LLC.

Excerpts from *Black*, *Blue*, *Gold*, *Red*, and *White* by George Elliott Clarke, Copyright © 2012, 2011, 2016, 2011, 2021 Gaspereau Press. Reprinted by permission of Gaspereau Press.

Excerpts from *Looking for Livingstone: An Odyssey of Silence and She Tries Her Tongue, Her Silence Softly Breaks* by M. NourbeSe Philip, Copyright © 1991, 2015 M. NourbeSe Philip. Reprinted by permission of the author.

Excerpts and image from *Zong!* by M. NourbeSe Philip, Copyright © 2011 M. NourbeSe Philip. Reprinted by permission of the author.

"Brothering Watching," "Fam Jam (Fe Sum Immigrins)," "A Good Name," Words and Music by Shad. Copyright © 2007, 2013, 2010 Black Box Recordings. Reprinted by permission of the artist.

"Out of Touch," Words and Music by Shad. Copyright © 2021 Secret City Records. Reprinted by permission of the artist.

Index

abolition: in Canada, 9, 20, 383n48; and *Zong*, 216
Achebe, Chinua, 146–47
Adorno, Theodore, 299, 306, 312, 412n31
aesthetic: 25, 36, 37–38, 100, 111, 119–20, 153, 163, 165, 179, 188–92, 196n♭, 234, 247; aesthetic vs. rhetoric, 65–68, 390n9; as beauty, 33, dub, 190, 195, 199, 236–37; hip hop 258, 341–42, 350. *See also* rhetoric
Afrosporic (NourbeSe Philip), 18, 380n32
African Canadian: as terminology, 17–18, 382n30, 382n35; literary history, 20, 25, 79, 83, 141, 383n57; settler history, 380n5. *See also* Black Canadian
African diaspora, 36, 58, 92, 156, 248
Africville, 20, 80, 83, 102–4
Afrological and Eurological (Lewis), 34
Agamben, Giorgio: on refugees, 11; "whatever being," 175–76
Allen, Lillian, 187–88, 197, 239n♭
analogue and digital, 57–61, 328, 359, 371
Andrisani, Vincent, on "sonic citizenship," 49, 290
Angélique, Marie-Joseph, 21
anitafrika, d'bi.young: on dub, 193, 400n30; on community, 194; "foolishness" (poem), 207; silence, 210; "young black" (poem), 367; on gender, 51

Anti-Black racism, 12–13, 109, 257, 206, 321, 356, 363, 373. *See also* racism
apartheid, Canada's support of South Africa, 55
archive: as "living repertoire" (Diana Taylor), 30, 383n76; the DJ as archivist 23, 47, 62, 303, 307; Black archive 26, 86, 90, 312–13, 407n36
Armstrong, Louis, 37, 75, 305
Austin, David, 72, 195, 377n3
avant-garde, 34, 153 (poetics), 163, 165, 182

Baker, Jr., Houston A.: 33, 76, 247; "the blues matrix," 33, 365
Baldwin, James, 28, 201, 210, 221, 365–66, 391n23
Baraka, Amiri: 28, 91, 108–10; aesthetic and rhetorical practice, 68; African continuum/"the changing same," 248, 307, 357, 363; on bebop, 160; on Black Arts movement, 108–10; on Langston Hughes, 77; liberatory potential of art, 26; *See also* Black Arts Movement
beauty: aesthetic and beauty, 33; beauty and justice, 66, 374, 388n9. *See also* Clarke, George Elliott: on beauty
Beckford, Sharon Morgan, 51, 154, 204
Bell, Alexander Graham, 298

Bernstein, Charles: on close listening and poetry, 47, 158, 184. *See also* close listening
Black Arts Movement: 53, 68, 124, 317n♭; "Black Arts" (Baraka), 91, 108–9. *See also* Baraka, Amiri
Black, Ayanna, 83, 129
Black Canadian: as terminology, 17–18, 382n30; cultural and literary history, 12–13, 17–29, 31, 33, 84–87, 92, 256, 311, 356, 361, 418n30; music and Black Canadian poetics, 42–46, 369. *See also* African Canadian
Black chant: book, *Black Chant* (Nielsen), 27, 249, 406n19; as poetic practice, 108–9, 208, 211
Black Lives Matter, 124, 379n4, 381n23
Black Loyalists, 23, 80, 83, 103-4, 383n48
Blackness: 35, 78, 102, 122, 130, 159, 171, 198, 253, 308, 321–22, 338, 347; as open-ended practice, 18, 24, 364, 371, 384n108; in relation to multiculturalism, 281, 290–91
blues: music, 32, 72–76, 77, 146; "blues matrix" (Baker), 33, 100, 117, 141, 365; "blues moment" (Clyde Woods), 279; and poetry, 128, 130, 142, 248, 393n67
Brand, Dionne: on history, 12, 20, 152-57; on Canada and CanLit, 26, 40; on poetry 66; on jazz, 158–59
Brand, Dionne—works: *The Blue Clerk*, 181–83; *Bread Out of Stone*, 158–59; *A Map to the Door of No Return*, 153; *No Language is Neutral*, 157; *Ossuaries*, 157–81; *Thirsty*, 401n100; *What We All Long For*, 163, 178
Brathwaite, Kamu: on dub 193, 208, 221; on jazz, 157; on "Nation Language," 208–9; "Vévé" (poem), 326–27. *See also* tidalectics (Brathwaite)
Brooks, Gwendolyn, 150, 372
Butler, Judith, 41, 231

Canaan: as promised land and reference to Canada, 9–16, 22, 51, 55, 62, 80, 102, 136, 238–39, 313, 373–74, 377n3, 381n48; as a reference to Palestine, 15
Canadian hip hop, 256–61, 395n9, 395n10. *See also* hip hop
Canadian jazz, 148–50. *See also* jazz
Canadian Literature (CanLit): debates, 12–13, 26, 28, 40, 87–88, 188, 340, 358, 361–63, 416n10; silence on NourbeSe Philip, 210–11
canon and canonicity, 15–16, 25, 89–93, 108–9, 113–14
censorship, 123, 245
citizenship: Black porters and, 13, 51; legal definition, policy, and exclusion, 48–57, 138, 234, 279, 313–14, 349, 361, 385n131, 385–86n135, 389n150, 415n109; multicultural citizenship, 56; as performance and sounding 16, 19, 37, 47, 48–49, 58, 62, 67, 75, 134, 154, 188, 197, 211, 286–88, 292–93, 318, 320–22, 357, 364, 369–71, 373, 388n9; "sonic citizenship," 49–50, 54, 63, 80, 141-42, 175, 180, 235, 242, 256–57, 290, 338
Civil Rights Movement: 7, 42, 54–55, 169, 361; "long civil rights movement," 377n4
Clarke, Austin, 23, 26, 31, 132, 364
Clarke, George Elliott: on African Canadian literature 20, 25; on beauty, 99, 123, 126, 131, 138, 140–42, 391n79; on harmonious dissonance, 123; on homage and dedication, 82–83; on Miles Davis, 70–72, 106, 128; on music and song, 93–97; on nationalism, 88, 90; on Ezra Pound, 111–12
Clarke, George Elliott—works: *Black*, 116–26; *Blue*, 100–116; *Blue Exile*, 79–80; *Gold*, 132–35; *Lush Dreams*, 79–81, 119; *Odysseys Home*, 25, 86–87, 92, 380n35, 380n36, 381n44; *Red*,

126–31; *Trudeau*, 85, 95; *White*, 135–39; *Where Beauty Survived*, 94, 136; *Whylah Falls*, 113, 391n67, 391n79
close listening, 47. *See also* Bernstein, Charles
Coleman, Ornette: on "harmolodic music," 167; on jazz and capitalism, 251
collective amnesia, 9
colonialism (including settler colonialism), 9, 237–38, 260, 274, 332, 361, 378n12, 413n108
Coltrane, John: 80, 115, 158, 160, 166, 177, 181–83, 244n♭, 337, 373
Coltrane, John—songs: Alabama," 7; "My Favorite Things," 7–8; "Naima," 115, "Venus," 144–45, 177, 182–83; "Violet for Your Furs," 80, 80n♮
community: 34, 36, 39, 44, 56–57, 61, 67, 76, 80–81, 93, 113–15, 139, 145, 159–60, 163, 175–76; 178–80, 187, 194, 202, 231, 234, 237, 255, 266–69, 272, 292, 297, 303, 334, 341, 348–50, 353–58, 365–71, 401n51, 415n169; "coming community" (Agamben), 159, 175–76
Compton, Wayde: on "Halfrican" (term), 316; on hip hop, 308, 342–43; on Hogan's Alley, 350–51; on repetition, 305, 310; on "schizophonophilia," 30, 318, 320; on tradition, 312
Compton, Wayde—works: *49th Parallel Psalm*, 309–10, 321–22, 325, 335; *Bluesprint*, 312–13; *Performance Bond*, 315–16, 319, 326–57, 362
conceptual poetry, 312
Constitution Act, 1982, 50
Cooper, Afua, 9, 21, 34, 195–98, 203
"Cosmopolitan Humanist" (Watkins), 41n♭

Dante, 125, 143, 166, 307
Davis, Andrea A., 55
Davis, Angela: on planetary citizenship, 52; on women and the blues, 75

Davis, Miles, 23, 69, 70–72, 81, 97–99, 106–8, 111, 119, 120–21n♭, 128, 151n♭, 158, 160; misogyny, 168
"deep listening" (Oliveros), 46–48, 184, 367
Desmond, Viola, 20, 81n♭, 131–32, 138, 255
"diasporic sensibility," 18–19
digital (and analogue). *See* analogue and digital
"discordant democracy" (Wolin), 57, 338
dissonance: "harmonious" (Clarke) 123; musical, 17, 148, 161, 165, 199–201; political, 284, 292, 340, 368
Douglas, James, 309-10, 313-14, 323
Douglass, Frederick: on Canaan, 374; on Canada, 11; improvisation, 44; on slavery, 10; on slave songs, 31–32, 371; "unmeaning jargon," 254
DJ Methodology, 29-36, 63, 366
DJ music and culture: 29, 74, 297–311, 317–18, 358, 383n76; on turntablism, 245, 296, 302, 304, 308, 320, 325, 342. *See also* remix
Du Bois, W.E.B.: 13, 37, 73–74; debate with Claudy McKay, 68
dub poetics, 187–88, 191–200, 237; improvised dub chant, 60, 186, 188, 195, 204–9, 213. *See also* reggae
Dunbar, Paul Lawrence, 78, 96, 208n♭
"duppy states" (Iton), 212, 223;
Dylan, Bob, 85, 96, 359, 391n72

Ellison, Ralph, 32, 37, 79, 159, 305, 316, 360, 384n106
exile, 19, 80, 155, 162, 166, 175, 178, 206, 209, 211, 265, 267, 273–75, 332

Foster, Cecil: on Blackness, 364, 369; on citizenship, 13, 51; on duppies, 402–3n82; on Martin Luther King, Jr. and Pierre Elliott Trudeau, 386–87n149; on multiculturalism, 54, 280, 284, 288, 290–92

Freire, Paulo, 23, 62
Frye, Northrop, 26, 51, 67, 156, 332, 388n5

Gates, Henry Louis, Jr., 78, 170, 363, 402n66
"geo-heterodoxy" (Iton), 53, 86, 314, 336
Gilroy, Paul, 20, 83, 92, 98, 245, 304
Guelph Jazz Festival, 370

Harlem Renaissance, 17, 35n♭, 90n♭
Harper, Stephen, 332
Hartman, Saidiya, 10, 232
"hauntological," 156, 212, 214, 229, 233–34, 340
Heble, Ajay, 24, 44, 67, 174, 180n♭, 199, 201, 292, 340, 370
Hendrix, Jimi, 312, 314–15, 356
hip hop: 8n♭, 33, 58, 62, 74, 92, 241–94, 296, 299–305, 308, 314, 321, 327, 330n♭, 341–48, 350, 406n19, 410n22.
See also Canadian hip hop
Hogan's Alley, 20, 39, 297, 308, 313-5, 326, 333–34, 341, 348-57, 369, 373, 411n50, 415–16n169
Holiday, Billie, 76, 183, 329n♭
hooks, bell, 160, 171n♭, 205n♭, 245, 263
Hughes, Langston, 17, 45, 66, 76–77, 193, 248, 385n120
Hurston, Zora Neale, 208, 301–2, 304, 323, 402n66

Ibrahim, Abdullah, 16, 176n♭
identity, 14, 17, 19, 29, 37, 40, 48, 49, 55, 67, 83, 87, 93, 100–101, 107, 120, 128, 140, 171, 178, 201, 211–12, 228n♭, 231, 235, 352, 267, 275, 288–89, 297, 305–6, 308, 314, 316–20, 327, 331, 336, 338-9, 343n♭, 358, 367, 391n83
improvisation, 41–46, 72, 78, 82, 94, 102, 114, 145–47, 158–62, 177–79, 208, 223, 224, 227, 231, 249, 254, 293, 302, 306, 308, 321, 327–28, 339, 345, 368, 384–85n119, 385n120

Indigenous: "Apache" (song), 343n♭; Black and Indigenous connections, 51, 55–56, 286n♭, 362, 364–65, 373, 383n96, 416n6; citizenship, 50, 85, 332; genocide and anti-Indigeneity in Canada, 15, 22, 288, 340, 360, 413n108; Pamela George, 135; hip hop, 260; and Palestine, 379n23; presence in BC, 314, 329; on reconciliation, 413n08, 413n127; resistance, 28, 246; *The Unjust Society*, 387n150. *See also* colonialism; *Constitution Act, 1982*
"infrapoetics" (Watkins), 29, 78, 118, 126
Iton, Richard, 48, 53, 212. *See also* geo-heterodoxy

jazz: music, 39, 45, 54, 58, 70, 82, 102, 111, 145–52, 165, 174, 176, 179, 185, 244, 315, 370, 384n106; jazz poetics, 34, 59, 77, 94, 95, 109, 120, 150, 153, 158–63, 168, 170, 181–82, 188, 200, 223, 406n19. *See also* Canadian jazz
Joseph, Clifton, 20, 191–92, 200
just society, 9, 11, 52, 55, 84–85, 134, 203, 275, 280, 287, 360–61, 371–72, 374, 387n150

Kelley, Robin D.G.: on Blackness, 364; on folk culture, 74; on hip hop, 248; "infrapolitics," 117; Thelonious Monk, 170n♭; on the COVID-19 pandemic, 43; redefining the political, 28; on Malcolm X, 383n73
Kid Koala, 74n♭, 259, 295–96, 300
King, Martin Luther, Jr.: assassination, 55, 85, 124; on Canada, 22; "fierce urgency of now," 360; Foster on King, 54, 386n149; interrelated nature of life, 363–34; just society, 11n♭, 292
King, Tiffany Lethabo: on Black and Indigenous connections, 51, 365
kinopoeia, 168, 202, 401n44

K'naan: on African stereotypes, 271; on using English, 274; on Somali tradition of song, 279; on success and fame, 289-90

K'naan—works: *Country, God, or the Girl* ("Better," 261; "Coming to America," 260–61);

The Dusty Foot Philosopher ("ABCs," 274; "The African Way," 272–73; "The Dusty Foot Philosopher," 261, "For Mohamoud," 271; "I Was Stabbed by Satan," 264; "If Rap Gets Jealous," 270; "My Old Home," 264–65; "Smile," 266; "Soobax," 273; "Strugglin'," 266–68; "Until the Lion Speaks," 262; "Voices in My Head," 294; "Wash it Down," 276–78, "What's Hardcore," 266); *Troubadour* ("15 Minutes," 274; "Fatima," 294; "I Come Prepared," 270; "Somalia," 252, 269; "Take a Minute," 262; "T.I.A," 274; "Wavin' Flag," 260, 280–87, 289, 291–92)

Kool Herc, 248, 303

L=A=N=G=U=A=G=E poetry, 196n♭, 211, 402n80

LGBTQIA2S+, 48, 243

listening, 23, 33, 35, 37–38, 45–47, 49, 59–62, 97, 102, 107, 115–16, 129, 131, 140, 143, 158, 160–61, 179–81, 184–85, 200, 213–14, 225, 233, 248, 264, 290, 297–98, 300, 328, 365–67, 373. *See also* close listening, deep listening

Lorde, Audre, 104, 131, 142, 203

Mackey, Nathaniel: on creative kinship, 16; on jazz, 39, 179; on orality, 31

Mandela, Nelson, 262

Marley, Bob, 36, 190–91, 196n♭, 272, 274, 286n♭

mashup, 30, 36, 297–98

Maynard, Robyn, 18, 51, 255, 281

McKay, Claude, 68, 89, 90n♭, 91, 390n54

Middle Passage, 9, 95, 155, 191, 198, 213, 221, 238, 253, 346

Miller, Paul D. (DJ Spooky), 29, 297, 305, 307

Mingus, Charles, 45, 79, 126, 129, 158, 172–74, 181, 342

modernism, 90n♭, 91, 96, 120, 168, 228, 304, 385n120. *See also* postmodernism

Montreal, 21, 149–50, 395–96n10

Morrison, Toni, 114, 150, 163, 172, 174, 344n♭, 379n22

Moten, Fred, 65, 185, 225

multiculturalism: 8, 17–18, 38, 40, 42, 44, 51, 54–56, 61, 82–84, 86, 88, 112, 141, 194, 197, 203, 237, 241–42, 257–58, 280–93, 316, 325, 329–30, 338, 340, 349–50, 355, 364, 369. 405n145; corporate, 282, 284; sonic multiculturalism, 41, 242, 287–92, 366, 370

"musicking" (Small), 30

Mutabaruka, 189, 194

naming, 228, 239

Nancy, Jean-Luc: on community to come, 57, 175, 368–69; on listening, 115; on multiculturalism, 56

nationalism, 18, 54, 108, 124, 243, 292; Black Nationalism (Clarke), 84–89, 141; Black Nationalism (Theophus Smith), 390n49; *See also* transnational

Nation Language, 195, 202, 208

Nazism, 53, 59, 105, 149–50, 238, 285, 319

negritude, 101, 130, 391n85

Nielsen, Aldon Lynn, 27, 167, 208, 249–50, 406n19

noise, 24, 59, 123, 221, 253–54

Northeast False Creek Plan (NEFC), 415–16n169. *See also* Hogan's Alley

"Northern Touch" (song), 258

Nova Scotia, 18, 20, 25, 80–81, 88–89, 102–4, 121, 138, 141, 255, 343, 381n48, 393n128

Oliveros, Pauline, 46–48, 184, 366. *See also* deep listening
Onoura, Oku, 193
orality, 31, 97, 141, 194, 207–8, 225, 246, 346, 410n22
ostranenie, 153

Palestine, 15, 373, 379n23
Parker, Charlie, 46, 145, 148, 164–69, 179, 195, 213n♭
Parker, William, 32, 42, 151
pedagogy: pedagogy of the oppressed, 62; hauntological pedagogy, 233–34; pedagogy of hope, 372
Peterson, Oscar, 94–95, 395n10
Philip, M. NourbeSe: on being Afrosporic, 18, 380n32; Black tradition in Canada, 88; on Black voice and song, 32, 220; Canada and colonialism, 237-8; on Canada as an adoptive mother, 206; on Carnival, 212; on citizenship, 19; on a hauntological pedagogy, 233; on history, 24, 381–82n57; jazz aesthetic, 59; *kinopoeia*, 168, 202; on multiculturalism, 281; on silence, 210–13
Philip, M. NourbeSe—works: *Blank*, 416n6; *A Genealogy of Resistance*, 196n♭, 199, 201, 207, 381n57; *Looking for Livingstone*, 209; *She Tries Her Tongue, Her Silence Softly Breaks*, 59, 195, 204, 206, 213, 219, 222, 235–36, 366; *Zong!*, 32, 60, 208, 212, 214–39
phonograph, 299, 302, 307; ear phonoautograph, 298. *See also* turntable
poetry: and citizenship, 16, 39, 47–48, 187, 191, 235, 363, 373; and music, 31, 34, 36, 42, 57–61, 65, 78, 94–97, 100, 102, 108, 132, 148, 182, 192–95; as political expression, 29, 62, 66–67, 108–9, 140, 264, 372; as remix, 310–11, 318–19; as risk taking, 227

polyphony, 110, 123
porters, 13, 51, 149, 314
postmodernism, 36, 85, 96, 208, 247. *See also* modernism
Pound, Ezra, 78, 99, 107, 126, 398n64

race: mixed-race experience, 121, 124, 259, 310, 313–22, 358, 407n44, 411n56; as social construct, 13, 321, 331
racism, 10–11, 13, 23, 42–43, 75, 105–6, 138, 185, 237–38, 257–58, 281, 308, 313, 332, 349, 355–56, 378n5, 378–79n17; and Canadian Acts and polices, 385n135. *See also* anti-Black racism
Rastafarian, 83, 196n♭, 202, 223
refugees, 11, 19, 32, 48, 50, 53n♭, 103, 121, 159, 242, 248, 261, 270, 273, 275, 282, 284, 288, 292, 294, 331–33, 339, 369, 381, 385–86n130
reggae, 97, 189-195, 223n♭, 286n♭. *See also* dub
remix, 8, 19, 23–24, 27, 37, 46–47, 56, 58, 73, 74n♭, 83, 120–21, 155, 167, 200n♭, 221, 247, 279–85, 296–97, 299–302, 305, 307, 310–11, 318, 321, 326, 332, 345–47, 352, 355, 360, 362–63. *See also* DJ music and culture; sampling
resistance, 17, 21–22, 25–29, 32, 34–35, 42, 57, 62, 87, 91, 101, 118, 138, 140, 145, 199, 202–3, 207, 228, 234, 236, 250–56, 263, 286n♭, 292, 307, 339, 348, 350, 354, 364, 371
rhetoric, 33, 35, 113; aesthetic vs. rhetoric, 65–68. *See also* aesthetic
Rockhead's Paradise, 395–96n10
Rose, Tricia, *Black Noise*, 59, 251–53
Roy, Arundhati, 43

Said, Edward, 15, 154, 339
sampling, 30, 82, 130, 141, 247, 330, 301n♭, 304–5, 318, 328, 344, 363; in K'naan's music, 272. *See also* remix
Sanders, Leslie, 12, 156, 173

"schizophonophilia" (Compton), 30, 318, 320
scopophilia, 171n♭
Scramble for Africa, 268–69
semiotics, 389n27
Shad, 97, 228–29n♭, 253, 293–94; "Fam Jam", 241–42
Shadd, Mary Ann, 21–22, 378n5
Shakespeare, William, 91–92, 101–2, 113–14, 390n54
Sharpe, Christina: on "Black visualsonic resistance," 350, 354; on Dionne Brand, 155; the wake, 19–20, 216
Siemerling, Winfried, 20, 53, 321, 325–28
signifying, 8, 78–83, 247, 263, 324
Simone, Nina, 7, 42, 302,
slave trade, 188, 215–16, 221, 224, 231, 233, 237, 276, 396n21
spirituals, 10, 73, 75, 251n♭, 253, 373, 377n3
Sun Ra, 47 ("the other side of nowhere"), 177, 180, 365

Thomas, Nigel, 34, 73, 88, 380n30
tidalectics (Brathwaite), 154, 311
Toomer, Jean: *Cane*, 35n♭
Toronto, 38–39, 89, 133–34, 196, 241–42, 257, 259, 275, 370–71, 384n104
tradition: Black literary tradition, 68, 71, 78–79, 81, 94, 100, 201, 211, 247, 312, 363, 389n27, 410n26, 412n78; importance of, 24, 32, 35, 88, 163–64, 192, 222, 236, 267, 279, 301, 307–9; mixing and revising, 101, 102, 106–7, 110–15, 118, 122, 141, 147, 166, 169, 294–97, 310; Western literary tradition, 67, 77, 90, 108, 378n12
transnational, 22, 53–54, 61, 83, 92, 176, 184, 206, 224, 238, 246, 285–87, 314, 316, 328, 336, 349, 383n76. *See also* nationalism
trickster, 79, 91, 139, 310, 323–28
Trudeau, Justin, 50

Trudeau, Pierre Elliott: just society and multiculturalism, 11n♭, 55, 85–86, 88, 280, 287, 387n150; and Martin Luther King, Jr., 54, 386n149; pluralism, 386n147; "The White Paper," 50
Tubman, Harriet, 10, 21–22, 136
turntable, 20, 62, 74n♭, 146, 287, 298–300, 302–4, 307, 309, 318–19, 322, 341, 345; technics, 120, 299, 354. *See also* phonograph

Underground Railroad, 10–11, 21–22, 251n♭, 281, 354, 373

Vancouver, 148, 258, 311, 313–15, 330, 333–36, 343, 349, 352–56
"versioning," 190
Vodou, 323–36, 341, 412n78

Walcott, Derek, 83, 92, 108, 113
Walcott, Rinaldo, 14, 17–18, 34, 51, 55, 159, 256–57, 340, 362
Wallace, David Foster: on hip hop, 247
Weheliye, Alexander G.: on W.E.B. Du Bois, 74; on hip hop, 246; on repetition, 304; on "sonic Afro-modernity," 35, 37
West, Cornel, 16, 146, 384n106
Williams, Mary Lou, 151n♭, 158
witness and witnessing, 33, 79, 105, 113, 225, 236, 263–64, 266
whiteness, 12–14, 23, 40, 50, 71, 122, 134–37, 290–91, 313, 318, 364, 378–79n17, 384n108
Wynter, Sylvia: on the human, 378n12

X, Malcolm, 76, 88, 97, 105, 124–25, 128, 383n73, 394n153

Zong massacre, 215–16

www.ingramcontent.com/pod-product-compliance
Lightning Source LLC
Chambersburg PA
CBHW071328080526
44587CB00017B/2771